James White

Ontario history

vol. 11-12

James White

Ontario history
vol. 11-12

ISBN/EAN: 9783741135323

Manufactured in Europe, USA, Canada, Australia, Japa

Cover: Foto ©ninafisch / pixelio.de

Manufactured and distributed by brebook publishing software (www.brebook.com)

James White

Ontario history

Ontario Historical Society.

PAPERS AND RECORDS.

VOL. XI.

TORONTO:
PUBLISHED BY THE SOCIETY
1913

OFFICERS, 1912-13

Honorary President:
THE HONORABLE THE MINISTER OF EDUCATION OF ONTARIO.

President:
JOHN DEARNESS, M.A., London.

1st Vice-President:
CLARANCE M. WARNER, Napanee.

2nd Vice-President:
SIR EDMUND WALKER, Toronto

Secretary and Acting Treasurer:
ALEXANDER FRASER, LL.D., LITT. D., Toronto.

Auditors:
J. J. MURPHY, Toronto.   FRANK YEIGH, Toronto

Councillors:
A. F. HUNTER, M.A.   W. STEWART WALLACE, B.A.
J. STEWART CARSTAIRS, B.A.   W. L. GRANT, M.A.
ALEXANDER FRASER, LL.D., LITT. D., F.S.A., SCOT. (Edin.)

The Ontario Historical Society does not assume responsibility for the statements of its contributors.

Place-Names in Georgian Bay

(Including the North Channel)

BY JAMES WHITE, F.R.G.S.

For convenience and on account of the historical connection, the North Channel names have also been included in this compilation.

Place-names in the area covered by this paper can be assigned to three distinct periods ; first, those given by Bayfield when he surveyed it in 1819-22 ; second, the local names given by fishermen, residents and others between the date of Bayfield's survey and 1883 ; third, the new survey by Messrs. Boulton and Stewart in 1883-93.

Before discussing the derivations of the first period, a few notes respecting Bayfield may be of interest. He was born in 1795, entered the Navy in 1806, on H.M.S. Pompee (80), Sir William Sydney Smith, and was in action with a French privateer, six hours after leaving Portsmouth. Later, he served in H.M.S. Queen (98), Admiral Lord Collingwood's flagship, and in the Duchess of Bedford, Lieut. Spilsbury. In 1806, he was appointed to H.M.S. Beagle, Capt. F. Newcombe, and, in 1811, he was midshipman in the Wanderer (21), Capt. F. Newcombe. He was promoted to Lieutenant, 1815, and was appointed assistant to Capt. William Fitzwilliam Owen, R.N., in the survey of Lake Ontario. The war of 1812-14 had shown the necessity for a hydrographical survey of the Great Lakes and Capt. Owen had been appointed for the survey. While the naval force at the beginning of hostilities was a negligible quantity, at the close there were upwards of 40 British war vessels, ranging from one-gun gunboats to the St. Lawrence, a ship of the line with 102 guns. To permit these vessels to navigate the lakes with confidence, a survey was absolutely necessary.

Owen was in charge of the survey of Lake Ontario till its completion in 1816, when he was succeeded by Bayfield who surveyed

*Read at the annual meeting of the Ontario Historical Society at Brantford June, 1911

Lake Erie in 1818, Huron and Georgian Bay in 1819-22, and Superior in 1823-25. In 1827, Bayfield was appointed to the survey of the St. Lawrence River and Gulf. This work was carried on in Gulnare I, 1827-51, and Gulnare II, from 1852 till his promotion to Rear Admiral in 1856. He retired with rank of full Admiral, 1867, and died at Charlottetown, P.E.I., 1885. For the quality of his work it is sufficient to quote Capt. Boulton : "While making a survey of Georgian Bay and the North Channel of Lake Huron . . . I had a good opportunity of witnessing the marvellous quantity and excellence of Admiral Bayfield's work. . . . I doubt whether the British Navy has ever possessed a more gifted and zealous surveyor than Bayfield. He had a marvellous combination of natural talent with tremendous physical energy."

The charts that were sufficient for navigation in the "twenties" when the largest vessel on Lake Huron measured a few hundred tons were inadequate for the vessels of a half-century later. In 1883, the Canadian Government secured the services of an Admiralty surveyor, Capt. J. G. Boulton, R.N. For ten years, 1883-93, surveys of Georgian Bay and North Channel were carried on under his direction. In 1893, he resigned to return to duty in the Navy and was succeeded by his principal assistant, the present Chief Hydrographer, Mr. W. J. Stewart.

So far as the names given by Bayfield are concerned, their derivation is a matter of inference, but the evidence, in some instances, almost amounts to a demonstration. At the date of his survey, George IV was King of Great Britain and Ireland, hence Georgian Bay and Lake George ; Prince William Henry, Duke of Clarence, was Admiral of the Fleet, 1811, and Lord High Admiral, 1827-28, hence Prince William Henry Island ; William Frederick, Duke of Gloucester, married Prince William Henry's sister, Mary, and was thus, both his cousin and his brother-in-law, hence Gloucester Point and Bay.

In 1822, Robert Saunder Dundas, 2nd Viscount Melville, Sir Wm. Johnstone Hope, Sir Geo. Cockburn and Wm. Robt. Keith Douglas were Lord High Admirals, hence Cape Dundas, Melville Sound, Hope Bay and Island, Cockburn Island and Point, and Douglas Bay and Point. Capt. Thos. Hurd was Hydrographer from 1808 to 1823, and Capt (afterwards, Admiral Sir) William Edward Parry, from 1823-29, and James Horsburg was Hydrographer to the East India Co. ; hence Cape Hurd, Parry Sound and Island and Horsburg Point. Barrow Bay is after Sir John Barrow, for 38 years, 1807-45, Second Secretary to the Admiralty, and Croker Cape and Island after John Wilson Croker, First Secretary, 1809-30 ; Dyer Bay, after John James Dyer, for many years Chief Clerk of the Admiralty ; Hay Island, after Viscount Melville's private secretary, and Amedroz Island after an Admiralty officia..

As there was a considerable naval establishment on the Great Lakes, Bayfield named a number of features after naval officers. James, Lucas and Yeo Islands, after Sir James Lucas Yeo, commander-in-chief on the Great Lakes, 1814 ; Barrie Island after Capt. Robt. Barrie, Acting Commissioner of the Navy at Kingston ; Bushby Inlet, Boucher Point Clapperton Island and Channel, Henvey Inlet, Wingfield Point and Basin, Worsley Bay, Grant Island and Thompson Point are al o named after officers of the Royal Navy serving on the Great Lakes.

Confiance Rock was named after the Confiance, gunboat on Lake Huron, formerly the U. S. S. Scorpion, captured Sept. 6th, 1814. This Confiance was the third bearing her name. The first was Yeo's first command, a French privateer captured by him at Muros Bay, and the second was Downie's flagship on Lake Champlain, captured by the Americans at Plattsburgh, Sept. 11th, 1814, five days after the capture by the British of what was, later, Confiance III. Bedford Island is, probably, after the Duchess of Bedford, the third ship in which Bayfield served, or, after Admiral William Bedford.

Colpoys Bay, Rous Islands, Mudge Bay and Byng Inlet are after British admirals, the last named being the admiral who was shot, in 1757, for his failure to relieve Minorca—"pour encourager les autres." Fitzwilliam Island and Owen Channel are after Bayfield's former chief in the survey of Lake Ontario, while Cape Commodore, Owen Sound, Point William, Campbell Cliff and Point Rich commemorate Owen's brother, Commodore Sir E. W. C. R. Owen.

Bayfield's assistants were : Midshipmen Philip Edward Collins and Vidal, "immortalized" in Philip Edward Island, Collins Inlet and Vidal Island. Till his death in 1835, Collins was Bayfield's assistant in his survey of the St. Lawrence, and Vidal was the grandfather of the late Gen. Vidal, Ottawa.

Franklin Inlet—now obsolete—and Parry Island and Sound were named after the famous Arctic navigators; Portlock Harbour is, probably, after Capt. Portlock, R.N., who commanded a fur-trading expedition to the Pacific Coast and published an account of his voyage ; Bigsby Island is after Dr. J. J. Bigsby, geologist to the Commission appointed under the Treaty of Ghent to define the International boundary through the St. Lawrence and the Great Lakes.

Of the Bayfield family there are : Henry Island, Wolsey Lake and Bayfield Sound after himself, Elizabeth Bay after his mother, Helen Bay after his only sister, Julia Bay and Point after a young lady of Quebec. Honora Bay and Juliet Cove are, probably, after other young ladies of his acquaintance, but nothing definite is known concerning them.

The other names given by Bayfield are either unimportant or of unknown derivation.

As already stated, during the second period local names were given to many features, but were only known locally. When Capt. Boulton commenced his survey in 1883, the only names on the charts were those given by Bayfield, sixty years earlier. Consequently, while there was a second "name-period," it is not possible to separate it from the third, namely, those given by Messrs. Boulton and Stewart. As the circumstances connected with the names given in the second period were, in nearly every case, of local interest only, they were incorporated in the charts and no description of them is necessary.

The names given by Messrs. Boulton and Stewart can be divided into a number of classes, only a few of which need be noticed. As Capt. Boulton was an officer of the Royal Navy, many features bear the names of Admiralty officials and naval officers. Thus, Brassey Island, Hamilton Rock, Hood Patch and Hotham Island are after Lords of the Admiralty; Dalrymple Rock is after Alex. Dalrymple, the first Hydrographer to the Admiralty, and Beaufort Island and Evans and Wharton Points after recent incumbents; Browning Cove and Island, Goalen Island, Harris Bank, Hoskin Island, Jamieson Island, Orlebar Rock, Pender Islets, Peter Islands, Pettey Rock, Richards Reef, and Scott Island are after naval surveyors. An island is named after Admiral Lord Charles Beresford of "Well done, Condor" fame, and another after Admiral Sir Thomas Sabine Pasley.

The war of 1812-14 is commemorated by features named after the Chesapeake and her captain, Lawrence, after the Shannon and Lieut. Provo Wallis. That there were gunboats on the lakes after the close of the war is commemorated by islands, etc., named Faith, Minstrel, Heron, Rescue, Gunboat, Britomart, Cherub, Danville and Drew. Naval officers who distinguished themselves in 1812-14 are not forgotten as evidenced by Barclay, Huntly and Finnis Rocks, Frederic Inlet, Spilsbury Island and Popham Point.

A study of the "First Conquest of Canada" resulted in the naming of islands after Thomas Kirke, after one of his captains, Brewerton, and after two of the vessels, the Gervase and Abigail. The "Life of Parry" has given numerous names to features. The Ardent, Borer, Griper, Hecla, Niger, Sceptre, Tribune and Vanguard were ships in which Parry served, and Baker, Capel, Cathcart, Coote, Cornwallis, Glyn, Powys, Quilliam and Ricketts were captains under whom he served; Hooper, Hoppner, Liddon, Lyon and Nias were subordinate officers during his Arctic expeditions;

the Christian names of his father and the Christian names and surnames of his mother and wife were also utilized.

The defence of Detroit, 1763, is commemorated by Beaver and Gladwyn Rocks ; the naval battle in Hudson Bay, 1693, by Dering, Hampshire and Pelican Rocks and French explorers and missionaries by Breboeuf, Champlain, Hennepin, Joliette, La Salle, Nicolet, Talon and Tonty Islands and Roberval Point ; Dauphine Rock is named after the vessel in which Verrazano made his discoveries in 1524.

The Camperdown-Victoria disaster, in 1893, furnished names for twenty features, nearly all of which were after officers of the ill-fated Victoria. The eldest son of King Edward VII—died 1892—is commemorated in Victor Bank, Albert and Clarence Channels and Duke Island. The Hudson Bay expeditions of 1884, 1885 and 1886, account for Neptune Island, Gordon Rock and Alert Point. Our Governors-General are represented by Aberdeen, Dufferin, Elgin, Lansdowne, Lorne and Stanley Islands and Monck Point, while Aide-de-camps Colville, Kilcoursie, Kindersley and St. Aubyn have not been forgotten. Lieutenant-Governors Aikins, Morris and Schultz of Manitoba, Beverly Robinson and Kirkpatrick of Ontario, Belleau, Masson, Robitaille and Letellier de St. Just of Quebec, and Laird and Royal of the Northwest Territories, have had their names attached to features, also Sir John Abbott, Sir Mackenzie Bowell, Sir Wilfrid Laurier, Sir Hector Langevin, Sir Francis Hincks, Sir A. T. Galt, Sir Charles Tupper and many other Ministers and about forty-five Members and Senators.

Of the remainder it is only possible to enumerate the classes of name-derivations. (1) Scores of features, principally rocks and shoals, have been named after lake vessels, usually because the danger has been reported by one of her officers or because she has achieved an undesired fame by striking it. Many others have received the names of captains and other officers of lake vessels and of officials of navigation companies. The families and near relations of Messrs. Boulton and Stewart and of the sailing-master, Capt. McGregor, account for thirty names. As Mr. Stewart is a graduate of the Royal Military College, Kingston, he attached the names of some twenty-five officers and cadets to rocks, etc., in the North Channel and St. Mary River. The surveys were carried on under the Department of Marine and Fisheries and the names of eighty officials of that and other departments have been given. Seventeen features are named after judges of the Supreme Court and of Ontario courts and many bear the names of residents of nearby towns, of clergymen, of citizens of Ottawa, of fishermen, lighthouse-keepers and Indian chiefs.

Place-Names in Georgian Bay and North Channel

ABBOTT.—Island, Parry Sound ; after Sir J. J. C. Abbott (1821-1892), Premier, 1891-92.

ABERDEEN.—Island, Muskoka ; after Lord Aberdeen, Governor-General of Canada, 1893-98.

ABIGAIL.—Island, North Channel, Algoma ; after one of Kirke's vessels at taking of Quebec, 1629.

ACADIA.—Rock, North Channel, Algoma ; after the propeller Acadia.

*ADAMS.—Point, Simcoe ; named by Bayfield ; possibly after an official of Penetanguishene naval station.

AFRICA.—Rock, North Channel, Algoma ; after steambarge Africa.

AIKINS.—Island, North Channel, Algoma ; after Hon. J. C. Aikins, Lieut.-Governor of Manitoba, 1882-88.

*AIRD.—Island and bay North Channel, Algoma ; derivation unknown ; named by Bayfield.

AJAX.—Islands, Parry Sound ; probably after a lake vessel.

ALBERT.—Channel, Parry Sound ; after Prince Albert Victor, Duke of Clarence, (1864-1892).

ALBERTA.—Rock, Parry Sound ; after the steamer Alberta.

ALEC CLARKE.—Rock Manitoulin ; after a fisherman of Collingwood.

ALERT.—Point, Cloche I., Sudbury ; after the Alert, an Admiralty vessel, loaned by the Admiralty to the Canadian Government for the Hudson Bay expeditions, 1885 and 1886 ; was the flagship of the Nares Arctic expedition, 1875-76.

ALEXANDER.—Island, Muskoka ; after private secretary to Sir W. C. Van Horne.

††Names distinguished by a †† have same derivation as the first feature bearing same name.
*Names preceded by an asterisk appeared in Bayfield's chart, and, unless otherwise stated, were given by him. All Bayfield's names are noted whether the derivation is known or unknown.

ALEXANDER.—Inlet, Parry Sound ; after Alexander Murray McGregor, sailing-master of the steamer Bayfield.
ALEXANDER.—Rock, Manitoulin ; after Wm. Alexander, clerk in Marine and Fisheries Department.
ALFRED.—Island, North Channel, Algoma ; after Alfred D. De Celles, General Librarian, Library of Parliament.
ALICE.—Rock, Muskoka ; after Christian name of Mrs. Libbs, a widow of Penetanguishene.
ALICE.—Island, St. Joseph Channel, Algoma ; after sister of John Woodman, C.E., Winnipeg.
ALICIA.—Rock, North Channel, Algoma ; after a daughter of George Marks, Bruce Mines.
ALLEN.—Rocks, Muskoka ; probably after Henry R. Allen, clerk to Secretary of the Victoria, sunk in collision with the Camperdown off Tripoli, June 23rd, 1893.
ALMON.—Island, St. John Channel, Algoma ; after late M. B. Almon, C.E., graduated from the Royal Military College, Kingston, 1883.
ALVES.—Point, Parry Sound ; after a resident.
ALWIN.—Rock, Key Harbour, Parry Sound ; after a seaman on the Bayfield.
*AMEDROZ.—Island, North Channel, Sudbury ; named by Bayfield after a clerk in the Admiralty.
AMELIA.—Rock, Parry Sound ; after Miss Amelia Johnson, daughter of a Parry Sound merchant.
AMERICAN CAMP.—Island, Muskoka ; a party from the United States camped on it.
AMYOT.—Rocks, North Channel, Algoma ; after late Lt.-Col. Amyot, M.P.
ANCHOR.—Island, North Channel, Algoma ; good anchorage near it.
††ANCHOR.—Island and rock, Parry Sound.
††ANCHOR.—Rock, Muskoka.
ANDERSON.—Ledge, Manitoulin ; after Col. Wm. P. Anderson, Chief Engineer, Department of Marine and Fisheries.
*ANNARELLA.—Islands Sudbury ; named by Bayfield ; derivation unknown ; name now obsolete.
ANNIE.—Rock, Manitoulin ; after the Annie Clark, fishing tug.
ANN LONG.—Bank, Manitoulin ; after the first vessel used in the hydrographical survey of Georgian Bay, 1883.
ANSLEY.—Island, Parry Sound ; after postmaster at Parry Sound.

ANTHONY.—Island, Manitoulin ; after an Indian of Wikwemikong.

APPELBE.—Island, Parry Sound ; after a physician of Parry Sound.

ARAXES.—Bank, Parry Sound ; after the Araxes, a lake vessel.

ARDENT.—Rock, Parry Sound ; after H.M.S. Ardent in which Parry (q.v.) served, 1815.

ARIEL.—Rock, Parry Sound ; after the schooner Ariel.

ARMSTRONG,—Rock, Parry Sound ; after a tourist, named Armstrong.

ARMSTRONG,—Rocks, Parry Sound ; after Judge Armstrong.

ARNOLD.—Point, Aird I., Algoma ; after a mill-owner, Spanish River.

††ARNOLD.—Rock, North Channel, Algoma.

ARTHUR.—Island, Muskoka ; after Arthur Street-Macklem, Toronto. Indian name *minnewawa*, meaning 'pleasant sound' (as of wind in the trees).

ARTHUR.—Point, Vidal I., Manitoulin ; after a son of Capt. Boulton.

ASHMEAD.—Point, Algoma ; after Ashmead Ellis Bartlett Burdett-Coutts, British politician, Lord of the Admiralty, 1885.

ASIA.—Rock, North Channel, Algoma ; after the steamer Asia, lost in Georgian Bay, 1882.

ATHABASCA.—Rock, Parry Sound ; after steamer Athabasca.

ATLANTIC.—Rock, St. Joseph I., Algoma ; after the steamer Atlantic.

AUGUSTA.—Rock, Parry Sound ; after a daughter of Capt. Cox, R.N., naval surveyor.

AURORA.—Bank, North Channel, Algoma ; after the schooner Aurora.

AVA.—Island, Muskoka ; after the late Lord Ava, eldest son of Lord Dufferin ; killed in the Boer war.

AZOV.—Ledges, Manitoulin ; after the schooner Azov, stranded on Squaw I.

BACON.—Island, North Channel, Algoma ; after late Lt.-Col. Bacon, Ottawa.

*BADGLEY.—Island and rocks, Manitoulin ; named by Bayfield, 1826, probably after Dr. Badgley, a prominent fur-trader who came to Montreal about 1788, d. 1841 ; possibly after Capt. Francis Badgley, 1st Batt., Montreal City Militia, on duty during war of 1812-14. 'Badgeley' on chart.

BAD NEIGHBOUR.—Rock, Manitoulin ; "the worst danger in the main channel."

BAILEY.—Rock, Parry Sound ; after a fisherman.

BAKER.—Group, Parry Sound ; after the captain of the Tribune, vessel in which Parry (q.v.) served.

BAKER.—Point, Clapperton I., Manitoulin ; after E. Crow Baker, sometime M.P. for Victoria, B.C.

BALD.—Island and rock, Parry Sound ; descriptive.

††BALD.—Rock, North Channel, Algoma.

BAMAGESECK.—Bay, St. Joseph Channel, Algoma ; after an Indian.

BAMFORD.—Island, St. Joseph Channel, Algoma ; after the lighthouse-keeper.

BAND.—Island, Muskoka ; after the Bursar of the Reformatory at Penetanguishene.

BANDIN.—Bluff, Manitoulin ; after a Roman Catholic priest, Wikwemikong.

BANSHEE.—Rock, North Channel, Algoma ; after the Banshee, a lake trading vessel.

BAR.—Island, Parry Sound ; descriptive.

††BAR.—Point, Simcoe.

BARCLAY.—Rock, Parry Sound ; after Com. Robert Heriot Barclay (1785-1837), British commander in the battle of Lake Erie, 1813 ; post captain, 1824.

BARIL.—Point, Parry Sound ; stated that the name commemorates the loss of a barrel of whiskey at this point—a doubtful explanation.

BARNARD.—Bank, Muskoka ; after William Barnard, acting boatswain in the Victoria, sunk in collision with the Camperdown off Tripoli, 1893.

BARREN.—Island, Sudbury ; descriptive.

BARRETT.—Bank, North Channel, Algoma ; after a boatman in surveying steamer Bayfield.

*BARRIE.—Island, Manitoulin ; after Commodore Robert Barrie, Acting Commissioner of the Navy at Kingston after the war of 1812-14 ; made a tour of inspection through Simcoe county about 1828.

*BARRIER.—Island, Bruce ; named by Bayfield ; descriptive.

*BARROW.—Bay, Bruce ; after Sir John Barrow (1764-1843) ; from 1807 to 1845, Second Secretary to the Admiralty.

BARTLETT.—Point, Algoma ; after Ashmead Ellis Bartlett Burdett-Coutts, Lord of the Admiralty, 1885.

BASS.—Group of islands, Muskoka ; noted fishing ground for bass.

BASSETT.—Island, North Channel, Algoma ; after the captain of a Georgian Bay vessel.

††BASSETT.—Rock, Parry Sound.

BATE.—Rock, Parry Sound ; after Sir Henry N. Bate, Chairman of the Ottawa Improvement Commission, Ottawa.

BATEAU.—Islands, Parry Sound ; after the passages between the islands, only passable by small boats (bateaux).

BATH.—Island, `Parry Sound ; after Bath, city, Somerset, England. Parry (q.v.) was educated in Bath.

BATOCHE.—Point, Bedford I., Sudbury ; after the action at Batoche, Sask., Riel rebellion, 1885.

BATTERY.—Bluff, Manitoulin ; descriptive, resembles a battery.

BATTURE.—Island, Manitoulin ; after the reef (batture) joining it to Vidal Island.

BAXTER.—Point, Aird I., Algoma ; after the captain of a Spanish River tug.

BAYARD.—Island and reef, Manitoulin ; probably after Thomas Francis Bayard (1828-1898), Secretary of State (U.S.) 1885-89 ; first U. S. ambassador to England, 1893.

BAYFIELD.—Bluff, Killarney harbour, Manitoulin ; from "the surveying steamer Bayfield having occasionally tied up to it during the progress of the survey in this locality."

††BAYFIELD.—Rock, Parry Sound.

BAYFIELD.—Sound, Manitoulin ; after Captain (later, Admiral) Henry Wolsey Bayfield, naval surveyor, who did so much excellent work upon the Great Lakes between 1817 and 1823.

††BAYFIELD.—Reef, Manitoulin.

BAY OF ISLANDS.—Bay, Manitoulin I. ; from the numerous islands.

BAYVIEW.—Point, Grey ; descriptive.

BEACH.—Point, Fitzwilliam I., Manitoulin ; "derives its name from the fact of its being the north-easterly termination of a long stony beach."

BEAR.—Island, Georgian Bay ; this name is also applied to numerous other features in Canada, usually owing to the unusual numbers of this animal frequenting the vicinity ; or to some unusual occurrence in connection with it at the time of naming ; or, it is the translation of the Indian name.

††BEAR BACK.—Island and shoal, Algoma.

††BEAR.—Head, Parry Sound.

BEAR'S RUMP.—Island and shoal, Bruce ; "the name given to an island having somewhat the outline of that animal."

BEATRICE.—Bank, Parry Sound ; after Miss Beatrice Johnson, daughter of a Parry Sound merchant.

BEATTY.—Bay, Clapperton I., North Channel ; after the manager of the Canadian Pacific lake steamship line, 1887.

BEAUDRY.—Point, Algoma ; probably after Hon. J. L. Beaudry, Montreal ; died 1886.

BEAUFORT.—Island and reef, North Channel, Algoma ; after Rear-Admiral Sir Francis Beaufort (1774-1857), Hydrographer to the Navy.

BEAUMONT.—Point, Algoma ; after Dr. H. Beaumont Small, Ottawa.

BEAUSOLEIL.—Island, Simcoe ; after a French-Canadian who came from Drummond Island ; he settled here in 1819. "Prince William Henry I." on Bayfield's chart.

BEAUTY.—Island, Goat Channel, Sudbury ; descriptive.

††BEAUTY.—Island, Parry Sound.

BEAVER.—Rock, Parry Sound ; after the schooner Beaver employed in the defence of Detroit during Pontiac's rebellion, 1763.

BEAVER.—Island, Strawberry I., Manitoulin ; probably contained many beaver in the early days.

††BEAVER ISLAND.—Harbour and bank, Strawberry I., Manitoulin.

*BECKWITH.—Island ; named by Bayfield, after Colonel Sir Thomas Sydney Beckwith, 95th Regt., served in the Peninsula : appointed Quartermaster-General, North America, Jan. 7, 1813 ; died 1831.

*BEDFORD.—Island, Sudbury ; named by Bayfield, probably after Admiral William Bedford, d. 1827. Or, after the Duchess of Bedford in which Bayfield had served.

BEER.—Point, Manitoulin ; after a clergyman, Manitoulin I.

††BEER.—Rock, St. Joseph Channel, Algoma.

BEGLEY.—Channel and rocks, Parry Sound ; after a fisherman.

BELCHER.—Rock, Algoma ; after Admiral Sir Edward Belcher (1799-1877), commanded a Franklin search expedition of four searching vessels and a store vessel, 1852-54 ; his officers, notably M'Clintock, Mecham, Richards and Osborn, discovered and surveyed thousands of miles of coast-line of the Arctic islands of Canada.

BELIZE.—Rock, Parry Sound ; after the tug Belize.

BELL.—Cove, Cloche I., Sudbury ; after Dr. Robert Bell, late Chief Geologist, Geological Survey.

BELLE.—Bay, Parry I., Parry Sound ; after Georgian Bay steamer Northern Belle.

††BELLE.—Rock, North Channel, Algoma.

BELLEAU.—Island, North Channel, Algoma ; after Sir Narcisse F. Belleau, Lieutenant-Governor of Quebec, 1868-73.

BEN BACK.—Shoal, Manitoulin ; after one of crew in surveying steamer Bayfield,

BENJAMIN.—Island, North Channel, Algoma ; after Christian name of lightkeeper at Clapperton Island.

BENNETT.—Bank, Simcoe ; after William Humphrey Bennett, M.P. for East Simcoe for many years.

BENSON.—Point, Manitoulin ; after Col. Thomas Benson, Master-General of the Ordnance, Ottawa ; graduated from Royal Military College 1883.

BERESFORD.—Island, Parry Sound ; after Admiral Lord Charles Beresford, K.C.B., G.C.V.O., Lord of the Admiralty, 1886.

BERGERON.—Point, John I., Algoma ; after J. G. H. Bergeron, M.P. for Beauharnois, 1879-1900.

BERGIN.—Rock, North Channel, Algoma ; after the late Darby Bergin, M.P. for Cornwall, 1872-74 and 1878-82 ; for Cornwall and Stormont, 1882-96.

*BERNARD.—Rock, Manitoulin ; named by Bayfield, probably after Alex. Bernard, R.N., Asst. Surgeon during war of 1812-14.

BEVERLY.—Island, Manitoulin ; after Sir John Beverly Robinson (1821-1896), Lieut.-Governor of Ontario, 1880-87.

BIG DAVID.—Bay, Muskoka ; after an Indian chief.

BIGGAR.—Rock, St. Joseph Channel, Algoma ; after Charles A. Biggar, D.L.S., Dominion Astronomical Observatory

*BIGSBY.—Island, North Channel, Algoma ; after John J. Bigsby, M.D., geologist to the International Boundary Commission, appointed under the Treaty of Ghent ; was author of "Shoe and Canoe."

BILLA.—Rocks, Aird I. Algoma ; after the late Senator Billa Flint, Belleville.

BIRCH.—Island, North Channel, Algoma ; descriptive.

BIRCHALL.—Island, Muskoka ; after maiden name of Mrs. Charles Band, Penetanguishene.

BIRD.—Island, North Channel, Algoma ; characteristic ; frequented by gulls, etc.

*BLACK BILL.—Islands, Parry Sound ; named by Bayfield ; descriptive of these black rocks rising a few feet above the surface of the water.

BLACKSTOCK.—Point, Manitoulin ; after Geo. Tate Blackstock, K.C., Toronto.

BLACKSTONE.—Point, Clapperton I., Manitoulin ; descriptive.

BLAIR.—Landing, Parry Sound ; "after the present occupant of the farm house at the mouth of the stream."

BLAKE.—Island, Sudbury ; after late Hon. Edward Blake, Minister of Justice, 1875-77 President of the Privy Council, 1877-78 ; M.P. for West Durham, 1867-75 and 1879-91 ; M.P. for South Bruce, 1872-78 ; elected member of the Imperial Parliament for Longford S.D., 1892.

BLIND.—Bay, Parry Sound ; descriptive.

BLIND.—River, and BLIND RIVER, post village, Algoma ; after the formation of the river mouth which is not discernable from the lake (Huron). Named by the French who settled here, 1837 ; Indian name *penebawabikong*, signifying "a sloping rock."

BLOCK.—Island, Western Islands, Parry Sound ; after blocks of stone on top of rock.

BLUE.—Mountains, Grey ; name given by the early voyageurs ; when seen from out in the lake, they have a bluish, hazy appearance.

BLUFF.—Point, Parry Sound ; characteristic.

BOAT.—Cove, Cloche I., Sudbury ; descriptive, navigable only by small boats.

††BOAT.—Harbour and passage, Cove I., Bruce.

††BOAT.—Harbour and rock, Manitoulin.

††BOAT.—Passage, Parry Sound.

BOGART.—Island, Parry Sound ; after Ven. James John Bogart, Archdeacon of Ottawa.

BOLD.—Point, Manitoulin ; "so called from the fact of there being good water close to it."

BOLGER.—Rock, Parry Sound ; after the late Francis Bolger, O.L.S.

BOLSTER.—Bank, Muskoka ; after Thomas Bolster, Fleet-Surgeon in the Victoria, sunk in collision with the Camperdown off Tripoli, 1893.

BONNET.—Island, Bruce ; "from its clump of dark coloured trees, somewhat resembling a plume."

BOOTH.—Rocks, North Channel, Algoma ; after J. R. Booth,. manufacturer and lumber merchant, Ottawa, late President of Canada Atlantic Railway.

BORER.—Bank, Parry Sound ; after H. M. brig Borer in which Parry (q.v.) served.

BORRON.—Rock, Parry Sound ; after E. B. Borron, Inspector of Mines, Ontario, 1872.

BOSWELL.—Island, St. Joseph Channel, Algoma ; after late Col. Boswell, 90th Regt., Winnipeg.

BOTTERELL.—Point, Manitoulin ; after Edward Botterell, sometime Distributor of Printed Documents, House of Commons.

*BOUCHER.—Point, Grey ; named by Bayfield after Capt. Wm. Boucher, in command of Lake Erie fleet, in 1816.

BOUCHER.—Rock, Muskoka ; after a land surveyor, resident of Penetanguishene.

BOUCHER.—Island, Parry Sound ; after a fisherman.

BOUCHIER.—Islands, Parry Sound ; after a naval surveyor of 1865.

BOULANGER.—Point, St. Joseph Channel, Algoma ; after the farmer who owned it.

BOULDER.—Bank, Manitoulin, and bluff, Bruce ; descriptive.

BOULTON.—Reef, Manitoulin ; after Capt. Boulton, in command of survey of Georgian Bay and North Channel, 1883-93 ; now residing in Quebec.

BOURINOT.—Island and rock, Algoma ; after the late Sir John Bourinot, Clerk of the House of Commons.

BOURKE.—Point, Muskoka ; after Hon. Maurice A. Bourke, captain of the Victoria, sunk in collision with the Camperdown, 1893.

BOWELL.—Cove, Manitoulin ; after the Hon. Sir Mackenzie Bowell, P.C., Premier, 1894-96.

BOWEN.—Island, St. Joseph Channel, Algoma ; after Major Aylesworth Bowen Perry, Commissioner, Royal Northwest Mounted Police ; graduated from the Royal Military College, 1880.

BOWES.—Island, Muskoka ; after a lawyer, Parry Sound.

BOWKER.—Point, Algoma ; after a merchant residing at Marksville.

BOYD.—Island, North Channel, Algoma ; after Sir John Alexander Boyd, Chancellor of Ontario.

††BOYD.—Islands, Parry Sound.

BOYLE.—Cove, Manitoulin ; after a draughtsman at the Admiralty, 1880.

BRADLEY.—Rock, North Channel, Algoma ; after late F. Bradley, Secretary, Department of Railways and Canals.

BRANDON.—Harbour, St. Joseph Channel, Algoma ; after a hotelkeeper, Richards Landing.

BRASSEY.—Island, Manitoulin ; after the late Lord Brassey, Lord of the Admiralty, 1880, 1882-83 ; First Secretary of the Admiralty, 1884-85.

BRAY.—Reef, Key Harbour, Parry Sound ; after a seaman in steamer Bayfield.

BREBOEUF.—Island, Muskoka ; after Rev. Father Breboeuf, Jesuit missionary, put to death by the Iroquois, 1649.

BREWERTON.—Island, North Channel, Algoma ; one of the captains of Kirke's squadron which captured Quebec, 1629.

BRIGGS.—Rock, North Channel, Algoma ; after a draughtsman at the Admiralty in 1887.

BRITOMART.— Point, Manitoulin ; after a British gunboat.

BROMLEY.—Island, Parry Sound ; after a mill-owner of Pembroke.

BROTHERS.—Islands, Alexander Inlet, Parry Sound ; descriptive of their resemblance to each other.

BROWNING.—Cove and island, Heywood I., Manitoulin ; after an officer in the British surveying service.

BRUCE.—Rock, North Channel, Algoma ; from its proximity to Bruce Mines which, probably, after James Bruce, Earl of Elgin and Kincardine (1811-63).

BRYMNER.—Bay, Manitoulin ; after the late Dr. Douglas Brymner, Dominion Archivist.

BURBIDGE.—Island, Manitoulin ; after the late George Wheelock Burbidge, Judge, Exchequer Court, Ottawa.

BURGESS.—Reef, Manitoulin ; after late A. M. Burgess, Deputy Minister of the Interior, 1883-97.

BURKE.—Shoal, Parry Sound ; after a Georgian Bay pilot.

BURTON.—Bank, Parry Sound ; after a mill-owner of Byng Inlet.

*BUSHBY.—Inlet, Muskoka ; named by Bayfield after Lieut. Bushby in command of the schooner Newash on Lake Erie, 1816.

††BUSHBY.—Point, Muskoka.

BUSHY.—Island, Alexander Inlet, Parry Sound ; descriptive.

*BUSTARD.—Islands, Sudbury ; named by Bayfield, probably after numerous wild fowl seen on them.

BUSWELL.—Point, Algoma ; after the owner of a mill on North Shore.

BUTCHER BOY.—Bank, North Channel, Algoma ; after the lake steamer Butcher Boy.

BUZWALES.—Cove. Manitoulin ; after an Indian at Wikwemikong.

*BYNG.—Inlet, Parry Sound ; named by Bayfield probably after Admiral John Byng (1704-1757), courtmartialed for his failure to take Minorca and shot, 1757, as a witty Frenchman said : "pour encourager les autres."

*CABOT.—Head, Bruce ; after John Cabot, famous explorer ; commissioned by Henry VIII, discovered Cape Breton and Nova Scotia, in 1497. Name appears on Bouchette's map, 1815.

††CABOT HEAD.—Shoal, Bruce.

CADOTTE.—Point, Parry I., Parry Sound ; after a boatman in steamer Bayfield.

CALEB.—Island, Parry Sound ; after Dr. Caleb Hillier Parry, father of Admiral Sir W. E. Parry, Arctic explorer.

CALF.—Island, North Channel, Algoma ; so named as it is a small island compared with others in vicinity.

CALLADY.—Reef, Parry Sound ; after a boatman in surveying steamer Bayfield.

CALVIN.—Island, Muskoka ; after Hiram A. Calvin, manager of the Calvin Co. ; M.P. for Frontenac, 1892-96 and 1900-04.

CAMBRIA.—Bank, St. Joseph I., Algoma ; after steamer Cambria.

CAMEL.—Rock, Parry Sound ; descriptive of appearance.

CAMERON.—Bay, Aird I., Algoma ; after an official of the Spanish River Lumber Co.

CAMERON.—Island, Parry Sound ; after late Chas. Cameron, Collingwood, manager, Northern Navigation Co., and owner of the island.

CAMP.—Point, John I., Algoma ; from W. J. Stewart having camped there.

††CAMP.—Cove, Strawberry I., Manitoulin.

CAMPANA.—Shoal, North Channel, Algoma ; after steamer Campana.

*CAMPBELL.—Cliff. Grey ; named by Bayfield after Admiral Sir Edward William Campbell Rich Owen (q.v.) ; name obsolete ; now called "The Claybanks."

CAMPBELL.—Island, Parry Sound ; after captain of a lake steamer.

CAMPBELL.—Rock, Parry Sound ; after D. C. Campbell, Department of Marine and Fisheries ; graduate, Royal Military College, 1883.

††CAMPBELL.—Rock, Manitoulin.

*CAMPEMENT D'OURS.—Island, St. Joseph Channel, Algoma ; this name, probably, commemorates an adventure with a bear. Probably a local name placed on the chart by Bayfield.

CAMPING.—Point, Vankoughnet Island, Manitoulin ; a hydrographical survey party camped here.

CAMPION.—Island, Georgian Bay, Muskoka ; after William H. Campion, Asst. Paymaster in Victoria, sunk in collision with the Camperdown off Tripoli, 1893.

CANADA.—Rock, St. Joseph Channel, Algoma ; after the fishery protection cruiser Canada.

CANDLEMAS.—Shoal, Muskoka ; named on Candlemas day.

CANOE.—Channel, Squaw Island, Parry Sound ; used by canoes.

††CANOE.—Point, St. Joseph Island, Algoma ; probably same as preceding.

CAPEL.—Rock, Parry Sound ; Lieut. W. E. Parry was in 1813, appointed to H.M.S. La Hogue, Capt. the Hon. Bladen Capel.

CARADOC.—Point, St. Joseph Island, Algoma ; after Christian name of Major-General Ivor John Caradoc Herbert, commanding Canadian Militia, 1890-95.

CAREY.—Rocks, Parry Sound ; after Lieut.-Col. H. C. Carey, graduate, Royal Military College, 1884.

CARIBOU.—Point, Algoma ; after the caribou seen on the island in early days.

CARLETON.—Point, Amedroz Island, Manitoulin ; after a clerk in Marine and Fisheries Department ; now superannuated.

CARLING.—Bay and point, Manitoulin ; after the late Sir John Carling, K.C.M.G., Postmaster-General, 1882-85 ; Minister of Agriculture, 1885-92 ; Senator, 1891-92 and 1896-1911.

††CARLING.—Rock, Parry Sound.

CARMONA.—Rock, St. Joseph Channel, Algoma ; after the steamer Carmona.

CAROLINE.—Island, North Channel, Algoma ; after a sister of W. J. Stewart, Chief Hydrographer.

CARON.—Point and reef, Manitoulin ; after the late Sir Joseph Philippe René Adolphe Caron (1843-1908), Minister of Militia, 1880-92 ; Postmaster-General, 1892-96.

CARPMAEL.—Island, Sudbury ; after the late Charles Carpmael, Director, Meteorological Service, Toronto.

CARTWRIGHT.—Point, Manitoulin ; after the late Hon. Sir Richard John Cartwright, K.C.M.G., Minister of Finance, 1873-78 ; Minister of Trade and Commerce, 1896-1911.

CASEY.—Shoal, North Channel, Algoma ; after late George Elliott Casey, M.P. for West Elgin, 1872-1900 ; d. 1903.

CASGRAIN.—Rock, North Channel, Algoma ; after P. B. Casgrain, M.P. for L'Islet, 1872-91.

CASTLE.—Island, Bustard Island, Parry Sound ; descriptive.

CATARACT.—Rock, Parry Sound ; after the schooner Cataract, wrecked there.

CATHCART.—Island, Parry Sound ; Lieut. W. E. Parry (q.v.) served in the Alexandria, Capt. Cathcart, 1811-13.

CATHERINE.—Rock, Parry Sound ; after Lady Parry, née Catherine Edwards Hankinson.

CAVE.—Point, Bruce ; 'from the number of small caverns in its cliffy face."

CEDAR.—Island, North Channel, Algoma ; from the cedar trees on it.

††CEDAR.—Point, Simcoe.

CELTIC.—Rocks, Manitoulin ; after the steamer Celtic.

CENTRE.—Island, and CENTRE ISLAND, bank, Manitoulin ; descriptive of position.

CHAIN.—Island, Parry Sound ; descriptive.

CHALLENGER.—Rock, Parry Sound ; after the Challenger, a famous British surveying vessel.

CHAMBERLAIN.—Island, Parry Sound ; after the steambarge Chamberlain.

CHAMBERLAIN.—Point, Manitoulin ; after the Rt. Hon. Joseph Chamberlain, British statesman.

CHAMPLAIN.—Island, Parry Sound ; after Samuel Champlain (1567-1635), famous French navigator and explorer.

CHANCELLOR.—Island, Parry Sound ; after Sir John Alexander Boyd, Chancellor of Ontario.

CHANNEL.—Point, Cove Island, Bruce ; descriptive of position near a channel.

††CHANNEL.—Point, Cockburn Island, Manitoulin.

††CHANNEL.—Rock, Fitzwilliam Island, Manitoulin, and rock, Parry Sound.

CHAPLEAU.—Cove and point,Manitoulin ; after the Hon. Sir Joseph Adolphe Chapleau (1840-1898), Lieut.-Governor of Quebec, 1892-98.

CHAPMAN.—Rock, North Channel, Algoma ; error for Chipman ; after C. C. Chipman, sometime Private Secretary to the Minister of Marine and Fisheries ; later, Commissioner, Hudson's Bay Co., Winnipeg.

CHARITY.—Point, Christian Island, Simcoe ; because on Christian Islands, which were, at one time, known as Faith, Hope and Charity.

CHARLES.—Inlet, Parry Sound ; after a son of Capt. McGregor (q.v.).

CHARLIE.—Island, Manitoulin ; after a son of Admiral Bayfield.

CHATWIN.—Rock, Algoma ; after a steward in surveying steamer Bayfield.

CHEROKEE.—Rock, French River, Parry Sound ; after the tug Cherokee.

CHERUB.—Rock, North Channel, Algoma ; after the Cherub, a British gunboat on Lake Huron.

CHESAPEAKE.—Rock, Georgian Bay, Parry Sound ; after the U. S. frigate Chesapeake, captured by the Shannon in war of 1812-14.

CHEVALIER.—Islands, North Channel, Algoma ; after Chevalier St. Onge, a French halfbreed who, at one time resided on the western, and larger, of the two islands.

CHICORA.—Island, North Channel, Algoma ; after the steamer Chicora.
††CHICORA.—Shoal, St. Joseph Channel, Algoma.
CHIEF.—Rock, Parry Sound ; after Solomon, an Indian chief.
*CHILES.—Point, Simcoe ; name obsolete ; now Sturgeon Point ; possibly after an official of Penetanguishene naval station.
*CHIN.—Cape, Bruce ; named by Bayfield ; descriptive.
CHINA.—Reef, Bruce ; after the schooner China, wrecked on this reef.
††CHINA.—Cove, Bruce.
CHIPPEWA.—Bank, North Channel, Algoma ; after a lake vessel.
CHOWN.—Island, Parry Sound ; after George Y. Chown, Registrar, Queen's University, Kingston.
*CHRISTIAN.—Island, Simcoe; so called because the Christianized Hurons and the priests, fleeing from the Iroquois, took refuge on these islands and endeavoured to found a new settlement, trusting that they would there be safe from attack ; name probably antedated Bayfield's survey.
CHRYSLER.—Rocks, North Channel, Algoma ; after F. H. Chrysler, K.C., Ottawa.
CHURCH.—Hill, Manitoulin ; after Roman Catholic church near the hill.
CHURCHILL.—Islands, Parry Sound ; after the late Lord Randolph Churchill (1859-95), British statesman.
CITY.—Rock, Parry Sound ; after the steamer City of Midland.
*CLAPPERTON.—Channel, Manitoulin ; probably after Lieut. B. Clapperton who was returned, Oct. 16, 1815, as Acting Lieutenant in the Star on Lake Ontario. Possibly after Hugh Clapperton (1788-1827) ; made extensive explorations in the Soudan and Niger, Africa.
††*CLAPPERTON.—Island, Manitoulin.
††CLAPPERTON.—Harbour, Manitoulin.
CLARA.—Island, North Channel, Algoma ; after Mrs. W. J. Stewart (q.v.)
CLARENCE.—Channel, Parry Sound ; after Albert Victor, Duke of Clarence and Avondale, eldest son of Albert Edward, Prince of Wales ; died, 1892.
CLARKE.—Rock, Muskoka ; after the captain of a lake tug.
CLARKE.—Rock, Parry Sound ; after a fisherman.
CLAUDE.—Rock, Parry Sound ; after Claude Johnson, son of a Parry Sound merchant.
CLAY.—Cliff, Manitoulin ; characteristic.

*CLOCHE.—Island, North Channel, Sudbury ; the name applied to the island by the French, from the rocks ringing like a bell (Fr. *cloche*) on being struck.

††CLOCHE.—Channel, peninsula, bluff and mountain, Sudbury.

††LITTLE CLOCHE.—Island, Sudbury.

*CLUB.—Island, Manitoulin ; named by Bayfield ; derivation unknown.

††CLUB.—Harbour, and CLUB ISLAND, ledge, Manitoulin.

COATSWORTH.—Island, St. Joseph Channel, Algoma ; after a well-known Toronto family.

*COCKBURN.—Island, Manitoulin ; after Vice-Admiral Sir George Cockburn (1772-1853), Lord of the Admiralty, 1834-35 and 1841-46. Parry says that he named the northern portion of Baffin Island after Cockburn, "whose warm personal interest in everything relating to northern discovery can only be surpassed by the public zeal with which he has always promoted it." Or, after Lieut.-Col. Francis Cockburn, Deputy Quartermaster General who was in attendance on the Earl of Dalhousie on a tour of inspection, 1822.

††*COCKBURN.—Point, Simcoe ; named by Bayfield ; name obsolete ; now called Gidley Point.

COFFIN.—Cove and hill, Grey ; after a farmer residing there.

COGANASHENE.—Point, Muskoka ; abbreviation of Minnacoganashene (q.v.).

COLBY.—Island, St. Joseph Channel, Algoma ; after Hon. C. C. Colby, M.P. for Stanstead, 1867-91.

COLE.—Bay, Manitoulin ; after a Church of England clergyman at Manitowaning.

COLIN.—Point, Algoma ; after D. Colin Campbell, assistant to Capt. Boulton during survey of Georgian Bay.

††COLIN.—Rock, Parry Sound.

*COLLINS.—Inlet, Manitoulin ; after Philip Edward Collins, assistant to Capt. Bayfield during the survey of Lakes Huron and Superior.

††COLLINS.—Bay and reef, Parry Sound.

COLLINS.—Reef, Nottawasaga Bay, Simcoe ; after the lighthousekeeper, Geo. Collins, Collingwood.

*COLLS.—Bay, Georgian Bay, Simcoe ; name obsolete ; now Hog Bay ; possibly after an official of Penetanguishene naval station.

COLMER.—Ground, North Channel, Algoma ; after J. G. Colmer, from 1881 to 1903, Secretary to the High Commissioner for Canada, London.

*COLPOYS.—Bay, Bruce ; named by Bayfield ; after Rear-Admiral Sir Edward Griffith Colpoys ; died 1832.

COLTER.—Island, St. Joseph Channel, Algoma ; after N. R. Colter, M.P. for Carleton, N.B., 1891-96.

COLVILLE.—Island and bank, North Channel, Algoma ; after Major the Hon. C. R. W. Colville, Secretary to Lord Stanley, 1888-1892.

*COMB.—Point, Algoma; named by Bayfield ; derivation unknown.

*COMMODORE.—Cape, Bruce ; after Commodore Sir E. W. C. R. Owen (q.v.) ; commanded naval forces on Great Lakes in 1815.

CONE.—Island, Georgian Bay, Parry Sound ; descriptive.

*CONFIANCE.—Rock, Bruce ; after the Confiance (2) gunboat on Lake Huron; formerly the U. S. S. Scorpion, captured Sept. 6th, 1814. The first Confiance was Yeo's (q.v.) first command, a French privateer captured by him at Muros Bay ; the second was a 36-gun ship carrying Downie's flag on Lake Champlain, captured off Plattsburg, Sept. 11th, 1814 ; the third was the namesake of Confiance rock ("shoal" on Bayfield's chart).

CONMEE.—Island, North Channel ; after James Conmee, Port Arthur ; M.P. for Thunder Bay and Rainy River, 1904-11.

COOK.—Bay, Manitoulin ; after the late John Cook, first settler there.

COOK.—Island, North Channel, Algoma ; after H. H. Cook, M.P. for North Simcoe, 1872-78 ; for East Simcoe, 1882-91.

COOPER.—Rock, St. Joseph Channel, Algoma ; after R. W. Cooper, clerk in Rideau Canal Office, Ottawa.

COOTE.—Island, Parry Sound ; Lieut. W. E. Parry commanded one of the boats during a "cutting-out" expedition up the Connecticut River in 1814. The expedition was under the command of Capt. Coote of H. M. brig Borer.

COPPER.—Island, St. Joseph Channel, Algoma ; this name is also applied to numerous other features in Canada, usually owing to the real or alleged discovery of this mineral in the vicinity.

COPPERHEAD.—Island and harbour, Parry Sound ; from copperhead snakes found on the island.

COPPERMINE.—Point, Algoma ; descriptive.

CORBIER.—Cove, West Bay, Manitoulin ; after a half-breed chief living at Honora Bay.

CORBMAN.—Point, Franklin Island, Parry Sound ; after a resident of the locality.

CORISANDE.—Rock, Parry Sound ; after the schooner Corisande.

CORNER.—Rock, Parry Sound ; descriptive.

CORNET.—Point, Griffiths Island, Grey ; after a fisherman.

CORNWALLIS.—Rock, Parry Sound ; after Admiral the Hon. W. Cornwallis, who was in command of the Channel fleet in 1803. Parry went to sea for the first time, in Cornwallis' flagship.

COSTIGAN.—Point, Manitoulin ; after the Hon. John Costigan, Minister of Inland Revenue, 1882-92 ; Secretary of State, 1892-94 ; Minister of Marine and Fisheries, 1894-96.

COUNTS.—Bank, Key Harbour, Parry Sound ; resident, Sault Ste. Marie.

COURSOL.—Bay, Algoma ; after the late C. J. Coursol, M.P. for Montreal East, 1878 till death in 1888.

COURTNEY.—Island and bank, Manitoulin ; after J. M. Courtney, C.M.G., I.S.O., late Deputy Minister of Finance.

COUTLEE.—Island, Thunder Bay ; after Chas. R. Coutlee, C.E., Chief Engineer, Ottawa River Regulation ; graduate, Royal Military College, 1886.

*****COVE.**—Island, Bruce ; descriptive.

††**COVE ISLAND.**—Harbour and ground, Bruce.

COVE OF CORK.—Bay, Bruce ; probably from fancied resemblance to cove at foot of bay, to Cove of Cork, Ireland.

COWIE.—Reef, Muskoka ; after F. W. Cowie, Chief Engineer, Montreal Harbour Commission ; sometime, Chief Engineer, St. Lawrence ship channel.

COWPER.—Island, Parry Sound ; after George B. Cowper, who was Chief Clerk, Crown Lands Department, Ontario.

COX.—Island, St. Joseph Channel, Algoma ; after a draughtsman in Department of Marine and Fisheries.

CRACROFT.—Rock, Parry Sound ; after Miss Sophia Cracroft, niece of Sir John Franklin, the famous Arctic explorer.

CRAFTSMAN.—Point, Algoma ; after the schooner Craftsman.

CRAWFORD.—Island, North Channel, Algoma ; after the Hon. Thomas Crawford, M.P.P. for West Toronto since 1898 ; Speaker of Legislature, 1907.

CREAK.—Island, North Channel, Sudbury ; after a naval officer, Admiralty 1890—probably Capt. Ettrick William Creak, C.B., retired, 1891.

CREASOR.—Bight, Manitoulin ; after Judge Creasor, Owen Sound.

CREBO.—Rock, St. Joseph Channel, Algoma ; after a Killarney merchant.

CREIGHTON.—Point, Manitoulin ; after David Creighton, M.P.P. for North Grey, 1875-90 ; Asst. Receiver-General, Toronto, 1895.

CRESCENT.—Island, Simcoe ; descriptive of its crescentic outline.

††*****CRESCENT.**—Island Manitoulin, and island, Parry Sound.

CRICKET.—Island, St. Joseph Channel, Algoma ; after Miss C. Clark, Henderson, N. Carolina.

*CROKER.—Cape, Bruce ; named by Bayfield, after John Wilson Croker (1780-1853), Secretary to the Admiralty 1809-30 ; he was an enthusiastic supporter of the search for the Northwest passage and of the Franklin search.

††*CROKER.—Island, North Channel, Algoma.

CROOKS.—Island, North Channel, Algoma ; after late Hon. Adam Crooks, M.P.P. for West Toronto and, later, South Oxford ; Provincial Treasurer 1872-76 ; Minister of Education, 1876-83.

CROSS.—Island, Serpent Harbour, Algoma ; "so-called because it lies athwart the channel into the harbour."

††CROSS.—Ledge, Parry Sound.

CROWLEY.—Reef, North Channel, Algoma ; after a fisherman at Grant fishery station.

CRUISER.—Rock, St. Joseph Channel, Algoma ; after the Cruiser, purchased from Allan Gilmour, Ottawa, and used in fishery protection service on Georgian Bay and Lake Huron.

CUBA.—Rock, Georgian Bay, Parry Sound ; after the steamer Cuba.

CUMBERLAND.—Rock, North Channel, Algoma ; after steamer Cumberland.

CUNNINGHAM.—Point, Manitoulin ; after Cyril Cunningham Boulton, son of Capt. Boulton.

CURRAN.—Rock, North Channel, Algoma ; after Hon. J. J. Curran, M.P. for Montreal Centre, 1892-95 ; Solicitor-General, 1892-95 ; Judge, Superior Court, Montreal District, 1895.

CUTKNIFE.—Cove, Bedford I., Sudbury ; after action at Cutknife Creek, Saskatchewan, Riel rebellion, 1885.

CYRIL.—Cove, Manitoulin ; after Cyril Cunningham Boulton, a son of Capt. Boulton.

††CYRIL.—Point, Parry Sound.

DALRYMPLE.—Island, North Channel, Algoma ; after Alexander Dalrymple (1737-1808), first Hydrographer to the Admiralty.

DALTON.—Reef, North Channel, Algoma ; after late Dalton McCarthy, M.P. for Cardwell, 1874-78 ; M.P. for North Simcoe, 1878-98.

††DALTON.—Reef, Nottawasaga Bay, Grey.

DALY.—Island, North Channel, Algoma ; after late Hon. T. M. Daly, Minister of the Interior, 1892-96.

††DALY.—Point, Christian I., Simcoe.

DANIEL.—Shoal, St. Joseph Channel, Algoma ; after Rev. A. W. Daniel, Rothesay, N.B. ; graduate, Royal Military College, 1881.

DANVILLE.—Ground, Manitoulin ; after commander of a gunboat on Great Lakes.

DARBY.—Rock, North Channel, Algoma ; after Darby Bergin, M.D. (q.v.), sometime M.P. for Cornwall and Stormont.

*DARCH.—Island, North Channel, Algoma ; named by Bayfield ; derivation unknown.

DARLING.—Reef, Bruce ; after a fisherman.

DART.—Rock, Alexander Inlet, Parry Sound ; after a British surveying vessel, 470 tons. Another Dart was with Nelson at Copenhagen.

DAUPHINE.—Rock, Parry Sound ; in 1524, Verrazano, in the Dauphine, explored the Atlantic coast of North America from lat. 34 degrees north, to Newfoundland.

DAVID.—Island, North Channel, Algoma ; after the late Hon. David Mills (1831-1903), Minister of Justice, 1876-78 and 1897-1902.

DAVIES.—Rock, North Channel, Algoma ; after Sir Louis Davies, K.C.M.G., Justice, Supreme Court of Canada ; Minister of Marine and Fisheries, 1896-1901.

DAVIN.—Point, John I., Algoma ; after Nicholas Flood Davin, K.C. (1843-1900) ; M.P. for Assiniboia West, 1887-1900.

DAVY.—Island and rock, Parry Sound ; after maternal parent of Mrs. W. J. Stewart.

DAWSON.—Island, St. Joseph Channel, Algoma ; after late S. E. Dawson, M.P., whose representations induced the Dominion Government to commence the survey of Georgian Bay.

*DAWSON.—Rock, Manitoulin ; named by Bayfield, probably after George Robert Dawson, Secretary to the Admiralty, 1834-35.

DEAD.—Island, Parry Sound ; "from the fact of its having been in olden times the burial place of the Indian tribes frequenting these parts."

DEAN.—Bay, Manitoulin ; after David and Thomas Dean who own timber lands here.

DE CAEN.—Rock, North Channel, Algoma ; after Emery de Caen, who received Quebec when restored by English, 1632, after capture by Kirke.

DE CELLES.—Island, North Channel, Algoma ; after Alfred D. De Celles, General Librarian of Parliament.

DEEP.—Cove, Huckleberry I., Parry Sound ; descriptive.

DEEP.—Point, Darch I. Algoma ; descriptive of water off point.

DEEPWATER.—Island, Fraser Bay, Manitoulin ; from having deep water nearly all around it.

††DEEPWATER.—Point, Parry I., Parry Sound.

††DEEPWATER.—Point, Griffith I., Grey.

DEER.—Island, Muskoka ; from its proximity to Moose Deer Point.

DELF.—Island, Muskoka ; from broken crockery found on it.

DELOS.—Island, Parry Sound ; probably after a half-breed. Possibly after Delos, an island in the Aegean Sea—the mythical floating island and birthplace of Apollo and Artemis.

DENISON.—Rock, North Channel, Algoma ; after Col. George Taylor Denison, police magistrate, Toronto.

DENNIS.—Island, North Channel, Algoma ; after Colonel Stoughton Dennis, C.M.G., Surveyor-General, 1871-78 ; Deputy Minister of the Interior, 1878-81.

DENT.—Bay and rock, Parry Sound ; after a resident of the locality.

DEPOT.—Bay, Parry Sound ; takes its name from being the landing place in past years of the supplies for the Parry Island Indians.

DERING.—Rock, Parry Sound ; after an armed Hudson's Bay Co. vessel, which took part in fight with French fleet under d'Iberville, 1697.

DE ROBERVAL.—Point, Algoma ; after Jean Francois de la Roque, Sieur de Roberval, first viceroy of New France, 1540.

DESJARDINS.—Bay, St. Joseph I., Algoma ; after Hon. Alphonse Desjardins, M.P. for Hochelaga, 1874-92 ; Senator for De Lorimier division, 1892.

DEVIL.—Gap, St. Joseph Channel, Algoma ; an experienced navigator states that it was so called because it is exceedingly difficult to navigate it.

††DEVIL.—Island, St. Joseph Channel.

DEVIL.—Island, Bruce ; the island is surrounded by shoal water and dangerous for vessels to approach.

††DEVIL ISLAND.—Bank and channel, Bruce.

DEVILS ELBOW.—Channel, Parry Sound ; from a sharp bend in the channel.

DEWDNEY.—Island and rock, North Channel, Algoma ; after the Hon. Edgar Dewdney, Minister of the Interior, 1888-92, and Lieut.-Governor of British Columbia, 1892-97.

DIGBY.—Bank, Muskoka ; after Hon. Gerald F. Digby, Lieutenant in the Victoria, sunk in collision with the Camperdown, 1893.

DIVIDED.—Island, Parry Sound ; descriptive.

DIXIE.—Rock, North Channel, Algoma ; after the tug Dixie.

DIXON.—Bank, Parry Sound ; after a fisherman.

DIXON.—Island, North Channel, Algoma ; after a naval surveyor.

DOBIE.—Point, Algoma; after James S. Dobie, merchant, Thessalon.

DOG.—Point, Mississagi Island, Algoma; from a dog being found there during the survey.

††DOG POINT.—Shoal, Algoma.

DOKIS.—Island, Parry Sound; late Chief Dokis, Nipissing band of Indians.

DOROTHY.—Inlet, Algoma; after Mrs. W. P. Anderson (q.v.), Ottawa.

DOT.—Island, North Channel, Algoma; descriptive (very small).

DOTY.—Rocks, Parry Sound; after a tug.

DOUBLE.—Island, Parry Sound; "divided into two parts, hence the name."

††DOUBLE.—Island, North Channel, Algoma, and island, Simcoe.

††DOUBLE.—Cove, island, and DOUBLE ISLAND, ledge, Manitoulin.

DOUBLE TOP.—Island, Western Islands, Parry Sound; "it is nearly divided into two small rocks."

DOUCET.—Rock, North Channel, Algoma; after Emile Doucet, C.E., District Engineer, National Transcontinental Ry.; graduate of Royal Military College, 1880.

*DOUGLAS.—Bay, Simcoe; named by Bayfield, probably after Wm. Robt. Keith Douglas, Lord of the Admiralty, 1822-27; name obsolete; now Thunder Bay.

DOUGLAS.—Point, Simcoe; after a marine surveyor (voyageur's statement, probably wrong).

DOWELL.—Rock, Parry Sound; after a merchant of Parry Sound.

DOYLE.—Rock, Smith Bay, Manitoulin; after one of the crew of the Bayfield.

DRAPER.—Island, Manitoulin; after Hon. W. H. Draper, Chief Justice of the Queen's Bench, 1863-68; Chief Justice of Ontario, 1868-77.

DREVER.—Rock, Parry Sound; after a fisherman.

DREW.—Island, North Channel, Algoma; after the commander of a gunboat on Great Lakes in 1838.

DRIFTWOOD.—Cove, Bruce; characteristic.

DUETT.—Rock, Georgian Bay, Parry Sound; after a boatman in steamer Bayfield.

DUFFERIN.—Island, Manitoulin; after the Rt. Hon. Frederick Temple Blackwood, Marquis of Dufferin and Ava (1826-1902), Governor-General of Canada, 1872-78.

DUFFY.—Island, Parry Sound ; after a fisherman.
DUKE.—Island, and rock, Parry Sound ; after Prince Albert Victor, Duke of Clarence (1864-1892).
DUNCAN.—Rock, St. Joseph Channel, Algoma ; after a Marksville hotelkeeper.
*DUNDAS.—Cape, Bruce ; named by Bayfield after Robert Saunders Dundas, 2nd Viscount Melville (1771-1851) ; First Lord'of the Admiralty, 1812-27, and 1828-30.
DUNLEVIE.—Point, St. Joseph Channel, Algoma ; after the late John Dunlevie, Winnipeg.
DUROQUET.—Point, Manitoulin ; after the R. C. priest at Wikwemikong.
DUTCHMAN.—Head, Manitoulin ; descriptive of outline.
DUVAL.—Island, St. Joseph I., Algoma ; after Prof. Duval, Royal Military College, Kingston.
DWYER.—Island, North Channel, Algoma ; after an engineer, Algoma Mills.
*DYER.—Bay, Bruce ; named by Bayfield after John Jones Dyer, Chief Clerk of the Admiralty.
DYMENT.—Rock, Algoma ; after a lumber merchant, Barrie.

EAGLE.—Cove and point, Cove I., Bruce ; after the schooner Eagle.
EAGLE.—Island and point, North Channel, Algoma ; probably same as Eagle rock.
EAGLE.—Rock, Parry Sound ; after the steamer Eagle.
††EAGLE.—Reef, Parry Sound.
EAGLE NEST.—Point, Algoma ; after eagle's nest on it.
EAGOR.—Bank, Muskoka ; after a boatman in steamer Bayfield.
EARL.—Patches, Bruce ; after an old resident (pilot) of Tobermory.
EATON.—Point, Manitoulin ; after a Church of England clergyman.
ECHO.—Island, Bruce ; characteristic.
EDITH.—Island, St. Joseph Channel, Algoma ; after Mrs. F. A. Beament, Ottawa, née Belford.
EDSALL.—Bank, Parry Sound ; old name of surveying steamer Bayfield.
EDWARD.—Island, Parry Sound ; after Admiral Sir William Edward Parry (q.v.).

EDWARDS.—Bank, Parry Sound ; after Lady Parry, née Catherine Edwards Hankinson.

*EGG.—Island, North Channel, Algoma ; many gulls' eggs were found on the island.

EIGHT-FATHOM.—Patch, Georgian Bay, Bruce ; after the depth of water on it.

EKOBA.—Bay, Algoma; corruption of Echo Bay ; which from Echo Lake ; latter named after the "echo" from the bluffs on its shores.

ELEVEN-FOOT.—Rock, Sudbury ; from having that depth of water on it.

ELGIN.—Rock, Parry S und ; after the Earl of Elgin (1811-63) ; Governor-General of Canada, 1847-53.

*ELIZABETH.—Bay, Manitoulin ; named by Captain Bayfield (q.v.) after his mother.

††ELIZABETH.—Point, Manitoulin.

ELLIS.—Point, Algoma; after Ashmead Ellis Bartlett Burdett-Coutts, British politician, son of Ellis Bartlett, U.S.A. ; m. Baroness Burdett-Coutts, 1881, and assumed the surname "Burdett-Coutts" ; Lord of the Admiralty, 1885.

ELM.—Island, Algoma ; "from a single tree of that nature which it still preserves."

††ELM-TREE.—Island, Parry Sound.

EMERALD.—Point, Serpent Harbour, Algoma; after the steamer Emerald.

EMERY.—Reef, Algoma ; after the U.S. tug Temple Emery.

EMILY.—Island, North Channel, Algoma ; after the wife of Col. Boswell, 90th Regt., Winnipeg.

EMILY MAXWELL.—R ef, Fitzwilliam I., Manitoulin ; after the U.S. schooner Emily Maxwell ; stranded on Fitzwilliam Island.

EMPIRE.—Ledge, St. Joseph Channel, Algoma ; after Canadian lake steamer, United Empire.

ENGLISH.—Point, Cloche I., Sudbury ; after a Little Current hotelkeeper.

ERIE.—Shingle, Manitoulin ; after the Erie, a trading vessel, wrecked on it.

††ERIE.—Channel and bank, Manitoulin.

ESTHER.—Cliff, Grey ; after the daughter of a farmer.

ESTHER.—Rock, Parry Sound ; after a sister of Capt. Boulton.

ETHEL.—Rock, Aird I. Algoma; after Capt. Boulton's daughter.

EULAS.—Ground, Algoma ; after Hon. George Eulas Foster,

Minister of Marine and Fisheries, 1885-88 ; Minister of Finance, 1888-96 ; Minister of Trade and Commerce since 1911.

EUROPA.—Reef, North Channel, Algoma ; after the Europa, a lake vessel.

EVANGELINE.—Patch, Algoma ; after Bishop Sullivan's yacht.

EVANS.—Point, Badgley I., Manitoulin ; after Sir Frederick John Owen Evans (1815-85), British hydrographer.

EVELYN.—Rock, Parry Sound ; after Evelyn Steele, Dept. of Secretary of State, Ottawa.

EVERARD.—Reef, Parry Sound ; after Commander Thomas Everard, R.N., who came from H.M. brig Wasp then lying at Quebec ; commanded expedition of Aug. 1, 1813, against Plattsburg and Saranac.

FAGAN.—Ground, Manitoulin ; after a waiter in steamer Bayfield.

FAITH.—Point, Beckwith I., Simcoe ; after the armed schooner Faith.

FALSE DETOUR.—Channel between Cockburn and Drummond Islands ; called "False" to distinguish it from the true Detour channel which is at the other—western—end of Drummond Island ; called "Detour" because it was the passage used by the fur-traders when going to Mackinac. As Mackinac was off at one side of the regular route from Montreal to Lake Superior, they were thus forced to make a "detour" to reach it.

FANNY.—Island, Manitoulin ; after Christian name of Mrs. Bayfield.

FARR.—Rock, Parry Sound ; after a fisherman.

FAWCETT.—Island, North Channel, Algoma ; after Thomas Fawcett, D.L.S., Niagara Falls.

FAWKES.—Rock, Muskoka ; after Ayscough G. H. Fawkes, midshipman in the Victoria, sunk in collision with the Camperdown off Tripoli, June 23, 1893.

FELIX.—Rock, Muskoka ; after Felix Foreman, fleet engineer in the Victoria sunk in collision with the Camperdown, 1893.

FINNIS.—Rock, Manitoulin ; after Capt. Finnis who was in command of the Queen Charlotte and was killed in the battle of Lake Erie, Sept. 10th, 1813.

FISH.—Point, George I., Manitoulin ; "derives its name from being the place where the fishermen of Killarney formerly deposited their fish refuse."

FISH CREEK.—Point, Rous I., Sudbury ; after the action of Fish Creek, Riel rebellion, 1885.

FISHER.—Bay and shoal, St. Joseph I., Algoma ; after a farmer, who lived on the shore of the bay.

FISHER.—Island, North Channel, Algoma ; after the Hon. Sidney Fisher, Minister of Agriculture, 1896-1911.

FISHERMAN.—Gut, North Channel, Algoma ; so called because frequented by fishermen.

††FISHERMAN.—Point, Simcoe.

*FISHERMAN.—Shoal, Simcoe ; name obsolete ; named by Bayfield.

FISHERY.—Island, North Channel, Algoma ; descriptive.

††FISHERY.—Island, Parry Sound.

††FISHERY ISLAND.—Cove, Manitoulin.

FISHERY.—Point, Manitoulin ; it "affords shelter to boats employed in attending the pound nets in the locality."

FISK.—Reef, North Channel, Algoma ; after the captain of a lake vessel.

FITZGERALD.—Bay, Parry Sound ; after a resident of Parry Sound.

*FITZWILLIAM. —Island, Manitoulin ; after Captain (later, Vice-Admiral) William Fitzwilliam Owen (1774-1857) ; died at St. John, N.B. Lieut. Bayfield was his assistant in the survey of Lake Ontario, 1816-17.

††FITZWILLIAM.—Channel, Manitoulin.

FIVE-FATHOM.—Patch, Manitowaning Bay, Manitoulin ; descriptive—"5¼ fathoms on it."

FIVE-MILE.—Bay, Parry Sound ; because supposed to be five miles long.

FLAT.—Island, Goat Channel, Sudbury ; descriptive ; numerous other features bear this name.

††FLAT ROCK.—Bank, Simcoe.

FLEMING.—Bank, Algoma ; after Sir Sandford Fleming, Ottawa, eminent Canadian civil engineer.

††FLEMING.—Rock, Nottawasaga Bay, Grey.

FLINT.—Rocks, Aird I., Algoma ; after the late Senator Billa Flint, Belleville.

FLOOD.—Island, North Channel, Algoma ; after the late Nicholas Flood Davin, M.P. for West Assiniboia.

FLOWER-POT. —Island, Bruce ; "derives its name from two remarkable isolated rocks close to the east shore, both being much eroded at the bases, with a few small trees on their summits, much resemble gigantic flower pots."

FLUMMERFELT. —Patch, Bruce ; after a fireman in steamer Bayfield.

FORBES.—Island, North Channel, Algoma ; after John Colin Forbes, artist, Toronto.

FOREMAN.—Islands, Muskoka ; after Felix Foreman, Fleet-Engineer in the Victoria, sunk in collision with the Camperdown, 1893.

FORSHAW.—Island, St Joseph I., Algoma ; after late Prof. Forshaw Day, sometime Professor of Drawing at the Royal Military College, Kingston.

FORT.—Channel, Algoma ; after the remains of a fort in the locality.

FORTIN.—Rocks, North Channel, Algoma ; after Pierre Fortin, M.P. for Gaspe, 1867-74 and 1878-87 ; Senator, 1887 ; d. 1888.

FOSTER.—Bank, Sudbury ; after Hon. George Eulas Foster, Minister of Marine and Fisheries, 1885-88 ; Minister of Finance, 1888-96 ; Minister of Trade and Commerce since 1911.

††FOSTER.—Rock, Parry Sound.

FOUL.—Bight, Algoma ; descriptive.

FOURNIER.—Islands, Serpent Harbour, Algoma ; after Hon. Telesphore Fournier, Minister of Inland Revenue, 1873-74 ; Minister of Justice, 1874-75 ; Postmaster-General, 1875 ; Judge, Supreme Court, 1875-95 ; d. 1896.

*FOX.—Islands, Algoma ; probably because numerous foxes found on these islands.

FRANCES.—Point, Par y Sound ; after steamer Frances Smith, which named by first owner after his wife.

††FRANCES SMITH.—Shoal, Key Harbour, Parry Sound.

FRANCIS.—Brook, Manitowaning Bay, Manitoulin ; after a doctor, Manitowaning.

*FRANCIS.—Point, Manitoulin ; named by Bayfield ; derivation unknown.

FRANK.—Rock, St. Joseph Channel, Algoma ; after Frank Marks, Marksville.

FRANK.—Ledge, Smith Bay, Manitoulin ; after Frank McGregor, a son of sailing master of the Bayfield.

*FRANKLIN.—Inlet, Parry Sound ; after Sir John Franklin, Captain, R.N. ; famous Arctic explorer ; in 1825, passed through Georgian Bay on his way to the Arctic and met Bayfield ; name practically obsolete ; usually called Shawanaga Bay.

*FRASER.—Bay, Manitoulin ; named by Bayfield ; derivation unknown.

††FRASER BAY.—Hill, Manitoulin.

FRASER.—Rocks, North Channel, Algoma ; after Hon. C. F. Fraser, Provincial Secretary 1873-74 ; Commissioner of Public Works, 1874-94.

FRECHETTE.—Bay and island, Manitoulin, and island, North Channel, Algoma ; after the late Louis Honoré Fréchette, French-Canadian poet.

FREDERIC.—Inlet, Parry Sound ; after Provincial Lieut. Chas. Frederic Rolette (1783-1831) ; "entered Royal Navy ; was at the battle of the Nile (wounded) and Trafalgar ; 1st Lieutenant in the Hunter, 1812 ; captured the packet Cuyahoga, 3rd July, 1812 ; was at Put-in Bay, taking command of the Lady Prevost when commander was wounded ; a prisoner of war and confined as a hostage in Frankfort penitentiary."

FREER.—Point, Manitoulin ; after the late Capt. H. C. Freer, South Staffordshire Regiment ; graduate of Royal Military College, 1880.

FREMLIN.—Island and reef, St. Joseph Channel, Algoma ; after a Marksville lumber merchant.

FRENCH.—Island, North Channel, Algoma ; so called because a number of islands in vicinity were named after early French explorers and missionaries.

FRENCH.—River, Parry Sound ; the waterway by which the early French traders came from eastern Canada to the western country.

FROST.—Point, Manitoulin ; after a clergyman at Sheguiandah.

GAFFNEY.—Island, St. Joseph I., Algoma ; after an officer of the U.S. engineers.

GAHAN.—Rock, Muskoka ; after Dr. Gahan, Penetanguishene.

GALBRAITH.—Point, Aird I., Algoma ; after Dr. John Galbraith, Dean of the Faculty of Applied Science, University of Toronto.

GALT.—Island, Sudbury ; after the late Sir A. T. Galt, G.C.M.G. (1817-1893), Minister of Finance, 1867 ; High Commissioner for Canada in the United Kingdom, 1880-83.

GAMON.—Rock, Nottawasaga Bay, Simcoe ; after a lawyer of Collingwood.

GARDEN.—Island, Goat Channel, Sudbury ; named by contrast, being a barren, limestone island.

GARDEN.—Bay, Algoma ; from Garden River, which from a cultivated or cleared spot at the mouth.

GARIBALDI.—Island, Serpent Harbour, Algoma ; after a trading vessel.

GARRISON.—Point, Simcoe ; where the first fort was built.

*GAT.—Point, Cove I., Bruce ; named by Bayfield ; derivation unknown.

††GAT POINT.—Reef, Cove I., Bruce.

GAUGE.—Islands, Parry Sound ; "The name was given to this small cluster on account of a beacon fastened to the eastern islet to indicate to the Midland and Parry Sound steamer the depth of water in South Channel."

GAUTHIER.—Point, Manitoulin ; after a resident.

GAVAZZI.—Island, North Channel, Algoma ; after Rev. Father Gavazzi, whose preaching in Montreal led to riots in 1854.

GAVILLER.—Island, Parry Sound ; after a Church of England clergyman, Rev. Hans Gaviller.

GEORGE.—Rock, Nottawasaga Bay, Simcoe ; after George Moberly, Collingwood.

*GEORGE.—Island, Manitoulin ; after King George IV, reigning monarch at date of Bayfield's survey.

††GEORGE.—Rocks, Manitoulin.

††*GEORGE.—Lake, St. Mary River, Algoma.

††*GEORGIAN. —Bay, Lake Huron.

GERALDINE.—Island, Muskoka ; after tug Geraldine.

GEREAUX.—Island, Parry Sound ; after the light-keeper on the island.

GERMAIN.—Island, Key Harbour, Parry Sound; after a launch owner, Byng Inlet.

GERTRUDE.—Island, Manitoulin ; after a daughter of Admiral Bayfield.

GERVASE.—Island, North Channel, Algoma ; after one of the ships in Capt. Kirke's squadron which captured Quebec, 1629 ; the vessel named after Capt. Kirke's father, Gervase Kirke.

*GIANT'S TOMB.—Island, Simcoe ; "from the appearance of the highest part, as seen from 'The Westerns,' when, usually, the hill appears out of the water, and resembles a huge tomb."

GIBBONS.—Point, Manitoulin ; after a retired naval officer, Little Current.

GIBRALTAR.—Cliff, Manitoulin ; fancied resemblance to the famous peak.

GIBSON.—Point, Manitoulin, and reef, Muskoka ; after a draughtsman at Admiralty in 1890.

GIDLEY.—Point, Simcoe ; after the owner.

*GIG.—Point, Cove I., Bruce ; named by Bayfield, probably after his gig (boat).

GILEAD.—Rock, Muskoka ; from balm of Gilead trees on rock.

GILLESPIE. — Island, Muskoka ; after a Mr. Gillespie, of Hamilton.

GILLFORD.—Rocks, Georgian Bay, Muskoka ; after Lord Gillford, Flag-Lieutenant in the Victoria, sunk in collision with the Camperdown, June 23, 1893

GILLMOR.—Point, Frechette I., Algoma ; after the late Arthur H. Gillmor, M.P. for Charlotte, N.B., 1874-96 ; Senator, 1900.

GISBORNE.—Point, Croker I., Algoma ; after the late Francis N. Gisborne, Superintendent, Dominion Telegraphs.

GLACIS.—Island, Muskoka ; after its "steep, bare, western face."

GLADMAN.—Rock, Parry Sound ; after a resident of Parry Sound.

GLADWYN.—Rock, Parry Sound ; the schooner Gladwyn assisted in defence of Fort Detroit, 1763 ; the fort was commanded by Captain Gladwyn.

GLADYS.—Island, Thunder Bay ; after a member of an Ottawa family.

*GLOUCESTER.—Bay, Simcoe ; after H.R.H. the Princess Mary (1776-1857), fourth daughter of George III. She was the last surviving of the fifteen children of George III. Or, after her husband, and first cousin, H.R.H. William Frederick, Duke of Gloucester and Edinburgh. Name appears on Bouchette's map, 1815, but is now obsolete ; now, Midland Bay.

*GLOUCESTER.—Point Simcoe ; name obsolete ; now Sucker Creek Point.

*GLOVER.—Point, Simcoe ; possibly after an official of Penetanguishene naval station.

GLYN.—Rock, Parry Sound ; after the captain of H.M.S. Vanguard, in which Parry (q.v.) served, 1808-09.

GOALEN.—Island. North Channel, Algoma ; after an assistant surveyor with Capt. Tooker in hydrographic survey of Newfoundland.

GODFREY.—Island, North Channel, Algoma ; after a friend of Captain Boulton.

GO-HOME.—River, Muskoka ; translation of the Indian name *kewanenashing*.

††GO-HOME.—Bay, Muskoka.

GOLD-HUNTER.—Rock, Smith Bay, Manitoulin ; after schooner Gold-hunter, stranded near here.

GOLDWIN.—Rock, Parry Sound ; after Prof. Goldwin Smith, "The Grange," Toronto.

GOOD CHEER.—Island, Parry Sound ; a descriptive name given by the owner of the island, Chancellor Boyd.

GORDON.—Point, Simcoe ; the site of an old trading post established by George Gordon, 1825.

GORDON.—Rocks, Parry Sound ; after Lieutenant Andrew R. Gordon, R.N., in command of Hudson Bay expedition, 1888.

††GORDON.—Rock, Sudbury.

GORE.—Bay, and GORE BAY, town, Manitoulin ; after the steamboat Gore which plied between Collingwood and Sault Ste. Marie in the "sixties" ; the steamboat named after Sir Charles S.

Gore, who assisted in suppression of the rebellion of 1837-38. Formerly called Janet Cove and named by Admiral Bayfield.

††GORE.—Rock, Simcoe ; the Gore struck on this rock.

GORREL.—Point, Manitoulin ; after a farmer of Gore Bay.

GOURDEAU.—Patch, Manitoulin ; after Colonel F. F. Gourdeau, late Deputy Minister of Marine and Fisheries.

GOW.—Point and shoal, Strawberry I., Manitoulin ; after a summer resident of the island.

GOWLAND.—Point, Parry Sound ; after a doctor, Parry Sound.

GRĀBURN.—Island, Parry Sound ; after an officer of the Department of Marine and Fisheries ; he made a survey of French River.

GRACE.—Bank, Muskoka ; after the tug Grace.

GRAND.—Bank, Manitoulin ; descriptive.

*GRANT.—EAST, MIDDLE and WEST, islands, North Channel, Algoma ; after an officer of the gunboat Confiance, on Lake Huron in 1826. Or, after Charles Grant (later, Lord Glenelg), Treasurer of the Navy, 1827-28.

GRANTHAM. —Shoal, Georgian Bay, Manitoulin ; after the schooner Grantham.

GRAVEL.—Point, St. Joseph I., Algoma ; characteristic.

††GRAVELLY.—Point and bay, Bruce.

GRAVEYARD.—Point, St. Joseph Channel, Algoma ; descriptive.

*GRAVIER.—Point, St. Joseph I., Algoma ; old voyageur name ; now translated into English form. See Gravel Point. Appears on Bayfield's chart.

GRAY.—Point, Manitoulin ; after Major Gray, formerly resident engineer, Public Works Department of Canada, Toronto.

GREEN.—Island, Parry Sound ; this and numerous other features so named after the green timber covering them.

GREENFIELD.—Reef, Bruce ; after the colour of the water enclosed by the reef.

GREENWAY.—Island, North Channel, Algoma ; after Thomas Greenway (1838-1908), som time Premier of Manitoba.

GRIEVE.—Rock, Muskoka ; after Arthur C. Grieve, midshipman in the Victoria, sunk in collision with the Camperdown off Tripoli, June 23rd, 1893.

GRIFFIN.—Bank, Manitoulin ; after M. J. Griffin, General Librarian, Parliamentary Library.

*GRIFFITH.—Island, Grey ; after Vice-Admiral Sir Edward Griffith Colpoys (q.v.).

GRIPER.—Bank, Parry Sound ; after one of Parry's vessels in his expedition in search of the Northwest passage, 1819-20.

*GRONDINE.—Point, Manitoulin ; named by the voyageurs after the grinding (grumbling) sound made by the rocks of the shore when affected by the waves.

††GRONDINE.—Rock, Manitoulin.

GUANO.—Rock, Key Harbour, Parry Sound ; so-called because much resorted to by gulls, etc.

GULL.—Rocks, Parry Sound ; this, and other features, so called because much frequented by gulls.

GULNARE.—Point, North Channel, Algoma ; after the steamer Gulnare, surveying vessel, Newfoundland. The first Gulnare was used by Bayfield during his surveys of St. Lawrence River and Gulf.

*GUN.—Point, Bruce ; named by Bayfield, probably to commemorate the loss of a gun or similar occurrence.

GUNBOAT.—Shoal, North Channel, Algoma ; after its position near Minstrel rock which named after a British gunboat.

GUNDERSON.—Shoal, Grey ; after a lake captain.

GUY.—Rock, Parry Sound ; after a son of Capt. Boulton.

GWYNNE.—Bay, Algoma ; after John Wellington Gwynne, Justice, High Court for Ontario, 1868-79 ; Judge, Supreme Court, 1879-1902.

HAGARTY.—Islands, North Channel, Algoma ; after Hon. Sir John Hawkins Hagarty (1816-1900), Justice of the High Court for Ontario, Queen's Bench Div. 1862-68 ; Chief Justice of Common Pleas, 1868-78 ; Chief Justice, Queen's Bench, 1874-84 ; Chief Justice for Ontario, 1884-97 ; knighted, 1897.

HAGGART.—Point, Parry Sound ; after late Hon. John Haggart, M.P. ; Postmaster-General, 1882-92 ; Minister of Railways and Canals, 1892-96.

HA-HA.—Rock, Muskoka ; after the tug Ha-ha.

HAIGHT.—Rock, Parry Sound ; after a lawyer of Parry Sound.

HAILSTONE.—Island, Parry Sound ; after a resident.

HALCRO.—Island, Parry Sound ; after Chancellor Boyd's yacht.

HALFWAY.—Islands, Waubuno Channel, Sudbury ; because situated about half-way through the channel.

*HALFMOON.—Island, Bruce ; descriptive of outline.

††HALFMOON.—Bank, Bruce.

HALKETT.—Rock, Manitoulin ; after J. B. Halkett, chief clerk, Department of Marine and Fisheries.

HALL.—Reef and rock, Parry Sound ; after a steam barge.

HALL.—Shoal, St. Joseph Channel, Algoma ; after one of the crew of the Bayfield.

HAMILTON.—Island, Manitoulin ; after Lord George Hamilton, First Lord of the Admiralty, 1885-92.

††HAMILTON.—Rock, Serpent Harbour, Algoma.

HAMPSHIRE.—Rock, Parry Sound ; after the Hampshire, an English vessel, sunk by d'Iberville in Hudson Bay, 1697.

*HANGCLIFF.—Cape, Parry I., Parry Sound ; named by Bayfield ; descriptive of appearance ; name obsolete ; now Lion Head.

HANG-DOG.—Point and bank, Parry Sound ; "as the name indicates is a broken-up foul point."

HANKINSON.—Bank, Parry Sound ; after Parry's brother-in-law, Rev. R. E. Hankinson.

HANNAH.—Rock, Parry Sound ; after Mrs. M. G. Poole, sister-in-law of W. J. Stewart, Chief Hydrographer.

††HANNAH.—Ground, St. Joseph Channel, Algoma.

HANS.—Rock, Parry Sound ; after a Church of England clergyman, Rev. Hans Gaviller.

HAPPY-GO-LUCKY.—Island, Muskoka ; so named by the owner of camp on island.

HARBOTTLE.—Islands Alexander Inlet, Parry Sound ; after late Capt. Harbottle, Steamship Inspector, Toronto.

HARBOUR.—Island, Clapperton Island, Manitoulin ; descriptive name applied to this and several other features.

HARD-HEAD.—Point, Hope Island ; from the boulders (hard-heads) scattered along the shore.

HARDIE.—Island, Parry Sound ; after late chief clerk, Department of Marine and Fisheries.

††HARDIE.—Rock, Manitoulin.

HAROLD.—Point, Parry Sound ; after a son of Capt. Boulton, late Hydrographer.

††HAROLD.—Point, Vidal Island, Manitoulin.

HARRIETTE.—Point, Algoma ; local name.

HARRIS.—Rock, Muskoka ; after a man who was lost in the Waubuno.

HARRIS.—Bank, Parry Sound ; after a naval surveyor.

HARRISON.—Bank, Parry Sound ; after a boatman in steamer Bayfield.

HARTNEY.—Cove, Manitoulin ; after E. P. Hartney, chief clerk, House of Commons.

HARTY.—Patches, Manitoulin ; after Patrick Harty, Kingston, Inspector of Lights, Department of Marine and Fisheries.

HASLEYWOOD.—Bank, Parry Sound ; after a lawyer, Charlottetown ; a friend of Capt. Boulton.

HAT.—Island, St. Joseph Channel, Algoma ; descriptive of outline of island.

HATTIE.—Island, St. Joseph Channel, Algoma ; after Miss Hattie Richards, Richards Landing.

HAWKES.—Shoal, St. Joseph Channel, Algoma ; after a cousin of Mrs. W. J. Stewart.

HAWKINS.—Island, North Channel, Algoma ; after Sir John Hawkins Hagarty ; see Hagarty.

*HAY.—Island, Bruce ; named by Bayfield, probably after the private secretary to Lord Melville, First Lord of the Admiralty.

HAYSTACK.—Rock, Parry Sound ; descriptive of appearance.

HAYTER.—Point, Christian Island, Simcoe ; after Hayter Reed, Indian Commissioner 1888-95 ; Deputy Superintendent-General of Indian Affairs, 1893-97.

HEAD.—Island, Parry Sound ; "supposed by some to take its name from the resemblance of the north-east island of the three to a bald-headed man."

HEART.—Bank, Parry Sound ; descriptive of shape.

HECLA.—Rock, Parry Sound ; after one of Parry's vessels in his Arctic expeditions, 1819-20, 1821-23 and 1824-25.

*HELEN.—Bay, Manitoulin ; named by Bayfield (q.v.) after his only sister, Lady Page Turner.

HELEN.—Island, North Channel, Algoma ; after Mrs. Hurt, sister-in-law of W. J. Stewart.

HENNEPIN.—Island, North Channel, Algoma ; after Father Hennepin (1640-1701), Recollet missionary and explorer.

HENRIETTA.—Point, Franklin Island, Parry Sound ; after the wife of H. B. Small, Department of Agriculture, Ottawa.

*HENRY.—Island, Manitoulin ; after Admiral Henry W. Bayfield (q.v.)

††HENRY.—Patch, Manitoulin.

HENSLEY.—Bay, Manitoulin ; after the late Capt C. A. Hensley of the Royal Dublin Fusiliers ; graduate of the Royal Military College.

*HENVEY.—Inlet ; named by Bayfield after Lieut. William Henvy (or Henvey), R.N., who, in October, 1815, was serving in the St. Lawrence.

HERBERT.—Island, North Channel, Algoma ; after Major-General Ivor John Caradoc Herbert, commanded Canadian Militia, 1890-95.

HERCULES.—Bank, Parry Sound ; after a lake vessel.

HERMAN.—Point, Serpent Harbour, Algoma ; after Herman H. Cook, M.P. (q.v.).

HERON.—Patch, Manitoulin ; after a gunboat on Great Lakes.

HERVEY.—Rock, Muskoka ; after Frederick W. F. Hervey,

Lieutenant in the Victoria, sunk in collision with the Camperdown, June 23rd, 1893.

HESSON.—Point, Innes Island, Algoma ; after S. R. Hesson, M.P. for North Perth, 1878-91.

HEWETT.—Shoal, Sudbury ; after late General Hewett, Commandant, Royal Military College, Kingston.

*HEYWOOD.—Island and sound, Manitoulin ; named by Bayfield ; derivation unknown.

††HEYWOOD.—Rocks, Manitoulin.

HIAWATHA.—Bank, Nottawasaga Bay, Grey ; after the tug Hiawatha.

HIESORDT.—Rocks, North Channel, Algoma ; after the manager of the Spanish River mill.

HIGH.—Beach, Badgley Island, Manitoulin ; characteristic ; name also applied to several other features.

HILLIER.—Island, Parry Sound ; after Dr. Caleb Hillier Parry, father of the Arctic explorer, W. E. Parry.

HINCKS.—Island ; after Sir Francis Hincks (1807-1885), Premier of Canada, 1851-54.

HOAR.—Point, Hope Island, Simcoe ; after the lightkeeper of Hope Island light.

HOFFMANN.—Bay, Algoma ; after Dr. George C. Hoffmann, late Chemist, Geological Survey.

HOLE-IN-THE-WALL.—Channel, Parry Sound ; "a remarkable cleft separating Huckleberry and Wall Islands. The narrowest place is 111 feet wide."

HOLMES.—Island, St. Joseph Channel, Algoma ; after Capt. Holmes of C. G. S. Cruiser.

*HONORA.—Bay, Manitoulin ; named by Bayfield ; derivation unknown.

††HONORA.—Point, Manitoulin.

HOOD.—Island, North Channel, Algoma ; after a boatman in surveying steamer Bayfield.

HOOD.—Patch, Parry Sound ; after Admiral Sir Arthur William Acland Hood, Lord of the Admiralty, 1885.

††HOOD.—Reef, Parry Sound.

HOOPER.—Island, Georgian Bay, Parry Sound ; after William H. Hooper, purser on Parry's three Arctic voyages.

*HOPE.—Bay, Bruce ; named by Bayfield after Admiral Sir Wm. Johnston Hope ; Lord of the Admiralty, 1807 et seq ; d. 1831.

*HOPE.—Island, Simcoe ; probably same as preceding ; possibly after Col. Henry Hope, Member of Legislative Council, Quebec ; Administrator, 1785, pending the return of Lord Dorchester from Great Britain ; died 1789.

HOPPNER.—Island, Parry Sound ; after Lieutenant Henry P. Hoppner, Commander of the Fury in Parry's third Arctic voyage, 1824-25.

HORACE.—Point, Manitoulin ; after a son of Admiral Bayfield.

HORNE.—Rock, North Channel, Algoma ; after a boatman in surveying steamer Bayfield.

*HORSBURG.—Point, Manitoulin ; after James Horsburg (1762-1836), hydrographer to the East India Company author of the celebrated "Directions for sailing to and from the East Indies, etc.," the basis of the present East India Directory.

††HORSBURG.—Hill, Manitoulin.

HORSE.—Island, Manitoulin ; after a shipwrecked horse that remained on the island for several years.

††HORSE.—Island, St. Joseph Channel, Algoma.

HORSLEY.—Island, Parry Sound ; after a friend of Captain Boulton.

HOSKIN.—Island, North Channel, Algoma ; said to be after a naval surveyor. Possibly should be Hoskins, after Vice-Admiral Sir Anthony H. Hoskins, Lord of the Admiralty, 1880-82 and 1885-88.

HOSPITAL.—Point, Serpent Harbour, Algoma ; "so called from its being the temporary site of a camp for the isolation of typhoid fever patients during an outbreak in the season of 1887."

HOTHAM.—Island, North Channel, Algoma ; after Sir Chas. Fred. Hotham, G.C.B., G.C.V.O., Admiral of the Fleet, Lord of the Admiralty.

HOUGHTON.—Bay and rocks, Algoma ; after the tug Houghton.

HOWLAND.—Rocks, North Channel, Algoma ; after William H. Howland, Mayor of Toronto, 1886.

HUDGIN.—Rock, Parry Sound ; after a fisherman.

HUMBUG.—Point, St. Joseph Island, Algoma ; after a back current that holds boats when in light wind or calm.

HUNGERFORD.—Point Manitoulin ; after a lake trading vessel.

HUNT.—Point, Cloche Island, Sudbury ; after the late Dr. T. Sterry Hunt, Geological Survey.

HUNTLY.—Rock, North Channel, Algoma ; after the commander of a British gunboat on the lakes.

*HURD.—Cape, Bruce ; after Capt. Thomas Hurd (1757-1823), appointed hydrographer to the Admiralty, 1808.

††HURD.—Channel, Bruce.

HURT.—Rock, St. Joseph Channel, Algoma ; after a brother-in-law of W. J. Stewart.

IMPERIAL.—Bank, Parry Sound ; after the steamer Imperial.

INDIAN.—Bight, Manitoulin ; this and other features so named because Indians live on the shores or frequent them.
††INDIAN.—Bight, Algoma.
††INDIAN.—Channel, Clapperton and Vankoughnet Islands, Manitoulin.
††*INDIAN.—Harbour, Georgian Bay, Muskoka.
††INDIAN.—Island, Serpent Harbour, Algoma.
††*INDIAN.—Islands, Parry Sound ; name obsolete.
INDIAN BELLE.—Rock, Simcoe ; after the steamer Indian Belle.
INDIAN JOHN.—Point, Algoma ; after a pilot, Spanish River.
INDIAN HARBOUR.—Point and reef, Fitzwilliam Island, Manitoulin ; "much resorted to by the Manitoulin Indians during the trolling season for trout in the autumn."
*INNES.—Island, North Channel, Algoma ; named by Bayfield ; derivation unknown.
IRELAND.—Point, Parry Sound ; after a resident of Parry Sound.
IRONSIDES.—Rock, Manitoulin ; after an officer of the Indian Department, at Manitowaning.
††IRONSIDES.—Reef, North Channel, Algoma.
IRWIN.—Island, North Channel, Algoma ; after Lieut.-Colonel de la C. Irwin, C.M.G. ; retired Colonel, R.C.A. ; was Inspector of Artillery, 1882-98.
ISAAC.—Rock, North Channel, Algoma ; after the steamer Isaac May.
ISABEL.—Rock, Algoma ; after Isabel Grant, Ottawa.
ISAIAH.—Rock, Parry Sound ; after an Indian.
*ISTHMUS.—Bay, Bruce ; descriptive ; name obsolete ; now, Whip-poor-Will Bay.
IVOR.—Rocks, North Channel, Algoma ; Major-General Ivor John Caradoc Herbert, commanded Canadian Militia, 1890-95.

JACKMAN.—Rock, Killarney Harbour, Manitoulin ; after a merchant at Killarney.
JACKSON.—Island, North Channel, Algoma ; after the Inspector of Fisheries, Georgian Bay.
*JACKSON.—Cove, Bruce ; probably after Lieutenant Jackson, in command of the Heron, 1816.
††JACKSON.—Shoal, Bruce.
JACQUES.—Island, Muskoka ; after the captain of the steamer Manitou.
JAGGED.—Island, Western Islands, Parry Sound ; descriptive.
*JAMES.—Bay, Manitoulin ; after James Horsburg (q.v.).

*JAMES.—Island, Manitoulin ; after Commodore Sir James Lucas Yeo (q.v.).

††JAMES ISLAND.—Reef, Manitoulin.

JAMES.—Rock, Parry Sound ; after an Indian.

JAMES FOOTE.—Patch, Manitoulin ; after Capt. James Foote of the steamer Athabasca.

JAMIESON.—Island, North Channel, Algoma ; after a naval surveyor.

JANE.—Island, Parry Sound ; after schooner Jane McLeod.

JANE.—Rock, Parry Sound ; after Capt. McGregor's wife.

*JANET.—Cove, Manitoulin ; named by Bayfield, probably after a friend ; derivation unknown ; now called 'Gore Bay' (q.v.)

††*JANET.—Head, Manitoulin.

JENKINS.—Point, Parry Sound ; after a resident of Parry Sound.

JENKINS.—Rock, Sudbury ; after S. V. Jenkins, sometime Secretary to Hon. George E. Foster, Minister of Marine and Fisheries.

JENNIE.—Rock, St. Joseph Channel, Algoma ; after Miss Jennie Marks, Bruce Mines.

JERMYN.—Rock, St. Joseph Channel ; after an Indian agent.

JESSIE.—Point, Manitoulin ; after Miss Jessie Grant, Ottawa.

JOE DOLLAR.—Bay, Algoma ; after a citizen of Bruce Mines.

*JOHN.—Island, Algoma ; named by Captain Bayfield (q.v.) after his father.

††JOHN.—Harbour, John I., Algoma.

JOHN.—Ledge, Manitoulin ; after John McNeil, coxswain in surveying steamer Bayfield.

JOHNSON.—Island, Parry Sound ; after George Johnson, late Dominion statistician.

JOLIETTE.—Island, North Channel, Algoma ; after Louis Jolliet (1645-1700), French explorer.

JOLY.—Rock, St. Joseph Channel, Algoma ; after Lieut.-Col. Alain Joly de Lotbiniere, C.S.I., C.I.E. ; graduated from the Royal Military College, 1883.

*JONES.—Bay, Simcoe ; named by Bayfield ; possibly after an officer of Penetanguishene naval station ; name obsolete ; now Sturgeon Bay.

JONES.—Bluff, Bruce ; after the Wiarton tug J. H. Jones.

JONES.—Island, Parry Sound ; after a former resident of Beeton, Ont.

JONES.—Point, Fox Island, Algoma ; after Charles J. Jones, Assistant Governor-General's Secretary.

PLACE-NAMES IN GEORGIAN BAY. 47

JOSEPHINE.—Rocks, Parry Sound ; after daughter of Capt. McGregor, sailing master of steamer Bayfield.

JUBILEE.—Island, Parry Sound ; named in 1887, the year of the late Queen Victoria's Jubilee.

††JUBILEE.—Shoal, Manitoulin.

JUDD.—Bank, Muskoka; after a sister of W. J. Stewart, Chief Hydrographer.

JUKES.—Island, Parry Sound ; after a resident of Parry Sound.

*JULIA.—Bay and point, Manitoulin ; named by Bayfield (q. v.) after, probably, Julia, eldest daughter of late Mr. Stevenson of Quebec. The latter "was an intimate friend of the Admiral's and for many years supplied the Gulnare." The schooner Julia was used by Bayfield in the survey of Lake Superior.

*JULIET.—Cove, Manitoulin ; named by Bayfield ; derivation unknown.

KALULAH.—Rock, North Channel, Algoma ; after a lake vessel.

KANGAROO.—Rock, North Channel, Algoma; after a lake vessel.

KAULBACH.—Rock, North Channel, Algoma ; after the late C. E. Kaulbach, M.P. for Lunenburg, 1878-82, 1883-87 and 1891-1904.

KEATING.—Island, Muskoka ; after a friend of Capt. Boulton, a resident of Penetanguishene.

KEEFER.—Island, Parry Sound ; after T. C. Keefer, Ottawa, prominent Canadian civil engineer.

KEEGAN.—Rock, Parry Sound ; after a boatman in steamer Bayfield.

KENNEDY.—Bank, Parry Sound ; after a fisherman.

KENNY.—Point and shoal, Innes Island, Algoma ; after Thomas Edward Kenny, M.P. for Halifax, 1887-96.

KENSINGTON.—Point. St. Joseph Channel, Algoma ; after Col. Kensington, late Professor of Mathematics, Royal Military College, Kingston.

KERBY.—Island, St. Joseph Channel, Algoma ; after Forbes M. Kerby, C.E. ; graduated from Royal Military College, 1883 ; now residing in Grand Forks, B.C.

KERLEY.—Island, St. Joseph Channel, Algoma ; after a Church of England clergyman.

KERR.—Island, Muskoka ; after Mark E. F. Kerr, Lieutenant in the Victoria, sunk in collision with the Camperdown, June 23rd, 1893.

*KEY.—Inlet, Parry Sound ; so named by Bayfield, because it is key-shaped.

KEYSTONE.—Rock, Parry Sound ; descriptive.

KIDD.—Bay and point, White Cloud Island, Grey ; "after the owner of sawmill here."

KILCOURSIE.—Bay, Parry Sound ; after Viscount Kilcoursie, Grenadier Guards, A.D.C. to Lord Stanley, Governor-General of Canada, 1888-93.

KILLALY.—Point, St. Joseph Channel, Algoma ; after H. H. Killaly, from 1875 to 1892 employed in the construction and enlargement of the St. Lawrence canals.

KILLARNEY.—Village, bay and peak, Manitoulin ; after Killarney, Ireland.

KILL-BEAR.—Point, Parry Sound ; probably commemorates an encounter with a bear.

KINDERSLEY.—Island, Muskoka ; after Captain Kindersley, A.D.C. to Lord Aberdeen, Governor-General, 1893-98.

KING.—Point, Muskoka ; descriptive of commanding position.

††KING.—Bay, Muskoka.

KING WILLIAM.—Island, Manitoulin ; after King William IV.

KIRKE.—Island, North Channel, Algoma ; after Sir David Kirke, who, in 1629, captured Quebec ; received a grant of Newfoundland, 1637 ; died 1655.

KIRKPATRICK.—Island, Sudbury ; after the late Hon. Sir George Airey Kirkpatrick (1841-99), Speaker, House of Commons, 1883-87 ; Lieut.-Governor of Ontario, 1892-97 ; K.C.M.G., 1897.

KLOTZ.—Island. North Channel, Algoma ; after Dr. Otto J. Klotz, LL.D., Asst. Chief Astronomer, Department of the Interior.

KNIGHT.—Point, Algoma ; after Staff-Commander Knight, R.N. (retired), Collingwood.

††KNIGHT.—Rock.

KNIGHT.—Shoal, Parry Sound ; after a fisherman.

KNIGHTSLEIGH.—Island, Parry Sound ; name given by owner.

KOKANONGIVI.—Island and shingle, Manitoulin ; Indian name of a small fish.

LABATT.—Island, Simcoe ; after a prominent citizen of Hamilton, Ont.

LABELLE.—Reef, North Channel, Algoma, Ont. ; probably after Lieut.-Col. A E. Labelle, commanded the 65th Rifles during Riel rebellion, 1885.

LA CLOCHE.—See Cloche

LAFFERTY HOUSE.—Rock, Nottawasaga Bay, Simcoe, Ont.; after a fisherman.

PLACE-NAMES IN GEORGIAN BAY. 49

LA FRANCE.—Rock, North Channel, Algoma, Ont.; after a lake captain.

LAIRD.—Rock, Parry Sound; after the Hon. David Laird, Minister of the Interior, 1873-76; Lieut.-Governor of the Northwest Territories, 1876-81.

LALLY.—Point, Algoma; after the Collector of Customs, Algoma.

LAMANDIN.—Point, Parry Sound; after a light-keeper, Byng Inlet.

LAMBE.—Island, St. Joseph Channel, Algoma; after Lawrence M. Lambe, Invertebrate Palaeontologist, Geological Survey; graduate, Royal Military College, 1883.

LAMORANDIERE.—Bay and strait, Sudbury; after an Indian trader who resided there about 1825.

LAMORANDIERE.—Bank, Bruce; after an Indian residing at McGregor Harbour.

LAMPEY.—Bank, Sudbury; after a draughtsman in Department of Marine and Fisheries.

††LAMPEY.—Island, Parry Sound.

††LAMPEY.—Rock, North Channel, Sudbury.

LANDERKIN.—Island, North Channel, Algoma; after Dr. George Landerkin (1839-1903), M.P. for South Grey, 1872-78 and 1882-1900; Senator, 1901.

LANDRY.—Point, Algoma; after Hon. A. C. P. R. Landry, M.P. for Montmagny, 1878-87; Senator, 1892.

LANGEVIN.—Rock, Strawberry I., Manitoulin; after Sir Hector L. Langevin, Secretary of State, 1867-69; Minister of Public Works, 1869-73 and 1879-91; Postmaster-General, 1878-79.

LANSDOWNE.—Channel, Manitoulin; after Sir Henry Charles (Fitzmaurice), 5th Marquis of Lansdowne; Governor-General of Canada, 1883-88; Governor-General of India, 1888-94.

††LANSDOWNE.—Rock, Algoma.

LAPTHORN.—Island, Manitoulin; after Dr. A. Lapthorn Smith, Montreal, son of late William Smith, Deputy Minister of Marine and Fisheries.

LA SALLE.—Island, North Channel, Algoma; after Robert Cavelier, Sieur de la Salle (1643-87); explored the Mississippi to its mouth, 1682.

LASH.—Island, Key Harbour, Parry Sound; after Z. A. Lash, K.C., Toronto, Senior Counsel, Canadian Northern Railway.

LASHER.—Island, St. Joseph Channel, Algoma; after Mrs. W. J. Stewart, née Lasher.

LAUDER.—Islands, Parry Sound; after the late Archdeacon J. S. Lauder, Ottawa.

LAURIER.—Island, North Channel, Algoma; after the Rt. Hon. Sir Wilfrid Laurier, Premier of Canada, 1896-1911.

LAWRENCE.—Bank, Parry Sound ; after Capt. James Lawrence, in command of the U. S. S. Chesapeake, captured by H. M. S. Shannon, June 1, 1813.

LAWSON.—Island, Parry Sound ; after light-keeper at Red Rock lighthouse, Parry Sound, 1890.

LEFROY.—Island, French River, Parry Sound ; after General Sir John Henry Lefroy (1817-90), an English soldier, administrator and a man of science, was occupied in taking magnetic observations at St. Helena 1840-1842 ; transferred to the Observatory, Toronto, 1842.

LEHAYE.—Point and rock, Manitoulin ; after a hotelkeeper, Killarney.

LEO.—Rock, North Channel, Algoma ; after a steward in the surveying steamer Bayfield.

LEONARD.—Island, Parry Sound ; after owner.

LEONARD.—Reef, St. Joseph Channel, Algoma ; after Major R. W. Leonard, Chairman, National Transcontinental Ry., graduate of Royal Military College, 1883.

LE SUEUR.—Island, North Channel, Algoma ; after Dr. W. D. Le Sueur, late Secretary, Post Office Department.

LETT.—Island, North Channel, Algoma ; after Mrs. Lett, widow of a clergyman, Collingwood.

LEWIN.—Island, Manitoulin ; after Hon. James D. Lewin, St. John, N.B., Senator, 1876 ; died 1900.

LIDDON.—Point, Parry I., Parry Sound ; after Lieut. Matthew Liddon, who commanded the Griper in Parry's Arctic voyage, 1819-1820.

LIMESTONE.—Point, Manitoulin ; "composed of rock of this nature."

LINTER.—Island, North Channel, Algoma ; after the chief engineer in surveying steamer Bayfield, 1886.

††LINTER.—Rocks, Manitoulin.

LION.—Head, Bruce ; descriptive of appearance.

††LION HEAD and LION RUMP.—Hills, Sudbury.

LISGAR.—Island, Manitoulin ; after Sir John Young, Baron Lisgar, Governor-General of Canada, 1869-72.

LISTER.—Island, North Channel, Algoma ; after Justice Frederick Lister, Sarnia , M.P. for West Lambton, 1882-98.

LITTLE DETROIT.—Algoma ; the strait (Fr. *detroit*) between Craftsman Point and Aird Island.

LLOYD.—Island, Parry Sound ; probably after Rev. G. E. Lloyd, chaplain to the Queen's Own Regiment during Riel rebellion, 1885.

LOADING.—Cove, French River, Parry Sound ; "from its being a convenient place for the large vessels to take in saw logs."

LOAF.—Rock, Bruce, and rock, Parry Sound ; descriptive.

LOCKERBIE.—Rock, Nottawasaga Bay, Simcoe; after harbourmaster at Collingwood.

LOGAN.—Bay and island, Manitoulin; after the late Sir William E. Logan, famous Canadian geologist; director of the Geological Survey of Canada, 1841-69.

LONE.—Rock, Parry Sound; descriptive of position with reference to other islands.

††LONELY.—Bay, Manitoulin.

††*LONELY.—Island, Manitoulin.

LONGUISSA.—Point and bay, Muskoka; name given by Mr. Campbell, owner of the point, to house which he built on it.

LOOKOUT.—Island, Parry Sound; has a commanding position over approach to the channel.

LORNE.—Rock, Algoma; after the Marquis of Lorne, Governor-General of Canada, 1878-83; *suc.* his father as Duke of Argyle, 1900.

LOTTIE WOLF.—Rock, Simcoe; schooner Lottie Wolf struck on this rock.

LOUGHLIN.—Island, North Channel, Algoma; after a merchant, Algoma.

LOUIS.—Island, North Channel, Algoma; after Sir Louis Davies, Judge, Supreme Court of Canada.

LOUISA.—Island and rocks, Parry Sound, and island, Sudbury; after the wife of Captain Boulton.

LUARD.—Rock, Cloche Island, Sudbury; after Major-General R. A. Luard; commanded the Militia of Canada, 1880-84.

LUCAS.—Island, Manitoulin; after Commodore Sir James Lucas Yeo (1782-1818).

††LUCAS.—Channel, Manitoulin.

††LUCAS ISLAND.—Reef, Manitoulin.

LUMSDEN.—Rock, North Channel, Algoma; after the late Alexander Lumsden, M.P., lumberman, Ottawa.

LYNCH.—Rock, Parry Sound; after a clerk in Department of Public Works.

LYON.—Rocks, Parry Sound; after George Francis Lyon, commander of the Hecla in Parry's second Arctic voyage, 1821-23.

LYON.—Cove, St. Joseph Island, and island, North Channel, Algoma; after Robert Adam Lyon (1830-1902), sometime Registrar of Deeds, Sault Ste. Marie.

*McBEAN.—Mountain, North Channel, Algoma; "an Indian trader, of the name of McBean, has been here many years and has given his name to the spot." (Bigsby.)

††McBEAN.—Channel and harbour, Algoma.

McBRIEN.—Island, Parry Sound ; after the owner of the island.

McCALLUM.—Islands, North Channel, Algoma ; after the late Hon. Lachlan McCallum ; Senator, 1887 ; d. 1903.

McCARTHY.—Point, and McCARTHY POINT, ledge, Fitzwilliam I., Manitoulin ; after the late D'Alton McCarthy, Q.C. ; M.P. for Cardwell, 1874-78, and for North Simcoe, 1878-98.

††McCARTHY.—Rock, Nottawasaga Bay, Grey.

McCLELLAND.—Rock, Parry Sound ; after a resident of Parry Sound.

McCORMICK.—Island, Parry Sound ; after a boatman in the steamer Bayfield.

*McCOY.—Island and shoal, Parry Sound ; named by Bayfield, probably after J. S. McCoy, R.N., who in October, 1815, was master in H.M.S. Champlain.

††McCOY.—Shoal, Parry Sound.

McCRACKEN.—Island, Serpent Harbour, Algoma ; after a resident of Serpent River.

McCURRY.—Rocks, Parry Sound ; after a magistrate, Parry Sound.

McDONALD.—Shoal, Manitoulin ; after a fisherman.

McELHINNEY.—Ground, Bruce ; after nautical adviser, Department of Marine and Fisheries.

McGLASHAN.—Patch, North Channel, Algoma ; after a fisherman at Grant Islands in 1890.

McGOWAN.—Rock, Parry Sound ; after a lightkeeper at Red Rock lighthouse.

McGREGOR.—Bank, Manitoulin ; after Capt. A. H. McGregor, sailing master of surveying vessel Bayfield.

††McGREGOR.—Channel, Bruce.

McGREGOR.—Harbour, Bruce ; after the father of Capt. McGregor, sailing master of the Bayfield.

McGUIRE.—Rocks, St. Joseph Channel, Algoma ; after a boatman in surveying steamer Bayfield.

McHUGH.—Rock, Parry Sound ; after an officer of the Department of Marine and Fisheries.

McINTOSH.—Bank, Parry Sound ; after a fisherman.

McKECHNIE.—Rock, Parry Sound ; after a camper.

McKENZIE.—Island, Goat Channel, Sudbury ; after a lightkeeper at Strawberry Island light.

McKERREL.—Rock, Parry Sound ; after the captain of a lake vessel.

McKINNON.—Rock, St. Joseph Channel, Algoma ; after a boatman in surveying steamer Bayfield.

McLAREN.—Island, Parry Sound; after the owner of the island.

McLEAN.—Shoal, Parry Sound; after a boatman in steamer Bayfield.

McLELAN.—Rock, Manitoulin; after the late Hon. A. W. McLelan, Minister of Marine and Fisheries, 1882-85.

McLEOD.—Island, Parry Sound; after schooner Jane McLeod.

††McLEOD.—Point, Muskoka.

McNAB.—Island and reef, St. Joseph Channel, Algoma; after John McNab, captain of the steamer United Empire in 1889.

††McNAB.—Rocks, Parry Sound.

McNEIL.—Ledge, Manitoulin; after the coxswain in steamer Bayfield.

McPHAIL.—Rock, St. Joseph Channel, Algoma; after the captain of the tug Kate Marks.

McQUADE.—Island, Parry Sound; after the engineer and the purser of steamer Manitou.

McQUEEN.—Island, St. Joseph Channel, Algoma; after the chief engineer, in 1889, of he United Empire.

McRAE.—Patch, Sudbury, and patch, North Channel, Manitoulin; after one of the crew of the surveying steamer Bayfield, 1884.

McTAVISH.—Island, Algoma; after D. McTavish, Hudson's Bay Co. factor at La Cloche.

MACKAY.—Point, Manitoulin; after a hotelkeeper, Little Current.

MACKEY.—Island, Parry Sound; after Rev. A. W. Mackey, Church of England clergyman, Ottawa.

MACOUN.—Rock, Parry Sound; after Prof. John Macoun, Chief Botanist, Geological Survey of Canada.

MACPHERSON.—Ledge, Bedford I., Sudbury; after late Sir David Macpherson (1818-97), Senator from 1867; Minister of the Interior, 1883-85.

MACRAE.—Cove, Manitoulin; after a mill owner, Mildrum Bay.

MAGANETAWAN.—Ledges, Parry Sound; after the Maganetawan River—a corruption of the Indian name, '*mawgawnetlewang*, meaning 'a long channel.'

MAGAZINE.—Island, North Channel, Algoma; contains the site of old Canadian Pacific Ry. powder magazine.

MAGAZINE.—Island, Penetanguishene Harbour, Simcoe; after "the remains of an old naval and military magazine."

MAGEE.—Point, Amedroz I., Manitoulin ; after Chas. Magee, Ottawa, capitalist and banker.

MAGGIE.—Rock, North Channel, Algoma ; after the tug Maggie.

MAGGS.—Island, North Channel, Algoma ; after Miss Shepherd, daughter of the light-keeper.

*MAIRS.—Point, Simcoe ; possibly after an official of Penetanguishene naval station ; name obsolete ; now Flat Point.

MAITLAND.—Bank, Algoma ; after a merchant of Owen Sound.

MALCOLM.—Bluff, Bruce ; after a son of Alex. McNeill, M.P. for North Bruce, 1882-1901.

MALTAS.—Island, Goat Channel, Sudbury ; after a merchant of Little Current.

MANITOBA.—Ledge, Manitoulin ; after the steamer Manitoba, wrecked here.

MANITOU.—Point, Muskoka ; Indian name meaning "Great Spirit."

MANITOU.—Gap, Parry Sound ; after the lake steamer Manitou.

MANITOULIN.—Island, Manitoulin ; according to Indian tradition it is the dwelling place of both the Good Spirit, *gitchi-manito* and of *matchi-manito*, the Evil Spirit.

††MANITOULIN.—District and bay.

MANITOWANING.—Bay and harbour, Manitoulin ; Indian name, signifying "home of the Great Spirit."

MANN.—Rock, Algoma ; after a draughtsman of Marine and Fisheries Department.

MANN.—Island, Key Harbour, Parry Sound ; after Sir Donald D. Mann, Vice-President, Canadian Northern Ry.

MARY.—Island, Aird I. Algoma ; after the tug Mary.

MARKS.—Bank, St. Joseph Channel, Algoma ; after George Marks, Bruce Mines.

*MARKS.—Point, Simcoe ; possibly after an official of Penetanguishene naval station.

MARTIN.—Reef, Manitoulin ; after one of the crew of surveying steamer Bayfield, 1884 ; lived at Mudge Bay.

MARTYR.—Islands, Parry Sound ; after Charles Martyr, Secretary to the Admiral commanding at Halifax, 1816, and an intimate friend of Parry (q.v.)

MARY.—Point, Algoma ; after Mary Moodie, authoress.

MARY GRANT.—Rock, Parry Sound ; after the secretary to the Deputy Minister of Marine and Fisheries, 1890.

MASSON.—Island, Manitoulin ; after the late Hon. L. F. R. Masson, Lieutenant-Governor of Quebec, 1884-87.

MARY WARD.—Ledges, Nottawasaga Bay, Grey; schooner Mary Ward wrecked here.

*MATCHEDASH.—Bay, Simcoe; name applied by the Indians to the shores of the bay; signifies 'marshy land.' Name appears on Bouchette's map, 1815.

MATHER.—Rock, Muskoka; after the late John Mather, capitalist, Ottawa.

MATHESON.—Island, Sudbury; after a boatman in surveying steamer Bayfield.

††MATHESON.—Shoal, Manitoulin.

MAUD.—Island, Parry Sound; after the tug Maud.

MAXWELL.—Island, Muskoka; after the steamer E. B. Maxwell.

MAY.—Reef, North Channel, Algoma; after the steamer Isaac May.

MAYO.—Island, St. Joseph Channel, Algoma; after Mayo Neeland, graduate of Royal Military College, 1883.

MAYNE.—Point, Christian I., Simcoe; after Hon. T. Mayne Daly, Minister of the Interior, 1892-96.

MAYNE.—Island, Parry Sound; after a naval officer.

MAZEPPA.—Rock, North Channel, Algoma; after the schooner Mazeppa.

MEAFORD.—Shoal, Parry Sound; fisherman came here from Meaford, Ont.

MEAFORD.—Harbour, Grey; after Meaford town, which after Meaford Hall, seat, Staffordshire, England; birthplace of Admiral Sir John Jervis (1734-1823) Earl of St. Vincent. Meaford town is in St. Vincent township.

*MELVILLE.—Sound, Bruce; after Robert Saunders Dundas, second Viscount Melville, First Lord of the Admiralty, 1812-27.

MELVIN.—Bight, Strawberry I., Manitoulin; after a summer resident.

MENOMINE.—Channel, Parry Sound; *mene*, good, and *min*, a grain—the Chippewa name for wild rice.

MERCER.—Rocks, Parry Sound; after a boatman in steamer Bayfield.

MERCIER.—Rock, Parry Sound; after late Hon. Honoré Mercier, Premier of Quebec, 1887-91.

MEREDITH.—Island, and rock, Manitoulin; after Sir William R. Meredith, Chief Justice of the Court of Common Pleas, Ontario.

MERIDA.—Shoal, St. Joseph Channel, Algoma; after a lake vessel.

METEOR.—Rock, Serpent Harbour, Algoma; after the steamer Meteor.

METHODIST.—Bay and point, Simcoe ; said to be named after a camp-meeting held at the point by a pioneer Methodist missionary in early days.

MIALL.—Patch, Manitoulin ; after Edward Miall, Commissioner of Inland Revenue, 1883-1901.

MICHAUD.—Point, Simcoe ; after a French-Canadian who settled there, 1840.

MICHEL.—Ground, North Channel, Algoma ; after Bernard Michel, half-breed, Killarney.

MIDLAND.—Bank, Parry Sound ; after the steamer City of Midland.

MIDLAND.—Bay, point and shoal, Simcoe ; after the town of Midland which last after the Midland Railway ; the railway so named because it traversed the middle of Ontario and name suggested by the Midland Ry., Eng.

MIDSHIPMAN.—Point, Manitoulin ; after Midshipman Philip Edward Collins, assistant to Capt. Bayfield.

*MILDRUM.—Bay and point, Manitoulin ; 'Mildram Point' on Bayfield's chart ; derivation unknown ; may be after Meldrum, parish, Aberdeenshire, Scotland.

MILFORD HAVEN.—Harbour, St. Joseph Island, Algoma ; after Milford Haven, village, Wales.

MILLER.—Point, Manitoulin, and rock, Parry Sound ; after a resident of Parry Sound.

MILLIGAN.—Island, Parry Sound ; after the owner.

MILLIGAN.—Rock, Manitoulin ; after a boatman in the Bayfield.

MILO.—Rock, Parry Sound ; after a boatman in steamer Bayfield.

MINER.—Rocks, Parry Sound ; one of crew of Bayfield.

MINNICOG.—Bank, Muskoka ; abbreviation of Minnicoganashene (q.v.)

MINNICOGANASHENE.—Island, Muskoka ; Indian name, meaning "point of many blueberries."

MINNIE.—Rock, Parry Sound ; after a tug.

††MINNIE.—Rocks, St. Joseph Channel, Algoma.

MINOS.—Bank, Simcoe ; in Greek legend, Minos was a king of Crete ; after his death, a judge in the lower world.

MINSTREL.—Rock, North Channel, Algoma ; after the Minstrel, a British gunboat on the Great Lakes.

*MISSISSAGI.—River, Algoma ; from Chippewa : *missi*, 'large,' and *sag* or *sank*, 'outlet' (of a bay or river) ; the word signifies "great outlet" and is applicable to any river estuary.

††*MISSISSAGI.—Bay and island, Algoma.

†††*MISSISSAGI.—Strait, Manitoulin.

MITCHELL.—Island, North Channel, Algoma ; after the Hon. Peter Mitchell (1824-1899), one of the 'Fathers of Confederation' ; Minister of Marine and Fisheries, 1867-73.
MOBERLY.—Rock, Sudbury ; after a lawyer of Collingwood.
MOCKING BIRD.—Island, Manitoulin ; after a tug.
MOHAWK.—Rock, Simcoe ; probably after a vessel.
MOILE.—Harbour, John I., Algoma ; after the owner of a sawmill here. The mill was seized by bailiffs, but was transported on scows from Detroit to this point.
MONCK.—Point, Manitoulin ; after Charles Stanley, fourth Viscount Monck (1819-94) ; appointed Governor-General of British North America, 1861-67, and of Canada, 1867-68. Incorrectly, 'Monk' on the chart.
††MONCK.—Point, Cockburn I., Manitoulin.
*MONTRESOR.—Point, Bruce ; named by Bayfield, probably after Capt. Henry Montresor who distinguished himself in the capture of U. S. gunboats at New Orleans, Dec. 12, 1815.
MOODIE.—Rock, North Channel, Algoma ; after Mrs. Susanna Moodie, authoress of "Roughing It in the Bush," etc.
*MOORE.—Point, Simcoe ; possibly after an official of Penetanguishene naval station.
MOORHOUSE.—Patch, Manitoulin ; after a boatman in surveying steamer Bayfield.
MOOSE.—Point, Georgian Bay, Parry Sound ; 'Moose Deer' point on Bouchette's chart, probably translation of Indian name.
MORDEN.—Rock, Parry Sound ; after a lake captain.
MORELAND.—Bank, Manitoulin ; after a steward in the Bayfield.
MORRIS.—Island, Manitoulin ; after late Hon. Alex. Morris (1826-89), Minister of Inland Revenue, 1869-72 ; Lieut.-Governor of Manitoba, 1872-77.
††MORRIS.—Island, Muskoka.
MORRISON.—Islands, Serpent Harbour, Algoma ; after a lawyer, Owen Sound.
MOSLEY.—Island and rock, Parry Sound ; after a Church of England clergyman.
MOUSE.—Island, North Channel, Algoma ; "derives its name from the quantity of mice that abounded on it at the time of the survey."
MOWAT.—Island, Parry Sound ; after Sir Oliver Mowat (1820-1903), Premier of Ontario, 1872-96 ; Lieut.-Governor of Ontario, 1897-1903.
††MOWAT.—Island, Manitoulin.
*MUDGE.—Bay, Manitoulin ; possibly after Lieut.-Col. R. J. Mudge, R.E. (1790-1854), Lieutenant-Colonel, Royal Engineers, one of the commissioners appointed in 1830 to report on Maine-Canada

boundary. Or, after Capt. Zacharie Mudge (1770-1852), first Lieutenant in the Discovery in Vancouver's voyage, 1791-92 ; Rear-Admiral, 1830 ; Admiral, 1849.

MULOCK.—Island, North Channel, Algoma ; after Sir William Mulock, Chief Justice, Court of Exchequer, Ontario ; Postmaster-General, 1896-1905.

MURIEL.—Island, Parry Sound ; after Muriel Welsh Boulton, Capt. Boulton's daughter.

††MURIEL.—Point, Manitoulin.

MURRAY.—Point, Parry Sound ; after Capt. Alex. Murray McGregor (q.v.)

††MURRAY.—Rocks, Parry Sound.

NADEAU.—Island, Parry Sound ; after a Roman Catholic priest at Wikwemikong.

††NADEAU.—Point, Smith Bay, Manitoulin.

NANTON.—Reef, St. Joseph Channel ; after Lieut.-Col. H. C. Nanton, R.E., a graduate of the Royal Military College, 1883.

NARES.—Point and inlet, Parry Sound ; after Admiral Sir George Strong Nares ; commanded an expedition to the Arctic, 1875-76 ; attained the then, 'farthest North.'

NARROW.—Island and point, Manitoulin, and point, Noble I., Algoma ; descriptive.

NARROWS.—Island, Parry Sound ; descriptive of position near narrow passage.

NEEBISH.—Island, and EAST NEEBISH, rapids, St. Mary River ; Indian name ; probably same derivation as Nabobish, Indian village, Mich., which from *nubobish*, "poor soup."

NEELAND.—Island, St. Joseph Channel, Algoma ; after Mayo Neeland, graduate, Royal Military College, 1883.

NELLES.—Island, North Channel, Algoma ; after the Rev. Samuel Sobieski Nelles, D.D., LL.D. (1823-87), President of Victoria University, Cobourg, now of Toronto.

NEPTUNE.—Island, Cloche I., Sudbury ; after the steamer Neptune in Hudson Bay expedition under Lieutenant Gordon, 1884.

NEW.—Bank, Nottawasaga Bay, Grey ; discovered during survey.

NEWBERY.—Cove, Manitoulin ; after Christian name of Capt. Boulton's son.

NIAS.—Islands and rocks, Parry Sound ; Lieutenant John Nias served on the Fury during Parry's Arctic voyage, 1821-23.

NICHOLAS.—Island, North Channel, Algoma ; after the late Nicholas Flood Davin (q.v.) M.P. for Assiniboia West.

NICHOLSON.—Rock, Manitoulin ; after Moses Vernon Nicholson, clerk in Department of Marine and Fisheries.

NICOLET.—Rock, Parry Sound ; after Jean Nicolet, the famous French explorer who reached Sault Ste. Marie.

NIGER.—Rock, Parry Sound ; Parry (q.v.) served as Lieutenant in the Niger (38) in 1815.

NEWBURN.—Rock, Parry Sound ; after a boatman in steamer Bayfield.

NISBET.—Rock, Sudbury ; after the chief engineer of the Bayfield.

NOBLE.—Bank, Manitoulin ; after James Noble, fish merchant.

††NOBLE.—Island, Serpent Harbour, Algoma.

NORQUAY.—Island, North Channel, Algoma ; after the late Hon. Joseph Norquay, Premier of Manitoba.

*NOTTAWASAGA.—Bay, Simcoe ; *Nottaway* (or *Nadowa*) 'adders'—a name applied by various Algonquin tribes to a number of their neighbouring and most detested enemies—*sag* or *sank* 'outlet' (of a river). On Bouchette's map, 1815, the western portion is called "Iroquois Bay."

NUMBER 9.—Island, Muskoka ; number given to the island by the surveyor.

††NUMBER 10.—Island, Muskoka.

OAK.—Islands, Parry Sound ; this name is also applied to numerous other features in Canada, usually owing to its predominence in the vicinity over the other varieties of trees.

O'BRIEN.—Islands, Parry Sound, and patch, Manitoulin ; after the late Col. W. E. O'Brien, M.P., in command of the 12th York Rangers and the 35th Simcoe Foresters in Riel rebellion, 1885.

O'CONNOR.—Rocks, Parry Sound ; after Rt. Rev. Richard Alphonsus O'Connor, R. C. Bishop of Peterborough.

O'CONNOR.—Island, North Channel ; probably after late Daniel O'Connor, K.C., Ottawa.

O'DONNELL.—Point and channel, Muskoka ; after the captain of a local passenger steamer.

O'DONNELL.—Island, North Channel, Algoma ; after a boatman in the surveying steamer Bayfield.

O'DWYER.—Island, North Channel, Algoma ; after an engineer of Algoma.

OGILVIE.—Island, North Channel, Algoma ; after late Wm. Ogilvie, D.L.S. ; Commissioner, Yukon, 1898-1901.

OLD TOWER.—Island, Parry Sound ; from old lighthouse on it.

OLIVER.—Rock, Sudbury ; after Major-General J. R. Oliver, sometime, Commandant, Royal Military College, Kingston ; C. M. G., 1889.

O'MEARA.—Point, Manitoulin ; after a former accountant, Department of Militia.

OMEMEA.—Island, Parry Sound ; Indian name, signifies 'wild pigeon.'

ONE-TREE.—Island, Nottawasaga Bay, Simcoe ; from a "single ash tree . . . blown down in 1894."

††ONE-TREE.—Island, Western Islands, Muskoka.

††ONE-TREE.—Island, Parry Sound.

††ONE-TREE.—Island, St. Joseph Channel, Algoma.

††ONE-TREE.—Island, Manitoulin.

ORLEBAR.—Rock, Parry Sound ; after Commander J. Orlebar, R.N., naval surveyor.

OSBORN.—Point, Manitoulin ; after chaplain to Bishop Sullivan.

OSLER.—Island, North Channel, Algoma ; after Hon. Featherston Osler ; Judge of Common Pleas, Ontario, 1875-83 ; Justice of Appeal since 1883.

OSPREY.—Bank, Muskoka ; after Capt. Osprey V. Spain, late Wreck Commissioner, Marine and Fisheries Department.

OTTER.—Islands, North Channel, Algoma ; after an otter seen swimming near the islands.

OTTLEY.—Island, Muskoka ; after Charles L. Ottley, Commander on the Victoria, sunk in collision with the Camperdown off Tripoli, June 23rd, 1893.

OUIDA.—Rock, Parry Sound ; after one of the children of Rev. H. Gaviller, Parry Sound.

OVERHANGING.—Point, Bruce ; "name given to a cliff with a projecting apex."

*OWEN.—Channel, Manitoulin ; after Capt. (later, Vice-Admiral) William Fitzwilliam Owen (1774-1857) ; in 1815 and 1816, Lieut. Bayfield was assistant to Capt. Owen in the survey of Lake Ontario. Owen entered the navy in 1788 ; was midshipman in the London, bearing the flag of Vice-Admiral Colpoys (q.v.) at the date of the great mutiny ; Lieutenant, 1797 ; Commander, 1809 ; Captain, 1811 ; in charge of survey of Great Lakes, March, 1815, to May, 1816 ; Vice-Admiral, 1854 ; died at St. John, N.B., 1857.

††*OWEN.—Island, Manitoulin.

*OWEN.—Sound, Grey ; after Admiral Sir Edward William Campbell Rich Owen (1771-1849) ; entered the navy 1786 ; in 1796, he was acting captain of the Impregnable with Rear-Admiral Sir Thomas Rich (q.v.), his godfather, and of the Queen Charlotte with Sir John Colpoys (q.v.) ; K.C.B., 1815 ; in October, 1815, he signed, as Commodore, a 'Return of officers serving on the Great

Lakes' ; Commander-in-Chief in the West Indies, 1822-25 ; Rear-Admiral, 1825 ; G.C.H., 1832 ; Vice-Admiral, 1837 ; G.C.B., 1845 ; Admiral, 1846. It has usually been assumed that Owen Sound, like Owen Channel, was named after his brother, William Fitzwilliam Owen, but Cape Commodore at the western entrance and Point William, Campbell Bluff and Point Rich at the eastern, practically demonstrate the accuracy of the above derivation.

††OWEN SOUND.—Town, Grey.

OWEN.—Island, Parry Sound ; after a former resident.

OXLEY.—Point, Heywood Island, Manitoulin ; after the late James Macdonald Oxley, author, and, sometime, clerk in Department of Marine and Fisheries.

PACIFIC.—Rock, Sudbury ; after the steamer Pacific, which struck on it.

PAGE.—Rocks, North Channel, Algoma ; after John Page, Chief Engineer of Public Works, 1868-79 ; Chief Engineer of Canals, 1879-90.

PALESTINE.—Island, Parry Sound ; "derives its name from the circumstance of its having formerly been used as a rearing place for bees from that country, a reminder of which is a couple of hive-shaped houses still remaining near the north-eastern side of the island."

PALLISER.—Point, East Rous I., Sudbury ; after Sir Edward Palliser, famous British gun-maker.

PANDORA.—Rocks, North Channel, Algoma ; after a Georgian Bay vessel.

PANET.—Point, Clapperton I., Manitoulin ; after late Col. Charles Eugene Panet (1830-98), Deputy Minister of Militia and Defence, 1875-98.

PAPINEAU.—Island, North Channel, Algoma ; after Hon. Louis Joseph Papineau (1786-1871), of Montebello, Que. ; the principal leader in the Rebellion in Lower Canada, 1837-8.

*PAPOOSE.—Island, Manitoulin ; because near a larger island, Squaw Island.

*PARRY.—Sound and island, Parry Sound. As Capt. Boulton named features in Parry Sound and vicinity after brother-officers and ships that Parry served in, and after Parry's relations, etc., a brief summary of his life is given below, the names that have been given to features in Georgian Bay being in capitals :

Rear-Admiral Sir William Edward Parry (1790-1855), son of Dr. CALEB HILLIER Parry and SARAH, his wife. His mother was the daughter of John RIGBY and grand-daughter of Dr. TAYLOR of Norwich. He received the first rudiments of education under Dr. MORGAN, then headmaster of the Grammar School,

BATH. In 1803 he joined as a Volunteer the flagship of the Channel fleet, commanded by Admiral the Hon. W. CORNWALLIS, Ville de Paris, Capt. RICKETTS. He contracted a friendship with the Hon. Chas. POWYS. In 1806, he was appointed midshipman on the TRIBUNE, Capt. (afterwards Sir Thomas) BAKER. In 1808, he was transferred to the VANGUARD commanded by Capt. BAKER, later, by Capt. GLYN. In 1810, Lieut. Parry joined the Alexandria, Capt. John QUILLIAM, later commanded by Capt. CATHCART. In 1813, he was appointed to La Hogue, Capt. the Hon. Bladen CAPEL ; took passage on the SCEPTRE to join his ship at Halifax. The following year he commanded one of the boats in a "cutting-out" expedition under Capt. COOTE of the BORER brig, up the Connecticut River. In 1815, he served in the ARDENT, Carron and NIGER ; was seized with a severe illness when on his way from Bermuda to Halifax, in the Menai, Capt. PELL. While at Halifax, he contracted an intimate friendship with the admiral's secretary, Chas. MARTYR. In 1818, he went to the Arctic as second in command of Capt. John Ross' expedition. In the same year, Lieut. John FRANKLIN sailed in the Trent, another Arctic expedition, as second in command under Capt. Buchan. In 1819, he was appointed to the command of an Arctic expedition in the HECLA and GRIPER with Lieut. LIDDON, as second in command. In 1821, he made his second voyage, with Commander LYON as second in command. Other officers were Lieuts. NIAS, H. P. HOPPNER and PALMER and Purser W. H. HOOPER. In 1841, he married CATHERINE EDWARDS, daughter of the Rev. R. HANKINSON, Lynn.

††PARRY.—Harbour, Parry Sound.

††PARRY SOUND.—Town and district.

PARSONS.—Island, North Channel, Algoma ; after a Georgian Bay captain.

PASTURE.—Point, St. Joseph Channel, Algoma ; in contrast to rugged shores in vicinity ; the point is low and flat.

PAT HOWE.—Patch, Manitoulin ; after a boatman in surveying steamer Bayfield.

PATRICK.—Point, Algoma ; after Col. W. Patrick Anderson, Chief Engineer, Department of Marine and Fisheries.

††PATRICK POINT.—Bank, Algoma.

PATTEN.—Island, Goat Channel, Sudbury ; after a merchant of Little Current.

PATTERSON.—Island, Parry Sound ; after a boatman in steamer Bayfield.

PATTERSON.—Point, Frechette I., Algoma ; after Hon. William Patterson, M.P. for South Brant, 1872-96, for North Grey, 1896-1900, for Wentworth and Brant North, 1900-04, and for Brant 1904-1911 ; Minister of Customs 1897-1911.

*PAULETT.—Cape, Bruce ; probably after Capt. Lord H. Paulett, R.N.

PAWSEY.—Rock, Muskoka ; after Charles J. Pawsey, Secretary in the Victoria, sunk in collision with the Camperdown, June, 1893.

PEASE.—Rock,. Parry Sound ; after a boatman in steamer Bayfield.

PELHAM.—Cove, Parry Sound ; probably after Capt. Frederick S. Pelham, Rear-Admiral, 1907 ; is now, Admiral Superintendent at Gibraltar.

PELICAN.—Rock, Parry Sound ; after one of d'Iberville's vessels. In 1697, d'Iberville sank the Hampshire in Hudson Bay and captured Fort Nelson.

PELKIE.—Rock, Smith Bay, Manitoulin ; after an Indian at Wikwemikong.

PELL.—Island, Parry Sound ; after Capt. Pell of H.M.S. Menai in which Parry sailed.

PELLETANS.—Channel, Algoma ; after a Canadian who long cultivated some land on an island at its east end.

PENDER.—Islets, Manitoulin ; after a naval surveyor, Capt Daniel Pender, R.N. ; surveyed coast of British Columbia, 1857-70.

PENETANG.—Rock, Muskoka ; "so called from the fact that the smaller craft using the passage east of Minnicoganashene Island, on their way to Penetanguishene, have to pass round this, or rather leave the main ship's track here."

PENETANGUISHENE.—Harbour, Simcoe ; Indian name meaning "the place of the white rolling sands" ; from a bank of sand on Pinery Point on west side of harbour.

PERKINS.—Rock, Key Harbour, Parry Sound ; after engineer on Canadian Northern Ry. surveys.

PERLEY.—Island, Manitoulin ; island, Sudbury, and rock, Parry Sound ; after the late Major Henry F. Perley, Chief Engineer, Department of Public Works, 1880-91.

*PERRIQUE.—Island, North Channel, Algoma ; appears on Bayfield's chart ; name probably given by French voyageurs to commemorate some occurrence in which a wig played a prominent part. A reference in Badgley's diary shows that the name was in use in 1792.

PERSEVERANCE.—Island, Owen Channel, Manitoulin ; after the gunboat Perseverance wrecked at, or near, here.

PETER.—Islands, North Channel, Algoma ; after Peter Scott, naval surveyor.

PETLEY.—Rock, George I., Manitoulin ; after a naval surveyor ; possibly, Eaton Wallace Petley, Nav.-Lieutenant, retired, 1886.

PHILIP EDWARD.—Island, Manitoulin ; after Philip Edward Collins, Assistant to Capt. Bayfield in survey of Lakes Huron and Superior.

PHILLIPS.—Shoal, Key Harbour, Parry Sound ; after William Phillips, late Gen. Freight Agent, Canadian Northern Ry.

PHIPPS.—Point, and PHIPPS POINT, shoal, Manitoulin ; after the Indian agent at Manitowaning.

PHOEBE.—Point, Fitzwilliam I., Manitoulin, and rocks, Parry Sound ; after the schooner Phoebe Catherine.

PICTURE.—Island, St. Joseph Channel, Algoma ; "derives its name from a couple of white patches resembling an Indian and squaw with snowshoes over their shoulders."

PIERCE.—Island, Parry Sound ; after caretaker of clubhouse of Hamilton Canoe Club on the island.

PIERCY.—Rocks, St. Joseph Channel, Algoma ; after Canon C. Piercy, Sault Ste. Marie, Church of England clergyman, formerly at Marksville.

PIG, THE.—Rock, Muskoka ; "named from the appearance of a large boulder lying on it."

PINCH.—Island, Manitoulin ; after a lumberman at Collins Inlet.

PINCH-GUT.—Point, Darch I., Algoma ; local name ; from the men working in a quarry at this point, having run short of food.

*PINERY.—Point, Simcoe ; from the pines that grew there. Labatte in his narrative of "The Migration of Voyageurs from Drummond Island," says : "The barracks of Penetanguishene were built of Norway pine from Pinery Point." "Pine Point" on Bayfield's chart.

PLOUGH BOY.—Rock, North Channel, Algoma ; after the steamer Plough Boy.

PLUMB.—Island, North Channel, Algoma ; after Hon. Josiah Burr Plumb (1816-88) ; Senator, 1882 ; Speaker of Senate, 1887.

PLUMMER.—Island and bank, St. Joseph Channel, Algoma ; after Wm. Plummer, sometime manager of the Bruce mines.

POLLARD.—Island, Parry Sound ; after Rev. Henry Pollard, Ottawa, Church of England clergyman.

POND.—Point, Manitoulin ; "so called from a lake immediately back of it."

POOL.—Rocks, Western Islands, Parry Sound ; from the pools of water in hollows in rocks.

POPE.—Rock, Manitoulin ; after the Hon. John Henry Pope, Minister of Agriculture, 1878-85 ; Minister of Railways and Canals, 1885-89.

POPHAM.—Point, Manitoulin ; after Capt. Stephen Popham, commanding H.M.S. Montreal (22) on Great Lakes, 1814.
PORTAGE.—Island and point, Muskoka ; from a portage across inner portion of the point.
PORTER.—Point, Algoma ; after R. Porter, M.P. for West Huron, 1887-91.
*PORTLOCK.—Harbour Algoma ; probably after Capt. Nathaniel Portlock (1748-1817) ; explored and traded on Pacific coast of Canada, 1785-88.
††PORTLOCK.—Island, Algoma.
POTVIN.—Point, Parry Sound ; after a merchant of Byng Inlet.
POWELL.—Cove, and POWELL COVE, bank, Heywood I., Manitoulin ; after Col. Walker Powell, Adjutant General of Militia, 1873-74 and 1875-95.
POWER.—Island, Manitoulin ; after late Augustus Power, K.C., Department of Justice.
POWYS.—Rock, Parry Sound ; after Lieut. the Hon. Charles Powys, who served in the Ville de Paris, Parry's (q.v.) first vessel.
PRAIRIE.—Point, Bruce ; descriptive, being a broad, flat, bare, low point.
PRATT.—Island and reef, Key Harbour, Parry Sound ; after the Engineer of Terminals, Canadian Northern Ry.
PRATT.—Shoal, Parry Sound ; after a resident of Parry Sound.
PRENDERGAST.—Island, North Channel, Algoma ; after a friend of Capt. Boulton.
PRESENT.—Island, Simcoe ; so named from the annual gathering of the Indians to receive the customary distribution of presents from the Government.
*PRINCE WILLIAM HENRY.—Island, Simcoe ; after Prince William Henry, Duke of Clarence, brother of George III, later William IV. Name obsolete, now called Beausoleil.
PROUT.—Rock, North Channel, Algoma ; after a customs officer, Bruce Mines.
PROVO.—Shoal, Parry Sound ; after Lieut. Wallis Provo of H.M.S. Shannon, which captured the U.S.S. Chesapeake, June 1st, 1813.
PUDDING.—Island, Muskoka ; after conglomerate (puddingstone) rock on this island.
*PUMPKIN.—Point, Lake George, Algoma ; probably a vegetable garden at this point.
PYETTE.—Point and hill, Grey, and point, Huckleberry I., Parry Sound ; after a resident.
PYM.—Rock, Parry Sound ; after a naval officer.

QUAI DES ROCHES.—Point, Christian Island, Simcoe; "name applied to a pile of stones."

QUARRY.—Island, Simcoe; from an old quarry on it.

QUEBEC.—Bay, St. Joseph Channel, Algoma; after the steamer Quebec.

QUEEN.—Reef, Parry Sound; after the tug Queen.

QUILLIAM.—Shoal, Parry Sound; Lieut. W. E. Parry served in the Alexandria, in 1810, under Capt. John Quilliam.

RAFT.—Point, Simcoe; rafts tie up to it for shelter.

RAGGED.—Point, Alexander Inlet, Parry Sound, and point, Squall I., Manitoulin; descriptive.

RAINBOTH.—Island, North Channel, Lake Huron; after J. E. Rainboth, D.L.S., Ottawa.

RAMSEY.—Island, North Channel, Algoma; after an engineer on Canadian Pacific Ry.

RANNIE.—Rocks, Manitoulin; after a fishing tug.

RASPBERRY.—Island, Manitoulin; characteristic.

RATTLESNAKE.—Islands, North Channel; from the number of these snakes formerly to be found there.

RED.—Rock, Muskoka; rock, Manitoulin; rock, Parry Sound, and REDCLIFF, bight, Manitoulin; "the moss on it gives it a reddish or orange colour."

REFORMATORY.—Point, Simcoe; from the Provincial Reformatory built on it.

*RENNIE.—Bay, Muskoka; named by Bayfield'; possibly after an official of Penetanguishene naval station; is not on Boulton's chart, but was not surveyed by him.

RESCUE.—Rock, North Channel, Algoma; after gunboat Rescue on Great Lakes.

RESTLESS.—Bank, North Channel, Algoma; after a lake vessel.

*RICH.—Cape, Grey; after Commodore Sir Edward William Campbell Rich Owen (q.v.) who was godson of Sir Thomas Rich.

RICHARDS.—Reef, Fraser Bay, Manitoulin; after a naval surveyor, Admiral Sir George Henry Richards (1820-1900); surveyed British Columbia coast, 1856-63; commanded the Assistance in the Belcher Arctic expedition in search of Franklin, 1852-54; Hydrographer, 1864-74.

RICHELIEU.—Island, North Channel, Algoma; after Cardinal Richelieu (1585-1642), principal adviser of Louis XIII of France.

RICHMOND.—Rock, Parry Sound; after the captain of a tug.

RICKETTS.—Island and reef, Parry Sound; after Capt. Ricketts of the Ville de Paris, in which vessel Parry (q.v.) first went to sea, 1803.

PLACE-NAMES IN GEORGIAN BAY. 67

RICKCORD.—Rocks, Muskoka ; after Valentine D. J. Rickcord, Fleet Paymaster in the Victoria, sunk in collision with the Camperdown off Tripoli, 1893.

RIDOUT.—Islands, Parry Sound ; after late F. Ridout, C.E., Inspecting Engineer, Department of Railways and Canals.

RIGBY.—Island, Waubuno Channel, Parry Sound ; after John Rigby, maternal grandfather of Parry (q.v.).

RIGG.—Rock, Parry Sound ; after Major Rigg, Royal Military College.

RILEY.—Patch, Manitoulin ; after a boatman in steamer Bayfield.

RITCHIE.—Point and rock, North Channel, Algoma ; after Sir William Ritchie ; Chief Justice, Supreme Court of New Brunswick, 1865-75 ; Puisne Judge, Supreme Court, 1875-79 ; Chief Justice of the Supreme Court, 1879-92.

ROBB.—Rock, North Channel, Algoma ; after the tug Robb.

*ROBERT.—Cape, Manitoulin I. ; named by Bayfield ; derivation unknown.

*ROBERTS.—Bay, Muskoka ; not on Boulton's chart, but was not surveyed by him ; named by Bayfield, possibly after an official of Penetanguishene naval station.

ROBERTSON.—Rock, North Channel, Manitoulin ; after Capt. Tate Robertson of the Frances Smith, who reported it.

ROBIN.—Island, North Channel, Algoma ; from fancied resemblance in outline, to a robin.

ROBINSON.—Bay, Manitoulin ; after Hon. John Beverly Robinson (1821-96), Lieut.-Governor of Ontario, 1880-87.

ROBITAILLE.—Point, Darch I., Algoma ; probably after Hon. Theodore Robitaille, Lieut.-Governor of Quebec, 1879-84.

ROB ROY.—Patch, North Channel, Algoma ; after a lake vessel.

ROSS.—Shoal, St. Joseph Channel, Algoma ; after A. B. Ross, graduate of the Royal Military College, 1880.

ROSE.—Rocks, North Channel, Algoma ; after a lake vessel.

ROSSEAU.—Island and shoal, St. Joseph I., Algoma ; after a former resident opposite the island.

*ROUS.—EAST and WEST, islands, Sudbury ; after Admiral Henry John Rous (1795-1877) ; Admiral of the White, 1864.

ROWLAND.—Bank, Nottawasaga Bay, Grey ; after a hotelman of Collingwood.

ROYAL.—Point, Innes I., Algoma ; after Hon. Joseph Royal, Lieut.-Governor of Northwest Territories, 1888-93.

RYKERT.—Point, Algoma ; after J. C. Rykert, M.P. for Lincoln 1878-82, for Lincoln and Niagara 1882-91.

ST. ANGE.—Island, North Channel, Algoma ; after Chevalier St. Ange, a French halfbreed who, at one time, resided on Chevalier Island.

ST. AUBYN.—Bay, Parry Sound ; after Major the Hon. J. T. St. Aubyn, Military Secretary to Lord Stanley, Governor-General, 1892-93.

ST. JOSEPH.—Island, Algoma ; so named from its position in the St. Mary River, which last named by French missionaries after the Virgin Mary.

ST. JUST.—Islands, North Channel, Algoma ; after the Hon. Luc Letellier de St. Just, Lieut.-Governor of Quebec, 1876-79.

ST. PAUL.—Rock, Aird Island, Algoma ; after a lake steamer.

SABINE.—Island, French River, Parry Sound ; after Admiral Sir Thomas Sabine Pasley (1804-84).

SACKVILLE.—Island, Manitoulin ; after Lionel (Sackville), 2nd Baron Sackville (1827-1903), British Minister at Washington, 1881-88.

SALT.—Point, Parry Island, Parry Sound ; "after the Indian Methodist missionary residing here."

SAM SMITH.—Rock, North Channel, Algoma ; after a boatman in surveying steamer Bayfield.

SANDFIELD.—Point, Manitoulin ; after the Hon. John Sandfield Macdonald (1812-72), Premier of Canada, 1862-64 ; opposed Confederation ; Premier of Ontario, 1867-71.

SANDFORD.—Ground, Nottawasaga Bay, Grey ; after Sir Sandford Fleming, an eminent Canadian civil engineer.

SANFORD.—Island, North Channel, Algoma ; after Hon. W. E. Sanford (1838-1899), Hamilton ; Senator, 1887.

SANKEY.—Island, St. Joseph Channel, Algoma ; after Major Sankey, sometime Professor of Military Engineering, Royal Military College.

SANS SOUCI.—Islands, Parry Sound ; after Sans Souci palace, Potsdam, Prussia, built by Frederick the Great, 1745-47.

SAPPER.—Island, St. Joseph Channel, Algoma ; after a graduate of the Royal Military College.

SARAH.—Rock, Parry Sound ; after a daughter of Capt. Cox, R.N., naval surveyor.

SARAH.—Island, Parry Sound ; after Sarah Rigby, mother of Parry (q.v.).

SAULT STE. MARIE.—Town, Algoma ; after the rapids in the St. Mary River which so named by the French missionaries after the Virgin ; previously called "Sault du Gaston" after Jean-Baptiste Gaston, younger brother of Louis XIII and son of Henry IV. According to the Indian legend, the great demi-god, Nanabozho, "when he found the waters of Lake Superior rising, put on his great boots and walked around the lake until he found at the Sault that the great White Beaver had built a dam and that he kicked away the dam and opened up" the water course. The Chippewa village was called Pawating (Bawiting), a cognate form of *bawi ligunk*, "at the rapids." The old village site is the most sacred spot known to the old-time Chippewa and a Chippewa who has been to the rapids has made a holy pilgrimage.

SAYER.—Island, North Channel, Algoma ; after a trader at Mississagi River.

SCEPTRE.—Bank, Parry Sound ; Parry (q.v.) travelled from England to Halifax in H.M.S. Sceptre in 1813.

SCHREIBER.—Island, Sudbury ; after Collingwood Schreiber, C.M.G., Deputy Minister and Chief Engineer, Dept. of Railways and Canals, 1892 ; now, Consulting Engineer of same Department.

SCHULTZ.—Island, North Channel, Algoma ; after the late Sir John Schultz, Lieut.-Governor of Manitoba, 1888-95.

SCOTT.—Island, Parry Sound ; after Peter Scott, naval surveyor.

††SCOTT.—Island, and SCOTT ISLAND, passage, North Channel, Algoma.

SEAGRAM.—Rock, near Pt. Magnet, Thunder Bay ; after Jos. Seagram, M.P. for Waterloo North, 1896-1904.

SEAMAN.—Bank, Muskoka ; after tug Seaman.

SECRETARY.—Island, North Channel, Algoma ; after the Sectary to the Admiralty, John Wilson Croker (q.v.).

SEDGEWICK.—Point, Parry Sound ; after Robert Sedgewick, Deputy Minister of Justice, 1888-93 ; Puisne Judge, Supreme Court, 1893.

SEGUIN.—Bank, Parry Sound ; after the steambarge Seguin.

SENECAL.—Point, Clapperton Island, Manitoulin ; after A. Sénécal, Superintendent of Printing, 1888-91.

*SERPENT.—Island, North Channel, Algoma ; probably voyageur name given because infested with snakes.

SERPENT.—Harbour and river, Algoma ; from a perpendicular rock at the mouth of the river, on which a huge serpent is carved.

SEVERN.—River, and PORT SEVERN, village, Simcoe ; after the River Severn bordering England and Wales. Indian name was *wai-nautkecheaing* meaning river running about in all directions.

SEXTANT.—Bay and point, Manitoulin ; a sextant was lost off this point.

SEYMOUR.—Rock, Parry Sound ; after a lake steamer.

SHANLY.—Island, North Channel ; after the late Walter Shanly, C.E., M.P. for South Grenville, 1867-72 and 1885-91.

SHANNON.—Rock, Parry Sound ; after the British vessel Shannon, which captured the U.S.S. Chesapeake, June 1st, 1813.

SHAWANAGA.—Bay, island and river, Parry Sound ; Indian name meaning "a long bay or strait."

SHEBASHEKONG.—Bay and river, Parry Sound ; from Indian name *nebeshekong* meaning, "at the place of leaves."

SHEPHERD.—Reef, North Channel, Algoma : after a lightkeeper at Sulphur Island.

SHICKLUNA.—Rock, North Channel, Algoma ; after propeller Shickluna, which named after owner.

SHIP.—Island, Muskoka ; "so called because vessels keep it close on board to avoid Otonabee shoal."

SHUT-IN.—Point, Manitoulin ; descriptive.

SICCORDE.—Point, Algoma ; after a local merchant.

SIDNEY.—Island, Parry Sound ; after Sidney Band, son of Bursar of the Penetanguishene Reformatory.

SILBOW.—Rock, Parry Sound ; local name ; after a dog.

SIMON.—Rock, North Channel, Algoma ; after the late Simon J. Dawson, M.P. (q.v.).

SIMPSON.—Rock, Manitoulin ; after Sir George Simpson, Governor of the Hudson's Bay Co., 1822-1860.

SIMS.—Point, Manitoulin ; after Capt. Sims, Sarnia.

SKINNER.—Bluff, Grey ; after a farmer residing there.

SKULL.—Island and point, Manitoulin ; a large number of skeletons were found in a pit in the rock on the island.

††SKULL POINT.—Reef, Manitoulin.

SKYLARK.—Rock, Muskoka ; after yacht Skylark owned by Dodge of New York and Waubaushene.

SMITH.—Bay, Parry Sound : after one of the crew of steamer Bayfield.

*SMITH.—Bay and capet Harbour, Algoma ; after late William Smith (q.v.), Deputy Minister of Marine.

††SMITH.—Rock, Manitoulin.

*SMITH.—Bay and cape, Manitoulin ; probably after Sir William Sidney Smith (1764-1840). Bayfield entered the Navy in 1806 as supernumerary volunteer in the Pompee, the flagship of Sir William Sidney Smith. 'Smyth' on Bayfield's chart.

SMITH.—Shoal, St. Joseph Channel, Algoma; after the steamer Frances Smith.

SNAKE.—Bank and island, and LITTLE SNAKE, island, Parry Sound ; noted for snakes.

SNIDER.—Island, Serpent Harbour, Algoma ; after a resident of Serpent River.

SOLITARY.—Rock, Georgian Bay, Parry Sound ; descriptive.

SOLOMON.—Point, Stewart Island, Algoma, and rock, Parry Sound ; after Chief Solomon, an Indian chief.

SOPHIA.—Rock, Parry Sound ; after a daughter of Capt. Cox, R.N.

SOW, THE.—Rock, Muskoka ; near "The Pig."

SOW AND PIGS.—Islands, North Channel, Algoma ; descriptive.

SPAIN.—Rock, Muskoka ; after Capt. O. V. Spain, late Wreck Commissioner, Department of Marine and Fisheries.

*SPANISH.—River, Algoma ; Bigsby says that the name "is given to it from its having been once occupied by Spanish Indians." This, however, is incredible. It was probably named "Spanish" in contra-distinction to the "French" river further east. Name appears on Bayfield's chart, but not on Bouchette's map, 1815.

SPARKS.—Island, Parry Sound ; after a well known Ottawa family.

SPARTAN.—Rock, North Channel, Algoma ; after the steamer Spartan.

SPECTACLE.—Island, Parry Sound ; from resemblance in form to a pair of spectacles.

SPILSBURY.—Island, Manitoulin ; after Capt. Francis Brockell Spilsbury, R.N., in command of schooner Melville on Lake Ontario, August 10th, 1815 ; commanded the Beresford at Sackett's Harbour ; was present in actions off Burlington, Sept. 28th, 1813, and at French Creek, Nov. 1st, 1813 ; Captain commanding Niagara, May 21st, 1814 ; present at Oswego, May 6th, 1814. In 1806 Bayfield was serving in the Duchess of Bedford, a hired armed vessel, commanded by Lieut. Spilsbury, and was slightly wounded in a severe action in the Strait of Gibraltar in which that vessel beat off two Spanish feluccas with double her crew.

SPLIT.—Rock, Muskoka ; descriptive.

SPOHN.—Spit, Muskoka ; after P. H. Spohn, M.P. for Simcoe East, 1891-92

SPOTTED.—Island, North Channel, Algoma ; "so called from the circumstance of its being patchy."

SPRAGGE.—Island, Algoma ; after the late Hon. John Godfrey Spragge, Justice of the High Court, Chancery Div., Ontario, 1850-69, and Chancellor, 1869-81 ; Chief Justice of Ontario, 1881-84.

*SPRATT.—Point, Simcoe ; named by Bayfield ; possibly after an official of Penetanguishene naval station.

SPRAY.—Rock, Muskoka ; from "being bold-to on the west side, every little sea causes spray to fly over it."

SPROULE.—Islands, North Channel, Algoma; after Dr. Thomas Simpson Sproule, M.P. for East Grey since 1878 ; Speaker since 1911.

*SQUAW.—Island, Parry Sound ; so named by Bayfield ; smaller islands near were named "Papoose."

STAIRS.—Island, Parry Sound ; after Capt. W. G. Stairs, graduate, Royal Military College, 1882 ; he accompanied Stanley through Africa.

STALKER.—Bank, Parry Sound ; after a fisherman.

STANLEY.—Island, Manitoulin ; after Lord Stanley, Governor-General of Canada, 1888-93 ; suc. his father as Earl of Derby, 1893.

STANLEY.—Island, Parry Sound ; after Sir Henry M. Stanley, noted African explorer.

STANLEY.—Point, Heywood Island, Manitoulin ; after Capt. Stanley, a naval surveyor, contemporary of Capt. Boulton.

STARVATION.—Bay, Parry Sound ; from a camping party having been wrecked here.

STEELE.—Rock, Manitoulin ; after Vivian H. Steele, clerk in Department of Marine and Fisheries.

STEEPLE.—Rock, North Channel, Algoma ; "derives its name from its pinnacly nature."

STEERS.—Rock, Muskoka ; after a resident of Penetanguishene.

STEPHENS.—Ground, Nottawasaga Bay, Grey ; after a merchant, Collingwood.

STEPHEN.—Cove, Manitoulin : after a physician at Manitowaning.

STEWART.—Island, Algoma, and rock, Owen Channel, Manitoulin ; after W. J. Stewart, Chief Hydrographer of Canada ; assistant to Capt. Boulton, 1883 to 1893, when succeeded latter.

STONY.—Island, Bayfield Sound, Manitoulin ; from being "connected to the point northward of it by a bank of dry stones."

STORY.—Island, St. Joseph Channel, Algoma ; after the tug Story or, after her owner.

STRANGE.—Bay and point, Bedford Island, North Channel ; after late Major-General Thomas Bland Strange ; in 1871 appointed to command of Canadian artillery ;/ commanded Alberta field force in rebellion of 1885.

STRAUBENZIE.—Point and reef, Bedford Island, North Channel ; after the late Lieut.-Col. Bowen Van Straubenzie, b. 1829 ; commanded the Infantry Brigade at the action of Batoche, 1885.

STRAWBERRY.—Channel and island, Manitoulin ; from the wild strawberries growing on the island.

STRUTHERS.—Island, North Channel, Algoma ; after a physician, Algoma.

SULLIVAN.—Patch, Algoma ; after the Rt. Rev. Edward Sullivan, late Bishop of Algoma.

*SULPHUR.—Island, North Channel, Algoma ; named by Bayfield ; derivation unknown, but probably in use before date of survey.

SULTAN.—Rock, Parry Sound ; after a lake vessel.

SUPERIOR.—Shoal, Muskoka ; after tug Superior.

SUPPLY.—Point, Algoma ; "derives its name from · a small cove on the west side of the point affording good landing for provisions sent in to the parties working on the railway."

SURPRISE.—Shoal, Bruce ; from being unexpected ; it is at a considerable distance from land.

SUSANNA.—Island, North Channel, Algoma ; after Mrs. Susanna Moodie, authoress of "Roughing It in the Bush," etc.

SUTHERLAND.—Shoal, Manitoulin ; after one of the boatmen on surveying steamer Bayfield.

SWEATMAN.—Island, Muskoka ; after the Most Rev. Arthur Sweatman (1834-1909), Archbishop of Toronto.

*SYDNEY.—Bay, Bruce ; possibly after John Thomas (Townshend), 2nd Viscount Sydney (1764-1831), Lord of the Admiralty, 1789-93 ; or, after Sir Sydney Smith (q.v.).

SYLVAIN.—Island, North Channel, Algoma ; after L. P. Sylvain, Chief Clerk, Library of Parliament.

SYLVIA.—Rock, Alexander Inlet, Parry Sound ; after a British surveying vessel.

SYMES.—Rock, North Channel, Algoma ; after a lake captain.

TABLE.—Rocks, Muskoka ; "from the flat appearance of the top of the highest one."

TACHE.—Island and TACHE ISLAND, reef, Manitoulin; after the Most Rev. Archbishop Tache, St. Boniface, Man.

TALBOT.—Islands, Muskoka ; after Col. O. E. Talbot, M.P. for Bellechase, 1896-1911.

TALON.—Rock, North Channel, Algoma ; after Jean Talon, Intendant of New France, 1663-68 and 1669-75.

TASCHEREAU.—Bay, North Channel ; after late Sir Henri Elzear Taschereau, Puisne Judge, Supreme Court of Canada, 1878-1902 ; Chief Justice, Supreme Court, 1902 ; died, 1911.

TAYLOR.—Island, Parry Sound ; after the great-grandfather of Parry (q.v.).

TEAT, THE.—Rocks, Muskoka ; "so called from the appearance of the southeastern one."

TECUMSEH.—Cove, Cove Island, Bruce ; the steamer Tecumseh was wrecked here.

TELEGRAM.—Rock, Parry Sound ; after the steamer Telegram.

TEMPLE.—Rocks, Algoma ; after an American tug, Temple Emery.

TENBY.—Bay, St. Joseph Island, Manitoulin ; after Tenby, town, Wales ; named by late Major Rains, one of the first settlers.

TEN-MILE.—Point and shoal, Manitoulin ; "derives its name from being nearly that distance from Manitowaning."

TENNANT.—Point, Parry Sound ; after Lady Stanley, née Dorothy Tennant ; married Sir H. M. Stanley, African explorer, 1890.

TEN-RIB.—Rock, St. Joseph Channel, Algoma ; a fisherman broke ten ribs of his boat by running on this rock.

TERN.—Island, North Channel, Algoma ; after the sea-swallow.

THEBO.—Point and cove, Killarney Harbour ; after a merchant, Killarney.

THE COUSIN.—Island, North Channel, Algoma ; descriptive ; the islands are close together and with shoal water between.

THESSALON.—River, Algoma ; said by the Chief of the Mississagi band to mean "slow" ; the Chief of the Thessalon band says it means "a long, narrow point" ; called by the Jesuits "Tessalon."

††THESSALON.—Island and river, Algoma.

THE TOOTH.—Rock, Manitoulin ; descriptive.

THE TRIANGLE.—Rocks, Manitoulin ; "name given to three sunken rocks."

THE TRIPLETS.—Islands, Muskoka ; descriptive.

THE WALL.—Reef, Manitoulin ; "on account of the steepness of its eastern side."

THISTLE.—Island, Parry Sound ; after the late W. R. Thistle, lumberman, Ottawa.

THOMAS.—Bay and point, Manitoulin ; after Col. Thos. Benson, Master-General of the Ordnance, Ottawa ; graduate, Royal Military College, 1883.

THOMAS.—Island, North Channel, Algoma ; after Thomas Kirke, in command of the George at capture of Quebec, 1629.

THOMAS LONG.—Shoal, Nottawasaga Bay, Grey ; after Thomas Long, Vice-President, Collingwood Shipbuilding Co., Toronto.

*THOMPSON.—Point, Cockburn Island, Manitoulin ; named by Bayfield after an officer then serving on the gunboat Confiance.

THOMPSON.—Point, Manitoulin ; after the Rt. Hon. Sir John S. D. Thompson (1844-1894), Minister of Justice, 1885-94 ; Premier of Canada, 1892-94.

THREE-MILE.—Point, Parry Island, Parry Sound ; from being "about three statute miles from the town of Parry Sound."

THREE STAR.—Shoal, Parry Sound ; marked by three crosses (stars) on old chart.

THUMB.—Rock, Western Islands, Parry Sound ; descriptive.

THUNDER.—Bay, Simcoe ; present Owen Sound was named Thunder Bay on Bouchette's map, 1815 ; probably the name was misplaced and is a translation of the Indian name.

TIE.—Island, Parry Sound ; "so called from the fact of tugs tying up to it with their rafts in southerly gales."

TILTON.—Reef, Bruce ; after Lieut.-Col. J. Tilton, Deputy Minister of Fisheries, 1884-91.

TINDALL.—Point, Parry Sound ; after a resident of Parry Sound.

TINY.—Beach and island, Simcoe ; name originally applied to the township, which named after one of Lady Sarah Maitland's pet dogs.

TOAD.—Island, Manitoulin ; from its shape ; resembles a toad.

TOBERMORY.—Harbour, Bruce ; after Tobermory, seaport, Argyllshire, Scotland, which from Gaelic and Irish, *tobar moire* "well of the Virgin Mary."

*TODD.—Point, Simcoe ; named by Bayfield ; possibly after an official of Penetanguishene naval station.

TODD.—Point and shoal, Amedroz Island, Algoma ; after late Alpheus Todd, LL.D., Librarian of Parliament, 1867-84.

TODDS.—Point, Simcoe; after an early surveyor of that name.

TOLSMA.—Bay, Manitoulin ; after ―― Tolsma, who carried on an extensive fishing business here.

TOMLINSON.—Islands, North Channel, Algoma ; after Joseph Tomlinson, Engineer and Superintendent of Lighthouses, Department of Marine and Fisheries, 1873-80.

TONTY.—Island, North Channel, Algoma ; after Henri de Tonti (or Tonty) (1650-1704), lieutenant of La Salle in his explorations of the Mississippi.

TOTTENHAM.—Shoal, Muskoka ; probably after Tottenham, parish, suburb of London, England.

TOWNSEND.—Island, Muskoka ; after the owner.

TRACK.—Island, Parry Sound ; it is near the track for steamers.

TRANCH.—Rock, Parry Sound, and rock, Manitoulin ; after a lake captain.

TREE.—Island, Parry Sound ; from a single large pine-tree on it.

TRENT.—Rock, Parry Sound ; after the vessel which Lieut. Franklin commanded in his Arctic voyage to Spitzbergen, 1818.

TRIBUNE.—Island, Parry Sound ; Parry (q.v.) was appointed midshipman in the Tribune in 1806.

TRITON.—Rock, Parry Sound ; after the Triton, British surveying vessel.

TROW.—Point, and TROW POINT, shoal, Algoma; after James Trow, M.P. for South Perth, 1872-92.

TRUDEAU.—Point, Manitoulin; after the late Toussaint Trudeau, Deputy Minister of Public Works, 1868-79; Deputy Minister of Railways and Canals, 1879-92.

TRUDEAUX.—Point, Simcoe; after Jean Baptiste Trudeaux; was blacksmith in the Navy; later, settled there.

TRYON.—Island, Muskoka; after Admiral Sir George Tryon, commanding fleet at time of the Victoria-Camperdown collision, June 23rd, 1893.

TUG.—Rock, North Channel, Algoma; after the tug Robb.

TULLY.—Island, Muskoka; after late Kivas Tully, C.E., Toronto, father of Mrs. Band (q.v.).

TUPPER.—Island, North Channel, Sudbury; after Sir Charles Tupper, Minister of Inland Revenue, 1872-73; of Customs, 1873; of Public Works, 1878-79; of Railways and Canals, 1879-84; High Commissioner for Canada, 1884-87, 1888-96; Minister of Finance, 1888; Premier, 1896.

TURNBULL.—Island, and TURNBULL ISLAND, passage, North Channel, Algoma; after Lieut.-Col. James F. Turnbull, Commandant, Royal Can. Dragoons, 1883; accompanied his corps to N. W. T. on outbreak of Riel rebellion, 1885; Inspector of Cavalry, 1895; retired, 1895.

TURNER.—Cove, Manitoulin; after postmaster, Little Current.

TURNING.—Island, Parry Sound; "as its name indicates, marks the turning point from the middle reach into the main body of Shawanaga Bay."

††TURNING.—Island, Bruce, and rock, Muskoka.

TURTLE.—Channel, Parry Sound; from a rock in the channel having a fancied resemblance to a turtle.

††TURTLE.—Rock, Muskoka, and rock, Algoma.

TWIN.—Island, Parry Sound; "as its name indicates, it is almost divided into two parts."

††TWIN.—Islands, Manitoulin.

††TWIN.—Rock, Parry Sound.

TWINING.—Island, St. Joseph Channel, Algoma; after Lieut.-Col. P. G. Twining, R.E., graduate of Royal Military College, 1883.

TWO-MILE.—Point, Parry Island, Parry Sound; from "being about two statute miles from the town of Parry Sound."

††TWO-MILE.—Narrows Parry Sound.

TYRWHITT.—Shoal, North Channel, Algoma; after Lieut.-Col. R. Tyrwhitt, M.P. for South Simcoe, 1878-1900.

UMBRELLA.—Islands and ledges, Parry Sound ; "presumably from a single large pine tree growing upon one of the inside islets."

UNDERHILL.—Point, Badgley Island, Manitoulin ; after H. H. Underhill, draughtsman in the Hydrographic Department, Admiralty.

VAIL.—Point, and VAIL POINT, shoal, Grey ; after a Meaford fisherman.

††VAIL.—Rock, Parry Sound.

VALENTINE.—Rocks, Muskoka ; after Valentine Rickcord, Fleet Paymaster in the Victoria, sunk in collision with the Camperdown, 1893.

VANGUARD.—Rock, Parry Sound ; Parry (q.v.) served in H. M. S. Vanguard, 1808-09.

VANKOUGHNET.—Island, Manitoulin ; after the late Lawrence Vankoughnet, Superintendent-General of Indian Affairs, 1874-93.

††VANKOUGHNET.—Ground, Parry Sound.

VARIATION.—Point, Beckwith Island, Simcoe ; "so called because the late Admiral Bayfield, when surveying Georgian Bay in 1822, observed here for variation of the magnetic needle."

VICTOR.—Bank, Parry Sound ; after H.R.H. Albert Victor Christian Edward of Wales, Duke of Clarence (1864-92).

· VICTORIA.—Island, Parry Sound, and harbour, Simcoe ; after late Queen Victoria (1819-1901).

*VIDAL.—Island, Manitoulin ; after an assistant to Capt. Bayfield ; he was the grandfather of late Gen. Beaufort Henry Vidal. On Dec. 6, 1815, Monroe, U.S. Secretary of State, wrote the British representative at Washington, reporting "an enquiry into the case of Lieutenant Vidal, who had been fined for riot while pursuing offenders into American territory."

††VIDAL.—Bay, Manitoulin Island.

VILLIERS.—Island, North Channel, Algoma ; after late Col. Villiers, D.A.G., Winnipeg.

VIVIAN.—Rocks, Parry Sound ; after a cook in steamer Bayfield.

VIXEN.—Rocks, St. Joseph Channel, Algoma ; after a lake vessel.

VOYAGEUR.—Channel, Algoma ; "it was by this mouth of French River that the canoes in the early days are said to have entered Georgian Bay from Lake Nipissing on their way westward."

WABOO.—Island, West Bay, Manitoulin ; Indian word meaning "rabbit."

WABOSON.—Island, Manitoulin ; Indian name meaning "little rabbit."

WAUBUNO.—Bank, St. Joseph Channel, Algoma ; after the steamer Waubuno, lost with all hands in a snowstorm, Nov. 22nd, 1879.

††WAUBUNO.—Channel, Sudbury.

††WAUBUNO.—Channel and rock, Parry Sound.

WAGSTAFF.—Rock, Parry Sound ; after a tourist.

WAIT-A-BIT.—Point, Simcoe ; from delay to sailboats by getting into an eddy here.

WALES.—Rock, Muskoka ; after tug Wales.

WALKER.—Point, Muskoka ; after John Walker, farmer ; prior to 1875, was known as Long Point.

*WALL.—Island, Manitoulin ; "from the south side of Wall Island, a reef, named The Wall (on account of the steepness of its eastern side), extends."

††*WALL.—Island, Parry Sound.

††WALL ISLAND.—Channel, Manitoulin.

WALLACE.—Island and rock, North Channel, Algoma ; after the late Hon. N. Clarke Wallace, M.P. for West York, 1878 to 1901.

WALLACE.—Rock, Parry Sound ; after a Parry Sound fisherman.

WALLIS.—Rocks, Parry Sound ; after Lieut. Wallis Provo, of H.M.S. Shannon which captured the Chesapeake, June 1st, 1813.

WARD.—Island, Muskoka ; after Hon. Cyril A. Ward, midshipman in the Victoria, sunk in collision with the Camperdown, June 23rd, 1893.

*WATCHER.—Islands, NORTH and SOUTH, and reef, Muskoka ; "two small islands acting as a kind of guard to the shore, hence the name."

WATERS.—Point, John Island, Algoma ; after late Dr. John Francis Waters, Department of the Secretary of State.

WATTS.—Rock, Heywood Island, Manitoulin ; after a boatbuilder, W. Watts, of Collingwood.

WEBBER.—Island, North Channel, Algoma ; after a draughtsman at the Admiralty.

WEDGE.—Island, Parry Sound ; descriptive.

WELDON.—Shoal, North Channel, Algoma ; after late Dr. C. W. Weldon, M.P. for St. John, N.B., 1878-91.

WELLER.—Island, St. Joseph Channel, Algoma ; after J. L. Weller, Superintendent, Welland Canal ; graduate of Royal Military College, 1883.

WELSH.—Island, Manitoulin ; after Muriel Welsh Boulton, daughter of Capt. Boulton.

*WESTERN.—Islands, Parry Sound ; most westerly of the "30,000 Islands," east coast of Georgian Bay.

WESTERN.—Reef, Manitoulin ; "from being the westernmost of all the patches, being near the west entrance of Clapperton Channel."

WHALESBACK.—Rock, Muskoka ; has "a round top that is supposed to resemble the back of a whale."

††WHALESBACK.—Channel and rock, North Channel, Algoma.

WHARTON.—Point, Heywood Island, Manitoulin ; after late Rear-Admiral Sir William J. L. Wharton, Hydrographer of the Admiralty.

WHEELER.—Bank, Nottawasaga Bay, Simcoe ; after a resident of Collingwood.

WHIP-POOR-WILL.—Bay, Bruce ; from the unusually large amount of whip-poor-wills frequenting the vicinity.

WHISKEY.—Island, Simcoe ; "it was the custom of the early voyageurs and Indians to halt there for their first drink of liquor."

WHITCHER.—Island, North Channel, Algoma ; after the late W. F. Whitcher, Commissioner of Fisheries, 1868-83.

WHITE.—Cove, Strawberry Island, Manitoulin ; after the late Hon. Thomas White, Minister of the Interior, 1885-88.

WHITEAVES.—Island, North Channel, Algoma ; after late Dr. Joseph Frederick Whiteaves, Assistant Director, Geological Survey, 1883.

*WHITE CLOUD.—Island, Bruce ; probably after an Indian, or translation of Indian name.

WICKSTEED.—Point, Algoma ; after G. W. Wicksteed, Law Clerk, Legislative Assembly, Province of Canada, 1841-67 ; Law Clerk, House of Commons, 1867-87.

WICKSTEED.—Rock, Key Harbour, Parry Sound ; after H. K. Wicksteed, Chief Engineer, Canadian Northern Railway.

WIKWEMIKONG.—Bay, Manitoulin ; Indian name meaning "beaver bay" ; at one time the beavers were numerous here ; sometimes called Smith Bay after a trader.

WILD GOOSE.—Island, Parry Sound ; "from . . . a sloping pine tree with a top branch resembling somewhat a goose on the wing, near the southern extremity."

WILFRID—Island, North Channel, Algoma ; after the Rt. Hon. Sir Wilfrid Laurier, Premier of Canada, 1896-1911.

*WILLIAM.—Island, Manitoulin ; probably after Sir William Sidney Smith (q.v.).

WILLIAM.—Island, Parry Sound ; after Admiral Sir William E. Parry (q.v.).

*WILLIAM.—Point, Grey; after Commodore Sir Edward William Campbell Rich Owen (q.v.); name obsolete; now Vail Point.

WILSON.—Channel and island, St. Joseph Channel, Algoma; after Major Wilson, Indian Agent at Sault Ste. Marie.

WILSON.—Point, Croker Island, Algoma; after christian name of John Wilson Croker (q.v.), Secretary to the Admiralty, 1809-30.

*WINGFIELD.—Basin and point, Bruce; after Lieut. David Wingfield, R.N.; in command of the transport Beckwith on Lake Ontario, 1816; Oct. 16th, 1815, was Lieutenant commanding the Surprise on Lake Huron.

WISE.—Cove and point, Bedford Island, North Channel; after the late Capt. Henry Ellison Wise, Scottish Rifles, A.D.C. to Major-General Middleton, 1884-90; graduate of Royal Military College, 1880.

WOLSELEY.—Rock, Parry Sound; after late Lord Wolseley, Commander-in-chief of the British land forces.

WOLSEY.—Lake, Manitoulin; named by Bayfield after himself —Henry Wolsey Bayfield.

WOLSTAN.—Point, Algoma; after a son of late H. B. Small, Department of Agriculture.

WOODMAN.—Point, St. Joseph Channel, Algoma; after John Woodman, C.E., Winnipeg; graduated from the Royal Military College, 1883.

WOODWARD.—Point, St. Joseph Channel, Algoma; after the schooner Mary Woodward.

WOORE.—Rocks, Muskoka; after Francis Woore, Surgeon in the Victoria, sunk in collision with the Camperdown off Tripoli, 1893.

*WORSLEY.—Bay, St. Joseph Island, Algoma; named by Bayfield after Commander Miller Worsley, R.N., who, in October, 1815, was commander of H.M.S. Star (14), Lake Ontario.

WRECK.—Island, Parry Sound; after the remains of the steamer Waubuno.

WRECK.—Point, Bruce; descriptive; (see China reef).

WURTELE.—Point, St. Joseph Channel, Algoma; after Lt.-Col. E. F. Wurtele; graduate of the Royal Military College, 1882.

*WYE.—River, Simcoe; after the Wye, an affluent of the Thames River, England.

*YARWOOD.—Point, Simcoe; named by Bayfield; probably after Lieut. Thomas Yarwood, 1st Battalion, Montreal City Militia; served during War of 1812-14.

*YEO.—Island, Manitoulin ; after Commodore Sir James Lucas Yeo (1782-1818) ; commanded the fleet on Lake Ontario, 1812-15.
††YEO.—Channel, Manitoulin.
††YEO ISLAND.—Spit, Manitoulin.
YOUNG.—Island, Parry Sound ; after Rt. Rev. Richard Young, Bishop of Athabaska.

Ontario Historical Society

PAPERS AND RECORDS

VOL. XII.

TORONTO
PUBLISHED BY THE SOCIETY
1914

Ontario Historical Society

(Incorporated by Act of the Legislature of Ontario,
April 1st, 1899.)

HOME OF THE SOCIETY
Normal School Building, St. James Square, Toronto

OFFICERS 1913-1914

HONORARY PRESIDENT
The Hon. Robert A. Pyne, M.A., LL. D., M.P.P., Minister of Education, Toronto.

PRESIDENT
John Dearness, M.A., ...London

VICE-PRESIDENTS
Clarence M. Warner ....Napanee
Sir Edmund Walker, C.V.O., LL.D., D.C.L., F.R.S.C., ...Toronto
and the Presidents of Affiliated Societies.

COUNCILLORS
Mrs. J. R. Simpson.... ....Ottawa
J. Stuart Carstairs, B.A. ....: ....Toronto
Alexander Fraser, LL. D., Litt.D., F.S.A.Scot. (Edinburgh), ...Toronto
W. S. Wallace, B.A., (McMaster University) ....Toronto
W. L. Grant, M.A., F.R.S.C., (Queen's University) ....Kingston
James Henry Coyne, LL.D., F.R.S.C., ... St. Thomas
Ex-President 1898—1902.
Charles Canniff James, C.M.G., LL.D., F.R.S.C., ...Toronto
Ex-President 1902-1904.
George R. Pattullo, Ex-President 1904—1906, ...Woodstock
Lt.-Col. H. C. Rogers, Ex-President 1906—1907, ...Victoria, B. C.
David Williams, Ex-President 1910—1912 ....Collingwood

TREASURER
C. C. James, C.M.G., LL.D.,.. .... 144 St. George St., Toronto

SECRETARY AND LIBRARIAN
A. F. Hunter, M.A., Normal School Building, St. James Square, Toronto

CONTENTS.

I. The Toon o' Maxwell—An Owen Settlement in Lambton County, Ont. THE REV. JOHN MORRISON, SARNIA - - - - - - 5

II. The U. E. Loyalists of the old Johnstown District. JUDGE H. S. MACDONALD, BROCKVILLE - - - - - - - 13

III. The Local History of the Town of Brockville. LT. COL. W. H. COLE. BROCKVILLE - - - - - - - - 33

IV. The War of 1812-15. J. CASTELL HOPKINS, TORONTO - - - 42

V. Reminiscences of the First Settlers in the County of Brant. CHARLES AND JAMES C. THOMAS, BRANTFORD - - - - - 58

VI. The Past and Present Fortifications at Kingston. GEO. R. DOLAN, B. A. 72

VII. Reminiscences. MISS AUGUSTA I. GRANT GILKISON, BRANTFORD - 81

VIII. Capt. Joseph Brant's Status, etc. MAJOR GORDON J. SMITH, BRANTFORD 89

IX. Chief Smoke Johnson. MISS EVELYN H. C. JOHNSON, - - - 102

X. Influence of the War of 1812. LAWRENCE J. BURPEE, OTTAWA - 114

XI. History of the Hospital, Penetanguishene. DR. G. A. MACCALLUM - 121

XII. The American Indians in Relation to Health. DR. P. H. BRYCE, OTTAWA 128

XIII. Feudalism in Upper Canada. MARJORIE J. F. FRASER, TORONTO - 142

XIV. Bush Life in the Ottawa Valley. JOHN MAY, M. A., FRANKTOWN - 153

XV. The Peter Perry Election. GEO. M. JONES, B. A., TORONTO - - 164

XVI. David Zeisberger and his Delaware Indians. REV. JOHN MORRISON, SARNIA 176

XVII. Tribal Divisions of the Indians of Ontario. THE LATE ALEX. F. CHAMBERLAIN, M. A., Ph. D. - - - - - - - 199

XVIII. Bear Customs of the Crees and other Indians. ALANSON SKINNER - 203

XIX. An Introductory Enquiry in the Study of the Ojibwa Religion. PAUL RADIN 210

XX. A Noted Anthropologist (Dr. A. F. Chamberlain). - - - 219

The Ontario Historical Society does not assume responsibility for the statements of its contributors.

"THE TOON O' MAXWELL"—AN OWEN SETTLEMENT IN LAMBTON COUNTY, ONT.

By The Rev. John Morrison, Sarnia

At many points in the world's history, men have stepped out from the ranks, having some ideal scheme for the reconstruction of society and the betterment of their fellow-men.

Plato, in his "Republic," declares "any ordinary city, however small, is in fact two cities, one the city of the poor, the other of the rich, at war with one another." It will be seen by this quotation, he was out of harmony with the social and economic tendencies of the age in which he lived. What was his proposal by which these should be changed? He proposed to alter the lives of the citizens of the state, from the day of birth. In fact, he proposed to go behind that, by declaring that marriage and the number of births, as well as the industrial occupations, were to be controlled by the guardians or heads of the state.

Of home life, as we understand it, there would be none. Theoretically he advocated "the emancipation of woman," and yet maintained that "the woman was part and parcel of the property of man," therefore, he advocates, "community of wives."

Children were to be taken away from their parents and reared under the supervision of the state. The old nursery tales, "the blasphemous nonsense (he calls them), with which mothers fool the manhood out of their children," was to be suppressed. There will be no rich and no poor, therefore no rivalry, for all are to be provided for by the state. He admits there are difficulties to be overcome, but adds by way of a stimulant to any wavering one, "nothing great is easy."

Sir Thomas More's "Utopia" has many of the characteristics of the "Republic," as community of goods and labor, and the forbidding the private use of money. He differs from Plato, however, in maintaining the sacredness of the family relation and fidelity to the marriage contract. There was to be no community of wives in Utopia. All meals were to be taken in common and to be rendered attractive by the accompaniment of sweet strains of music, while the air was to be filled by the most delicate of perfumes, thus adding to the enjoyment of life.

Robert Owen, an uncrowned king in the industrial world, philanthropist and founder of the Owen system of socialism, was born in the Village of Newtown, Montgomeryshire, North Wales, in 1771. At the age of nine years he had completed his school education, and at ten went to service in a draper's shop in Stamford, where he served three or four years. He then went to Manchester and entered the cotton mills. His industrial and executive ability are seen in that, at the age of nineteen years, he was made manager of a cotton mill employing five hundred hands, and speedily proved himself the first cotton spinner in England. A business trip to Glasgow brought him in contact with Mr. Dale, proprietor of the New Lanark mills, with whose daughter he promptly proceeded to fall in love and afterward marry. Owen induced his partners (for he was now part owner of the Chorlton Twist Company, Cotton Mills, Manchester), to buy out the New Lanark Mills, which they did, and he settled there as manager.

Here, with about two thousand people, one-quarter of that number being children, he began his plans for their betterment. He improved their houses, he opened a store where goods of undoubted quality could be purchased by his employees at little over cost price. The sale of drink was placed under the strictest supervision. Educational facilities were provided for the young. He was the founder of infant schools in Great Britain. He began to write essays advocating his social and community theories, and in 1817 presented his views, in form of a report, to the Committee of the House of Commons, on the Poor Law. The essays and report brought him into the eye of the people, not alone in Britain, but throughout Europe. Industrial leaders, social reformers, philanthropists, titled men, and even Royalty itself, visited New Lanark to see and learn. While thus leading a remarkable industrial reform movement, his business enterprises were not allowed to flag, and he proved that it paid to deal as he was doing with his work-people and their children, for from his business enterprises he amassed a fortune.

Like Plato and Sir Thomas More, whose disciple he undoubtedly was, imbibing some of the principles of each system, he outlined his ideal community. He recommended that communities of about twelve hundred persons each, should be settled on quantities of land, of from one thousand to fifteen hundred acres, all living in one large building in the form of a square, with public kitchen and dining room. Each family should have its own private apartments, and the entire care of the children till the age of three, after which they should be brought up by the community, their parents, however, having access to them at meals and all other proper times. Work and the employment of its results should be in common. These communities might be established by individuals, parishes, counties or the state itself.

At this time he had gained the ear of the country, and one of his warmest friends and supporters was the Duke of Kent, father of Queen Victoria. He had the prospect before him of becoming one of the greatest of social reformers and world benefactors, for in his personal character then, and to the end of his life, he was above reproach. Unfortunately, in the heyday of his grip of the national heart strings, he began to advocate a very lax view of marriage, which gave offense to many and alienated them from him. Also at a great gathering in London, where he was the lion of the hour, he deliberately went out of his way to declare his hostility to all the received forms of religion, and advocated a creed or religion of his own, the chief points of which were—"That man's character is made not by him, but for him. That it has been formed by circumstances over which he had no control. That he is not a proper subject either of praise or blame." In plain English, that man is not a responsible, but an irresponsible, being, wholly controlled and governed by circumstances and environment. From the moment of that pronouncement, Owen's theories were, in the popular mind, associated with infidelity, and the tide of popular public opinion turned against him. Particularly true was this among our dour Scotch, the descendants of the men who had opened their veins and with the ink of their own blood, subscribed to the solemn league and covenant. They could, and would, if need be, live on crowdie and oat meal bannocks in limited quantity, but perish the thought that they should follow a man of infidel tendencies. In the bitterness of his disappointment he cried out—"Lanark people, I meant you to have a taste of heaven below, but you would have none of the methods."

Owen died at his native village in 1858, aged eighty-seven years, but was buried at New Lanark, where most of his life was spent and his socialistic theories worked out. His body lies in a quiet corner back of the church of St. Kentigern.

Henry Jones, Esq., of Exeter, England, was a retired officer of the British navy, having held the office of purser. He met and heard Robert Owen when the latter was touring England and speaking before the public on his social and communistic theory. Jones became fascinated with Owen's scheme, and about 1825 went to New Lanark, Scotland, to attend Owen's lectures and study his theory, and also the practical workings of such portion of the scheme as he was there carrying out among his work people. His decision was soon made; he would visit the new land across the sea—Canada—make a selection of land, then return and gather together a sufficient number of families, bring them out and establish an "Owen settlement or community."

Mr. Jones proceeded to carry out his plan, bringing with him one Alexander Hamilton as his valet and travelling companion. The landing was made at New York; then by such modes of conveyance as offered in that day across the state, the newly opened Erie Canal to Buffalo being part of the route, then by the waters of Lake Erie, Detroit River, Lake and River St. Clair to Lake Huron, and having skirted the shores for some miles, being much impressed by the high, dry and heavily timbered shore line, the mouth of the River Aux Perches, then a considerable stream as it was the outlet of Lake Wawanash, a shallow body of water, in what is now Sarnia Township, of about two thousand acres and from four to six feet in depth. This river he found to be literally alive with wild duck, the marshy ground around Lake Wawanash being an ideal breeding ground for them. This settled the matter for Mr. Jones, as here was abundant opportunity for sport, while the land seemed to him an ideal location for his proposed colony.

Returning to the old country, Mr. Jones proceeded to the securing of the necessary land in what are now the Townships of Sarnia and Plympton, Lambton County, then an unsurveyed wilderness. From the Crown Lands Department of Ontario we quote the following: "The Township of Sarnia was surveyed partly by Deputy Surveyor Roswell Mount, under instructions from the Surveyor General, bearing date 8th of April, 1829, and partly by Deputy Surveyor Peter Carrol, under instructions from the Commissioner of Crown Lands, bearing date 23rd of April, 1835.

"The Township of Plympton was surveyed partly by Deputy Surveyor Charles Rankin, under instructions dated 5th June, 1829, and partly by Deputy Surveyor Peter Carrol, under instructions from the Surveyor General, of the 29th of May, 1832."

Be it well understood there was no Lambton then, but the unsurveyed portion, on which Mr. Jones had fixed his mind, formed a part of Kent, being the nineteenth county under the proclamation of John Graves Simcoe, dated 16th July, 1792, and which by the terms of that proclamation was to "comprehend all the country not being territories of the Indians, not already included in the several counties hereinbefore described, extending northward to the boundary line of Hudson's Bay."

John Collier Jones, Vice-Chancellor of Oxford University, was a brother of Henry Jones. He was married to a sister of Lady Colborne, wife of Sir John Colborne, who in 1829 was to become Governor of Upper Canada. Henry Jones was enabled by this matrimonial tie with his family to induce Sir John Colborne to plead in his behalf at the Colonial Office, that he might be granted ten thousand acres on the shore of Lake Huron, where he might plant his community and work out his Utopian scheme along the lines laid down by Robert Owen. He was guaranteed the grant and then proceeded to carry out his plan.

Mr. Jones went to Scotland and began the gathering together of a goodly number of families who were willing to join in his scheme. With these he sailed for Canada. By what port he entered and by what route he came we do not know, but may presume, I think, that it would be by the same route he had previously pursued. Sometime, perhaps, some diary will be unearthed and discovered, musty with age, in which that trip was recorded. What a splendid bit of history it would be!

That band of pioneer men, women and children, in 1827, with a firmly seated conviction of bettering their condition, was led by a man of independent means, willing in behalf of his fellow-men to invest time, labor and wealth in this manner. Night after night they would pull up their boats on the shore and make their camp. Soon the campfire would blaze brightly, around which they would gather and prepare their evening meal, then roll up in their blankets, women and children in the boats, the men on the shore, and sleep and dream of the Arcadia they were going to establish in the wilderness of the new world.

Having reached their destination, they proceeded to establish themselves. Mr. Jones named his communistic colony "The Toon O' Maxwell"—Maxwell being the name of the residence at New Lanark, Scotland, of him whose follower he was—Robert Owen.

A member of the Jones family who began in 1831 (would that he had begun a few years earlier) a very comprehensive diary, gives the location of the community house as being on Lot fifteen, lake shore, Sarnia Township, and in 42 degrees, 58 min. N. Latitude, and 82 degrees, 30 min. W. Longitude.

The buildings erected were one storey high, of logs, and boards cut out with a whip-saw. The residence must have covered a considerable amount of ground, as a goodly number of families made their home within it. Each family had separate apartments, thus recognizing the family tie, but the cooking was done in one common kitchen, and they all met in one common dining-room for their meals. While the women thus worked in common together, in preparing the food, the men also went out together as a community to their daily toil in the new and strange work of clearing off the timber and cultivating the soil. Superannuated military stores had been drawn upon to help furnish the community for its backwoods life. Artillery harness, to which were attached chains which once had done service on board the men-of-war, and these in turn hitched to ponderous carts brought by the community from Britain. The motive power was Indian ponies, the only representative of the equine race then found in those parts. A member of the Jones family of a later generation, and still living, has told us that in his boyhood days some of that ponderous equipment was still extant, and an Indian pony must have been almost hidden from sight by the harness, and had load enough in the cart without anything being added thereto. About fifty acres were cleared and got under cultivation. The fencing of their fields by those honest but innocent pioneers, was a weary and almost interminable task. What knew they about a Virginia snake-fence? Never had any of them seen, much less split, a rail, and so in a manner as though for a king's palace they hewed out posts, and with two-inch auger and chisel, cut a number of mortices right through them, Then setting them firmly in the ground, they proceeded to fit into them rails or bars hewn out with elaborate precision, with well made tenons which were fitted into the morticed posts. A hard day's toil by all the men would only construct a few rods of fence, built in that manner, while the same amount of labor expended in splitting rails out of the timber they were burning up, and building them into a regular rail fence, would have enclosed as many acres. But they did not know and ought not to be sneered at because of their ignorance.

At a little distance from the community dwelling house they erected a building to be used as a store, from which all supplies might be obtained. Another building was put up which was the school in which the children of the community were to receive an education, for scholastic training of the young was one of the strong features of the Owen philosophy.

Thus they toiled on in their isolated location, for, except a few French families on the River St. Clair front, where now the south side of Sarnia is situated, there were no other white people on Canadian soil nearer than Baldoon, Lord Selkirk's colony, on the Chenal Ecarte, near the south-west corner of the present county of Lambton.

In the "Life and Journals of Kah-ke-wa-qua-na-by," (Rev. Peter Jones), Indian Methodist missionary to his own people, now a very rare book, we find the only printed reference dating right back to the time of the colony, we have been able to find. We quote from the above work, page 244: "Saturday, Aug. 1st, 1829. Started for St. Clair this morning. Called a few minutes at Kettle Point, so called from a number of rocks or stones projecting from the precipice overhanging the waters, resembling iron pots of various sizes. In the afternoon we passed a new settlement of white people eight or ten miles west (this is an evident typographical error, it should be east) of the mouth of the lake. This settlement was formed by a Mr. Jones, who tried to carry out what is called the **Owen system** of having all things common; but I was informed the thing did not work well here, as the colonists one after another left their leader.'' It is evident by this that the settlement was a short-lived one; only two years had gone by since its founding until the record was made in Rev. Peter Jones' journal, and already the community was showing a thinning of the ranks by desertion.

The complete failure of the attempt was all too evident, when a fire caught the community house and totally destroyed it. The date of this disaster we have been unable to place. A goodly number of the colony then left it, having learned by that time that each family could for a very small sum own a hundred acre farm for themselves; then why should they submerge their personality in a community in which they formed only a part? Two community houses were built after the fire for those who still remained true to the original idea, but on a much smaller scale than the former house. These were placed one on either side of the road they had made through their clearing. It was not very long, however, until Mr. Jones and his own family were left alone, as the exodus continued until all the others were gone.

During the period of its continuance as a community, the United States military post on the Michigan shore, ten miles away, Fort Gratiot, was their post office and point of contact with the outer world they had left behind them to establish a **Utopia** or **Arcadia** where the ordinary cares of humanity were not to be known, and by emancipation from them they were to be taught not to look back to the old life. The attempt ended, as most such have ended, in proving itself fruitless.

It was a costly experiment for the founder, Mr. Jones, who expended no less a sum than ten thousand pounds sterling, fifty thousand dollars, on the experiment, vindicating his singleness of purpose and sincerity of belief in the system, which he believed was to be a panacea for the ordinary troubles that commonly beset the path of the traveller in the journey of life.

After the extinction of the colony, objection being made in some quarters to Mr. Jones holding the large tract of land granted him by the Colonial Office and Provincial Government, now that his community was gone, he, with that high honor characteristic of the true Britisher, especially one of good family and birth, as he was, voluntarily relinquished nine-tenths of the grant, refusing to hold it, and retaining only the one thousand acres to which, as a retired officer of the navy of the rank of purser, he was entitled. So ended one of the most striking settlement or colonization schemes ever attempted in our Province. Romantic in its beginnings, tragic and disastrous in its ending, was "The Toon O' Maxwell, the Owen settlement in Lambton County."

Among the number of those who composed the community we have been able to glean a few names only, as Alexander Hamilton (valet to the founder), Henry Young, Thomas Steen, John McFarlane and brother, the Burys and McPhedrans. Descendants of some of these are prominent in the life of the county at the present day.

John Hamilton, Esq., of Forest, grandson of Alexander Hamilton mentioned above, has a neat little article which links to that Owen settlement, a silver pencil-case about four and one-half inches long, with a seal on the end. The seal is seven-sixteenths of an inch across, having a quill pen and the word Truth upon it. This belonged to Henry Jones, Esq., founder of "The Toon O' Maxwell," and as his personal seal was highly prized by him, and was specifically left by will to him who had made the preliminary voyage and exploration tour with him to Canada, and then as one of the company, helped establish the settlement. Needless to say it is highly prized by his grandson, to whom it was left when the grandfather died, as a trinket linking itself to a rich bit of our early pioneer history.

Let it be clearly understood we consider this paper to be suggestive only, not by any means exhaustive, and hope that we, or some other person, from this preliminary base, may yet be able to gather from as yet undiscovered, and we will hope, somewhere hidden away records, an exhaustive store of historic detail regarding "The Toon O' Maxwell" to which this paper will prove but the A. B. C.

Alvinston, Lambton Co., Ont., 1909.

II.

THE U. E. LOYALISTS OF THE OLD JOHNSTOWN DISTRICT.

By His Honor Judge H. S. MacDonald, Brockville

In June, 1884, at the meeting held in Adolphustown, Ontario, to celebrate the centennial of the first settlement of Upper Canada by the United Empire Loyalists, one of the speakers intimated that the celebration had been set on foot in order (to use the words of Dr. Ryerson) "to do, at least, a modicum of justice to the memory of a Canadian Ancestry, whose historic deeds and unswerving Christian patriotism, form a patent of nobility more to be valued by their descendants than the coronets of many a modern nobleman." Concurring as I do—as I trust you do—entirely in the truth of this tribute to those who may justly be called the forefathers of the great Province of Ontario, it is at once a pleasure and a privilege to speak of them, as I am to do in this paper.

It is impossible for us, at this remote period of time, to enter into the feelings and to appreciate the conduct and action of those who are known as the United Empire Loyalists. It has been so much the habit to have the virtue of true patriotism accorded to the American Revolutionists, and to hear the Loyalists, under the name of Tories, depicted as men who were false to their country, and cruel and cowardly in their actions, that many, even the descendants of the latter, have not known the truth of the matter. For this state of things United States writers have been largely responsible, and the thanks of the Canadian people are justly due to the late Rev. Dr. Egerton Ryerson, for having in his work entitled "The Loyalists of America and their Times," done justice to the Loyalists, and exposed the cruelty and injustice with which they were treated.

Mr. Lecky, the distinguished historian, says: "There were brave and honest men in America, who were proud of the great and free Empire to which they belonged, who had no desire to shrink from the burden of maintaining it, who remembered with gratitude the English blood which had been shed around Quebec and Montreal, and who, with nothing to hope for from the Crown, were prepared to face the most brutal mob violence, and the invective of a scurrilous press, to risk their fortunes, their reputations, and sometimes even their lives, to avert civil war and ultimate separation. Most of them ended their days in poverty and exile, and as the supporters of a beaten cause, history has paid a scanty tribute to their memory; but they composed some of the best and ablest men America has ever produced, and they were contending for an ideal which was at least as worthy as that for which Washington fought. The maintenance of our free, industrial and pacific Empire, composing the whole of the English race, may have been a dream, but it was at least a noble one.''

Rev. Dr. Egerton Ryerson says: "From the beginning the Loyalists were deprived of the freedom of the press, freedom of assemblage, and under an espionage universal, sleepless, malignant, subjecting the Loyalists to every species of insult, to arrest and imprisonment at any moment, and to the sacrifice and confiscation of their property. They were represented as 'the dregs of society,' as 'social outcasts,' as 'fiends in human shape opposed to all human liberty.' ''

And again: "The Americans inaugurated their Declaration of Independence by enacting that all adherents to connection with the Mother Country were rebels and traitors; they followed the recognition of 'independence' by England by exiling such adherents from their territories. But while this wretched policy depleted the United States of many of their best blood, it laid the foundation of the settlement and institutions of the then almost unknown, and wilderness, provinces which have since become the widespread, free, and prosperous Dominion of Canada.''

When the independence of the United States was recognized, and a treaty of peace came to be considered, one of the most difficult questions that faced the Commissioners was the treatment which should be accorded to the Loyalists. Lord Mahon says that it was "a main object with the British Government to obtain, if possible, some restitution to the men who, in punishment for their continued allegiance to the King, had found their property confiscated and their persons banished." The United States Commissioners said that they had no such power, nor had even Congress; that it rested with the individual States of the Union, that they (the Commissioners) were willing that Congress should, with certain modifications, recommend those indemnities to the several States, and it is said they to the last "continued to assert that the recommendation of Congress would have the effect" proposed. The 4th, 5th and 6th Articles of the Treaty made provision that Congress should earnestly recommend to the several Legislatures to provide for the restitution of all estates belonging to real British subjects who had not borne arms against them; that all other persons were to be at liberty to go to any of the Provinces, and to remain there for twelve months to wind up their affairs, the Congress also recommending the restitution of the confiscated property, and the repayment of the sums for which they had been sold. No impediment was to be put in the way of recovering bona fide debts; no further prosecutions were to be commenced; no further confiscations made. Congress is said to have urged, in strong terms, the propriety of making restitution to the Loyalists, but be this as it may, it was not made, the citizens generally objecting to their return to their former places of residence and to the proposal for reimbursing their confiscated estates. In some sections Committees were formed to oppose their peaceable residence, and outrages were committed on their persons and property. The result was that the United States lost and Canada gained a population at once, hardy, intelligent, and possessed of high principles.

May I be allowed to quote here the following lines written by Mr. Kirby.

The U. E. Loyalists.

The war was over, seven red years of blood
Had scourged the land from mountain top to sea:
(So long it took to rend the mighty frame
Of England's empire in the western world.)
Rebellion won at last, and they who loved
The cause that lost, and who had kept their faith
To England's Crown, and scorned an alien name,
Passed into exile, leaving all behind
Except their honour, and the conscious pride
Of duty done to country and to King.

Broad lands, ancestral homes, the gathered wealth
Of patient toil and self-denying years,
Were confiscate and lost; for they had been
The salt and savour of the land; trained up
In honour, loyalty, and fear of God.
The wine upon the lees decanted, when
They left their native soil with sword belts drawn
The tighter; while the women only wept
At the thought of old fire-sides no longer theirs,
At household treasures reft, and all the land
Upset, and ruled by rebels to the King.

Not drooping like poor fugitives they came
In exodus to our Canadian wild,
But full of heart and hope, with heads erect

And fearless eyes, victorious in defeat.
With thousand toils they forced their devious way
Through the great wilderness of silent woods,
The gloomed o'er lake and stream, till higher rose
The northern star above the broad domain
Of half a continent still theirs to hold,
Defend and keep forever as their own,
Their own and England's to the end of time.

The virgin forests carpeted with leaves
Of many autumns fallen crisp and sear,
Put on their woodland state: while overhead
Green seas of foliage roared a welcome home
To the proud exiles, who for empire fought
And kept, though losing much, this northern land
A refuge and defence for all who love
The broader freedom of a commonwealth
That wears upon its head a kingly crown.

The mills of the gods grind slowly, but they grind surely and exceedingly small.

In 1812-13 the United States, finding Great Britain engaged in war single-handed against much of Europe, as Europe then was—Napoleon Bonaparte being as yet unconquered—declared war against her, and Canada was promptly invaded. To its defence there sprang to arms many of the survivors and sons of the United Empire Loyalists, and Lundy's Lane, Queenston Heights, Chrysler's Farm, and other well-fought fields were witness to their courage and prowess.

In 1788 Lord Dorchester divided Upper Canada into four districts. General Simcoe afterwards adopted a new division into districts, counties and townships, one of these being the district of Johnstown, which was formed by Act 38, George III., Chapter 5, passed in 1798. Originally it included territory somewhat in excess of that comprising the United Counties of Leeds and Grenville, but for the purpose of this paper the United Counties are taken as they now are. The County-town was Johnstown—two or three miles from Prescott. There is in existence a record of the names of Justices of the Peace—all of them, I doubt not, U. E. Loyalists, or sons of such, who were present at a Court of General Sessions of the Peace holden at Johnstown on the 14th October, 1800, George the Third then being King, and of the oaths which they subscribed and took. This is of special interest at the present moment, when the public mind in the United Kingdom and in the British Dominions over the sea, is concerned with the oath to be taken at his Coronation, one hundred and ten years later, by His Majesty, George the Fifth, a great, great grandson of George the Third.

The record is as follows:

Province of Upper Canada,

District of Johnstown.

At a Court of General Quarter Sessions of the Peace, held at the Court House in the Town of Johnstown, the following oaths were administered to the subscribers, 14th October, 1800.

Oath of Allegiance.

I do sincerely promise and swear that I will be faithful and bear true allegiance to His Majesty, King George. So help me God.

Oath of Supremacy.

I do swear that I do from my heart abhor, detest, and abjure as impious and heretical that damnable doctrine and position that princes excommunicated or deprived by the Pope or any authority of the See of Rome may be deposed or murdered by their subjects or any other whatsoever; and I do declare that no foreign prince, person, prelate, state or potentate hath or ought to have any jurisdiction, power or superiority, preeminence, or authority ecclesiastical or spiritual within this realm. So help me God.

Oath of Abjuration.

I do truly and sincerely acknowledge, profess, testify and declare, in my conscience before God and the world, that our sovereign lord King George is lawful and rightful King of this realm and all other His Majesty's dominions and countries thereunto belonging. And I do solemnly and sincerely declare that I do believe in my conscience that not any of the descendants of the person who pretended to be Prince of Wales during the life of the late King James the Second, and since his decease pretended to be and took upon himself the stile and title of King of England by the name of James the Third, or of Scotland by the name of James the Eighth, or the stile and title of King of Great Britain, hath any right or title whatsoever to the Crown of this realm or any other the dominions thereunto belonging: and I do renounce, refuse and abjure any allegiance or obedience to any of these: and I do swear that I will bear faithful and true allegiance to His Majesty King George, and him will defend to the utmost of my power against all traitorous conspiracies and attempts whatsoever which shall be made against his person, crown or dignity. And I will do my utmost endeavor to disclose and make known to His Majesty and his successors all treasons and traitorous conspiracies which I shall know to be against him or any of them. And I do faithfully promise to the utmost of my power to support, maintain and defend the succession of the crown against the descendants of the said late King James and against all other persons whatsoever, which succession by an Act entitled "An Act for the further limitation of the Crown and better securing the rights and liberties of the subject" is and stands limited to the Princess Sophia, electress and duchess dowager of Hanover and the heirs of her body being Protestants. And all these things I do plainly and sincerely acknowledge and swear according to these express words by me spoken and according to the plain common sense and understanding of the same words, without any equivocation, mental evasion, or secret reservation whatsoever. And I do make this recognition, acknowledgement, abjuration, renunciation and promise heartily, willingly and truly upon the true faith of a Christian.

So help me God.

Ye shall swear that as justice of the peace in the District of Johnstown in all articles in the King's Commission to you directed, you shall do equal right to the poor and to the rich after your cunning, wit, and power, and after the laws and customs of the realm and statutes thereof made. And ye shall not be of counsel of any quarrel hanging before you. And that ye hold your Sessions after the form of the Statutes thereof made. And the issues, fines and amerciaments that shall happen to be made and all forfeitures which shall fall before you, ye shall cause to be entered without any concealment (or embezzling) and truely send them to the King's exchequer. Ye shall not let, for gift or other cause, but well and truely ye shall do your office of justice of the peace in that behalf. And that you take nothing for your office of justice of the peace to be done, but of the King, and fees accustomed, and costs limited by Statute. And ye shall not direct nor cause to be directed any warrant, (by you to be made) to the parties, but ye shall direct them to the bailiff of the said District or other the King's officers or ministers or other indifferent persons to do execution thereof.

So help you God.

The justices who signed were:

WM. FRASER
SOLOMON JONES
JAMES BRECKENRIDGE
TRUMAN HICOCK
THOS. FRASER
SAML. WRIGHT
HUGH MUNROE
WILLIAM SOWLES
EPHM. JONES
EDWARD JESSUP
JOEL STONE
STEPHEN BURRITT
RICHARD ARNOLD
THOS. SMYTHE
HENRY ARNOLD

It may be mentioned that the oaths of office and of allegiance administered to Justices of the Peace at present are of a simple and wholly uncontroversial character. They read as follows:

Oath of Office.

I, A. B., of the   in the United Counties of Leeds and Grenville, do swear that I will well and truly serve our Sovereign Lord King George the Fifth in the Office of Justice of the Peace, and I will do right to all manner of people after the laws and usages of this Province without fear or favour, affection or ill-will. So help me God.

Sworn before me at the
of   in the
United Counties of Leeds and
Grenville, this
day of   A. D. 19

Oath of Allegiance.

I, A. B.,   of the
in the United Counties of Leeds and Grenville,
do sincerely promise and swear that I will be faithful and bear true allegiance to His Majesty King George the Fifth as lawful Sovereign of the United Kingdom of Great Britain and Ireland, and of the British Dominions beyond the Seas, and that I will defend him to the utmost of my power against all traitorous conspiracies or attempts whatever which may be made against His Person, Crown and Dignity, and that I will do my utmost endeavor to disclose and make known to His Majesty, his Heirs or Successors, all treasons or traitorous conspiracies or attempts

which I may know to be against Him or any of them. And all this I do swear without any equivocation, mental evasion or secret reservation. So help me God.

Sworn before me at the Town
of Brockville in the said
United Counties this
day of   A. D. 19

In 1810 Brockville became the county town. Above the Judge's bench in the present courtroom is the painted representation of the Royal Arms which was in place in the old Johnstown Court House more than a hundred years ago. It is said that a strong party in the eastern part of the District opposed to the removal to Brockville laboured under the impression that no legally constituted court could be held without the Royal Arms and determined to resist its removal by force. By some stratagem the coveted ensignia was secured by the Brockville representatives, and then followed a hand to hand struggle for its possession which terminated in a victory for those representing the new court house.

His Honor Judge Pringle (of Cornwall), in his interesting book concerning the United Counties of Stormont, Dundas, and Glengarry—"The old Eastern District"—describes the system adopted in the allotment of lands to the Loyalists as follows:

They had their farms allotted to them on the lottery principle, i. e., each one would draw from a hat or box a slip of paper on which was marked the number of a lot, and of the lot so drawn he became the owner. Each soldier received a grant of 100 acres fronting on the river, and 200 at a point removed from it. As soon as possible after the division of the land was made, the owner took possession. As they landed in June, 1784, they had several months in which to make some preparation, rude though it might be, for the coming winter. Those on adjoining lots would join together to put up for each settler a log house as a shelter. These houses were small, the largest not more than 20 feet by 15, built of round logs notched at the corners, and laid one upon the other to a height of seven or eight feet. The roof was made of elm bark, an opening for a door and one for a window were cut; the floor was made of split logs, the hearth of flat stones, the chimney of field stone laid up with hard clay for mortar as high as the walls, above which it was made of small round sticks plastered with clay. The spaces between the logs were "chinked" with small pieces of wood and daubed with clay, a blanket did duty as a door until a few boards could be cut with a whipsaw, the window was fitted in course of time with a rough sash and four lights of glass, seven and a half inches by eight and a half, and the log house would be complete. Bed and bedding the settlers in most cases brought with them, but chairs, tables and bedsteads had to be manufactured by each man for himself. Blocks of wood might serve for seats, the lid of a chest could do duty as a table, and a few poles could be put together to form a bedstead. Shelter having been provided, each family proceeded as best they might to clear a space of ground on which to raise a scanty crop the following year.

The Hungry Summer—In the year 1787, the universal cry that arose from Upper Canada was "bread! bread! bread!" though the height of the famine was not reached until the summer of 1788. The sad condition of the Province was brought about by a failure of the crops and by the government ceasing to grant the usual supplies to new settlers, who came into the country totally unprovided for, and, unable to raise crops, were reduced to the greatest straits, and in many instances experienced all the horrors of a famine. In the vicinity of Maitland there was raised a field of wheat which escaped the frost and came to maturity at an early period in the summer. The people flocked to the field in large numbers, even before the wheat ripened, taking the milk-like heads and boiling them into a kind of gruel Half-starved children haunted the banks of the river, begging sea-biscuits from the passing boatmen. It is related that one gentleman who was en route from the Lower Province was so touched with the plaintive appeals that he gave up his last crust and had not a mouthful for himself for three days. Money was sent to Montreal and Quebec for flour, but the answer came back, "We have none to spare." Salt rose in some localities to the enormous price of one dollar a quart. Indian cabbage or kail, ground nuts, and even the young buds of trees were eagerly devoured. Fish and game, when caught, were frequently roasted in the woods, and eaten without pepper or salt. Families existed for months on oat porridge; beef bones were boiled again and again; boiled bran was a luxury; farms were offered for a few pounds of flour. Fish were caught with a hook made from the backbone of the pike, and speared in the small creeks with a crotched pole. In the Province, five individuals were found dead, including one poor woman with a live infant at her breast. The infant was carried away and protected.

"The following are the names of some of the early settlers: Joseph White, Asa Webster, David Kilborn, Reuben Mott, Henry Mott, Conrad Peterson, Jonathan Mills Church, Edward Leehy, Henry Elliott, Bartholomew Carley, Livius Wickwire, Jonathan Wickwire, William Buell, B. Buell, Jonathan Buell, Samuel Wright, William Wright, Abraham Elliott, Adam Cole, John Cole, Jonathan Fulford, Captain Joseph Jessup, Ensign Thos. Smith, Enoch Mallory, Elisha Mallory, Jos. Buck, Asa Landon, Alexander Bernard, Henry Manhard, Lieut. Jas. Breckenridge, Ruggles Munsell, Matthew Howard, Stephen Howard, John Howard, Peter Freel, Terrence Smith, James Miller, Daniel McEathron, John McEathron, Daniel Shipman, Joseph McNish, Levi Hotchkiss, Robert Putnam, James Cooney, Henry McLean, Robert McLean, Allan Grant, Joseph White, Jr., William Clow, John Munroe, the Hecks, and Levi Comstock." Many members of Jessup's Corps, after being disbanded, also became settlers, and among these were: Thomas Sherwood, the Frasers, Solomon Snyder, Gideon Adams, Simon Coville, Benoni Wilton, the Jones, the Jessups, and other well known names, descendants of some of whom are still living in the United Counties. It is impossible within the limits of this paper to do more than refer to some of them.

The Sherwoods.—Thomas Sherwood, father of the late Adiel Sherwood, who settled in Elizabethtown, below Brockville, in 1784, is said to have been the first settler in the United Counties. He had been a subaltern officer in Major Jessup's Corps, and located lot number One in the First Concession of Elizabethtown, about the first of June, 1784, and continued to live there until his death in 1826. His son Adiel Sherwood was Sheriff of the United Counties, within my memory, and died between twenty-five and thirty-five years ago full of years. In a written memoir furnished by him to Dr. Canniff, of Toronto, he said:

After the first year, we raised a supply of Indian corn, but had no mill to grind it, and were therefore compelled to pound it in a large mortar, manufacturing what we call "Samp," which was made into the Indian bread called by the Dutch "suppawn." The mortar was constructed in the following manner: We cut a log from a large tree, say two and one-half feet in diameter, and six feet in length, planted it firmly in the ground, so that about two feet projected above the surface; then carefully burned the centre of the top so as to form a considerable cavity, which was then scraped clean. We generally selected an ironwood tree about six inches in diameter from which to make the pestle. Many a time I have pounded with one until the sweat ran merrily down my back. Although this simple contrivance did well enough for corn, it did not answer for grinding wheat. The Government, seeing this difficulty, built a mill back of Kingston, where the inhabitants, for seven miles below Brockville, got their grinding done. In our neighborhood they got along well enough in summer, by lashing two wooden canoes together. Three persons would unite to manage the craft, each taking a grist. It generally took about a week to perform the journey. After horses were procured, kind Providence furnished a road on the ice until the road was passable by land. What is wonderful is that during the past fifty years it has not been practicable for horses and sleighs to traverse the ice from Brockville to Kingston, such a way having been provided, only when absolutely necessary, for the settlers.

The Buell Family.—Among the United Empire Loyalists who sought refuge in Canada were the original pioneers of the Buell family. From the hour when the first rude shanty was built on the site of Brockville, down to the present time, the descendants have been intimately associated with the control of public affairs, not only in the town, but also throughout the county.

Wm. Buell, Sr., was of English descent, both upon his father's and mother's side. He was the son of Timothy Buell, and his wife Mercy Peters, and was born at Hebron, in the then English Colony of Connecticut, on the 5th of October, 1751. His mother was a descendant of the Rev. Dr. Samuel Peters, who at the commencement of the American Revolution was the Bishop of Connecticut, and wrote a history of that colony which has recently been re-published under the editorship of his great-grandson, S. Jarvis McCormick, Esq.

When the war broke out, Mr. Buell remained loyal to the British Crown, and as soon as was practicable made his way through the wilderness to Montreal, where he received an ensign's commission in the "King's Rangers," subsequently becoming lieutenant. His service extended over a period of seven years, and during a portion of the time he acted as quarter-master. He was frequently detailed to carry important despatches from the authorities in Canada to the British Commander at New York, and on many occasions met with hair-breadth escapes. He was twice taken prisoner by the insurgents, but succeeded in effecting his escape, and was also present at the surrender of General Burgoyne.

On the 10th day of March, 1782, he was married at St. Johns, Lower Canada, to Martha Norton, whose father was an U. E. Loyalist who had removed to Canada from Farmington, Connecticut. A family of nine children was the result of this union.

After the termination of the revolutionary war, Mr. Buell, Sr., was placed upon the half-pay list, and retired from military service. In 1785, accompanied by his wife, he removed to Upper Canada, settling upon the present site of the Town of Brockville, then a wilderness. He received a grant from the Crown of the land upon which the central portion of the town was subsequently built, where he settled and erected the first house.

About the year 1800 Mr. Buell, after a contest with Reuben Sherwood, a Provincial Land Surveyor, was elected a member of the House of Assembly for Upper Canada, for a term of four years.

Mr. Buell was upright and honest, and very kind to the poor. He was generous in his character, liberal in his politics, and highly respected. He died at Brockville on the 8th day of August, 1832, in the 81st year of his age. Of his children, William Buell the younger was a Lieutenant Colonel of the Militia, and held the medal with clasps for the Battle of Chrysler's Farm, 1813, and was one of the representatives for the County of Leeds in the Upper Canada Assembly from 1828 to 1836, (having been thrice elected).

His son, Lieutenant Colonel Jacob Dockstader Buell, was born in Brockville in 1827, and was called to the Bar of Upper Canada in 1854. He took a deep interest in Canadian military affairs, and was for several years Lieutenant Colonel of the 42nd Battalion, Brockville Infantry. He represented Brockville in the House of Commons of Canada for two Parliamentary terms, and was elected Mayor of Brockville for several terms. He died in 1895. His son, Mr. William Senkler Buell, of Brockville, Barrister, has been Mayor of Brockville. He has inherited the military instincts of his great-grandfather, grandfather, and father, and after service for some years as Adjutant of the 41st Battalion of Brockville Rifles, has recently, with the great goodwill of the officers and men, as well as of the community, become Colonel of that excellent Corps, whose traditions and honour could not be in safer hands than in his.

Joel Stone.—Joel Stone was the founder of the Town of Gananoque, which is beautifully situated on the banks of the River St. Lawrence, almost in the heart of the Thousand Islands.

In 1774 he was engaged in the business of a merchant, in Litchfield, Connecticut. He says, "I soon had the happiness to discover myself in the confidence and esteem of my neighbours, and the public in general. By dint of an unwearied diligence, and close application to trade, I found the number of my friends and customers daily increasing, and a fair prospect of long happiness rose to my sanguine mind, in one of the most desirable situations, beneath the best of laws, and the most excellent Government in the Universe.

"But alas, the most dreadful commotions that commenced about this period quickly involved that unhappy country in all the dreadful horrors of an unnatural war, and filling the pleasant land with desolation and blood, removed all my fair prospects of future blessings; yet amidst all this anarchy and rage I was fixed in my resolve, rather to forego all I could call my property in the world, than flinch from my duty to the best Sovereign, sooner to perish in the general calamity than abet in the least degree the enemies of the British Constitution."

Entertaining such sentiments it may readily be supposed that his life soon became a disturbed one. In 1775, being suspected of unfriendliness to the provincial or continental party, he was cited to appear before a Committee, possibly a "Vigilance Committee," and was accused of having supplied those whom we would call Loyalists with sundry articles of provisions, and with having supported and assisted the British prisoners confined in Connecticut. It was with much difficulty that he at the time escaped a very severe examination at the hands of the emissaries of Congress. His aged father appears to have occupied much the same position as his son, for we are told that he was repeatedly imprisoned, threatened, and harassed "for his steady perseverance in maintaining with all his ability the true liberty of the country, and just cause of his rightful Sovereign."

At length, in 1776, Joel Stone discovered that it was impracticable for him any longer to conceal his sentiments. He was required to declare without further hesitation whether he would immediately take up arms himself against the British Government or procure a substitute. Having declined to do either the one or the other, a warrant was issued for his apprehension, and having been informed of it, and that men were actually on their way to his house, he took flight upon horseback, and the night being a dark one, he had the good fortune to elude those who were searching for him, and escaped. The party seeking him was attended by a mob, and his house was broken up, and all the property which could be got at was seized.

Mr. Stone made his way to New York, which was then in possession of the British, and here he resided for several years. He took up arms for his King and served him from 29th June, 1777, until the evacuation of New York. Having gone to Huntingdon, Long Island, to recruit men, he was surprised, while asleep, on the 12th of May, 1778, by a company of whale-boat men and carried to Fairfield, Connecticut, where he was committed to close custody upon a charge of treason. He escaped on the 23rd of July, 1778, from what he calls "that town of terrors," and with great difficulty made his way to Long Island. After the evacuation of New York by the British, and in or after July, 1783, Mr. Stone went to England, arriving there on 23rd December, 1783, after a long and tedious voyage. In 1786 he sailed for Canada, and having first settled where the Town of Cornwall now stands, eventually, in 1792 or 1793, removed to the Gananoque River, and is said to have been the first white man who resided on the peninsula on the west side of that stream. Here he lived until his death, which took place on the 20th of November, 1833.

Justus Sherwood and His Descendants.—Justus Sherwood, who was a captain in the Colonial Militia on active service during the American war of independence, came into the Province of Quebec about the year 1777, and remained at St. John's for some time. His second son, the late Mr. Justice Sherwood, was born there. Justus Sherwood afterwards settled in the Township of Augusta, on a farm near where the old blue church was afterwards erected. He was one of the first members of the House of Assembly of Upper Canada, that met at Newark, now the Town of Niagara. He had two sons, Samuel Sherwood, Esq., and Mr. Justice Sherwood, before mentioned, who were educated for and became members of the Bar of Upper Canada. Mr. Justice Sherwood was elected by the County of Leeds to the House of Assembly in 1822, and became Speaker of that body, and in 1825 was appointed a Puisne Judge of the Court of King's Bench for Upper Canada. He served in this capacity for a number of years and afterwards retired. In 1841, during the administration of Lord Sydenham, he was appointed Speaker of the Legislative Council of Canada. He died in 1850 leaving four sons and three daughters. Henry, the eldest son, at one time represented the Town of Brockville, and afterwards the City of Toronto, and held the offices of Solicitor and Attorney-General. George, his second son, represented Brockville for about twenty years. He held the offices of Receiver-General and Commissioner of Crown Lands, in the Cartier-McDonald Ministry, and retired from Parliament about the year 1863. He was, in 1865, appointed Judge of the County of Hastings. Samuel, his third son, was Registrar of the City of Toronto at the time of his death in 1867, and Edward, the fourth son, was, at the time of his death, 1877, Registrar of the County of Carleton.

The Jessups.—Edward Jessup, Major Commandant of a Colonial corps, which was known as the "Loyal American Regiment," was born in the parish of Stamford, in the County of Fairfield, State of Connecticut, in the year 1735. He was the son of Joseph Jessup who died in Montreal in 1779, and grandson of Edward Jessup, who emigrated from England at the close of the Seventeenth Century, and settled in the colony of New York. At the breaking out of the Revolutionary War, Major Jessup and his family resided at the City of Albany, New York.

A staunch Loyalist, Major Jessup promptly sacrificed his fortune by taking up arms for the King, and entering upon the struggle for the maintenance of the British supremacy in the revolting colonies. With his corps he joined the army under Burgoyne, who was then marching upon Ticonderoga (1777), and continued in the service until the close of hostilities.

After the defeat of Burgoyne, the major proceeded to Canada with his corps, which then became known as "Jessup's Rangers." They were first stationed at Isle aux Noix, and subsequently at St. Charles, St. Denis, River du Chene, Vercheres, and Sorel. When peace was declared in 1783, large tracts of land were granted by the Crown to the officers and men who, accompanied by their families, in the Spring of 1784, proceeded up the St. Lawrence in a brigade of boats, thus commencing the settlement of Leeds and Grenville, Addington and the Bay of Quinte.

After completing the location of his men, Major Jessup proceeded to England, where he remained for several years. When he returned to Canada, he settled in the Township of Augusta, County of Grenville, selecting lots numbers 1, 2 and 3 in the First Concession, they having been granted to him by the Crown.

In the year 1810 the Major had a town plot surveyed, on the front of lots numbers 2 and 3, in the 1st Concession, which he named Prescott, in honor of a distinguished British officer of the name.

Immediately after the survey had been completed, Major Jessup built a school house, and also a residence for the teacher. Previous to that date, the present site of Prescott contained only three houses, the residence of Major Jessup, the residence of his son, and a house which he had built for the manager of his farm.

He died at Prescott in February, 1816, at the advanced age of 81 years. His life was spent in the defence of Crown and country, in creating a new Empire, under the old flag, upon the northern bank of the St. Lawrence, in fostering British institutions, and carving out of the primeval forest homes for future generations.

Edward Jessup, only son of Major Jessup, was born in the City of Albany, Province of New York. He was a lieutenant in the Royal Rangers commanded by his father, and after the close of the Revolutionary War was placed on the half-pay list. He visited England with his father, and with him returned to Canada, settling on the present site of Prescott.

He was elected representative for the Eastern District in the Legislative Assembly of the Province. In January, 1800, he was appointed by Lieutenant-Governor Hunter, Clerk of the Peace for the District of Johnstown. Lieutenant-Governor Gore issued a commission to him in 1809, as Lieutenant-Colonel of the first Regiment of Leeds Militia. Mr. Jessup died at Prescott in the year 1815, leaving a wife and seven children.

The Jones Family of Fort Edward.—At or about the commencement of the revolutionary struggle, there lived on the Rogers' Farm, opposite Fort Edward, on the Hudson River, a widow lady named Sarah Jones, the mother of seven sons, all of whom, but one, are said to have been officers in the royal army, one of whom lost his life and others their homes and property because of their loyalty to their King. His Honor Judge Pringle, in his book "Lunenburg, or the Old Eastern District," furnishes information showing that Jonathan Jones, David Jones, and Solomon Jones were respectively a Captain, a Lieutenant, and a Surgeon's mate in Jessup's Corps, having joined it on 4th November, 1776. Of five who survived the war, the eldest, Jonathan, settled in Nova Scotia, and the other four made their homes in the Johnstown District, Daniel drawing land in Elizabethtown, within the limits of the present Town of Brockville. He died in 1820, and his body lies in the family plot in the old cemetery on the banks of the St. Lawrence. His sons, David and Daniel, became barristers. David represented the County of Leeds and also the Town of Brockville, in the Upper Canada Legislature, and was for a time the Judge of the Eastern District Court at Cornwall. He was also for many years Registrar of the County of Leeds. The younger son, Daniel, was born in the year 1794, and died at Brockville in 1838. In 1835 he visited England, at which time he received the honour of Knighthood from His Majesty, King William IV., being the first native of the Province of Upper Canada who had received so distinguished a mark of royal favour.

Solomon Jones, one of the four brothers who sought refuge on the banks of the St. Lawrence, served with Burgoyne's army in the capacity of surgeon, to which profession he had been educated, and, effecting his escape at the time of the surrender at Saratoga, made his way to Canada, tendered his services to the Commander of the British forces, then having headquarters at Three Rivers, and continued to serve in Lower Canada until peace was declared.

Dr. Jones was a man of note in his locality and generation, and his memory is still cherished as that of a gentleman of high worth and marked capacity. His professional services were eagerly sought along the sparse settlements, all the way from Kingston to Cornwall. He was a member of the first Parliament of Upper Canada, and Judge of the Johnstown District Court. He died in 1822. His great-grandson, Mr. Harold Jones, occupies the old homestead on the bank of the St. Lawrence, between Brockville and Prescott.

David, another of the four brothers, and the sixth son, was a lieutenant, and served in General Burgoyne's army. He had become affianced before the war commenced to Jane or Jean McCrea, who, according to one report, was the daughter of one who espoused the cause of the revolutionary party, and, according to another, was the daughter of the Rev. James McCrea, a New Jersey Loyalist. Supposing that the troubles would soon be ended, Mr. Jones and Miss McCrea decided not to be married until peace should have been made. It soon appearing that the war was likely to last longer than had been expected, it was agreed that the marriage should not be further delayed, and on the 27th day of July, 1777, Miss McCrea, in company with a lady friend, left her home at Fort Edward to go to General Burgoyne's headquarters, at which the marriage ceremony was to be performed by a clerk in holy orders—probably a chaplain to the forces. Between the American post at Fort Edward and the advanced English posts at or near Glen's Falls, or Sandy Hill, was a debatable ground over which it was necessary for Miss McCrea and her friend to pass. Scouting parties of Indians being then frequently out, Lieutenant Jones feared that one of these might meet Miss McCrea and cause her alarm, if not injury, and, owing to his anxiety, he engaged an Indian chief, in whose good faith and intelligence he had confidence, and to whom he told the object of her coming, to go out and keep watch over her, at such a distance, however, as not to alarm her, and yet near enough to render her assistance if needed. It so happened that she was taken prisoner by a party of Indians, who were returning from a marauding expedition, and the friendly chief, fearing for her safety, drew near to protect her.

At this time she met with her death—how will never be known. On the one side it is said that a dispute arose between the Indians as to who should have the honour of conducting Miss McCrea to the British headquarters, and that this waxed so fierce that a savage belonging to the party which had made her prisoner drew his tomahawk and killed her before the arm of the friendly chief could be raised in her behalf. On the other hand, the Indians who composed the scouting party contended that she was killed by a shot fired by one of a party of American soldiers then in pursuit of them for the purpose of avenging the death of an American officer whom they had surprised and killed that day, and that the shot intended for them, by mischance, killed Miss McCrea. Be this as it may, the Indians took off her scalp, and, leaving her body where it was, made their way to the British camp. Here they told their story. Dr. Solomon Jones, the brother of David Jones, and surgeon in General Burgoyne's army, learning what had occurred, sought the bereaved lover to inform him of the fate of his betrothed. But he found that his brother had seen the Indians coming into camp with the scalp, and knew but too well from whose head the beautiful tresses had been taken.

An investigation was held by General Burgoyne, or under his authority, but without result, so far as it is known. The body of the unfortunate girl was buried at or near the bank of the Hudson River, not far from Fort Edward. From this place it was removed to the old burying ground, and again removed to the union cemetery between Fort Edward and Sandy Hill, where it now rests.

Lieut. Jones was overcome by the shock caused by the tragic event, and was not known by his relatives or intimate friends ever afterwards to have smiled. Subsequently to the peace of 1783 he settled in Upper Canada, in the Township of Augusta, not far from where the Town of Prescott now stands, and made his home with his brother Solomon. He died suddenly in or about 1790, and his body was buried at the old blue church burying ground, near the bank of the River St. Lawrence, and not far from his Canadian home.

Another family of the name of Jones were emigrants from the Mohawk Valley, in the Colony of New York.

Ephraim Jones, a member of this family, during the Revolution, made his escape to Montreal. Two of his brothers at about the same time succeeded in reaching Nova Scotia. In 1790 Ephraim (better known as Commissary Jones, in consequence of his having charge of the supplies granted to the settlers by the British Government) arrived in Upper Canada. He received a grant of 300 acres of land in the Township of Augusta, and built a house on the farm now or lately owned by Thomas Murdock, situated a short distance east of Maitland. Returning to Montreal he married Miss Coursoll, of which family the late Judge Coursoll was a descendant. The fruit of the union was a family of four sons and four daughters.

Of the sons, Charles, born in 1781, afterwards the Honourable Charles Jones, was a merchant in Brockville and a mill owner, and for many years one of the most prominent men in public life in the eastern portion of the Province. Having been called to the Legislative Council, he held many offices of trust and emolument under several Administrations. He died in 1840.

Jonas, the third son, was educated, as were the others, by the late Bishop Strachan, at Cornwall. He studied law, and practiced many years at Brockville, being successful in his profession and attaining its highest honors. He served during the war of 1812 and was at the taking of Ogdensburg. He received the first Commission as Lieutenant of Cavalry, (attached to 1st Regiment Leeds Militia, Colonel Breckenridge), June 22nd, 1812—commission under seal of Sir Isaac Brock; his second commission as Colonel 3rd Regiment Leeds, June 18th, 1822. He was for some years Judge of the District Court of the then Bathurst District, and also of the Johnstown District. Subsequently, he was appointed one of Her Majesty's Judges of the Court of Queen's Bench, which required his removal to Toronto, A. D. 1837, where he died in 1848, aged 57 years. His great knowledge of the manners and ways of the people caused his decisions and judgments, both in the District Courts and in the Queen's Bench, to give great satisfaction. His manliness of character and honesty of purpose caused him to be much beloved by the people of the United Counties of Leeds and Grenville, and his removal from Brockville was much regretted by all classes.

But I must pass on to a conclusion.

What is the great lesson which we are to learn from these United Empire Loyalists—from their sufferings, their struggles, and their trials? Surely it is a lesson of loyalty. They labored, and we have entered into the fruits of their labors.

They passed unto us a heritage great and goodly, and by force of circumstances, and by virtue of geographical position, that heritage has become greater and more goodly. Of Great North Western Canada, and of the lands and waters beyond the Rockies they knew nothing. These have been added to that older Canada which was, when they came to it, a wilderness—a wilderness which they had done much to reclaim before they passed over to the great majority. And now we Canadians possess a land of immense resources, of immeasurable possibilities. On our eastern and western shores and seas, fisheries, the finest in the world; in the older Provinces, forests and water powers and mineral resources, the value of the last of which we are but beginning to know. In the newer portions, Manitoba and the North-West Territories, lands which are as a field which the Lord hath blessed—lands so rich, so fertile, "that they are covered with corn," and of them it may indeed be said, "they shout for joy, they also sing;" and in British Columbia, and the new lands beyond, a wealth in forests and minerals. To this land, to this Canada of ours, let us be loyal. To the great Empire of which it forms a part—a colony and something more—let us be loyal.

To the memory of these illustrious forefathers who, for loyalty's sake gave up their homes, and comforts, and wealth, who faced troubles and endured hardships, and who made mighty sacrifices, I say to their memory, let us be loyal, and may the good Hand of their God and ours be upon us as a people, and above all to Him may we be loyal in heart and purpose and service. "Righteousness exalteth a nation; but sin is a reproach to any people."

III.

THE LOCAL HISTORY OF THE TOWN OF BROCKVILLE.

By Lt. Col. W. H. Cole, Brockville

The inhabitants of Brockville have always been noted for their loyalty to Crown and Flag of England; they could not be otherwise; it was the call of their blood; a large number even now are descendants of the U. E. Loyalists or other soldiers of the Empire, who, after the expiration of their services, made this place their home.

The land now included within the Corporate limits of the Town are from lots Eight (8) to Fifteen (15) both inclusive from east to west, about two miles in extent; and from the international boundary line in front to the north line of the Corporation, nearly one and a half miles. The First Presbyterian Church is geographically the center of the Town.

There were no settlers in Ontario before 1783, except the few attached to the Military Posts at Frontenac, Niagara (Fort George) and Amherstburg (Fort Malden). To the advance guard of the U. E. Loyalists who came up the River in 1783, the silence of nature over the surface of the vast River must have been oppressive. No wonder they pressed on. But in 1784 a larger number came, forming quite a fleet of canoes and batteaux, and landing just where they pleased. Of those who landed in the vicinity of what is now Brockville were William Buell, Ephraim Jones, Daniel Jones, Thomas Sherwood, Seth and Adiel Sherwood (3 brothers), and many others; but we will only refer to a few of those who acquired the land now within the limits of Brockville, and who seemed to have the power of shaping its destiny. William Buell located upon and afterwards received the Patent or Government Deed of the West half of Lot Eleven and East half of Lot Twelve. The widow, two daughters and son of Lieutenant Peter McLaren received the Patent of Lot Ten and east half of Lot Eleven in March, 1805, which land was purchased from the McLarens by Charles Jones, the eldest son of Ephraim Jones. The west half of Lot Twelve and all of Lot Thirteen was patented to Daniel Jones. You will thus see that all that part of Brockville from Ford Street to a little west of Ann Street, was in possession of three men, Daniel Jones, William Buell and Charles Jones, the two latter being owners of what was the business portion.

In 1791, the Imperial Parliament passed an Act dividing Canada into two Provinces, Upper and Lower Canada, and Col. John G. Simcoe was appointed Lieutenant Governor in the Spring of 1792. He landed in Quebec and proceeded with his staff by canoes to ascend the River to Kingston, where he organized his Government on the 8th day of July, and on the 21st July they left for the place that had been selected for the capital of the new Province, called Newark, afterwards called Fort George and now known as Niagara-on-the-Lake. He issued instructions for the people to elect representatives to form the first parliament, which they did, and they were called together on the 17th September, 1792. The first person to represent the County of Leeds was John Booth. The House was again in session in 1793. During this year it was decided to remove the seat of Government farther from the frontiers, and York was selected, steps being taken to carry out that decision by erecting suitable buildings. In the meantime Governor Simcoe removed to York himself, and Parliament was to meet there in June of 1797; but before that time arrived the Governor was promoted to be Lieutenant-General and Governor of St. Domingo. Honourable Peter Russell was his successor. At the session of 1795, the Legislature passed the first Act making provision for registering all documents affecting land and the appointing of Registrars for the different Registry Divisions. In 1796, the first Patents for land were issued to the U. E. Loyalists in the County of Leeds. In 1797, Alexander Campbell was appointed the first Registrar for Leeds, Grenville and Dundas. Subsequently Dundas and Grenville were set off in separate divisions and also all land north of the Rideau River set off to Lanark and Carleton, leaving the County of Leeds as it is to-day. During the 113 years the County of Leeds has had six Registrars. Before leaving this part of my subject I will say that from the beginning we have had legislators who recognized the fact that the land was the basis of a nation's prosperity and wealth, that all laws, forms and documents affecting land should not only be plain and easily understood, but also so elastic that the legal transfer of the right to the land could be made the basis of the individual, as well as the National, credit. So with that end in view, our law makers have improved our land and registry laws from time to time, and I think Ontario to-day has the best Registry system and laws in the world.

In the year 1800, William Buell was elected to represent Leeds in the Legislative Assembly for four years.

The first administration of justice in its crude way was by Magistrates supposed to be appointed by the Governor under the authority of

THE LOCAL HISTORY OF THE TOWN OF BROCKVILLE. 35

what was called the Quebec Act, passed in 1774 by the Parliament of England. As the men first appointed lived adjacent to the first stopping place after passing the Rapids of the St. Lawrence, their Courts were then held in the Village of Johnstown, in the eastern part of the District of Johnstown. An effort was made about 1805 to have the Courts held in a more central part of the District, and by this time the Township of Elizabethtown was recognized as the place where the public business should be transacted. And as Charles Jones and William Buell were then the owners of the land forming the central part of the village, they (while opposed to each other in many other things) were a unit in endeavoring to carry forward this matter. Offers were made to give the land necessary for a Court House and Gaol on Lots 10, 11, or 12 in the First Concession, on the 16th March, 1808. An Act was passed for the building of a Court House and Gaol in the Township of Elizabethtown, in the District of Johnstown, the building to be erected on Lot Number 10, 11, or 12, in the First Concession. The land selected was that offered by William Buell. The deed was given on the 16th day of May, 1809, to our Sovereign Lord George the Third, whereby the said William Buell, in order to make a good and sufficient title to his Majesty "of the land hereinafter mentioned, for a site on which to erect a Gaol and Court House for the District of Johnstown." That deed included the land commencing on the North side of King Street, taking the land now called the Court House Avenue and Court House Square from the Bank of Montreal on the east to Court Terrace on the west, and as far north to within 40 feet of Gaol Street. This land comprised four acres, with a road sixty feet wide leading from the centre point of the said space to the River St. Lawrence, provided that "in case the said Gaol and Court House shall not be built according to the provisions of an Act in said Deed the said premises to revert to the said William Buell." On the first of June, 1833, Andrew N. Buell, the second son of William Buell, gave a deed to our Sovereign Lord King William the Fourth of the following lands for streets: what is now known as Wall Street, sixty feet in width, extending from the north-west corner of the Methodist Church to south limit of Pearl Street; also what is known as William Street, 60 feet wide, extending from the north-east corner of the Presbyterian Church lot to the southern limit of Pearl Street. This deed contains a gift of land eighty feet in width, running from William Street on the west to Wall Street on the east, the north forty feet for a street now known as Gaol Street, the south 40 feet to be added to the Court House Square and used for same purposes as Court House Square.

I find this further reference made to the Courts: Journals of House of Assembly, Feb. 12th, 1811, there was read the petition of certain inhabitants of the District of Johnstown to the effect that an effort was being made to have the Courts sit alternately at Johnstown and Elizabethtown in that district, that the Court now sat by law at Elizabethtown, which is central, and a large Court House and Gaol had been lately erected at a great expense.

February 13th, 1811, motion for a Bill to hold the Quarter Sessions and District Courts alternately at the Town of Johnstown, in the County of Grenville, and in the Township of Elizabethtown, in the County of Leeds.

February 27th, 1812, a petition read respecting the public disadvantage of holding Courts of Justice for the District alternately at Elizabethtown and Johnstown, signed by Adiel Sherwood, Andrew Smith, William Buell and six hundred and sixty-four others. We find nothing further done to remove the holding of the Courts from Elizabethtown. This being the legal name of the Township, the people thought that the size and importance of the collection of residences and business buildings was worthy of a name distinct from the Township, and as the larger portion of the land still belonged to Charles Jones and William Buell, they were expected to settle on a name. Mr. Jones' friends wished to have it called Charlestown, and Mr. Buell's friends suggested Williamstown; and he had a plan made by Jeremiah McCarthy, a Surveyor for Upper Canada and signed Sept. 12, 1811. This plan was not registered.

The last deed registered in the Registry Office in which the name of Elizabethtown is used, prior to the word Brockville being used, as intimating it was the name agreed on, is as follows: Deed dated 1st June, 1812, and registered the 9th July, 1812, by Charles Jones, of Elizabethtown, to Henry Jones of the same place, being lots No. 3 and 42 on the west side of Bethune Street, from King Street to Pine Street.

The first intimation that we have that Brockville was settled as the future name of the pretty village is contained in a report made by Colonel Lethbridge to Major-General Brock, dated Kingston, August 10th, 1812. This report was to explain to General Brock why a vessel called the Julia had been allowed to escape from Ogdensburg. Col. Lethbridge had just returned (so his report shows) from Prescott and Brockville. The time of the change in name is thus brought down to within two months. We have no record of General Brock ever having been here, as we find his time fully taken up elsewhere after coming to Upper Canada up to the time of his death; and we do not know whether

THE LOCAL HISTORY OF THE TOWN OF BROCKVILLE. 37

any private correspondence had taken place between himself and Mr. Jones, Mr. Buell, or any other person with respect to the name, but it is gratifying to know that General Brock was made aware by the above mentioned report and by what he must have heard in Kingston (for he was there on the 4th Sept., 1812), that his name had been adopted as the designation of the town.

On 3rd December, 1812, Charles Jones gave a deed of gift to the Church Wardens of the Episcopal Church of a lot for Church purposes, being Lot 19, Block 10. A building was erected in which Mr. Denroche, the Rector, lived for many years, but it was sold by the Church Wardens of St. Peter's Church in 1854 for £500, and in 1852, Mary E. Jones, the widow of the late Honourable Jonas Jones, gave a deed of gift of Lot 67, Block 15, for a Rectory for St. Peter's Church, now used by them for that purpose. Also the estate of Charles Jones gave to St. Peter's Church what is now known as Victoria Park, on the east side of Park Street.

The above was the first gift of land in Brockville for Church purposes. On the 6th May, 1819, William Buell gave a deed to William Smart of the Lot on which the Presbyterian Manse or Parsonage now stands, in which deed he recites that "the eastern boundary is along the western line of the lot deeded to the said William Smart and Peter Purvis on which said Presbyterian Church is erected," and William Smart, on the 12th April, 1871, gave a deed to the Trustees of the Church of both the Church lot and the Parsonage lot, being Lots 42 and 43 in Block 31.

In the Public School Act of 1807, it says that the Public School for the District of Johnstown shall be opened and kept in the Township of Augusta. This does not appear ever to have been carried into effect. In the Act to repeal Public School Acts (passed in 1819) it says the Public School for the District of Johnstown shall be opened and kept in the Village of Brockville. In the year 1819, the Hon. Charles Jones appears to have given parts of Lots 82 and 86 on which a building was afterward erected for a Public School. These Public Schools were afterwards called Grammar Schools, and one was supposed to be in each district. This property was afterward transferred by the High School Board to the Public School Board of Brockville for $4,500.00, and is that on which the Horton Public School is built.

Apparently the first Court House and Gaol erected under the Act of 1808 were not very substantial, evidently being wooden buildings. On the 19th January, 1824, an Act was passed including in its purpose the building of a Court House and Gaol for the District of Johnstown, and to build the said Court House upon the ground allotted for that purpose in Brockville. The buildings were erected, the Court House of red brick, with the gaol in rear of the east part.

On the 21st March, 1826, William Buell gave to Alexander McDonnell, Catholic Bishop of Upper Canada, and others, a deed of the land on which to build a church for the use of the Catholic congregation in Brockville. This land is now Lot 31, Block 35; while on the same day David Jones and Daniel Jones, only sons and heirs of Daniel Jones, the Patentee, gave a deed to Alexander McDonnell, Catholic Bishop of Upper Canada, and others, for the use and benefit of the Roman Catholic Church in Brockville. This land is now Lot 30, in Block 35.

On February 23, 1828, at a meeting held by the Methodists of Elizabethtown, it was decided to build a church in Brockville. William Buell had intimated that he would give them the site. The first Methodist Church in Brockville was built and dedicated on the 14th February, 1830, Mr. Buell giving them the deed on the 18th August, 1830, for what is now Lot 61, in Block 31, in which he recites "the lot on which the Church is now built, lot 80 ft. x 140 ft."

On June 28th, 1832, an Act was passed to establish a body Corporate and Politic in fact and law by the name of the President and Board of Police of Brockville. The first members were Jonas Jones, Henry Sherwood, Samuel Pennovk and John Murphy, Daniel Jones being President.

On the 19th October, 1833, Charles Jones, as a free gift, gave the Market Square, from the south side of King Street to the River St. Lawrence, and from the Revere House on the west to the brick block on the east (being 240 ft. on King Street with a depth of 460 ft. to the River), on which a frame Market Building was built and used for many years until replaced by part of the present City Hall.

In 1836, an Act was passed to establish a Market in the West Ward of the Town of Brockville. On the 14th November of that year Pamelia Jones, a daughter of the first Daniel Jones, deeded to the President and Board of Police of Brockville for £50 a site for a Market House on the corner of King Street and St. Paul Street. The Board of Police caused to be erected a stone building two stories high, the lower one for a market, the upper one for a Town Hall, used for the meeting of the Board and also as a school house and for all public meetings. The Methodist Episcopal Church for many years were allowed to use it for

Church and Sunday School purposes, and after Brockville bought its second fire engine, it was used as a fire station until the building was taken down to make room for the present brick building on the Lot.

As I have said before, the west half of Lot 12 and all of Lot 13 was patented to Daniel Jones (the first). One of the side roads running to the rear of the Concession was between Lots 12 and 13; but it was impossible at the time to get over the high rock where the stone school house was afterward built on Perth and George Streets, so Mr. Jones, as owner of all the land, opened the road which is now Perth Street, and afterward gave a deed of the road allowance. The first deed he gave of any part of this land was of a lot 200 feet square, in the year 1815, to Nehemiah Seaman, for £100, on which Mr. Seaman built the first stone house in Brockville, and it stands there to-day. The building has been used for many purposes—store, tavern, school-house and residence. A short time afterward he erected a frame house on the west end of this lot with veranda, and when finished he moved from his farm (which was part of Lot 16 in the first Concession, where the Park now is). In his frame house he lived until his death in 1830, and his widow for many years after. The property afterward came into my possession, and in 1895 I had the old building torn down to make room for the present brick building. The carpenter, on removing the roof, the partitions, and the floor of the second storey, found lying on top of one of the timbers under the floor, and the partition right over that, a copper coin or medal of 1806, evidently placed there when the building was erected and left undisturbed for nearly 80 years. I will just say here, before leaving this part of my subject, that the deed of this lot is the only deed given by Daniel Jones of any land on King Street west of Perth Street that defines where the street line is. Taken in connection with a map in the Registry Office, made by John Booth in 1824, it shows the north line of King Street from Perth Street to the Kingston bridge.

On the 6th March, 1838, an Act was passed to authorize the erection of a Court House and Gaol at Brockville on the site of the building used for that purpose, and giving power to the Magistrates of the District, in Quarter Sessions assembled, to levy a tax of one penny on the pound (as a special rate) each year until the buildings were paid for. Nothing was done by the Sessions for over two years. At the Sessions held on the 11th August, 1840, to 10th Nov., 1840, the question was considered, and preparation was made at the Session of 18th May, 1841, when a building committee was appointed to procure plans and take all necessary steps to have the work carried out. Paul Glassford,

Esquire, was appointed Chairman of the Committee; the plans were procured and submitted to the Commissioners appointed by virtue of an Act to regulate the future erection of Gaols in this Province and approved by them on 18th November, 1841; and on the 27th of December, 1841, the building committee entered into a contract with Benjamin Chaffey, Esquire, for the erection of a Court House and Gaol. The use of the Town Hall on the corner of King and St. Paul Streets was given by the President and Board of Police for the use of the Courts and for District purposes.

At the Session of the Legislative Assembly of the Province, held in the latter part of the year 1841, the first general Municipal Act was passed creating District Councils, the Government retaining the power of appointing the Warden or Chairman. The Hon. William Morris was the first Warden, and he called the District Council together on the 8th day of February, 1842. The work of organizing and settling the many things connected with Municipal Government in a large District occupied the attention of the Members of Council for some time before they were able to give the question of Court House and Gaol any attention; then they made some change in the Committee, but very wisely retained Paul Glassford, Esquire, as Chairman and financial head of the Committee, during the whole period of construction. The buildings were finished and occupied in the latter part of 1843, being about two years in construction. The accounts were all referred to a special finance committee, who reported on the 14th of August, 1844, that they "had examined the accounts and vouchers of the Chairman of the Building Committee, Paul Glassford, Esquire, and they appear to your committee clear and satisfactory." The total cost of the building appears to be £9262.3.4.

Mr. William Holmes, an architect and contractor, had been retained by the committee to give them a sketch of a figure of Justice, which he did, offering to complete the figure as proposed for £38; but should they not accept his proposal, his claim for services rendered would be £5. The figure of Justice was ordered, completed, and put for the ensuing year, making the total cost £9300.3.4.

The County Buildings have been greatly enlarged and improved since that time by the erection of a new building to the west of the Court House for meetings of the County Council, offices for some of the County Officers, and also by the erection of a residence for the Gaoler, and by all the latest improvements in the Gaol for the safety and care of the prisoners.

May the 30th, 1849, the Act establishing a President and Police

Board for Brockville was repealed, and the first Municipal Act governing the town was passed, enlarging the limits of Brockville, creating three Wards, electing three members each, who chose a Mayor from their number, Robert Peden being the first Mayor.

On the 2nd May, 1874, the Council made application to have the limits extended, and the town divided into five Wards, each electing two members, with a Mayor to be elected by the whole vote, and on 21st Aug., 1875, a proclamation issued to take effect on Jan. 3, 1876, and this form of Municipal Government has continued to the present time.

As I have said in the beginning of this paper, the two principal men who seemed to be in a position to largely control the future destiny of the town were men of large and liberal views. Where land was required for public or church purposes, they were prompt and liberal in their giving. Mr. Buell's gifts to the public were the Court House Square and Avenue, the land for the Presbyterian Church, the land on which the first Catholic Church was built, and the land on which the Wall Street Church was built. While the Hon. Charles Jones gave to the public the Market Square from King Street to the River, the lot for the site of St. Peter's Church and for the first Rectory, together with the gift to St. Peter's Church of what is now known as Victoria Park or Square; while the widow of the Hon. Jonas Jones gave the land on which the present rectory of St. Peter's Church now stands. Mr. Ephraim Jones, father of the Hon. Charles Jones, did not own land in Brockville, being a resident of, and large land owner in, the adjoining Township of Augusta, but did business in Brockville, and with his whole family was largely interested in its welfare. And I presume that his descendants, and those of William Buell, have filled as many, if not more, important positions of trust and responsibility than those of any other two men connected with the early history of the town, leaving behind them many tokens of their desire for the welfare of town, province and Empire.

IV.

THE WAR OF 1812-15.

By J. Castell Hopkins, Toronto

The aggressive war through which the United States, in the early years of the century expressed in active form its hostility toward Great Britain had a more important effect upon the development and the history of British North America than is generally supposed. It meant more than the mere details of skirmishes, battles and the rout of invading armies. It involved considerations greater than may be seen in any ordinary record of campaigns in which Canadian militia and British regulars were able to hold British territory intact upon this continent during a period of over two and a half years of struggle. That a population of 500,000 people, scattered over widely-sundered areas, should be able, almost unaided for a long time, to successfully oppose the invasions of an organized Republic of six millions, was an extraordinary military performance, and it is only natural, and, indeed, inevitable, that in considering the result, it should have been regarded chiefly from the military standpoint.

In the upbuilding of Canada, however, this struggle holds a place similar in national import to that of the Revolution in American history. It consolidated the British sentiment of the whole population from the shores of Lake Huron to the coasts of the Atlantic. It eliminated much of a disloyal element which was beginning to eat into the vitals of Provincial life in Upper Canada, and it modified in some measure the force of the American spirit which remained in the hearts of some sections of the settlers. It checked the growth of republicanism amongst the French of Lower Canada and prevented the Rebellion of 1837 in that Province from being the rising of a whole people united in political sympathies with the great population to the south. It made the authorities of the Roman Catholic Church in the same part of the country feel once more as they did when the Continental Congress of 1775 attacked the Quebec Act, that the only visible danger to what they considered the sacred rights and privileges of their faith came from the other side of the international line. It, for a time, brought Canadians of French and

British and American extraction together in defence of their hearths and homes, and laid in this way an almost invisible foundation for that seemingly vain vision—the permanent Federal union of British America for purposes of common interest, defence and government. It effected religious organizations which were becoming dependent on American pulpits, supplies, and polity. It influenced social life and customs by drawing a more distinct line against innovations from the other side of the border. Finally, it greatly affected political development and assured the ultimate success of those who strove honestly, though often unsuccessfully and mistakenly in detail, to preserve and promote the permanent acceptance of British as opposed to American principles of government upon the northern half of the continent.

It was an unjust, unnecessary, and, to both the United States and Great Britain, an unsatisfactory war. To the British settlements and French colonists of the present Dominion it proved, however, a blessing in disguise, and produced a page of glorious history which few would now like to see eliminated and which all patriotic Canadians treasure as one of their dearest national possessions. The nominal causes of the struggle were simple and yet world-wide in their environment. During many years Great Britain had been facing the perils of Napoleon's stormy progress over Europe. One great Power after another had been shattered by his military genius, and always before the eyes of his towering ambition was the recognized and steady policy of ultimately subjugating the British Isles. The British had fought him on the ocean from the earliest days of his sweeping career, and with a success which his proud spirit found it hard to brook. She had subsidized his opponents with enormous sums of money, and on the sands of Egypt, the plains of Hindostan and the fields of the Iberian Peninsula had presented her thin red line of armed men as the great preservative of European liberty. On November 1st, 1806, Napoleon had issued from Berlin, where he was newly installed as the victor of Jena and Austerlitz, the "Decree" by which he proclaimed the British Isles to be in a state of blockade, and merchandise from Britain to be a prize of war. He, at the same time, arrogantly commanded the cessation of all intercourse with Great Britain by neutral nations. Great Britain naturally retaliated, and early in the following year her Orders-in-Council proclaimed a blockade of the coasts of Europe from Brest to the Elbe, and declared all traffic with France in neutral vessels to be contraband and the vessels and cargoes liable to seizure.

These proceedings affected greatly the large carrying trade of the

United States, and, as Great Britain practically controlled the seas, it was from her privateers and men-of-war that the American shipping interests suffered the most. Hence the "Non-Intercourse Act" of Congress in 1808, by which all commerce with either France or Great Britain was prohibited until the obnoxious regulations were repealed. Another point in dispute was the claim made by Great Britain to search ships upon the high sea, suspected of having deserters from the British Navy amongst their crews, and to remove such as might be found. It was a claim which had for centuries been enforced as a right. Its assertion at this time was rendered necessary not only by the enormous expansion in the number of British ships but also by the fact that in 1805 it was estimated that at least 2,500 deserters of this kind—chiefly from merchant vessels—were in the American service. The practice was naturally unpleasant to a highstrung nation such as the people of the United States, but had there been any real desire to smooth over difficulties forced upon Great Britain by her strenuous struggle with France, a means of returning deserters to their legitimate service might easily have been found. A minor cause of trouble was the publication of some unimportant correspondence between Sir James Craig, Governor-General of British America, and an adventurer named Henry who had been sent by the former, rather unwisely, though not unreasonably, to ascertain the condition of public feeling in the States. Henry reported a disposition on the part of New England to secede from the Union, and then—finding himself unable to force money from the authorities at Quebec—had sold the letters for $50,000 to the American Government.

These were the nominal causes of the war. They sufficed to inflame the smouldering embers of pre-revolutionary dislike and distrust and enabled President Madison, when an opportune moment of apparent British weakness arose, to accept the dictum of the war party in the Republic and to receive the Democratic nomination for a second Presidential term upon the pledge that a conflict should be precipitated. That the New England States were averse to the policy; that a Convention held in Albany, N. Y., in September, 1812, composed of delegates from various counties in the State, denounced the action of the Administration in this respect; that the best element in the general population was opposed to it; that the British Orders-in-Council were revoked five days before the declaration of war—did not affect the carrying out of the hostile policy on Madison's triumphant re-election to the supreme place in the national councils. That such was the case is due to the avowed reasons for the war not having been the real ones.

The truth is, that despite the lack of consideration shown to the

United States in many directions by Napoleon, and despite his creation of an arbitrary system of government, which was absolutely the antipodes of democracy, there had been during all these years a feeling of sympathy towards France in the minds of the mass of the American people, which arose, perhaps naturally, from the cherished memories of Lafayette and of French assistance at the most critical juncture of their war for independence. Added to this was an admiration for the military achievements of the Emperor which in later days has resulted in a sort of literary deification of his career. Still more to the point was a feeling of continuous irritation against Great Britain arising out of internal discontent and the lack of material progress; increased by the dominating influence of British manufactures and goods in the local markets and a consequent depression in local industries; inflamed by the voice of demagogues who exaggerated every issue and incident into handles for personal popularity and political power. Back of all, and influencing all, was the partially concealed, but none the less strong, desire of the leaders of the day to round off the Republic by the possession of northern America.

When war was declared by the American President on the 18th of June, 1812, the action afforded an exultant moment of anticipation to the American Republic, an added depression to greatly-burdened Great Britain, and proffered many tragic possibilities to the little British population scattered along the 1,800 miles of the United States frontier. Never in her prolonged struggle with Napoleon had public opinion in Great Britain been so depressed. She stood absolutely alone in Europe. The French Emperor was the practically acknowledged master of Prussia and the minor States of Germany as well as of Switzerland, Italy, Austria, and Spain; and with an immense army had begun a march into Russia which promised to be a final triumph before the realization of his intention to combine the forces of the conquered continent in a supreme attack upon British power. No wonder if thoughtful men in the British Isles drew their breath in doubt when the announcement came that the United States had thrown its weight into the scale against their country, and wondered how long the titanic struggle could be maintained by their population of eighteen millions.

Little wonder, also, if Americans thought that their time had come, as well as that of the French, for the complete subjugation of a continent. As to Canada, it was not believed that she could offer anything but a nominal resistance. Jefferson declared the expulsion of Great Britain from the continent to be "a mere matter of marching." Eustis, Secretary of War, announced that "we can take Canada without soldiers." Henry Clay thought the Canadas "as much under our command as she (Great Britain) has the ocean." Part of this impression had, no doubt, been created by the false reports of American settlers in Upper Canada as to the existence of internal disloyalty; part by the fact that there were only 4,450 regular British troops in the whole country; part by the tremendous disparity in population and strength between the Republic and the Provinces; part by the belief that France would practically keep Great Britain out of the struggle.

Two factors had, however, been overlooked. One was the indomitable spirit of a people fighting in a just cause for their homes, their institutions, and their country. The other was the presence in their midst of a soldier possessed of magnetic personal qualities, combined with a real, though unknown, genius for war. Major-General Isaac Brock was forty-three years old when the struggle began—he had been born in the same year as Wellington and Napoleon—and had served in Holland and at Copenhagen before he came to Canada with the 49th Regiment in 1802. He had held command of the troops in Upper Canada since 1806 and had also assumed the Administration of the Provincial Government in 1811. He had done his best to prepare for the war which to his mind was inevitable—as it had also appeared to Simcoe away back in 1794—and to meet the undisguised gathering of American troops and militia in New York and other border States. But the British Government naturally hoped against hope to avert this additional burden upon the overstrained resources of its people, and really seems to have believed that the arbitrament of war might be avoided. In February, 1812, Brock had opened the Upper Canada Legislature with a patriotic speech in which he expressed the desire to adopt "such measures as will best secure the internal peace of the country and defeat every hostile aggression." His difficulties, however, were very great. Arms and equipment were exceedingly scarce. A certain proportion of the militia was cold and even disloyal, and there was a distinctly American party in the House of Assembly led by a man named Wilcocks, who afterwards fled to the United States and was killed fighting as an American officer. Through his influence the House actually refused to suspend the Habeas Corpus Act so as to enable the Government to deal peremptorily with the disaffected element in the population.

Under such circumstances, when the news of the declaration of war reached Brock through a private source, he knew that everything would depend upon swift and sweeping action. He promptly sent some regulars to try and hold the Niagara frontier, summoned the Legislature, called out the militia and made such preparations as he could pending the receipt of official information regarding the action of the United States. It did not come, but on July 12th General Hull crossed the River from Detroit to Sandwich with 2,000 men and issued a braggadocio proclamation announcing protection to all non-combatants, declaring the certainty of conquest and of relief from British "tyranny and oppression," and stating that if the British Government accepted assistance from its Indian subjects in resisting his invasion "instant destruction" would be the lot of all who might be captured fighting beside an Indian contingent. Brock replied with a most eloquent, dignified and patriotic manifesto, and, on July 27th, met the Legislature with an address which was a model in sentiment and expression.

By the 8th of August, Hull had returned again to Detroit on hearing of the capture of the important American position at Michilimackinac, by Captain Roberts in pursuance of orders from his chief. One week later, Brock, with 320 regulars and 400 militia from York and Lincoln, assisted by the gallant Indian chief Tecumseh and some six hundred followers, was crossing the St. Clair in pursuit of his enemy. Hull had been startled, first by a summons to surrender and then by seeing the little British army crossing the River—General Brock, "erect in his canoe, leading the way to battle," as Tecumseh, in graphic Indian style, afterwards described the event. Before an assault could be made, however, Hull and his entire force of 2,500 men, including the 4th United States Regiment and its colours, surrendered. With the capitulation went the entire Territory of Michigan; the town and port of Detroit, which had practically commanded the whole of Western Canada; the Adams war brig; many stands of arms, a large quantity of much-needed stores, 33 pieces of cannon and the military chest. It had been a bold and venturesome action on the part of Brock and the result affected almost the entire struggle. It inspirited the militia from end to end of the Provinces; it showed many of those having disloyal tendencies that it might be safer to at least appear loyal; it electrified the masses with vigour and fresh determination.

Following this all-important success, Brock turned to meet greater difficulties than were presented by the enemy in the field. He had to encounter the weakness and vacillation of Sir George Prevost, who, as Governor-General and Commander-in-Chief of the Forces, was directing affairs from Quebec in the spirit of one who believed hostilities would soon cease and knew that the Ministry at home was anxious to do nothing that would intensify difficulties in that connection. An armistice arranged by Prevost neutralised many of the benefits of the capture of Detroit; orders from the same source prevented Brock from destroying American shipping on the Lakes which was in course of building and which he foresaw might endanger the control of that most vital part of the situation; commands were actually issued for the evacuation of Detroit, though they were fortunately capable of evasion; while the very documents and general orders written by Prevost were dispiriting and unfortunate in terms. But Brock turned to his militia, and, though refused the right of aggressive action, which might have changed the whole tide of events, proceeded with a system of organisation which soon made his volunteer force as effective in health, drill, condition and spirit as well-equipped regular troops. And, through the summary measures of imprisonment or practical banishment accorded to those who showed an overt inclination to the American side—coupled with the magnetic influence of his own character and strong personal confidence in the result of the struggle—he obtained full control over the population of Upper Canada as well as the Legislature. He made every effort to give the volunteers an opportunity for getting in their crops, and all over the Province the women themselves helped by working in the fields. Throughout this conflict, indeed, the signal devotion of noble women was continuously added to a record of determined defence of their country by the men, and the incident of Laura Secord walking many miles through a rough and gloomy forest region to give a British force warning of the enemy's approach, was by no means an isolated case of devotion.

On the 18th of September, while his preparations were still in progress, Brock wrote to his brother that in a short time he would hear of a decisive action, and added: "If I should be beaten the Province is lost." This reference to the gathering of 8,000 American troops upon the border for invasion, by way of Niagara, illustrates the tremendous importance of the ensuing conflict at Queenston Heights. Their intention was to take and hold this strong position as a fortified camp and from thence over-run the Province with troops brought over at leisure from the large reserves behind. At the same time General Dearborn, with a considerable force, was to menace Montreal from New York State by way of Lake Champlain; General Harrison was to invade the Upper Province from Michigan with 6,000 men, and Commodore Chauncey was to take a force across Lake Ontario. The first part of the programme commenced on October 13th with an attempted movement of 1,500 regulars and 2,500 militia across the Niagara River. About eleven hundred troops, slowly followed by other detachments, succeeded in getting over and climbed the Heights at Queenston in the face of what slight resistance could be offered by a small British outpost. If the Americans could have held this position the result was certain and would no doubt have been much in line with their expectations.

Meantime, Sir Isaac Brock—unknown to himself he had been gazetted an extra Knight of the Bath one week before as a recognition of his victory at Detroit—had arrived from the post at Fort George from which he had been watching events. But before he could do anything further than show himself to his troops, size up the situation and shout an order to "Push on the York Volunteers!" in resistance of an American contingent which was making its way up the Heights, he fell with a ball in his breast, and only had time to request that his death be concealed from the soldiers. The event was amply avenged. Reinforcements under Major-General Sheaffe, which had been ordered to the front, arrived shortly afterwards, and with 800 men in hand a bayonet charge was made upon the enemy which forced them over the Heights down towards the shore—many in their headlong retreat being dashed to pieces amidst the rocks, or drowned in attempting to cross the waters of the Niagara. The survivors surrendered to the total of 960 men, and included Major-General Wadsworth, six colonels and 56 other officers, together with Winfield Scott, afterwards celebrated in the Mexican contest. The British loss was trifling in numbers.

Although the victory was great and its result exceedingly important to Upper Canada, nothing could counterbalance the mournful death of the hero of the war. The inspiration of his memory remained, it is true, and was lasting in its effects, but the presence of his fertile intellect, his powers of rapid movement, his genius for military organization, were forever lost. Had he lived his name would have been a great one in the annals of the British army and the world. As it is, although his place is secure in the web and woof of Canadian history and in the hearts of the people, it has in too many British and American records of war been relegated to the position held by myriads of gallant officers who simply did their duty and died in some obscure outpost skirmish. The vast import of the issues and influences decided by these first events of the struggle have in such cases been disregarded or unknown.

Winter was now at hand, and, after a futile invasion from Buffalo under General Smyth, which was repulsed by a few troops commanded by Colonel Bishop, the scene of the conflict moved for a brief moment to Lower Canada. Prevost had his difficulties there, as well as Brock in the other Province, but he was without the latter's vigour and determination. He had succeeded to the troubles of Sir James Craig's Administration, and found a community violently stirred by frothy agitations and by influences which had been developing from peculiar conditions during some years past. So great was the apparent discord that it had helped the war party in the States to spread the belief that the passive French-Canadians of 1776 were now at last active in their antagonism to British rule. When war was once declared, however, the local Legislature showed no hesitation in supporting the Government—and in this proved superior in its loyalty to the little Assembly at York which had allowed Wilcocks and his followers to momentarily block procedure. The Governor-General was authorized to levy and equip 2,000 men, and, in case of invasion, to arm the whole militia of the Province.

The members voted £32,000 for purposes of defence and at the next session granted £15,000 a year for five years in order to pay interest on the issue of army bills. It may be stated here that the Upper Canada Legislature had in February, 1812, also recognized the immediate need of money by authorising General Brock to issue army bills to the extent of £500,000 currency—two million dollars. The payment of the interest was guaranteed, and in January, 1814, the authorised amount of issue was increased to £1,500,000 currency, or six million dollars. The total circulation of these bills does not appear to have ever exceeded $4,820,000. The financial arrangements in both Provinces were excellently made. No public officer was allowed to profit by the use of the notes, and the payment of the interest was carefully attended to. In December, 1815, it may be added, the bills were called in and redeemed by Sir Gordon Drummond, then Lieutenant-Governor of Upper Canada, on behalf of the Imperial Government. Meanwhile some ten thousand men, under General Dearborn, had threatened the Lower Province from near Lake Champlain, but, after a brief demonstration, which was checked by the Montreal militia under command of Major de Salaberry, the American forces all along the line retired into winter quarters and the Canadas found that they had come through the first campaign of war without a defeat or the loss of a foot of ground, although some progress was made by the Americans in obtaining that command of the Lakes which Brock had been so wisely anxious to avert.

The campaign of 1813 was not quite so pleasant an experience. It opened successfully for the British and Canadian forces. On January 19th Colonel Procter with 500 British regulars and 800 Indians under the Wyandot Chief Roundhead crossed the frozen Detroit and three days later attacked General Winchester who had about an equal number of men under him. After a severe battle, in which he lost by death or wounds 182 men, Procter won a decisive victory and took 495 prisoners. The loss to the enemy in killed was between three and four hundred men. It was a dearly purchased success, however, as it won for Procter a reputation which he sadly failed to live up to. Colonel McDonell, who had raised a strong regiment amongst the Highland Catholics of the Glengarry settlement, on February 23rd attacked Ogdensburg in New York State—from which some predatory excursion had come during the winter—and captured eleven guns, a large quantity of ordnance and military stores and two armed schooners. Four officers and 70 privates were taken prisoners. In April there was a change. Commodore Chauncey with a fleet of fourteen ships and 1,700 troops sailed from Sackett's Harbour on the New York coast of Lake Ontario for York (Toronto), which was then a small town of some 800 population, containing the Government buildings of the Province. Under the immediate command of Brigadier-General Pike the American forces landed on April 27th, but were for a short time held in check by the determined resistance of two companies of the 8th Regiment and about 200 Canadian militia. The Fort, situated at some distance from the little town, was finally captured, after an accidental explosion in which Pike and 260 of his men were killed. As the advance was continued, General Sheaffe with his small force of regulars withdrew and retreated to Kingston. The town then surrendered with about 250 militia, and, despite the terms of capitulation, was freely pillaged and all its public buildings burned. Even the church was robbed of its plate and the Legislative Library looted. In this latter connection Chauncey expressed indignation and made a personal effort to restore some of the stolen books.

Incidents of importance now came swiftly one upon the other. On May 27, Fort George, on the British side of the Niagara River, was captured by the Americans, and two days later Sir George Prevost was repulsed in an attack upon Sackett's Harbour on Lake Ontario. Early in June two American gunboats were captured on Lake Champlain, and on the 5th of the same month Colonel Harvey—a soldier with some of Brock's brilliant qualities, and afterwards Lieutenant-Governor of New Brunswick—attacked in the night a large force of at least 3,500 Americans encamped at Burlington Heights, near the Hamilton of later days, and captured a number of guns, two general officers, and over a hundred other officers and men. On the 24th of June, Lieutenant Fitzgibbon, of the 49th Regiment, by a clever concealment of his number, obtained the surrender of 544 American soldiers under Colonel Boerstler, not far from Fort George and Queenston. He had only 66 troops and 250 Indians in his command. During the next two months the British captured Black Rock, where they lost the gallant Colonel Bishop and Fort Schlosser—both on the Niagara Frontier. Plattsburg, on Lake Champlain, was captured and the public buildings burned in memory of York. The latter place was taken a second time by the Americans. Then came the disastrous British defeat on Lake Erie, where Captain Barclay, with six vessels and 300 seamen, was taken by Commodore Perry with nine vessels and more than 600 men. Not only disastrous, but disgraceful, was the ensuing defeat of General Procter, near Moraviantown, by General Harrison, who had driven him from Detroit and Amherstburg. Procter was retreating steadily with about 400 troops and 800 Indians, under Tecumseh, pursued by the American force of 4,000 men. The battle was fought on October 5th and the natural result followed, with the important loss of Tecumseh. The disgrace of Procter, who fled early in the day and who was afterwards court-martialled, censured, and deprived of all command for six months, was not in defeat under such circumstances, but in the utter lack of all proper military precautions either at the time of the conflict or during his previous retreat. The death of the great Indian chief was one of the severest blows to the Canadian cause in the whole campaign. It was more important even than the fact that this victory placed the entire western part of the Province in the hands of the Americans. The territory might be won back; the leader never. Tecumseh was a savage of heroic mould—one who inspired victory, and who, when acting with men like Brock or Harvey, was almost invincible. His Indians would do anything for him—even refrain from massacre or cruelty.

The next two months saw some events of brighter import, and attention must now be transferred to Lower Canada. The French-Canadians earnestly and enthusiastically showed their love for the land of their birth and home by turning out in large numbers. By October an army of 8,000 men had been collected at Sackett's Harbour, N. Y., under Generals Wilkinson and Boyd for a descent upon Montreal by way of the St. Lawrence. As these forces descended the river they were followed by a small and compact body of British troops under Colonels Pearson, Harvey, Morrison and Plenderleath, accompanied by eight gunboats and three field-pieces, which did much damage to the enemy. On Nov. 11th, Wilkinson and his main army were with the flotilla near Prescott and on their way to effect a junction with an army under General Hampton which was to meet them at the mouth of the Chateauguay.

General Boyd, with 2,500 men, was marching along the shore, followed by 800 British troops under Colonel Morrison, who had resolved to attack the enemy at a place called Chrystler's farm. The result was one of the most complete victories of the war—the Americans leaving many prisoners besides 339 officers and men killed or wounded. The British loss was 181. Boyd immediately retired to the boats and joined Wilkinson. They then proceeded to the place at which the junction with Hampton was to be made and whence they were to advance upon Montreal.

Meanwhile Hampton had marched from Lake Champlain with 7,000 men toward the mouth of the Chateauguay. At this point, and amidst the natural difficulties of forest surroundings, he was met on the night of October 25th by Colonel de Salaberry in command of 300 French-Canadian militia and a few Indians, supported by Colonel McDonell with another French-Canadian contingent of 600 men, who had made the most rapid forced march in Canadian history and had reached Chateauguay the day before the battle. The Americans advanced upon the first line with 4,000 men, but, on driving it back, they met the second line under Colonel McDonell and here encountered the stratagem of buglers placed at great distances from each other and sounding their instruments so as to give the impression of large numbers, while at the same time the bewildering yells and war-cries of some fifty scattered Indians greatly increased the tumult. The immediate result was the defeat of the American forces, their retreat on the next day and consequent failure to meet Wilkinson. The latter result was the collapse of the attempted invasion of Lower-Canada—the defeat of an elaborate campaign made by some 15,000 men through the timely gallantry and clever leadership of less than 2,000. An unpleasant incident was the manner in which Prevost endeavoured, in his despatches, to take the whole credit of this victory for himself. Despite this the facts became known in some measure and at the end of the war McDonell and De Salaberry were each decorated with the C. B.

In Upper Canada during this period there had been another glaring evidence of Prevost's incapacity. Frightened by the apparent results of Procter's defeat near Moraviantown, he had ordered the British Commander at Burlington and York (General Vincent) to abandon all his posts and retire upon Kingston. Had this been done the Upper Province would have been practically in American hands. Instead of doing so, however, Vincent maintained his ground, and Colonel Murray, with some 378 regulars and a few volunteers and Indians was given permission some weeks later to advance upon the enemy, who, with

2,700 men under General McClure, was holding Fort George. On December 10th the latter evacuated the Fort, but before doing so wantonly burned to the ground the neighboring village of Newark (now Niagara). It was a cold winter's night, and the beautiful village contained chiefly women and children—as the men were either away at the front or had been sent as prisoners across the river. The unfortunate inhabitants were turned out in the snow without shelter and in many cases very scantily clothed. British retribution was swift. The American Fort Niagara, just across the river, was promptly stormed and held till the end of the war and the neighboring villages of Lewiston, Youngstown, Manchester and Tuscarora were burned. Fort Schlosser was destroyed, and Buffalo captured and burned. These events closed the campaign of 1813, at the end of which the Americans only held possession of Amherstburg on the frontier of Upper Canada, and, besides losing all the benefits of Harrison's success against the incapable Procter, had also lost Fort Niagara on the American side, and with it the control of the frontier in that direction.

General Sir Gordon Drummond, a brave and able officer, had meanwhile become Administrator and Commander in Upper Canada, and this fact had much to do with the succeeding successes of 1814. This campaign commenced with another advance from Lake Champlain by 4,000 Americans under General Wilkinson. It was checked and, eventually, repulsed on March 30th by a gallant handful of some three hundred men commanded by Major Handcock at Lacolle's Mill—a small stone building on the Lacolle River and about a third of the way between Plattsburg and Montreal. Wilkinson retired again to the former place. A little later Michilimackinac was relieved by Colonel McDonell, and in May Sir Gordon Drummond and Sir James Yeo, the new naval commander, captured Fort Oswego on the New York side of Lake Ontario, together with some valuable naval stores. Meantime some minor defeats had been encountered by British detachments, and early in July Major-General Brown with 5,000 troops, backed by 4,000 New York militia which had been ordered out and authorised for the war, invaded Upper Canada from Buffalo. To meet this attack Drummond had about 4,000 effective regulars, depleted, however, by the necessity of garrisoning a number of important posts. His difficulties in meeting this invasion had been increased by the seeming impossibility of making Prevost understand the situation and the need of reinforcements. The latter could only see the menace offered to Lower Canada by the massed forces at Lake Champlain

Fort Erie surrendered to the Americans on July 3rd and General

Riall was defeated at Chippewa two days later with the loss of 511 men killed and wounded. The victorious American advance was checked, however, at Lundy's Lane, where Sir Gordon Drummond, who had come up from Kingston with about 800 men, assumed command and fought on July 25th, within sound of the roar of Niagara Falls and in the most beautiful part of a fertile region, the fiercest battle of the whole war, and one which continued during the greater part of a dark night. The victory is variously claimed, but the bare facts are that, after trying for six hours with 5,000 men to force a British position held by half that number, Brown had to retire to Chippewa with a loss of 930 men as against Drummond's loss of 870. On the 26th he retreated to Fort Erie, and was there, shortly after, attacked unsuccessfully by the British with a loss to the latter of 500 men. Here, until September, he was blockaded within the walls of the Fort.

Meanwhile, the struggle with Napoleon in Europe being temporarily over, 16,000 trained and experienced British soldiers had landed at Quebec. Prevost advanced with a force of 12,000 of these troops to Plattsburg, where he was to meet and co-operate with the British fleet on Lake Champlain. The latter was defeated, however, and the British General, with an army which under Brock might have threatened New York City itself, ignominiously retreated in the face of two or three thousand American soldiers. So far as the Canadas were concerned, territorially, this practically ended the war. Despite Prevost's disgrace at Plattsburg the campaign for the year had terminated with the British in control of Lake Ontario—although the Americans were masters of Lake Erie—and with their possession of several forts on American soil, to say nothing of the border portion of the State of Maine. In the Maritime Provinces the struggle had not been severely felt. Major-General Sir John Cope Sherbrooke was Lieutenant-Governor of Nova Scotia, and through the vicinity of the British fleet at Halifax and the presence of a sufficient number of regulars, he was able, in 1814, to make a series of attacks upon the coast of Maine until the whole region from the Penobscot to the Ste. Croix was in British hands. At the same time Sherbrooke had kept sending troops up to Canada whenever possible, and the march of the 104th Regiment in February, 1813, through hundreds of miles of frozen wilderness, was of special interest as well as importance. Elsewhere on sea and land the war had been equally varied. A number of naval victories had been won by the United States as well as by Great Britain, but, excluding the actions fought in Canadian waters, there seems in every case of American success to have been great superiority in men, guns and tonnage. The purely British part of the campaign of 1814 included the capture of the City of Washington and the burning of its public buildings in revenge for the previous harrying of the Niagara frontier and the burnings at York and Newark. An unsuccessful attempt was also made upon Baltimore. Early in 1815 General Pakenham was defeated in an attempt to capture New Orleans. The terrible bloodshed of this last struggle of the war—over 2,000 British troops having been reported killed, wounded, or missing—was the result of ignorance of the fact that on December 24th, 1814, a treaty of peace had been signed at Ghent.

The ultimate result of this war upon the destinies of Canada have been briefly indicated. Its immediate effects upon the various countries concerned were more clear. The Americans obtained not a foot of British territory and not a solitary sentimental advantage by the struggle. Their seaboard was insulted and injured, their capital city partially destroyed and three thousand of their vessels captured. The immense gain to their carrying trade which had accrued to them as a result of Great Britain's conflict with Napoleon, was neutralised, while their annual exports were reduced to almost nothing and their commercial classes nearly ruined. A vast war-tax was incurred and New England was rendered disaffected for many years to come. The twin questions of right of search and the position of neutrals in time of war, which had been the nominal causes of the conflict, were not even mentioned in the Treaty of Ghent. Some military and naval glory was won, but the odds were in favour of the United States throughout the struggle, and, when Great Britain's hands were finally freed by Wellington's march upon Paris, the war ceased. In many of these conflicts, however, both on sea and land—notably in the famous duel of the Chesapeake and the Shannon, when Sir Provo Wallis, of Nova Scotian birth, laid the foundation of fame and fortune—United States soldiers and seamen showed all the courage and skill of the race from which they had sprung. To Great Britain the war was only one more military and naval burden. It added to her difficulties in fighting France, subsidising Europe and holding the seas against the sweeping ambitions of Napoleon. But her struggle for life and death had been so prolonged in this connection, and the shadows of its wings so dark and menacing, that the conflict in Canada did not then, and has not since, attracted the attention it deserved.

While this was natural enough at that period, the time has now come when the position should be changed, and the memories of Brock and De Salaberry, Morrison and McDonell, Harvey and Drummond, be given their place in the historic pantheon of Empire. Canadian difficulties in this struggle should be understood, the courage of its people comprehended, the results of the conflict appreciated. Out of their tiny population over five thousand militiamen in Upper Canada and twenty-three thousand in Lower Canada were under arms during some portion of the period, and to these Provinces many and many a vacant seat at the fireside, many a ruined home and shattered fortune, many a broken life and constitution, remained after peace had been long proclaimed. Few had hoped for success in the struggle, still fewer had expected to gain by it. Through the influx of money from Britain, and by the good fortune of holding the greater part of the country free from conquest, there was a degree of prosperity prevalent during the last two years of the war. But it was the fleeting result of partial successes, and with the termination of the conflict came reaction and a realisation of the stern bed-rock of misery which all invasions must cause the population of the country attacked. And that suffering was sufficient to finally build into Canadian life and Canadian institutions a sentiment which has made independence of the United States absolute and has helped to make unity with Great Britain the great factor in the history of Canada in these early years of another century.

V.

REMINISCENCES OF THE FIRST SETTLERS IN THE COUNTY OF BRANT.

By Charles and James C. Thomas, Brantford

While reading the papers written for the Brant Historical Society, which were published in the daily newspapers, it struck us very forcibly that some statements therein contained were not altogether in accordance with the facts as we understood them. Consequently we thought it proper to place before the Society a synopsis of the contents of the books, documents and other papers left by our great-grandfather and grandfather, and which were inherited by us on father's demise.

Great Britain, by signing the Treaty of Paris, in April, 1783, acknowledged the independence of the thirteen rebel colonies, and the Revolutionary war was at an end.

In consideration of the early attachment to the King's cause manifested by the Six Nations Indians, and of the loss of their settlements which they thereby sustained, the British, through Sir Frederick Haldimand, then Governor and Commissioner-in-Chief of the Province of Quebec and territories depending thereon, etc., by an instrument in writing by him subscribed with his seal-at-arms annexed dated the twentieth day of March, 1784, assigned to them, through their agent, Capt. Joseph Brant, a tract of land extending six miles on each side of the River Ouse, or Grand River, at the mouth and extending in proportion to the head of the river. This document Capt. Brant journeyed to Quebec city by canoe and on foot to receive at the hands of the Governor.

Capt. Brant persuaded John Smith (great grandfather) and John Thomas, merchant, (grandfather) to come with them to their new home. The children of John Smith, who journeyed with him to the Grand River, were: William Kennedy Smith; Joseph Smith; Eleanor Smith, who married John Thomas; Mary Smith, who married Benjamin Wintermute, of Fort Erie; Harriet Smith, who married Mr. Macklem, of Chippewa; and John Smith, jun. Taking these up in chronological order—Wm. K. Smith married a sister of Capt. Jos. Brant and had two children—Abram Kennedy Smith, and Margaret, who subsequently married William Kerby, sen., who for a great many years ran a grist mill which was located nearly opposite Kerby's Island. He was the father of James Kerby who built the Kerby House. To A. K. Smith and Margaret Kerby the Six Nations Indians granted the Smith and Kerby tract containing 1100 acres of land, which in addition to the 200 acres previously granted to Wm. K. Smith made a total of 1300 acres of land, the site of the present City of Brantford. Joseph Smith married Charlotte Douglas of Blenheim Township, and had three sons, viz., John Smith, first Sheriff of the County, Joseph and Absalom, and several daughters, whose Christian names we have failed to obtain, with the exception of Harriet, who married Absalom Griffin, of Waterdown, and Mary, first wife of George Keachie, first governor of the gaol, who had four children, two girls and two boys. His second wife was Miss Yardington, daughter of the late Henry Yardington.

The Old Bible.—This is a quarto edition, bound in full calf, and bearing the imprint—

Edinburgh:
Printed by Mark and Charles Kerr,
His Majesty's Printers,
MDCCLXXXIX.

In addition to the copies of the Old and New Testaments, it contains an index to the Holy Bible in which time is divided into seven ages, an alphabetical table of proper names, with the meaning of those words in their original language, tables of weights and measures, of money, of offices and conditions of men, of kindred and affinity, and of time, together with the Psalms of David in metre. In the family Bible we find recorded John Thomas and Eleanor Smith, his wife, were married on the 2nd April, 1791, Sunday.

John Smith Thomas was born 19th October, 1798, 5 o'clock p. m., Friday.

Joseph Thomas was born January 23rd, 1801, 12 o'clock, Friday.

William Thomas was born December 23rd, 1804, 6 o'clock p. m., Friday.

Eleanor Thomas was born 22nd July, 1809, 2 o'clock a. m., Saturday.

John S. Thomas and William died when comparatively young men (between 20 and 30 years of age).

Many facts were told us by father, the late Joseph Thomas, J. P. (1801-88), when in a conversational and reminiscent mood, which was more especially the case when one or more of his boyhood friends visited him. Having heard these statements, not once only, but repeatedly, they are indelibly impressed on our memories; such facts as the Christian names of the children of the late John Smith, sen., the names of the persons to whom they were afterwards married; that all the members of the family were regular attendants at the Mohawk Church (which was erected in the year 1786), when service was held therein; that in this church they had been baptized by itinerant clergymen from the frontier, Rev. Robert Addison, and Revds. Ralph and Wm. Leeming, for this church had no regular pastor until the advent of the Rev. Mr. Luggar, who was sent here from England by the Society for the Propagation of the Gospel; and that these transient ministers were their guests during their stay.

Grandfather was married in 1791, and father, his second son, was born 23rd January, 1801, in the two-storied frame house erected by the Smiths and John Thomas, for John Smith, jun., was a carpenter by trade, and had brought his chest of tools with him from the States. Some of these tools, at the present date, are in a good state of preservation, and are used by us when needed. They must have been located on the lot for some time previous to the erection of this house, as most of the lumber used in its construction had to be whip-sawed, i. e., by one man under the log and another above it. This house was located on a 200 acre lot fronting at where the village of Cainsville is now, on part of which lot the Methodist Church stands. To be more explicit, the house was built a little to the west of the church. The bricks for the chimneys of this house were made by mixing the wetted clay and tramping it with oxen, and, when at the proper consistence, placing it in moulds, hand-pressing and sun-drying until they had enough for a kiln.

This lot of land was in all probability the first lot of land covered by a Brant lease, for Brant was about to issue deeds when he was told by our great-grandfather that as he (Brant) had no deed, he could not issue deeds, but would advise him to grant leases for a term of years. Brant took his advice and leases were issued for 999 years at a rental of one dung-hill fowl per year if the same be asked for and demanded. One reason for considering this lot as being covered by the first Brant lease issued is that the starting point given in the lease is the "village or church on the river." Another reason (and the two taken together are irrefutable), is that when the Government of

Upper Canada recalled all the Brant leases, a corner stone with the initials J. T. chiseled on one side thereof was placed at the south-east corner of the lot in the exact place where the stake had been planted that is referred to in the Brant lease, and the government surveyors in running the lines for adjoining lots used this stone as a starting point.

John Smith, Sen.—From the papers and documents in our possession and from what father told us, it appears great-grandfather was a tall man, over six feet, and physically strong in proportion—a great pedestrian, which is evident from his repeated trips to Bertie, Fort Erie, Niagara-on-the-Lake, Toronto, and other distant points. These trips were made on foot, there being no wagon roads of any great length in those days, so that the only means of locomotion was on foot or on horseback. He despised the latter means as being too effeminate for a man of his standing and condition of life. (It may be interesting to state here that the saddle which we used in our boyhood days had silver-plated staples inserted in its front edge, one on each side of the pommel, for strapping fast the saddle bags or any other article.) That he was a man of integrity and great business tact in his dealings with his fellow-man is shown not only by his handwriting and letters, but is also proven by the large number of Powers of Attorney which we have in our possession, not only from his immediate friends and neighbours, but also from settlers extending from east of Hamilton, as far west as London, south to Long Point, and north to the northern boundaries of Blenheim.

Parchment Deeds.—These are formidable documents 22x14½ in., and the seal attached thereto of goodly size, being 4½ in. in diameter and one-half inch in thickness, composed of beeswax with white paper on each side, one side being stamped in relief with the British coat-of-arms and surrounding it the usual Latin inscription. On the other side, in relief also, is stamped what seems to be the Naval coat-of-arms, as it contains the Union Jack, crown, shield, mace, anchor, halberd, two cornucopias, etc. In the edge of the seal are inserted two strips of parchment by which it was attached to the deed.

The Mohawk Church.—After the close of the Revolutionary war, Capt. Joseph Brant went to England, and while there collected money to build a church. On his return to the Grand River he caused to be erected the first Protestant Episcopal Church in Upper Canada. This Church was completed in 1786 and a bell hung in its tower. We learn from a memoir of the late Bishop Mountain, first Bishop of the Canadas, "that he arrived in Quebec City on November 1st, 1793, and found that there was no church there nor in Montreal; but there were six clergymen in the Province and but three in the whole of Upper Canada." This memoir also contains the statement "that the Mohawks upon the Grand River have a church, and, what many of the English churches are without, a bell."

The War of 1812-15.—War was declared by Congress under President Madison on the 18th June, 1812. Among the earliest to turn out in defence of their homes and firesides were the Six Nations Indians, under the command of Capt. Jacobs and Capt. John Brant, son of the late Chief, upon whose shoulders the mantle of his father seemed to have fallen. "The affray at Beaver Dam," says Thos. Cross in "The Iroquois," "is said to have been planned and executed by this intrepid young man, eighteen years old, which resulted in the capture of Col. Boerstier and six hundred men."

In 1810, father was sent to school at Fort Erie, and he told us that he well remembered the fact that, in the summer of 1812, the late James Cummings, J. P., of Chippewa, rode into Fort Erie crying aloud, "There is war; war is declared between the King and the Congress." In consequence of this event he had to be brought home to the Grand River, but the family were not allowed to remain in peaceable possession of their home, as the British Government required the house, barn, and other out-buildings for His Majesty's stores and other military purposes. Upon the premises a regiment was stationed, probably the 37th Fusiliers, for we remember that a door of the house which was incorporated in the dwelling erected in later years having "37th Fusiliers" cut into it with a knife. The officers took up their quarters in the house, while the barn (36x50) served as barracks for the privates. The family retreated to the backwoods of Blenheim (known as the "Queen's Bush" at a later period), taking such portions of their furniture as they could conveniently convey. Amongst the articles left in the custody of the new-comers was a fall-leaf table of walnut, the leaves and top of which we have had placed on an extension dining-table. An officer, in want of a candlestick, dropped some of the melted tallow on the table and stood the candle thereon. He allowed it to burn so low that it burnt a hole in the table, still visible.

Capt. John Smith, our great uncle, was gazetted a Captain, and, as he has often told us, had captains serving under him as privates. He went through the war without receiving a wound, although in active service at Queenston Heights, Lundy's Lane, and other engagements in that neighborhood. When we were boys he made his home at father's, and having become almost entirely blind from the growth of cataracts on his eyes, one of us used to have to lead him when he wished to go on the road. Should any mention of the war be made, uncle would state, in language more forcible than elegant, though very expressive of his feelings at the time, how they had driven the enemy over the Heights at the point of the "bagonet"—these old settlers having mistaken the "y" in the word bayonet for a "g"—and that some of their bodies were in view, hanging in the shrubs and undergrowth, for two or three days. He was not married.

Mother's elder brother, the late John Ramsay, sen., of West Flamboro, served also during the war and escaped without a wound, but near the close of the war was, with an Indian, taken prisoner. They were marched to Greenbush, on the Hudson, and, as their guard were mounted, they were obliged to do some very fast walking to keep ahead of those in charge. On their arrival they were placed in the guard-house, but, when they found their guards dozing off, made their escape, ran the sentries at the outposts, and made their way back as far as Buffalo. Having no means of crossing the river at their disposal, they were recaptured and marched back to prison. They would have been shot had not the war been brought to a close by the ratification of the Treaty of Ghent on Dec. 24th, 1814. Thus the enemy did not have the opportunity to try them by court-martial on the charge of being prisoners of war who had attempted to escape.

Mrs. Joseph Thomas, mother of the compilers of this paper, whose maiden name was Deborah Ramsay, was born at Chippewa previous to the outbreak of the war of 1812, but all records of that event were destroyed when the U. S. troops burned the church as well as the houses of the inhabitants, in consequence of which she never knew her age. While living at Chippewa she saw the Falls run dry so that people walked out to the centre of the Horseshoe Falls, and one plucky young lady, Miss Ensign, planted a Union Jack in a fissure of the rocks, where it remained for nearly twenty-four hours.

Close of the War.—After the close of the war, the family returned from the place of their retreat, the backwoods of Blenheim, and found their homestead in a very delapidated condition, far different from what it was when they left it, in 1812. At that time they had forty acres cleared and under cultivation, well fenced with rails, staked and ridered; but on their return they found the house with panes of glass out and boards off here and there from all the buildings. The planks used for approaches to the barn doors were gone, as well as many from the floor; the rails used in fencing the cleared land had disappeared, as if by magic, for it seems the soldiers stationed here soon learned that the well-seasoned fence-rails were more combustible and portable than the standing timber near by. So when they had ascertained the sad condition of affairs, and to a certain extent realized the losses they had sustained by the occupation of the premises by the British and Indians, they made out a claim. This document bears the date of 20th Sep., 1815, and the following is certified as being a true copy:

"Amount of losses sustained by Eleanor Thomas in the late war, in consequence of His Majesty's troops and Indians being stationed at the Grand River, and buildings occupied for His Majesty's stores and other military purposes:

		£	s.	d.
1813 Oct.	One and one-half tons of hay on Gen. Proctor's retreat	4	10	0
	30 bus. potatoes	5	12	6
	5 hogs	5	12	0
1814	By the troops and Indians, and at the time Gen. McArthur (U. S.) came through from Detroit to the Grand River .. 4,800 rails in fences.	35	0	0
1814-15	The loss of the use of the farm by the destruction of the fences	40	0	0
		£91	2	6

It will be noticed that no price is put upon the 4,800 fence rails consumed. Father explained it in this way: The officer who was left in charge of the premises, and who was also empowered to settle the claim for damages, thought he could book the rails as oven wood, and consequently the family would get a higher price therefor than they otherwise would. But his plan failed to materialize, for the officer, after a very careful examination of the books of the commissariat department, failed to find any item establishing the fact that bread had been baked on the premises. Although the officer was well aware that bread had been baked here, yet, as there was no entry in the books of the commissariat department to that effect, the British Government would not pay the claim if inserted, so the rails had to go as fire-wood, and a lump sum for them and 900 ft. of planks to repair the barn floor, etc., was agreed upon, making the total amount of the claim £115, which was paid.

About the middle of September, 1815, three wagons, loaded with kegs filled with sovereigns, half-sovereigns, etc., arrived at the Grand River to pay the soldiers. When one of us in a bantering way asked father why he didn't take a few gold pieces, he replied: "Leaving honesty out of the question, one would have had little chance of so doing, for each wagon was guarded by fifty soldiers, their muskets loaded with ball cartridge, and bayonets fixed, and those on guard being aware of the fact that if they should allow this money to be despoiled they might have to wait a long time for their pay.

During the war of 1812 an epidemic of typhoid broke out at Kingston, which was attributed to the impurity of the water. Dr. Dunlop, a surgeon belonging to one of the regiments stationed at that town, and a newcomer to the place, having complained of a slight indisposition, when he was told by a sympathizing friend that it was owing to the water, earnestly replied: "It's no the water wi' me, for I aye tak' it weel diluted wi' brandy."

As the Six Nations Indians had commenced to locate themselves on this Grand River tract as soon as the war closed, April, 1783, and as great-grandfather with his family came in with them, the Township of Brantford must have been the first municipality in the County of Brant to be settled by people of the Anglo-Saxon race.

The Mohawk Church was erected soon after that date, probably in 1786. The two-storied frame house erected on the Cainsville lot was the first frame dwelling erected in the County.

The village or church on the River is used as the starting point for the first Brant lease issued to a white man, for the Lot is described as "being on the northerly part of the great bend below the village or Church on said river, beginning at a stake standing by the fence at the South-east angle of said tract," etc., etc.

From the words "a stake standing by the fence" we deduce the fact that the family must have been in actual possession of this lot of 200 acres for some time or they would not have had fences erected.

In these papers there are also recorded transfers of tracts of land from one person to another.

Father, in his boyhood days, and until he was 10 or 11 years old, had none but Indian children to play with, in consequence of which he could speak the Mohawk language as fluently as English. Even in his older days when he chanced to meet one of that race he invariably addressed him in the Indian tongue.

A Summerless Year.—The year 1816 was a memorable one for those living at that time. It was usually referred to by the old-timers as the year without a summer, for there was frost during every month of the year except the month of August. This, following the close of the war, made itself severely felt by the settlers, for the little grain they had on hand did not suffice till they gathered the next harvest, and many people were reduced to a state of semi-starvation. The first man to secure some ripened sheaves of rye, flailed out the grain and shared it with his less fortunate neighbours.

The Indians suffered also, but in all probability in a lesser degree, for game was plentiful. One of the younger Indians having found a bee-tree was voraciously devouring the honey, but was stopped by one of his race of more mature years and told that by eating it thus it was likely to produce colic. He got some dry wood, and after cutting it as small as possible, pounded it in a mortar (home-made) until it looked like sawdust. The honey was then mixed with it and partaken of with safety. On being questioned as to why he mixed the wood with the honey, he replied "that he knew of but one reason, and that was that the belly must be filled."

Father having mentioned that in his youth he had often loaded his wooden cannons so heavily that they exploded, we were anxious to know how he obtained his powder, as we were aware that money was not very plentiful then. "Oh," he replied, "just give an Indian hunter a piece of bread and at the same time let him know that you are out of powder, and he will take off his powder-horn and pour out enough to last you two or more days."

Post-Offices.—In 1809 there were few post-offices in Upper Canada, and no exchange of mail matter between our P. O. department and that of Uncle Sam. So if a person wished to mail a letter from any part of the U. S. to this Province he was compelled in the first place to seek some one who was journeying northward and get him to put the letter in the nearest P. O. in the Province after he arrived in it.

In a letter written at Hopkins' Court House, Tennessee, dated Dec. 11th, 1809, we find that John Thomas, the writer, had gone there on business, but found great difficulty in getting a settlement, as he states, "I am afraid of a war with the U. S., as the people are much exasperated at the conduct of the English in general, and Jackson in particular. Should this be the case, business done or not, you may expect my immediate return before any stroke can be made on either side. Goods begin to sell very high here. I fear I shall not be able to get a bill on New York as business begins to slacken and merchants are distrustful of a war and its consequences." As envelopes had not been invented at the time of writing, the letter had to be folded in such a manner that one side could be tucked into the other, and then, to secure it there, it was sealed with wax. It is addressed to Mrs. Eleanor Thomas, Grand River, Upper Canada, care of Capt. Brant to Niagara, and marked 2 S. postage to convey it to Ancaster.

Slaves in Upper Canada.—It is probable that it was on his return home from this trip that grandfather brought with him two slaves, a negro and his wife. They lived in a log house on the lot at Cainsville until their death, working for, and being cared for by grandfather. The woman died first and was interred by her husband close to the east side line of the lot, where he planted a seedling apple tree and a hickory tree at the head of the grave to mark its location. Subsequently the negro died and was buried beside his wife. In due course of time the Hamilton and Brantford Electric Railway was laid out, and its course ran directly over the spot where these two trees had been planted. The men engaged in grading the line found the skull of the negro to be still pretty solid, but the remainder of the bones had returned to mother earth.

Father told us that the only time in his life he was very strongly tempted to steal was in his boyhood days. His mother had sent him and a hired man, each mounted on a horse, and having a bag of wheat in front of him, to Malcolm's mill in Oakland, via Brant's ford, and along a footpath through the dense forest, now traversed by the serpentine Mt. Pleasant Road. Grandmother had entrusted the man with money for their dinners, as well as for provender for the horses, but he spent it for rum en route, so there must have been dram-shops in Brantford even as early as this. When they arrived at their destination it was time for dinner, but they had nothing to eat and the money spent. On seeing through a window some loaves of bread and plates overladen with newly-baked cakes, father said he was strongly tempted to steal some of them to satiate his appetite, but resisted the temptation. Mrs. Malcolm, wife of the miller, on questioning him, ascertained the plight in which he was placed, and took him in to dinner to his great delight, for which he was very thankful.

Grandfather Thomas was a member of the A. F. and A. M., No. 6, Barton Lodge. This lodge held meetings periodically in an upper chamber of the two-storied house on the lot at Cainsville. After the close of the War of 1812, John Thomas journeyed southward to Virginia and Tennessee to get his business settled, but was accidentally drowned while fording a river in that country, and his body could not be traced, although many efforts were made with that purpose in view.

Strange to say, no record can be found of the death of great-grandfather (John Smith, sen.). But we have his last will and testament, dated 13th Sept., 1827, and on comparing his signature thereto with that of other documents, we have concluded that he did not live many years after signing his will. From father we learned that on his demise his corpse was interred in the Mohawk Church graveyard, his body being that of the first white man interred therein.

Which of us, with our much vaunted Collegiate education, could go into the dense forest, having no other instrument than a surveyor's chain and a compass, and strike a line a mile and a half in length, so nearly due north and south that the Government surveyors, in making the surveys of the land contained in the old Brant leases, declared that the East line of the lot at Cainsville deviated so slightly from absolute north and south that they deemed it unnecessary to make any alteration thereof? Yet that was done by great-grandfather in 1801.

Education in Brant.—It has been already stated that father was at school at Fort Erie in 1812 when war was declared by the U. S. Congress, that he was hurried home, and that soon after his arrival the family were induced by circumstances over which they had no control to remove to the backwoods of Blenheim and take up their abode in a shack in which there was found but one corner dry enough to place a bed. Here they remained till the close of the war in Sept., 1815, father being then 14 years old.

About this time a schoolhouse was erected on the site of the one in what is now known as School Section No. 16, but at the time we are speaking of was called, at least by the pupils, Bunnell's schoolhouse, because the site was taken from a lot of land afterwards deeded by the Crown to Mr. Bunnell, grandfather of A. K. Bunnell, Treasurer of the City of Brantford. The first teacher was a Yankee adventurer named Forsyth, who, with many others, had followed the army. The textbooks he introduced were Mavor's Spelling-book, the English Reader, Morse's Geography, and Daboll's Arithmetic—all works of Yankee origin.

The spelling-book opened up with the alphabet and gradually advanced; a few illustrations of the commonest of our domestic animals were given, with a brief descriptive article of each. These were interspersed nearly to the end, where were found columns of words of five or more syllables, the first being "abominableness." The so-called English Reader was almost entirely made up of extracts from the best English authors, but it also contained extracts from speeches made by

Ben. Franklin, Patrick Henry, etc. The geography seemed to be made up especially to extol and enlarge the U. S. at the expense of Canada. To give an instance: the little State of Rhode Island was allotted more space in that work than could be spared for Canada, although the latter consisted of two Provinces. The Arithmetic proved to be the best of the books, and was a work of decided merit. After the war father became a pupil of this school, and frequently referred to his schoolmates—the late Malachi File, the late John J. File, etc., the last mentioned being the father of Levi File of the Township of Brantford, and also grandfather of Mrs. John D. McEwen of Mt. Pleasant Road. It was not long after the advent of the Rev. Jas. C. Usher, the founder and first rector of Grace Church, Brantford, before he held Divine service in the schoolhouse on Sunday afternoons. These services were heartily welcomed by the settlers who signified their appreciation by the regularity of their attendance.

[In 1834 the Rev. James C. Usher served Barton and the village of Hamilton. Mr. Usher was obliged to take the long journey to Quebec to be ordained in 1834. On his return he was preferred to Grace Church, Brantford.—From Wentworth Historical Transactions, 1902, p. 64.]

Means of Cooking.—Our "foremothers" had no such conveniences as "cookstoves," with the numberless utensils accompanying them, but were forced to do their cooking by means of the old-fashioned fireplace, with its crane and pot-hooks of various lengths for hanging the pot and tea kettle on. Those who had not brick ovens, when they wished to roast meat or bake bread, used a reflector made of bright tin, in shape somewhat like an open shed. When in use this was set upon a frame of iron with four legs, the open side towards the fire, and the frame filled with live coals. It is scarcely necessary to state that the food to be cooked was placed inside the reflector. The frying pan had long legs and a long handle for convenience. The smoothing irons (sad irons) were heated by standing them on end in proximity to the red-hot coals, and consequently required to have the ashes removed from their faces before using. They also provided themselves with a sheet-iron round pan, with an iron handle about six feet in length, for baking short cakes and pancakes of buckwheat, corn meal or wheat flour. To prevent themselves from getting overheated they improvised a jack made of iron, about five feet in height, and having notches at intervals of about six inches apart to rest the handle at such a height as would keep the pan level. Some bakers became so proficient in its use that they were enabled to grasp the handle with both hands, give it a toss and turn its contents (one cake) upside down, when cooked sufficiently on the lower side, and catch it in the pan.

Stoves and Ovens.—Some time about the year 1830, a man, J. Vannorman by name, started a foundry at Long Point. Its chief products were "The Farmer's Cook Stove," with its attendant furniture, and box stoves for heating purposes. The castings in these stoves were much thicker than those in use nowadays, and rods for holding the stove together were not used, so one had to be very careful in putting in wood or he might knock the back plate out on the floor. Many farmers, as soon as bricks could be obtained, erected brick ovens at a short distance from the kitchen, and thus were enabled to bake a batch of bread that would last the family eight or ten days. We have several pots made at Long Point and occasionally make use of them.

Clothing.—Our ancestors had not the opportunity to buy at Saturday bargains "$7.50 suits reduced to $4.98," but were compelled, owing to circumstances over which they had no control, to raise sheep, whose wool was taken to the nearest carding mill, where it was made into rolls. These were taken home and spun into skeins of yarn; thence it was taken to the weaver to be made into cloth, which was given to itinerant tailors to make into suits befitting the various members of the family. In a similar manner with regard to footwear, the farmer traded the pelts of animals to the tanner for leather, which was fashioned into boots and shoes by shoemakers who travelled from house to house with their kits of tools on their backs.

As reference was made to the "Stone Age" in a paper read before the Society, we not only believe that there was a people inhabiting this continent before the advent of the Indians, but have some proof thereof, for on the lot at Cainsville we, in our boyhood days, found a stone axe, which is of better shape, and in a better state of preservation, than any specimen on exhibition in the public museums of the Province.

About 12 years before Brant County was separated from the united Counties of Wentworth, Halton and Brant, father and the late William Holmes, J. P. (from whom we get the name Holmedale) were gazetted commissioners of the Court of Request, a court of equity as well as law. They continued to hold sessions of this court periodically until the establishment of County and Division Courts.

If it were possible for the late Capt. Joseph Brant, Thayendanegea,, to rise from the tomb, and standing upon some elevated spot of land, say Tutela Heights, view the city lying beneath him, with its railroads, steam and electric, its telegraph, telephone and trolley lines, its public buildings, its extensive and numerous manufacturies, private dwellings, and parks, its bridges, etc., he would be likely to exclaim in his native tongue the words of the Latin poet Horace: "I have reared to myself a monument more enduring than brass" (bronze), or he might select the words engraven by Sir Christopher Wren, architect of St. Paul's Cathedral, London, England, on that edifice, Si monumentum quaeris, circumspice—"If you seek my monument, look around."

> The memory of the red man,
> How can it pass away,
> While their names of music linger
> On each town, and stream, and bay.—Anon.

VI.

THE PAST AND PRESENT FORTIFICATIONS AT KINGSTON.

By George R. Dolan, Calgary, Alta.

The busy Canadian of to-day knows Kingston only as the home of the penitentiary, or the seat of Queen's University, or perhaps as a stagnant looking community. Its appearance of stagnation is due to the numerous small frame dwellings in the older wards, the crumbling walls of the various forts, and their grim looking towers. Its past growth and historic traditions have been due in a great measure to the erection of these military works, and to the probability that upon two occasions it was likely to be chosen as the provincial capital. This paper deals especially with the various fortifications of Kingston, and the two threatened attacks during the War of 1812.

The importance of the city during the war lay in its intermediate location between Montreal and the Niagara district, its selection as the depot of supplies for the troops in Upper Canada, and in the dockyard being located in its neighborhood.

From the year 1759 until 1784 the land about old Fort Frontenac had been entirely abandoned by English settlers, as well as soldiers. But in the latter year, Capt. Grass, who, though a German, had served in the British Army during the Seven Years War, and had been held a prisoner in Fort Frontenac in 1757, landed with a few U. E. Loyalist families on Mississauga Point, the land now occupied by the Canadian Locomotive Works. Their selection apparently was quite favorable, for many families followed them during the ensuing years, and in 1792, when Lt.-Governor Simcoe held his first government council in a log house, still standing on Queen St., there were about 120 houses, almost all of wood, scattered along the shore for a few hundred rods back, northeast of the present West Street. Among the earlier settlers were the Macaulays, Cartwrights, Fergusons and MacLeans, many of whom held commissions during the war. During the struggle the village made remarkable progress, and in 1821 had a population of 5,000, of all classes. Its progress at that time was due to its freedom from attack during the war, the settlement of many of the regulars in the neighborhood having naturally attracted many of the immigrants, whom they had known in

THE PAST AND PRESENT FORTIFICATIONS AT KINGSTON.

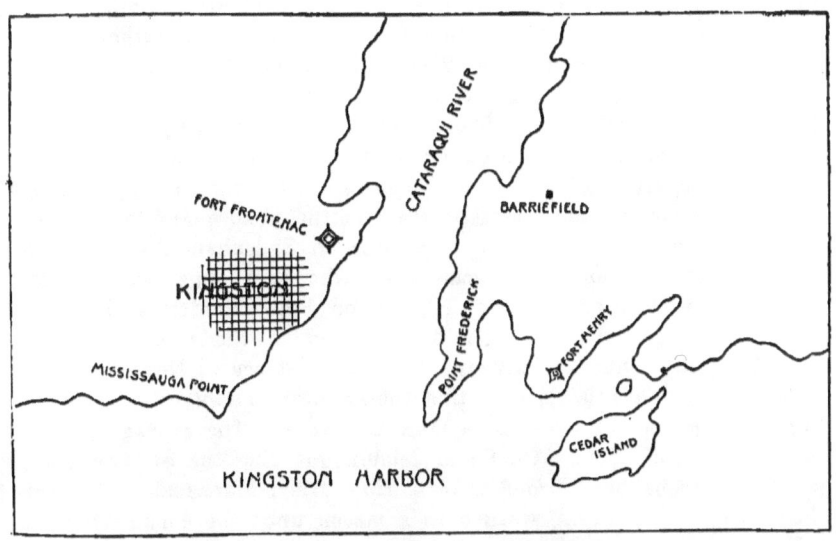

OUTLINE MAP OF ENVIRONS OF KINGSTON HARBOR.

the motherland. Then the Imperial Government had spent large sums in the purchase of provisions and clothing, and in the construction of the vessels of the Navy on Lake Ontario. Probably in the histories of this war we have been rather narrow-minded in the praise of our own militia. But we must not forget the great sacrifices the mother country had undertaken in sending out thousands of soldiers, sailors and marines, and practically paying almost all the expenses of the war, even when she was struggling for her commercial existence against the insatiable hatred and ambition of Napoleon.

Bad feeling existed between the mother country and the newly separated states from 1783 till 1791, on account of the treatment accorded to the U. E. Loyalists. Great Britain retained a few posts in American territory, and war clouds began to gather. So, upon the advice of the War Department, Lord Dorchester, the Governor-General at that time, ordered Surveyor John Collins in 1788 to make a survey of all the harbors in the inland lakes. He selected Carleton Island, south of Wolfe Island, as possessing most advantages in shelter, water and defence. Lt.-Governor Simcoe, after a personal inspection, supported Collins' choice against the views of Carleton, who had picked upon Kingston. In his report, Collins claimed that Kingston was open to attack from the rear; the old French fort was useless as a source of defence, and the harbor was exposed to the prevailing south-west wind. There is no doubt of the truth of the first two objections. The authorities in 1812 ran a palisade wall along West to Sydenham St., across Princess, or Store St., to Raglan Road, thence north-east to the site on the Cataraqui River of the cotton mill. This line was strengthened by the erection of two log blockhouses, one on Princess Street, and one on Montreal Street, but no traces of wall or blockhouses can be found to-day. Later, in 1845, five modern blockhouses were constructed to guard the various roads, and many may remember the one on Sydenham Street, which unfortunately was sold a few years ago. About the same year, to complete the fortifications at Fort Henry and Point Frederick, Martello towers were erected at Macdonald Park, and on the shoal near the Kingston and Pembroke Railway. The upper storey of these was constructed with movable sides, so that the artillery, mounted upon travelling carriages, could sweep both land and water. The average cost of these was about £8500. On Cedar Island, guarding the St. Lawrence, was the famous bomb-proof tower. Hon. Alex. Mackenzie, who was then living in Kingston, worked as a mason upon the construction of this in 1846.

Many have read in the shorter histories of Canada that LaSalle built Fort Frontenac, and later it was reconstructed as a western post of defence by Frontenac. But both of these men were essentially traders, and the location on level ground at the mouth of the Cataraqui River rendered it an excellent post for barter with the Indians. In an ancient map is marked an Indian store on the shore near the fort, which must have plied a busy trade as late as 1812. Like all other military works near Kingston, this fort passed through three distinct changes. The first fort planned by LaSalle was oblong in shape, each side being 250 feet long, with projecting bastions at each angle. It was constructed of upright logs, or palisades, with earth and stone packed between. There were log buildings erected inside and also near the fort to accommodate the garrison and traders. In 1689, during the terror-stricken rule of the weak Denonville, the fort was abandoned, and soon destroyed by the revengeful Iroquois. In 1695, Frontenac, during his second term as Governor, with a great retinue, re-visited the spot, and rebuilt it of stone, using simpler plans than before. Later, in 1720, a wooden gallery connected each bastion, so that the defenders would always be under cover. The walls were loopholed for musketry, but there was no surrounding ditch or terrace. The fort was taken without much difficulty by Gen. Bradstreet in 1758. He planted his cannon upon the site of the present market place, and in a few hours had battered the walls down.

THE PAST AND PRESENT FORTIFICATIONS AT KINGSTON. 75

For almost twenty-five years the spot was untouched by the British, till the coming of Capt. Grass in 1784. Five years later Kingston was chosen as the chief military depot, and wooden barracks were constructed for the men, with one storey houses for the officers, within the curtains of the fort. According to the prevailing custom, a stockade was constructed to surround the enclosure. The old French tower in the north-east angle was used as a magazine, and was torn down in 1832. The British Government never regarded the spot as of much defensive value, for in 1819 they permitted the local military authorities to tear down the fort to permit the extension of Ontario Street. The present barracks, called Tete-du-Pont, were erected with quarters for officers and men from 1831 till 1842. This is now occupied by B. Battery of the Royal Canadian Artillery.

In the selection of Navy Bay for the site of the proposed dockyard, a compromise was really effected between the opposing views of Collins and Lord Dorchester. Kingston harbour was passed over, and the bay enclosed by Points Frederick and Henry was chosen. The stores were to be kept on the narrow tongue of land now occupied by the Royal Military College. This spot must have possessed a decided superiority over the neighboring harbor, as the land was practically a wilderness; the forest must be cleared, and cottages, storehouses and docks constructed. There was no bridge crossing the mouth of the Cataraqui. A ferry, connected with a wire cable, carried the farmers and their wagons across. Later the marines used a scow rowed with long sweeps to cross the harbor, which at the points of crossing was about one-third of a mile. But the supplies and heavier equipment could be brought directly to this point by the Gananoque Road. A glance at the plan will show that the whole bay was sheltered from the objectionable south-west wind by Point Frederick. The water was sufficiently deep for any draught of sailing vessel, and the gradually receding shore permitted the construction of docks and ways.

The shape of Point Frederick, and its location almost surrounded by water, rendered its defence comparatively easy of solution. The narrow isthmus near the head of Navy Bay could easily be protected by the guns of the ships patrolling on either flank, so that it could easily be defended from a land attack in the rear. The waterfront was guarded by three strong batteries. On Mississauga Point a battery of six twenty-four pounders was erected, protected by a log casement and earthworks. Bouchette, who commanded the dockyard in 1792, describes a furnace erected here to heat the balls, so as to set fire to hostile ships.

In searching among the old stores in Fort Henry, I discovered a portable iron furnace, probably used in 1839 for a similar purpose. On the opposite shore at Point Frederick was a similar battery mounted upon earthworks. Surrounding this, close to the water's edge, was a line of cheveaux du frise, or a palisade fence with sharp iron spikes, pointing outward. Inside of this was a blockhouse, commanding a survey of both bays, mounted with heavy artillery.

So strong was this point considered that in 1842, the home Government constructed the present fort, which is rather oblong in shape, to suit the outlines of the shore. It is about 600 ft. deep by 750 ft. wide, and on the water side consists of thick walls twenty feet high, banked by earthworks twenty-five feet thick, mounted with heavy rifle guns, and carronades on revolving platforms. A few of the heavy guns used in 1812 are strewn about the fort. Among the interesting features of this structure are the sally ports, 25 feet long by 7 feet high and five feet wide, arched and cased with stone, which tunnel the walls on the waterside. By these the garrison could rush out upon an attacking or retreating force. In the centre was a very strong stone tower, mounted with heavy cannon, with a stone cased moat surrounding, so that even if the enemy should scale the walls, this deep and wide moat must be crossed before the garrison could be captured. Even now such walls, banked with thick mounds of earth, could offer a serious resistance to heavy artillery. I have been unable to find any historical incident connected with this battery.

On the eastern side of this point, within a stone-throw of the Royal Military College, is the site of the busy dockyard of 1812. A few posts still mark this historic spot, which was probably the busiest centre in Canada during the whole war. Here about 200 carpenters, 300 helpers, and 800 marines and sailors, from the Atlantic ships, were stationed during 1813 and 1814. During the winter of 1812-13 six warships were constructed, from 125 to 200 feet in length, most of them sloop rigged, and carried from the twelve guns of the "Beresford" to the 23 of the "Wolfe." In the following winter two larger ships, the "Princess Regent" and "Princess Charlotte," were built; while in 1814, the "St. Lawrence," the giant of the fleet, 300 feet long and carrying 100 guns, was launched. Many accounts have been written about this vessel, but there is the strongest evidence that she never took part in any fight, was drawn up again on the ways, where she remained roofed over for many years. Later she was sold, and while being towed to Amherst Island a storm drove her ashore. An oak chair, made from her huge stern posts, is now in the possession of the present member for Kingston, Mr.

W. F. Nickle. One of these ships, the schooner "Psyche," furnishes an interesting story of the conduct of the war office. She was first constructed in England, every single piece numbered and described; then she was taken apart, placed on board a transport ship, and carried to Montreal. Thence all the parts were carried by wagon or batteaux up the St. Lawrence, and refitted at the dockyard. All these exertions went for naught, as the ratification of peace cut off her active career. The records also show that four large casks to hold fresh water, and an apparatus for distilling the briny water of Lake Ontario were sent out to be used on board the navy. This paternal red tape spirit of the War Office is also shown in the official correspondence of five letters which passed back and forth, about the simple matter of a useless thirty cent lock on the door of an officer's room.

These vessels, though made of green elm and oak, were very well constructed, and show the difference between the English and American workmen. They were well shaped, with smooth sides, braced with copper and iron fastenings. There was not a great disparity in their weight of metal, nor in their sailing qualities. The American authorities at Sackett's Harbor rushed their ships together, regardless of finish, speed or size of guns. Thus, Sir James Yeo, with fewer ships, and carrying far less metal, with smaller crews, was on the whole able to keep control of Lake Ontario. In 1818 the famous Rush-Bagot Treaty was signed, restricting armed vessels on the lakes. So all the ships, including two captured American vessels, were sold to junk dealers, who, after stripping them of their copper, iron, and everything moveable, towed them a short distance from the shores and set them on fire. Their blackened timbers lie beneath the waters of Navy Bay, where they may still be seen on a calm day.

The only building still standing which had any connection with the War of 1812 was the large stone structure near the old dockyard, now used as a dormitory by the cadets. It was erected in 1816 to store the sails, ropes and guns of the ships. It was used as a storehouse till 1838, when Capt. Sandom and a force of marines were sent to reopen the dockyard. As the cottages for the soldiers and officers, used in 1812 had been sold, the old storehouse was cleared out, each floor fitted up as in a warship, hence its name—the stone frigate. After the Rebellion of 1837 a few steam gunboats were constructed, the most noted being the "Experiment."

The entrance to Navy Bay on the eastern side is at present guarded by the well known Fort Henry, which stands on a rising elevation at the entrance to the St. Lawrence. Here in the year 1813, a battery of six twenty-four pounders was erected, protected by logs and earthworks. A blockhouse was also constructed and all the surrounding woods cut down to permit the enemy landing and masking their guns. A captain of the Voltigeurs, who was stationed here in 1813, speaks with the most abject disgust of the forlorn looking stumps, rocks and shrubs, which were infested with mosquitoes, gnats and reptiles. Later in the same year officers' quarters, stone magazines and an armory were erected. The position was considered so advantageously situated that two strong towers of rubble stone were erected and surrounded by a palisade. A stone building about 80 feet long, used for officers' quarters, was erected. In 1818 the garrison must have been increased, as stone barracks 230 feet long, and two others 80 feet long, were built; so that a considerable permanent force was maintained there from 1818 till 1860.

The present fort, shown on the sketch, was erected in 1832, and with the advanced battery was not finished till 1842. It is erected on the crest of the hill, about 100 feet above the lake level. Unlike the first fort, built by the Royal Engineers, this was built by contract by Messrs. McAdoo, Duff and Noble. The late Sheriff Ferguson of Kingston had the contract of cutting the stone. Immense quantities of limestone were used, which was procured in the neighborhood, as the many nearby quarries show. A great many of those working on its construction perished from the cholera epidemic. The fort from rear to front towards the lake is about 800 feet long, and 500 feet broad. The walls of the inner fort are from 10 to 12 feet thick of solid masonry, and 20 to 25 feet high. Heavy rifle guns and carronades, a few marked 1811 and 12, are mounted on carriages, travelling on semi-circular tracks cemented into the rocky foundations. These guns, having a range from 800 to 1500 yards, all, of course, muzzle loaders, commanded the Gananoque Road and the St. Lawrence. Lining the inner walls are the stone quarters for officers and men. An interesting sight in many of the rooms is the brick fire-place, while in others furnaces were used. As these thick walls were continuously sweating, heat would be necessary during the warm months, and stalactites may be seen in almost all of the former mess-rooms. In the north wall was the cook-house, with fire boxes built in the brickwork, with huge iron pans for making soup or boiling meat. Some of these iron doors must have been used in the first fort, as they are stamped 1812. In another damp, mouldy room is a great quantity of hammers, files, tongs, scissors, cannon wads, rammers, cant hooks, bellows, meat saws, powder buckets of 1812 fame, all of which must have been used at various times by the garrison. If this Society is able in the near future to erect a suitable building, sufficient material alone could be furnished by the discarded stores at this fort to fill a military museum. Unfortunately most of these relics are being destroyed by rust, and judging from past experiences, the Militia Department might give an order for these weapons and tools to be sold as old iron. So that the least the Society might do is to notify the Department that if these are to be disposed of, it should be given the first selection.

The fort is tunneled under its walls and moat. The powder was kept below ground, and could be flooded at a moment's notice. The quarters for men and officers were ranged close to, and forming part of, the wall, to give greater protection and more room for parade grounds in the centre. Even the windows are strongly barred, so that if the enemy scaled the walls the garrison would still have a shelter. The advanced battery upon the water side, built about 1842, was a serious military blunder. The walls facing the lake are only about four feet thick, and not sufficiently high. A hostile fleet could see within the enclosure, train its guns upon the soldiers' quarters, without the wall offering any obstruction. Many have heard of the story of the engineer in charge of the work, discovering this serious mistake, after its completion, then in despair shooting or drowning himself. But the facts are that the mistake was made by Col. Wright, who had charge of the work. He was recalled to England and cashiered out of the army. The work was completed by Sir Richard Bonnycastle who had charge of the fortifications at Penetanguishene as well as Navy Bay.

The walls were surrounded by a moat 24 feet wide and twenty feet deep, with perpendicular stone sides. These were crossed by drawbridges, which were specially defended by heavy cannons. By underground passages the garrison could fire from both sides of the moat, so that even if an enemy scaled the hill they would be subject to a deadly fire from both sides of the moat. By means of open sally ports the garrison could descend to the water under cover. At the shore the mouths of the sally ports were protected by strong towers, mounted with heavy cannon, and loopholed for rifle fire. These were used in case of retreat, or for the temporary confinement of prisoners who were taken in a rush. The guns not only commanded the waterfront, but could be trained upon a land force, so that an attack from the rear was exposed to fire from three sides.

There have been many interesting incidents in connection with this strong fort, but I shall relate three in connection with the Rebellion of 1837. In February, 1838, a plan was formed by an American Confederate, Van Rensellaer, to attack Fort Henry. It was known that it was garrisoned by civilians, and among these a traitor had agreed to spike the guns, and even to open the gates upon the approach of the "Patriots." The plan leaked out, and 1600 militia were placed in the enclosure. An American force, which had collected at French Creek, near Clayton, to the number of 1800 men, took possession of Hickory Island, near Gananoque. But VanRensellaer proved to be a low fellow, and the force melted away.

In the dungeons during part of the month of November was confined the misguided Von Schultz, or Van Shultz, who, urged on by the notorious Bill Johnson, led about 500 men across the river to Prescott, and after four days' fighting was captured by Col. Dundas of Kingston. He was tried by court-martial, and was hanged at the north-west corner of the fort, just outside the walls. His body was claimed by a Kingston sympathizer, John Cicolari, and was buried in St Mary's cemetery, beside his friend Capt. Woodruff, who met the same sad end.

Here also were confined John Montgomery, and several others, who were captured after the skirmish at Montgomery's Tavern, sentenced to death, which was afterwards commuted to banishment to Van Dieman's Land. While being taken to Fort Henry for safe keeping, they formed a plot on board the "Sir Robert Peel" to overpower the guard and seize the vessel, but the plan was abandoned. They were then confined to Fort Henry for a few days. They planned their escape by means of information secretly conveyed to them. Their plan succeeded, except that Parker, a resident of Kingston, deserted them, and Montgomery broke his leg by a fall in the sally port. But after terrible suffering and starvation for five days, all except Watson and Parker, who were taken, reached Cape Vincent, where they were given a public dinner and every kindness shown them.

As these forts would furnish good material for a museum collection, so the stirring incidents connected with them, and the weed-covered charred hulls at the bottom of Navy Bay, open up a boundless field for historical and romantic story, which has hitherto been scarcely touched.

VII.

REMINISCENCES OF EARLIER YEARS IN BRANT.

By Miss Augusta I. Grant Gilkison, Brantford

The Brant Historical Society, which was organized at the Conservatory of Music on Nelson Street, May 11, 1908, welcomes you to this historical city of Brantford, renowned as being named after the great warrior, Thayendanagea, Capt. Joseph Brant, who was a captain in the British army. This part of the country was first inhabited by the Ojibways or Mississagas, the government buying part of their land for the Six Nations, through which the River Ouse, now the Grand River, ran.

When Brant arrived here in 1783, he settled at the bend of the river where the old Mohawk Church now stands, which was to be the Indian Village and his home for the future; and there he built his double log house, known as "Mohawk Castle," on the south side of the church. While living there he became an influential British subject, much honored and admired by all classes.

His portrait was painted by Romnèy, the English artist, in London, in 1776. Brant had neither the aquiline nose nor the copper complexion, nor the coarse jet black hair of the Indian race. His only Indian feature was the prominent cheek bone. This is true of the whole family of Brants, from Joseph Brant's grandfather, who visited England with Peter Schuyler early in the reign of Queen Anne. In the London Magazine for July, 1776, there is a sketch of Capt. Joseph Brant, in which it is stated that he was the grandson of one of the five Sachems who had visited England in 1710. Three of the latter were Mohawks, one of whom was Joseph Brant, Chief of the Canajoharie clan. These Sachems, or Indian "Kings," as they were called, had been taken to England by Col. Schuyler, and they created a great sensation, people following them wherever they went. The chiefs were dressed in black clothes after English manner, and instead of a blanket they each had a scarlet ingrain cloth mantle edged with gold lace, thrown over their other clothes. These court dresses were given them by Queen Anne, a more than ordinary solemnity having attended the audience they had of Her Majesty.

They were conducted to St. James' Palace in two royal coaches, and introduced into the royal presence by the Duke of Shrewsbury, Lord Chamberlain. The speech delivered by them was preserved by Oldmixon, the historian. Sir Richard Steele mentions these chiefs in the Tattler of March 13th, 1710, and Addison in the Spectator of the same week devotes a special article to the five Indian "kings" from North America.

Capt. Joseph Brant was a great letter-writer—wrote many letters on business, and on private or domestic concerns. His fame was co-extensive with England and the United States. In one of his letters to Thos. Eddy he says: "I was born of Indian parents, lived while a child among those whom you please to call savages. I was afterwards sent to live among the white people and educated at one of your schools, since which period I have been honored much beyond my deserts."

The saintly Rev. Robt. Addison of Niagara visited the Mohawks and baptized about a hundred and fifty of them. He and other missionaries were greatly assisted by Capt. Brant. When Lieut. Gov. Simcoe arrived at Niagara in 1792 he brought a letter from the Duke of Northumberland to the Mohawk Chief, Thayendanagea. This Duke had served in the Revolutionary War as Lord Percy and had been adopted by the Mohawks with the name Toughwegeri, or the "Evergreen Brake." Lieut.-Governor Simcoe delivered a brace of pistols to Brant from the Duke, and in a letter his Grace added: "I preserve with great care your picture which is hung up in the Duchess' own room." A close intimacy was thereupon formed between Lieut.-Gov. Simcoe and Capt. Brant.

George Washington also recognized the great influence of Capt. Brant over all the Indian tribes. He invited Brant to attend the great Council held at Philadelphia, the seat of Government, in the winter of 1792, and on May 23rd of that year the newspapers announced: "On Monday last arrived in this city from the settlement on the Grand River, Capt. Joseph Brant of the British Army, the famous Mohawk Chief who so eminently distinguished himself during the late war as military leader of the Six Nation Indians. We are informed that he will pay his respects to the President of the United States." The United States offered him a thousand guineas down and half pay pension, the reward he received from the British Government doubled, if he would endeavor to bring about peace with the tribes, but Brant refused as he thought it would be detrimental to the British interests, as also to the advantage and credit of the Indian Nations until the Americans should make the necessary concessions.

Brant sailed for England in 1786. He was well received and his society courted by gentlemen of rank and station, statesmen, scholars and divines. He was dressed in European clothes, but had a splendid Indian dress of his own nation. He was a great favorite with the Royal family. He proudly refused to kiss the King's hand, but he remarked with gallantry and address that he would gladly kiss the hand of the Queen. King George III. smiled, as he loved his Queen too well to be offended. Brant was accompanied about England by two negro servants.

Thayendanagea is described as having been a man of animal courage and as having the noble qualities of a brave soldier. He was tall, erect and majestic, with the air of one born to command, and his name was a tower of strength among the warriors of North America. He translated the gospels, prayers and psalms into the Mohawk language. His last words were: "Have pity on the poor Indian if you can get any influence with the great, endeavor to do them all the good you can. Oh, my Father, my Father, the chariot of Israel and the horsemen thereof."

No people are more painstaking in paying honor to their dead than the Indians. The funerals are marked with deep and affectionate solemnity. When Brant's remains were removed in 1850 from Wellington Square to the Mohawk Church, the old bell (the first bell that was rung to call the people to the house of God in Upper Canada), tolled for 24 hours, until the body, which had been carried on the shoulders of relays of six warriors at a time, walking through the forest until they reached the old Mohawk Church, was laid, with that of his son, Capt. John Brant, in the tomb erected to their memory. The removal of their remains and the erection of the beautiful monument is due to the untiring energies of Mr. Allen Cleghorn, who was an honored and beloved friend of the Six Nations.

Among the many persons who knew Brant from 1792 to the day of his death, Nov. 24th, 1807, were the first Gov.-Gen. Lord Dorchester, Gen. Amherst, Commodore Alex. Grant of Grosse Pointe near Detroit, Father Macdonell (who afterward was the first Roman Catholic Bishop of Kingston), Col. Thos. Talbot, Sir Isaac Brock, Capt. William Jarvis (Provincial Secretary), Wm. Osgoode, Jas. Baby, Chief-Justice Powell, Duparon Baby, Alex McKee, Wm. Robertson, Major John Richardson, Peter Burpree, Bishop Strachan, Tecumseh, and many others.

In 1884 there were only three warriors living who had fought with Brant: John Smoke Johnson, 94 years; Jacob Warner, 93; John Tutela,

92. John Smoke Johnson's last appearance in public was at the laying of the corner-stone of Brant's monument; he died shortly afterwards.

Mohawk Village, also known as Brant's Ford, was, in the earliest years of this province, the only inhabited place between the village of Niagara and Detroit. Gov. Simcoe, after having settled in Niagara, thought it was his duty to know the land over which he had been made governor, so he started with Capt. Wm. Jarvis and suite in Feb., 1792, marching through forests where towns and cities are now built, including Hamilton and others, until he came to the Mohawk Village, extending to where Cainsville stands and around the Mohawk Church. Brant received Gov. Simcoe and suite, entertained them for three days, accompanied them on their journey to Detroit many miles through the forest, and supplied them with food and horses. On arriving at Detroit he was received by Commodore Grant, who was then in command of the British fleet on the Upper Lakes. Gov. Simcoe returned in March, 1793, and was again the guest of Brant at the Indian Village, and was entertained with the usual dances, the calumet, buffalo, feather and war dances, the visitors being also given Indian names. On the 13th Feb., 1793, Mrs. Wm. Jarvis entertained Brant at dinner in her log house at Niagara.

Among the first persons who settled in Brantford were John Stealts, Enos Burnnell, Arnah Huntington, John A. Wilkes and others. Wm. Richardson was the first post-master and also Indian Superintendent after the death of Capt. John Brant. He was also Lieut.-Col. of the 10th Gore Regiment in 1837-38, had married Jane Cameron Grant, 11th daughter of Commodore Grant, in 1824, at Chippewa, and resided in Brantford until his death in the fifties.

Brantford is known as the "Telephone City," the telephone having been invented by Dr. Graham Bell at his residence on Tutela Heights. It once had a palisade in the early days; this passed the corner of Market and Colborne streets of the present time, with a high embankment, surmounted by fifteen-foot pickets. This place was divided into town lots in 1830, and it was then that it was called Brantford. An interesting account is given by Adam Ferguson, of Wood-Hill, Scotland, who visited Brantford with Mr. Wm. Dickson from Galt. They rode on horseback from Galt, May 15th, 1831. (Mr. Ferguson's Notes of his tour are reprinted in the Transactions of the Brant Historical Society.)

Mrs. Joseph Brant returned to her old log house next to the Mohawk Church after Brant died, and was seen every Sunday in the Church, dressed in a black velvet skirt, black silk over-dress, a black cloth blanket and black velvet cap with a fur band. Her two daughters lived with her, Mrs. John and Mrs. Powless. Brant was married three times. His first wife, Margaret, left issue, Isaac and Christina. Christina married Chief Joseph Sawyer of the Mississagas, a venerable chief. The second wife, Susannah, died shortly after they were married. His third wife, Katharine, had issue, Joseph, Jacob, John, Margaret, Katharine, Mary and Elizabeth. Margaret married Powless and had several children. Katharine married Peter John and had three children. Mary married Seth Hill and had one child. Elizabeth married Wm. Johnson Kerr and had four children.

The corner-stone of the Brant Memorial was laid Aug. 11th, 1886, by Chief Clench, and unveiled the 13th Oct., 1886, by the Hon. J. B. Robinson, Lieut.-Gov. of Ontario. There were present at the unveiling seven North-West Indian Chiefs, Blackfeet and Crees—Red-crow, Chief of the Blood Blackfeet; North-Axe, Chief of the Piegan Blackfeet; One Spot, pipe-bearer of Crowfoot, who was too ill to be present; Ah-tah-ta-coop, or Star Blanket, Cree Chief; Mist-ta-was-sis, or Big Child; Kah-kee-wis-ta-haw, or Flying in a Circle, Cree Chief from Crooked Lake; Osoap, or Back Fat, from Crooked Lake, a great grandson of Thayendanagea. He said he was glad to come and see his great-grandfather, Thayandagea, with his braves around him. He got short notice and could not dress himself like the other chiefs. He was ploughing when he was told to come. He at once handed the plough to his son and told him to go on, and started off. Had he notice he might have brought a dress which he could have left with his friends.

I must refer to Brant's enemy, Red-jacket, Sa-go-ye-wat-ha, Keeper Awake, a Seneca Chief, whose remains were reinterred by the Buffalo Historical Society in Forest Lawn Cemetery on October 9th, 1884, with those of five other Seneca chiefs, and Capt. Pollard. At this re-interment were thirteen chiefs of the Six Nations Indians of the Grand River, accompanied by their superintendent, Col. Gilkison. These chiefs, with Chief John Buck, the hereditary keeper of the Wampum Belts and also Fire-keeper, performed the funeral Indian dirge over the graves of Red-jacket and the other chiefs. Among those present were Miss Jessie Osborne, great-grand-daughter of Capt. Brant, Misses Evelyn H. and Pauline Johnson, daughters of Chief Geo. H. M. Johnson; the present writer, and many delegates from the Indian Reserves of the United States. Red-jacket was most intellectual, and well posted in Indian affairs. His word was bond; he was a great orator and the faithful friend of the missionaries. His last words, with his loving family around his bed, were: "Where is the missionary?"—and clasping his beloved little step-daughter, Ruth Stevenson, to his bosom, he passed away to his long rest.

Mrs. Catherine John died at Wellington Square, Feb. 8th, 1867. Latterly she had lived in the house of her childhood, Wellington Square. Her remains were brought to the Mohawk Church and buried beside those of her father, Capt. Brant. The service was read by the venerable Rev. Abraham Nelles. At the funeral were present Simcoe Kerr, Jacob Lewis, Mr. Osborne, her nephews, Chief Smoke Johnson, Geo. H. M. Johnson and many others, old and young, of the Six Nations. The pall-bearers were Mr. Allen Cleghorn, Honorary Chief, Dr. Dee, Mr. Gilkison, and Mr. Matthews.. Mrs. John in her old age, being over eighty, was tall, handsome and of queenly bearing. No one could look at the aged lady without being impressed with feelings of respect and admiration.

On July 31st, 1868, service and a picnic were held in the old Mohawk Church for the purpose of raising funds to restore the old church. It was beautifully decorated and crowded with Indians and white people. Prayers were read by the Rev. Mr. Elliot, of Tuscarora, many years missionary to the Six Nations, in the Indian tongue, followed by Rev. Mr. Roberts, Canon Ussher, Rev. Dr. Townley, Rev. Dr. Reid, Rev. Mr. Duane, Rev. Mr. Clotsworthy, all of whom took part in the service, Ven. Archdeacon Nelles preaching an excellent sermon. Chants and psalms were sung by the union choir, accompanied on the melodeon by Mrs. Dr. Dee, and a handsome collection was taken up. After service the people adjourned to the Indian Institute where the Indian boys and girls were educated, and there they enjoyed a feast of good things. Again Mr. Allen Cleghorn was the principal mover in this good work in restoring the old church for Sunday service. Addresses were given by him, explaining his views, Dr. Bown, M. P., and the Rev. Dr. Reid, of Grimsby. Chief Smoke Johnson, speaker of the Council, also gave an eloquent address. There were addresses too by Rev. Mr. Duane and other clergymen, and by Mr. Gilkison, Chief Seneca Johnson, Wm. Jacobs, John Buck, John A. Beaver, Rev. Isaac Barefoot, Chief Geo. H. M. Johnson.

On the 26th of March, 1869, a most interesting ceremony took place at the Indian church, Onondaga, when the fine old Indian chief, Seneca Johnson, and his wife (who were pagans) were baptized and received into the church by the Rev. Mr. Nelles, and afterwards united in the holy bonds of matrimony. The sponsors were Mr. Gilkison, Chief J. Smoke Johnson, Mrs. David Carpenter and Miss Johnson (Indian women). After an excellent discourse from the Rev. Mr. Roberts,

Chief Seneca Johnson rose and addressed the congregation, some of
whom were pagans, saying: "My dear friends, I wish to thank you
kindly, all of you who are present to witness this change I have made.
This may be all new to you, but it is not the case with me. I have carefully observed for some years the different churches, and I have learned
to understand and come to the conclusion to be baptized and join the
Church of England, and that church I only acknowledge. I now wish
to say to you all, my Indian friends, let us try and set a good example
to our young, and to you white people—teach us and lead us in the
right way. I cannot read the Bible; if your example be good and kind,
our little children will follow and profit by it and grow up good people.
Your presence here to-day assures me that you are all kind and friendly
to me. It is said I have left my tribe and people; I have not left my
people. I shall now take even more interest in them with better feeling
than ever." The chief (now known as John Seneca Johnson) was
dressed in a deer-skin coat, and looked extremely well, wearing his
Prince of Wales medal. He and his wife shook hands with many, receiving congratulations in the most cheerful and happy manner. The
ceremony was most impressive. There were from time to time during
the ministry of the Rev. Adam Elliot, missionary at Tuscarora, about
170 pagan adults baptized by him. At one time a pagan Cayuga chief
and his whole family were baptized by him and they continued exemplary members of the church.

Lieut.-Col. J. T. Gilkison met the chiefs in council for the first time
at Middleport, May 23rd, 1862, and was honored with the Indian name
that was given to their former superintendent, Col. Claus, Shaonwenjow-nach, meaning "United Lands." The Mississagas also gave Col.
Gilkison the name Pis-kah-yausk, the Sea-gull.

A pleasing event took place at the Indian Council House, Oshweken,
on Dec. 6th, 1887, when the chief warriors and Indian women presented
their superintendent with an address of congratulation upon the completion of his 25th year of service to them, accompanied by an Indian
sash of honor which was placed across his breast, and also a copy of
the Holy Bible. (That Bible is now placed in the new Church of England at its opening at Oshweken by his daughter, the present writer.)
Mr. Gilkison, on rising, was sensibly affected, and spoke in terms of
affection, referring to his pleasure in the performance of his various
duties in behalf of the people. Individually, he would prize the gifts,
and especially, pointing to the Bible, that guide to all. The sash he
would wear on all occasions when with the Six Nations. The chiefs,

warriors and Indian women filed past him and warmly shook him by the hand.

Shortly after one of the early Indian raids into Ohio and Kentucky, Mrs. Alex. Grant of Grosse Pointe heard that a band of savages had camped at Belle Isle, five miles up the river (now Detroit's beautiful Island Park). The Indians were going to hold a Pow-wow to celebrate their exploits and to torture and burn a young white boy, whose mother they had killed. The Commodore was away at York (now Toronto), but his wife's motherly instincts were aroused, and knowing the love and esteem of the Indians for her family, she determined to make an effort to save the boy from so terrible a fate. She was rowed in a canoe to Belle Isle and made her way to the camp, and asked the amount of the ransom for the child. The Indians, who were making preparations for their horrible feast, would not at first listen to her. The courageous woman was not to be baffled, and at last, partly by presents, and by threats that the black gown (priest) would bring calamity on them, she succeeded in her mission. The little boy was brought home and adopted by his humane deliverer, who already had a large family of twelve children. She gave him the name of John Grant. The grandchild of that boy, John, still lives and remembers his mother's account of Mrs. Grant's trip to the Island. This lady was Theresa Barthe, who married the Honorable Commodore Alex. Grant, 1774, and died Nov., 1810, aged 53, her remains being buried in Detroit. Commodore Grant was one of the first members of Parliament called by Lieut.-Gov. Simcoe, and was President of Upper Canada in 1805-6. He died at Grosse Pointe May 11, 1813, aged 79 years, and was buried in St. John's churchyard, Sandwich.

There died in Windsor on Monday, May 15th, 1911, Mrs. Emilie Veronique Labadie Jacob, who resided her life of 87 years in that vicinity. The deceased was born on the old Labadie homestead, Sandwich East, March 27th, 1824. She married Geo. Alex. Jacob, a grandson of Commodore Grant, in 1844. Mr. Jacob was a member of the first Michigan Cavalry, and was killed in the battle of Wilderness. The deceased was a direct descendent of Des-comptes Labadie, prominent in the early history of Detroit.

VIII.

CAPT. JOSEPH BRANT'S STATUS AS A CHIEF, AND SOME OF HIS DESCENDANTS.

By Major Gordon J. Smith, Brantford
Superintendent Six Nations

His Status as a Chief.—In recent years the status of Joseph Brant amongst his own people has been the subject of much interest. Historians of his own and later times cannot agree, and there has always been an expression of doubt, or rather, it has never been said with absolute certainty, that Joseph Brant was an hereditary chief of the Six Nations. That he was a great man, a leader of his people, and the greatest Indian ever produced by the Six Nations, has not been denied. His force of character, strength of intellect, and physical prowess brought him to the front and proclaimed him the leader of the Six Nations, or of such of them as remained loyal to the British flag during the Revolutionary War. His shrewdness enabled him to secure a satisfactory home for himself and his people upon the conclusion of that war upon the Grand River Reserve in Upper Canada, now the Province of Ontario, and he led them forth into their new home and acted as their business adviser and plenipotentiary until the time of his death, in 1807.

The word "Chief" can be, and is, used in many senses.

1. Civil Chief—Royaner.

The League of the Iroquois was founded about the middle of the fifteenth century, but as there is nothing but tradition to guide us it is not possible to fix the exact date. The object of this League was not warlike; on the contrary, it anticipated the Hague Tribunal and the International Peace Commission by several centuries in banding the various tribes of the Iroquois into a confederation having for its object peace amongst its members. Thus was formed the Great League of the Five Nations—Mohawk, Oneida, Onondaga, Cayuga and Seneca. The government of this League was placed in the hands of fifty sachems or royaners, divided amongst the tribes as follows: Mohawks, nine; Oneidas, nine; Onondagas, fourteen; Cayugas, ten; and Senecas, eight. To each sachemship was given an appropriate name, and this name was assumed by each sachem upon his appointment, and borne until his death, resignation or deposition. The same names have been used by successive generations of sachems down to the present day, and are hereditary in the several tribes to which they belong, passing through the female line. There was absolute equality of rights, privileges and powers among this body of rulers. There was no principal, or head chief. Their jurisdiction was entirely of a civil character and confined by their organic laws to the affairs of peace. They constitute the aristocracy of the Six Nations. Their line of descent is claimed to be unbroken, save in a few instances, from the foundation of the League to the present day, and unless a man belonged to the royal branch of his clan, through his mother, he could never expect to be a sachem.

2. Assistant Chief, or Messenger.

Each sachem was entitled to an assistant, raised up in the same manner and from the same line of descent as his principal.

3. War Chief.

A war chief became such through his martial ardor, physical strength, or force of character. He was the creation of circumstances. When war occurred, Indians grouped themselves into independent bands and followed one of their members, who, from his character and disposition, showed the qualities of a leader, and thus became a so-called war chief.

But only two war chiefs were officially recognized. They were assigned to the Senecas; all others were independent and without status.

4. Pine Tree Chief.

On occasion a man, through his native ability, zeal for the public good and general high standing, is elected by the Six Nations Council to the office of Pine Tree Chief, but his office is not hereditary, it dies with him. Originally he had a voice but no vote in the council, but now he has a vote.

5. Chief. With the partial disruption of the Six Nations Confederacy during the troublous period of the revolutionary war, the civil power of the Six Nations was largely usurped by their military leaders, and these leaders by their force of character and ability practically constituted themselves the ruling body of the Confederacy. In the sense that they were leaders they were chiefs, in the same sense as a successful merchant is designated a merchant prince, a successful stock-broker a Napoleon of finance, or a Rockefeller an oil king.

CAPT. JOSEPH BRANT'S STATUS AS A CHIEF. 91

A chief in this sense does not inherit the title nor is he elected to it, but has it given to him as a courtesy title, or else assumes it.

Behind all these sachems, assistant sachems, war chiefs, and chiefs, were the warriors.

The object of this paper is to review all the evidence obtainable, and from it ascertain to which class Thayendanegea, Capt. Joseph Brant, belonged.

Brant's parentage is not a matter of absolute certainty. He was born on the banks of the Ohio in 1742. His father, according to Stone in his life of Brant, published in 1838, was a full blooded Mohawk Chief, referred to by Sir William Johnson, the first superintendent of the Six Nations, as "Old Nickus," or "Old Brant," but his mother's name was not mentioned. Sir William Johnson in his will, published in the second volume of Stone's Life of Johnson, refers to Brant as "that half-breed Joseph Brant." The author of this work is the son of the author of the Life of Brant.

A book entitled "Travels in the interior of the uninhabited parts of North America in the years 1791 and 1792," published by John Guthrie, Edinburgh, states that "This renowned warrior (Brant) is not of any royal or conspicuous blood."

The English historian, Weld, in his "Travels through the States of North America during the years 1795, 1796 and 1797," states that "here he (Brant) distinguished himself by valor in many different engagements, and was soon raised not only to the rank of war chief, but also to that of a war chief in His Majesty's service."

The Rev. Dr. Strachan, afterwards Bishop Strachan, published a brief account of Brant's life in the Christian Register of 1819, in Kingston, in which he says that "nothing was known of Brant's father among the Mohawks." He does not refer to his mother.

Thos. L. McKinney of the Indian Department, Washington, and James Hall of Cincinnati, in 1841 published in Philadelphia a History of the Indian Tribes of North America, in which they state that Joseph Brant was not a chief by birth, but that in 1776 he was appointed principal war chief of the Six Nations, it being an ancient usage to confer that dignity on a Mohawk.

Lewis H. Morgan, probably the most accurate and authentic writer on the Six Nations, states that there were but two war chiefs created to take general supervision of the affairs of war when the nations were prosecuting a common war. As the Senecas were the door-keepers of the Long House, these chieftaincies were assigned to them. Morgan further says: "During the Revolution Thayendanegea, Joseph Brant, commanded the war parties of the Mohawks, and from his conspicuous position and the high confidence imposed in him rather than from any claim advanced by himself, the title of military chieftain of the League has been conceded to him by some writers. But this is entirely a mistake, or rather a false assertion, which is expressly contradicted by all of the Iroquois nations, including the Mohawks themselves." (See his "League of the Iroquois," 1851.)

From these historic reocrds, some made during Brant's life and some made at various times down to thirty-five years after his death, when means were available for obtaining authentic information, we must come to the conclusion that Thayendanegea was not born of distinguished parents, that he was a half breed, and therefore, if his father was a full blooded Mohawk, as Stone says he was, his mother could not have been an Indian, and therefore her son, according to the laws of the League, could not inherit a sachemship. In any event his mother was of so little importance that she received no notice from the historians. Had she been of the royal line the presumption is that mention would have been made of it and her name or clan given.

That he was not an authorized war chief is proved by the fact that he was a Mohawk. Only Senecas could be representative war chiefs.

Evidence from Official Documents.—In addition to what has been written by historians and travellers in regard to Brant we will examine a few documents which are on the official files of Canada and the United States.

In 1788 a deed of territory along the Mohawk River was executed by sixty-five chiefs and witnessed by Colonel John Butler and Joseph Brant. Had Brant been a chief he would have signed as such and not as a mere witness.

In 1798 a deed of surrender was executed by Captain Brant as Attorney for the Six Nations beginning as follows: "I, Captain Joseph Brant, Thayendanegea Sachem and Chief Warrior of the five nations."

On the 20th of May, 1796, at the Mohawk Village on the Grand River a conveyance of 2000 acres in the Township of Brantford to Nancy Kerr and Mary Margaret Kerr, grandchildren of Mary Brant, Joseph's sister, was executed by "the Sachems, War Chiefs and Principal Women." In this deed Captain Brant's name does not appear, although he was then living at his Mohawk Village. Had he been a Sachem and Chief Warrior, as he described himself in the Deed of Surrender of 1798 above referred to, he would undoubtedly have been a party to the deed.

In 1804 "The Sachems and Chiefs of the Mohawks and others of the Six Nations of Confederate Indians residing on the Grand River, or River Ouse. . . . . do make, constitute and appoint our beloved brother and Principal Chief Captain Joseph Brant (Thayendanegea) our true and lawful attorney, representative and Agent." The wording of this Power of Attorney implies a difference between sachems and chief. Both sachems and chiefs signed this document, and amongst the signatures many of the hereditary names of the Sachems appear. Brant is described as "our beloved brother and principal chief." Had he been a sachem he would have been properly described as such, and he would have naturally taken steps to insure that he was so described.

Local Evidence.—Upon Brant's tomb at the Mohawk Church near Brantford is the following inscription:

"This Tomb is erected to the memory of Thayendanegea, or Capt. Joseph Brant, principal Chief and Warrior of the Six Nations Indians, by his fellow subjects, admirers of his fidelity and attachment to the British Crown. Born on the Banks of the Ohio River, 1742; Died at Wellington Square, U. C., 1807.

"It also contains the remains of his son Ahyouwaighs, or Capt. John Brant, who succeeded his father as Tekarihogea and distinguished himself in the war of 1812 and 15. Born at the Mohawk Village, U. C., 1795, Died at the same place 1832. Erected 1850."

This epitaph, written in 1850, appears at first sight a strong argument in favour of the contention that Joseph Brant was a chief, but when we read that John Brant succeeded his father as Tekarihogea we must at once conclude that the author of the epitaph either wilfully intended to deceive or did not know anything about the Six Nations Confederacy. It is as impossible for a son to succeed his father as a chief as it is for water to run up hill. At his father's death John was only thirteen years of age, too young to be made a chief. Later on he was made a chief, as his mother Catharine was of the Turtle clan, and through her he attained that dignity, not through his father. As the second paragraph is so manifestly incorrect little credence can be placed in the accuracy of the first paragraph.

The following is a portion of the inscription upon that beautiful and artistic monument erected to the memory of Captain Joseph Brant in Victoria Park, Brantford, in 1886.

"This National Monument erected by the Brant Memorial Association—Incorporated 41 Vic. Cap. 62, to

Thayendanegea

Captain Joseph Brant, born 1742, died 1807, interred at Mohawk Church, and to the Six Nations Indians, for their long and faithful services on behalf of the British Crown and their observance of Treaties. Contributed to by the Six Nations Indians, the Chippewas, The Dominion of Canada, The Province of Ontario, The City of Brantford, The Counties of Brant and Bruce, and private subscriptions. The British Government presented bronze cannon for the statues.

* * * *

Chiefs.

Ska-na-wa-dih	Ah-wen-in-neh	Ska-ko-ka-nyes
Ken-eh-da-geh-ka-non	Kwe-yo-teh	A. G. Smith, Interpreter."

It will be noticed that Brant is no where in this inscription mentioned as a chief. His highest title, that of Captain in the Army, is used. Towards this monument the Six Nations subscribed $5000.00, and consequently they were made parties to its erection and consulted in all details. Chief John Smoke Johnson, a Mohawk and a veteran of the war of 1812, was present at the laying of the corner stone of the monument. He was then in his ninety-fourth year and the only living Indian who had known and remembered the great Thayendanegea. If Brant had been a Chief and recognized as a Chief by the Six Nations, Chief Johnson and those Indians associated with him in the erection of this monument would not have allowed Brant's name to have appeared without all the honours to which he was entitled, and to an Indian the title of chief is a much greater one than that of a captain.

Miss Evelyn H. C. Johnson, a daughter and a grand-daughter of Chiefs (John Smoke Johnson above mentioned being her grandfather), and a diligent student of Indian history, in a paper recently presented before the Brant Historical Society, says: "A born leader of men, Brant became a leader of leaders of the Six Nations. A commander of the Six Nations he was not. The constitution of their government prohibited any one head of the whole Confederacy. Nowhere has the writer been able to learn of Brant leading as a chief in the deliberations of the great councils of the Six Nations. That assembly of inflexible legislators would never permit it. True he was present at their councils; so were other warriors. That he frequently spoke in council was his right. That he of course called a council is without question. His position as Interpreter and as deputy of the Superintendent and finally leader in war, would give him the right, and with Indians, as with all other nations, they glorified their great leaders who excelled in war and followed them to death and the grave..........

That Brant in his day was the Chief man of the Six Nations is indisputable. It may be said of him that he was born to fame. He acquired fame, and fame was thrust upon him. He was not a hereditary Chief. There is no hereditary chieftainship in the Brant family in the Six Nations Reserve, as any chief to-day will affirm. He was not a Pine Tree Chief. On the contrary, the Six Nations themselves do yet and always have denied absolutely that Brant was a Chief.

The writer has not been able to find any person on the Six Nations Reserve, either among the Chiefs or old men, who will affirm positively that Brant was a Chief.

This investigation was begun with a mind predisposed to find Joseph Brant a Chief; but the historical, documentary, and local evidence leads but to one conclusion, and that is that Captain Joseph Brant, Thayendanegea, was not of the royal line, and was not a Chief, not a Royaner. The name Thayendanegea was his private given name, and is not the name of any hereditary sachem.

That he was not an assistant chief or messenger is equally conclusive, as he was not of the royal line.

That he was not an official war chief is established by the fact that he was of Mohawk and not of Seneca descent.

That he was not a Pine Tree Chief is not so clearly established as the other contentions; but in view of the fact that he has nowhere been designated a Pine Tree Chief, that he never officially executed any Six Nations documents, and that he was not given the title of Chief on the monument is evidence sufficient to deprive him of this title.

That he was a chief by courtesy—a leader of leaders, a great warrior, a great Indian—no one will deny. There are to-day many leading Indians on the Six Nations Reserve who are called chiefs by white men and by the press because they think that being prominent Indians they must be chiefs; but the Indian never makes that mistake, nor will he ever give that great title to any one who is not entitled to it.

Brantford, June 2nd, 1911.

Captain Joseph Brant
Died 1807.

His Children and Descendants.

1. Isaac, died 1795—had issue.
2. Christina, married Aaron Hill—had issue.
3. Joseph died 1830—had issue.
4. Jacob, died 1846—had issue.
5. John, died 1832—had no issue.
6. Margaret, married Powless Powless—had issue.
7. Catherine, married Peter John—had issue.
8. Mary, married Seth Hill—had issue.
9. Elizabeth, married Wm. Johnson Kerr—had issue.

- **ISAAC** d. 1795
  - Isaac
  - Margaret m. Jacob Lewis
    - Isaac
      - Elizabeth m. Jas. Wilson
        - Annie
        - Edward
        - Lewis
          - Lewis
          - Beula
          - Bryce
          - Nellie
          - Evelyn
        - Henry
        - James
    - Mary m.
      1. Dan Doxtater
      2. Samson Hess
      3. Rev. A. Sickle
      - Chf. Dan Doxtater
        - Dan
          - Lizzie
          - Fred
          - Norman
          - Ellen
          - Matthew
        - Julia m. Uriah Marlin
          - Laura
          - Mary
          - Raymond
          - Aggie
          - Lillie
        - Job — Gordon
        - Mary
          - Stuart
          - Hilton
        - Samson
          - Harry
          - Samson
          - Russell
      - John Hess
        - Isaac
          - Clayton
          - Osler
        - Maggie
      - Enoch Hess
      - William Hess
        - Nellie m. John Vanevery
          - Florence
          - Eleanor
          - William
          - George
          - Mary
          - Stanley
    - Margaret m. John Sawyer, a missionary of the Credit.
      - Esther
      - John
      - Alexander
      - Peter
      - Jacob
      - Levi
      - Dan
      - Sarah
      - Mary
      - Isacher
        - Jemima m. Peter Hill
          - Albert
          - Hiram
          - Flora
          - Stephen
          - Jemima
          - Mary
  - Ellen m. Joseph Lottridge
    - Lydia Cornelius
      - Mary m. Festus Johnson
        - Richard
        - William
        - Josephine
        - Festus
        - Susie
        - Angus
      - Susan m. Aaron Hill
      - Maggie m. John Bennett
      - Lena m. Kittridge (white)
      - Angeline
        - Mary
        - David
        - Lucy
        - Andrew
        - Birdie
        - Hilton
        - Susan
        - Sarah
    - Esther m.
      1. Peter Powle
      2. Rev. Thos Funn
      3. Peter Scholer
      4. Isaac Claus
      - Chf. Peter Powless
        - Elizabeth
        - Isaac — Eveley
        - Joseph
        - James
        - Richard
        - Samson
      - Ellen m.
        1. Denis Sero
        2. Peter Martin
        - John
        - Alfred
          - Elizabeth
          - Alfred
          - William
          - Mary
          - John
        - Adeline m. Peter Miller
          - John
          - Thomas
          - Gertrude
      - Elizabeth m. Samson Newhouse
        - Lillie
        - Henry
          - Alexander
          - Evelyn
          - Helen
        - Cassie — Gordon Roy
      - Catharine m. Jacob Smith
        - Albert
        - Jonas
        - Emy
        - Mary
        - Cissy

ONTARIO HISTORICAL SOCIETY.

2.
CHRISTINA m.....
Henry Aaron Hill
- Solomon Hill
- Joseph Hill
- Mary m.,............
  1. Joseph Monture
  2. John Johnson
  3. Joseph Sawyer
  - Isaac Monture
  - Peter Monture......
  - Jacob Monture
  - Catherine Monture
  - Christina Johnson
  - Elizabeth Johnson...
    m. Elijah Johnson
    - John........
      - Clarence
      - Lydia
      - Matilda
      - Julia
      - Susan
    - Henry!...... Henry Gorde
    - Ansley
    - William .... Vera / Clara
    - Catherine

3.
Joseph Brant—Catherine (a)...
d. 1830.   m. John W. Hill
- William Hill
- Joseph Hill........ William
- Ann m............. Simcoe Loft / Ellen
  Alex. Loft
- Elizabeth
- Ellen m .... Acland / Catherine
  Dr. Oronhyatekha
- Lydia
- Susan m............ Clara / Harriett / Ethel
  John Loft
- Mary m .... Mary / Ellinor / Margaret
  Nelson Maracle
- Sarah m........... Gertrude
  Isaac Green

a) Catherine's descendants are members of the Bay of Quinte Reserve.

CAPT. JOSEPH BRANT'S STATUS AS A CHIEF.

4.
JACOB BRANT
d. 1846

- Jacob .... Mrs. Herkimer
- John..
  - John R.
  - Henry....... ...... { Peter H.
  - Joseph   { Lizzie Kelso
  - Jacob .... { Elias E.
                        { Maggie Thompson
  - Robert .... Alice
                        Marion Herkimer
                        Cameron
                        Ethel
                        John
                        Robert
                        Effie
                        Jos. Alex.
- Squire
- Peter
  - Sidney .... { Edith Elliott
  - Margt. Crane   { Edna Elliott
                       { Irene
                       { Austin
                       { Hazel
                       { Elgin
  - Christina Jones { Henry Jones
                    { Elizabeth
                    { Anna Foster
                    { Ella
  - Peter M .... { Frank
  - Alexander   { Arthur
                       { Peter H.
                       { David
                       { Reginald
                       { Huron
                       { William
                       { Fannie
- Charlotte Smith { Elizabeth m... .... { Kate Von Buskirk
                    Robt Dee, M.D.   { Fanny
                    (white)
                  { Mary m............ { Frank
                    Frank Dee, (white) { Elizabeth
                  { Charlotte

6.
MARGARET m ...
Powless Powless

- George Powless
  - Joseph Powless ...... Geo. Powless ...... Geo. Powless
  - Mrs. Nick Porter ...
    - Charles
    - Lucy
  - Mrs. Jos. Porter ...
    - Joseph
    - Mary Isaac
    - Henrietta Hill
- Susannah Lewis ...
  - Joseph
  - Jacob ...
    - Joseph
    - Lydia Brant
    - Christina Martin
    - Susannah Davis
  - David
    - Jacob
  - Chf. Abram Lewis ...
    - Abram
    - Charles
  - Chf. Elias Lewis ...
    - Isaac
    - Lawrence
    - Alexander
    - Susan
  - Margaret
  - Elizabeth m .. ..
    - Eli Burning
    - Nelson Hill
    - Abram Hill
    1. Burning
    2. Hill

CAPT. JOSEPH BRANT'S STATUS AS A CHIEF. 101

7.
CATHERINE m....
Peter John
- Chf. Wm. John..
  - Wm. John
  - Joseph John
- Isaac John
- Peter John

8.
MARY m. ......
Seth Hill
- Moses
- Seth
- Elinor
- Sarah m....... Elizabeth m.
- Jos. Lottridge   Wm. Thomas

9.
ELIZABETH m..
Col. Wm. Johnson Kerr
- Walter Kerr
- Joseph Kerr
- Chf. Wm. Simcoe Kerr
- Catherine m..........
- John Osborne
  - Wm. John Kerr Osborne
  - Jean m.........
    - Edwin Osborne Kerby
    - Wm. F. Kerby
    - John Brant Kerby
    - Kate
  - Don Kerby
  - Jessie m.
    1. Jos. C. Young
    2. Edwards

IX.

CHIEF JOHN SMOKE JOHNSON.

Sakayengwaraton—"Disappearing of the Indian Summer Mist."

By Miss Evelyn H. C. Johnson

Chief John Sakayengwaraton Johnson, more familiarly known in the Six Nations' Reserve as "Smoke" Johnson, was of pure Mohawk blood. His Mohawk name, Sakayengwaraton, signifies "Disappearing of the Indian Summer Mist," or "the haze that rises from the ground in an autumn morning and vanishes as the day advances." The Indians call this haze or mist "smoke," as the supposition is that it is caused by burning brush-wood; hence, this poetical Mohawk name was curtailed in English to "Smoke," and so widely did this grand old Indian chief become known by this name alone, that, as he advanced in years he was referred to simply as "Smoke," and all of his descendants bearing his name at the present day are known in the reserve as the "Smoke-Johnsons." So affectionately was he regarded by the Six Nations that he might well have been called the "Grand Old Man" of the Reserve.

John "Smoke" Johnson was the first of the family to be known and recognized by the English name Johnson, although his father, Jacob Johnson Tekahionwake—was the first to bear the name. He was, however, always known by his Mohawk name Tekahionwake, which is the family name of this particular family of Johnsons, the English meaning of which is "Double Wampum,' or "Double Wampum belts;" and, as there is a history in connection with this English name Johnson, and how it was derived, it will be traced here, as it is the earnest wish of the writer to refute the statements of some historians that this family are descendants of Sir William Johnson.

In reference to this subject, therefore, some years ago I entered into correspondence with that eminent philologist, Mr. Horatio Hale, for the purpose of having him make a correction of his explanation in the Iroquois Book of Rites of how this particular family derived their English name Johnson, which Mr. Hale claims is "from no less distinguished an ancestor than Sir William Johnson." In his letter of reply, Mr. Hale said he had never heard the story of how this English family name Johnson originated, and before the question could be adjusted and the correction made, Mr. Hale's death took place.

At the time the Six Nations Indians occupied their original territory along the Mohawk River, the country was one vast forest slowly being opened up by the white settlers, with here and there a small town. Indian trails intersected the forest, and wherever possible the water route, great or small, was utilized. Lakes, rivers and streams were the great highways of travel by canoe, practically every man possessing his individual canoe, whether for the purpose of pleasure or as a means of conveyance for his family, and altogether apart from the great war-canoes of the nations, which were their man-of-war ships.

It is doubtful if any Indian nation north of Mexico was ignorant of the great Falls of Niagara and the inland seas which empty their huge bulk of fresh water over the great cataract. "Niagara" is a Mohawk word meaning a "great fall of water," and without doubt it was the capital of the forest and the centre of meeting places for all the Indian nations in the vicinity of the great lakes and south-eastward to the Atlantic.

The early missionaries made Niagara their place of appointment for meetings with the Indians, and as travel through the forest as well as by water was slow and difficult, the missionaries were accustomed to periodically visit certain sections of the country to instruct the Indians in the Christian religion, baptize the children, and hold services in the forests for the benefit of the people. As all of the Indians knew the Falls of Niagara, it is but natural that Niagara became the leading place for these gatherings. The Indians came from far and near, no doubt for many reasons other than for the purpose of attending the missionary meetings. It is not unlikely that presents were given to them by their instructors, and that the opportunity was taken to hold councils with other nations. Regiments of British soldiers were stationed at Niagara, which helped to enliven the proceedings, and the people were always sure of meeting their friends from distant places.

The missionaries were earnest workers. All of the nations had their own marriage ceremonies and general rites, but they naturally enough knew nothing of Christian baptism. At regular intervals of two or three years, perhaps even a longer time, the missionaries made their rounds, and the children were brought to them to be baptized. It was at one of these periodical gatherings that the grandparents of John "Smoke" Johnson brought their son, Jacob, to be baptized. It must have been a special and noteworthy gathering, as the British Superintendent General of Indian affairs, Sir William Johnson, was present. Johnson Hall, the residence of Sir William, was situated in the vicinity of the source of the Mohawk River, among the Upper Mohawks. There were present for baptism some of the Lower Mohawks who came from a long distance, at the outlet of the river, to Niagara.

The Mohawk Nation is divided into two great sections, the Upper and Lower Mohawks, the upper being those of the nation whose homes were nearest the source of the Mohawk River, and the Lower being those who lived nearest the mouth of the river, where it empties into the Hudson. After the Six Nations removed to Canada and settled in the Grand River Reserve, the Mohawks retained their distinctive appellation, and are so known at the present day, even on the books of the Department of Indian Affairs, the designation being merely the same as Upper and Lower Canada, the Highlands and Lowlands of Scotland. Tekahionwake and his wife were Lower Mohawks. They had brought their son to Niagara to be baptized, and had already selected the name Jacob, but they were anxious to give the child a second name. There was some delay over the decision of a second name for the child, and learning the cause, their Superintendent-General, Sir William Johnson, came forward and said, "Name him Johnson after me." This was immediately done, and the boy was baptized Jacob Johnson.

Chief William Smith says his mother declared that Sir William Johnson stood godfather for this child, who was a lad some years old, not an infant in arms. Be that however as it may, my father, Chief G. H. M. Johnson, whose father was Chief John "Smoke" Johnson, told the same story of how the English family name Johnson was derived. My aunt, Mrs. Margaret Elliot, now in her ninetieth year, also tells the same story; and Mrs Mary Johnson-Davis, whose father was Aaron Johnson, a brother of Chief John "Smoke" Johnson, and a son of this infant boy, also tells the same story. This boy, Jacob Johnson Tekahionwake, had a sister Mary, two years his senior. Their father died when they were quite young, and his wife, the mother of these two children, married a second time to a Wyandot. In the Iroquois Book of Rites, Mr. Horatio Hale refers to the Wyandots as follows: "The Wyandots resided in ancient times near the present site of Montreal, in close vicinity to the Iroquois; this being recorded as a well remembered portion of their history. They emigrated to the Indian territory, a remnant of the tribe dwelling near Amherstburg in Canada." A few Wyandots remained living near the Six Nations and then removed to a great distance, these two children accompanying their mother and step-father to this distant country, which some of the Six Nations say was Kansas. It is altogether probable that this remnant re-joined their nation in the Indian Territory. Be that however as it may, their mother did not live long after her second marriage. After her death the Wyandots sent word to the Six Nations that these two children had lost their mother and that they were there friendless and alone, and they asked the Six Nations to send for them. After the receipt of this news the matter was discussed by the Six Nations, and a distant relative offered to go for the children. This woman set out on horseback and travelled many days. Chief William Smith says his mother told him that this woman called her pony "Spotty," but whether this name was in Mohawk or English does not appear. In the course of her travels she came to a great river; she selected a place to cross and made her horse swim the river with her on his back. After travelling still further she at last reached the country of the Wyandots, where, after resting, she prepared for her return journey. She set out with the two children on horseback; one sat in front and one behind her. When she reached the river she had crossed on her way to the Wyandots' Country, she left one of the children on the bank, and taking the other with her she made her horse swim the river as before. Leaving this child on the opposite shore she returned for the other one, and thus brought them safely across the river, and continuing her journey finally reached her home and people in the Mohawk Valley.

When the war clouds of the Revolution were darkening the sky, these children were orphans, and they were in care of the Six Nations. Sir William Johnson, as Superintendent, or else as god-father, said to Joseph Thayendanegea (Brant), "Here, you look after these children; you can take care of them better than I can." Joseph Brant then sent them on horseback, in care of two chosen Indians, to Sandusky, Ohio, where they were placed in charge of Indians. At the close of the war, and after the Six Nations were settled on the Grand River in Canada, they sent to Sandusky for these two orphans and had them brought back to the Mohawks, the girl Mary being then about twenty and the boy Jacob eighteen years of age. They lived, married, and died in the Grand River Reserve. Mary Tekahionwake's Mohawk name was Kah-heh-elo-leh; the English meaning is "Cornstalks shaking in the wind" ("just as if she herself does the shaking"). This girl married Oneida Joseph, whose Indian name was Teh-wah-seh-ela-keh, meaning "Two Axes." He was a very fine old Indian, well known throughout the reserve. They were the grandparents of Mrs. George Loft, now living and over eighty years old.

Jacob Johnson Tekahionwake married twice. His first wife was the mother of Chief John "Smoke" Johnson, but her name is not now known. His second wife was nicknamed in Mohawk "Chee-toh-leh," and was generally known by this nickname. She was hoeing corn on the cornfield flats, about where the Waterous Engine Co.'s works are situated, when a thunderstorm came up, and was struck unconscious by lightning. When a person is shocked by lightning, it is the Indian custom to cover them with some covering, leaving them where they fall until they regain consciousness, when they are at once removed.

Jacob Johnson Tekahionwake was little known in the Reserve by his English name. He was generally known as Tekahionwake, which is the Smoke Johnson's family name. At his death, however, his youngest daughter, Mrs. Ellen Powless, had the headstone erected at his grave in the old Mohawk churchyard, just to the left of the gate, on which is lettered his name, Jacob Johnson. His son, John "Smoke" Johnson, therefore, as already pointed out, was the first of the family of Tekahionwake to be known by the English name Johnson. He was born December 14th, 1792, at Johnson Settlement, which was north-west of Cainsville. He was a Lower Mohawk, of the Bear clan, and of pure Mohawk blood. His sister was Chief William Smith's mother, who survived her brother, and had often told her granddaughter, Mrs. George D. Styres, that she believed herself to be the last of the pure blood Mohawks.

John "Smoke" Johnson, when a boy, accompanied the great Thayendanegea, with a party of other Indians, to Montreal. He used to relate the story that he danced Indian dances for the amusement of the party. He knew Thayendanegea well, both of them being regular attendants at the old Mohawk Church.

For many years after the close of the Revolutionary War, the Six Nations and other Indian people were very restless. Those Indians remaining south of the great lakes claimed the Ohio River for the boundary, and the Six Nations upheld the claim and in every way possible endeavored to aid their red brethren to enforce this claim which the Americans refused to recognize. Whenever the disturbed conditions seemed to be settling down, some one Indian nation would go on the war path, others would join them, the Americans would use force to suppress the outbreak, and councils were convened both with other Indian nations and the American government, with always the demand "the Ohio for the boundary." These conditions were simmering for years, and when Great Britain and the United States resorted to arms in 1812, the Indians, led by the great Tecumseh (Captain Joseph Brant having died some four years previous), espoused the cause of Great Britain and took up arms in her behalf; and it is altogether probable that Canada owes to Great Britain's Indian allies the proud position she holds to-day as the eldest daughter in the British Empire. At one time during the War of 1812 the Six Nations assembled their women and children for safety at what is known as "Smoky Hollow," north of Cainsville, from which place could be heard the firing of cannon at different points east.

John "Smoke" Johnson was then twenty years of age. He quickly enlisted with the Six Nations in the service of the mother country and fought with conspicuous bravery in all the engagements of the Niagara frontier, taking part in the Battles of Queenston Heights, Stony Creek, Lundy's Lane, etc. He was present when General Sir Isaac Brock fell at Queenston. The Battle of Queenston Heights, it appears, began during the night or very early morning. Under cover of darkness the Americans crossed the Niagara River and scaled the heights. John "Smoke" Johnson used to relate with much laughter the following story of the commencement of the battle. As it was dark the Six Nations resorted to stratagem to enable them to distinguish their own warriors from those Indians who were fighting on the American side. They tied bands of white cloth, or white handkerchiefs, over their foreheads and around their heads. When hostilities began and foe met foe great confusion prevailed. It was discovered that the American Indians had resorted to a similar ruse and they also wore white bands around their heads for the purpose of distinguishing their warriors from the Canadian Indians. Of course the British and American uniforms were unmistakably different in appearance, but so great was the resultant confusion that the commanders on either side were compelled to withdraw their troops and await daylight.

This incident may be the one referred to in Stone's "Border Wars of the American Revolution" when he says, "The narrowness of the river, without the aid of spies enabled them to make these observations; added to which the sound of the oars had been heard, so that instead of being surprised the enemy was measurably prepared for Van Rensselaer's reception," and again, "The heights having been cleared of the enemy, who retired upon the village of Queenston, the Americans were allowed to repose a short time upon their laurels. But the respite was brief. General Brock being at Niagara when the action commenced was startled from his pillow by the roar of the artillery, but so rapid were his movements that he had arrived at Queenston ere the gray of the morning had passed, accompanied by his provincial aide-de-camp, Lieutenant-Colonel M'Donell." Stone's references to the "sound of the oars being heard," and "the grey of the morning," in a measure corroborate the foregoing narrative.

At the close of the battle my grandfather, John "Smoke" Johnson, was climbing over the steep cliffs, and as he rounded a huge boulder he came upon a Kentuckyan sitting on the ground. When the man saw my grandfather he rested his gun in the crotch of his arm, moving it about as my grandfather moved to get a good aim at him. My grandfather said he saw at once that the man's arm had been broken and he could not handle his gun freely, but, as he was endeavoring to aim, and my grandfather knew it was death for one of them, he shot the Kentuckyan. He then removed the Kentuckyan's shot-bag of leather, fringed at the edges by the leather being cut, and carried it himself during the remainder of the war. It is now in the possession of our family.

The conflagration of Buffalo took place Dec. 30th, 1813, and, from my grandfather's story of the war I have understood that he, in company with two other Indians crossed the Niagara River in a canoe, and landing upon the American shore they climbed to a place of vantage. Taking out his flint and steel and piece of punk, which he always carried, he then and there kindled the fire which burned Buffalo. Ten or twelve years ago, when I was living in that city, I was one evening dining with Mr. and Mrs. W. C. Bryant. The conversation led to mention of Chief John "Smoke" Johnson. Mr. Bryant turning to me said, "Your grandfather was the man who burned Buffalo." "Yes," I said, "I remember now—I had forgotten. But we have forgotten all that. It is past and gone with those who lived then. But how did you know it?" I asked. "After my father's death I found the notes he had made and which he got from your grandfather," he replied. "I was present," I said, "and I heard my grandfather tell your father when he was visiting us at Chiefswood, grandfather having come purposely at his request to give him information he was collecting about the Six Nations."

Mr. William C. Bryant, senior, barrister, whose home was in Buffalo, was a great lover of the Indians. So greatly did he admire Miss Kate Kerr, granddaughter of Thayendanegea, that before her marriage to Mr. John Osborne, of Hamilton, Mr. Bryant made her an offer of marriage. I have heard her laughingly tell the story of the first time they met, when he followed her into the garden where he made her an offer of marriage, and which she laughingly rejected, thinking he was demented. Throughout her after life he was one of the best friends she, as the granddaughter of Thayendanegea, possessed.

CHIEF JOHN SMOKE JOHNSON.

In 1815 John "Smoke" Johnson married Helen Martin (or Martyn, as my father said the name was spelled), eldest daughter of George Martin Onh-yea-leh and Catherine Rallston Martin (Wan-o-wen-re-teh) who had been taken captive by the Mohawks in her youth near Philadelphia. Helen Martin was born at the old homestead about two miles southeast of Cainsville, where it is still standing. It is estimated that it is about one hundred and twenty-five years old, and is, without doubt, the most historical spot, with the exception of the old Mohawk Church, in the County of Brant. In 1815 the Grand River Reserve was almost a trackless forest, and for the convenience of the missionaries several marriages took place at one time in the same house. It was either Rev. Mr. Howe (or Hough), or else Rev. Mr. Luggar, who married my grandparents. Their daughter, Mrs. Margaret Elliot, now in her ninetieth year, is uncertin which it was. The marriages were always arranged by the parents of the groom and bride, the latter having absolutely no choice in the matter. There were several marriages to take place in an Indian house which stood only a few years ago quite near the railroad at Cainsville. A large attendance of friends was always assured, and Helen Martin most unconsciously went to her fate accompanied by her parents, riding on horseback to her wedding, although she knew nothing of what was in prospect for her. After the other marriage ceremonies had been performed, she was told by her mother to go forward to the improvised altar and become the wife of John "Smoke" Johnson. She cried bitterly and entreated her mother not to insist upon her marriage, but her parent was inexorable, and she was married to the young warrior John "Smoke" Johnson, her mother removing her own wedding ring from her finger which her husband, George Martin, had purchased in New York, when he lived in the valley of the Mohawk, and it became for the second time a wedding ring, this time for her daughter. This ring is a plain band of probably plated gold having a square stone of ordinary glass. After the marriage, Helen Martin Johnson returned to her home, as she had left it, on horseback. It is the custom of the Indians for the bride to return to her parents' home, where the groom joins her. They live with the parents of the bride until after the birth of the first child, when the husband prepares a home for his family and takes them to it. Their eldest son, George Henry Martin Johnson, my father, was born at the old Martin homestead in 1816. John "Smoke" Johnson secured a property about a quarter of a mile north, to which he removed his little family and where he lived until the surrender of that portion of the Reserve in the beginning of the seventies. The log house in which he lived was some years ago razed, and a brick residence erected on the site. It was in this home that his wife died in 1866. He continued to live here with his married daughter, Mrs. Richard Davis, but finally removed to the portion of the Reserve near Kenyengeh.

John "Smoke" Johnson many a time took up the "death cry" of the Six Nations as its weird and blood-curdling sound echoed throughout the forest, and was carried down the water "telegraph-wire," the Grand River, past his home high upon the banks, to convey to all the people the dread news of the death of one of their great chiefs, or the terrible tidings of murder or war. On one of these occasions the official strings of purple wampum borne by one of the Indian runners when he entered the house and handed it to my grandfather, broke in two, and the wampum was scattered over the floor. My grandmother was obliged to restring it before my grandfather could proceed with it to meet the next runner. His daughter Margaret, Mrs. William Elliot, was present and witnessed the delay of the "telegram" caused by the accident.

The Pine Tree is the emblem of the Great League of the Iroquois. Mr. Hale says: "In general, the rank of the Pine Tree chief was personal; it was gained by the character and achievements of the individual, and it died with him." A Pine Tree chief is created a chief for life only by the great council of hereditary chiefs. John "Smoke" Johnson was not a member of one of the fifty noble families of the Iroquois confederacy, but he married into one of the noble families, that of Teyonhehkwen, i. e., "Double life." He being of the Bear clan could not, by the laws of the Confederacy, marry in the same clan. His wife was, therefore, of the Wolf clan, and as rank in the noble families follows the female, not the male, line, the hereditary chieftainship was on her side. Athough he spoke English well, his wife, my grandmother, was unable to speak a word of English.

So highly had John "Smoke" Johnson distinguished himself in the War of 1812 that the British Government requested the Six Nations to bestow upon him the honour of chieftainship. After due consideration of this request, and, taking into consideration the fact that he was a regular and deeply interested attendant at the councils of his people, the Six Nations Indians created John "Smoke" Johnson Sakayengwaraton a Pine Tree chief in their great confederacy. In the Iroquois Book of Rites, Mr. Hale refers to this incident in part as follows: "Sakayengwaraton is not an elected chief, nor does he bear one of the hereditary titles of the Great Council, in which he holds so distinguished a station. Indeed, his office is one unknown to the ancient constitution of the Kanonsionni. It is the creation of the British Government, to which he owes, with the willing consent of his own people, his rank and position in the Council. ...... He was known as a brave warrior, a capable leader, and an eloquent speaker. In the War of 1812, at the early age of twenty, he had succeeded an elder brother in the command of the Indian contingent, and had led his dusky followers with so much skill and intrepidity as to elicit high praise from the English commander. His eloquence was noted, even among a race of orators. I can well believe what I have heard of its effects, as even in his old age, when an occasion has for a moment aroused his spirit, I have not known whether most to admire the nobleness and force of his sentiments and reasoning, or the grace and flowing ease with which he delivered the stately periods of his sonorous language. He has been a worthy successor of the distinguished statesmen, Garagontish, Garangula, Decanasora, Canasatego, Logan and others, who in former years guided the destinies of his people. He is considered to have a better knowledge of the traditions and ancient usages of the Six Nations than any other member of the tribes, and is the only man now living who can tell the meaning of every word of the 'Book of Rites.'"

The grace, the beauty, the elegance, the poetry of the oratory won for him from his own people, themselves a race of orators, the title of "the Mohawk Warbler," and the tones of his voice were as the music of the rippling waters. For many years had he been affectionately known in the Reserve by this name, nor was he made aware of it by his silent and serene associates. It was some time in the sixties that his daughter-in-law, my mother, told him of his nickname, which greatly amused him. It has been suggested that his grand-daughter, E. Pauline Johnson (who died at Vancouver, B. C., March 7th, 1913), inherited from her grandfather the melody of her poems. For forty years Sakayengwaraton was Speaker of the Great Council of the Six Nations Confederacy.

In 1869, when the boy-Prince Arthur visited Canada, the Six Nations Indians, themselves never a conquered people, as allies of Great Britain, desired to confer upon their Sovereign's son the honour of a Pine Tree Chief of their Confederacy. Prince Arthur, now the Duke of Connaught, accepted the invitation to the Reserve, at that time extending to Cainsville, and the ceremony of installation took place at the old Mohawk Church and the old Mohawk Institution in the presence of all the chiefs and hundreds of people from the Reserve and surrounding cities and towns. Chief John "Smoke" Johnson, as Speaker of the Great Council and a Chief of the Mohawks, the leading nation of the confederacy, together with Chief George Buck, the leading chief of the

Onondagas, the brothers of the Mohawks, were appointed by the Great Council as their leading men to represent it in honouring the son of their Sovereign-Mother, and the great Confederacy to be honoured by a Prince of Great Britain becoming one of its chiefs.. They therefore, together with my father, Chief George H. M. Johnson, as the Six Nations' Interpreter, conducted the ceremony of installing the young Prince a chief of the Iroquois.

The copy of the original Iroquois "Book of Rites" was made by Chief John "Smoke" Johnson in 1832, upon the advice of an old chief who was stricken with Asiatic cholera and not expected to live. Not long after he had made the copy, the original was destroyed when the old chief's house wsa accidentally burned. Mr. Horatio Hale's "Iroquois Book of Rites" is, in part, the English translation of this Book to which he refers as "an Iroquois Veda," and was by him first discovered in 1879. After this book, "The Iroquois Book of Rites," was published in 1883, Mrs. Erminnie A. Smith, of New York, who was interested in the welfare of Indians, made a trip to the Grand River Reserve in Canada, with the intention of securing this Indian copy of the original. She offered Chief John "Smoke" Johnson ten dollars for it. As he was then ninety years of age he let her have the book, not knowing its value. As she was leaving our home, Chiefswood, for her home in New York, we learned of the transaction of our American guest, and, although we made every effort to recover the book from her, we were unsuccessful. I was told in New York that she, who loved the Indians so much, made some hundreds of dollars by the sale of this book to the Smithsonian Institution in Washington.

Sakayengwaraton was a zealous member of the Church of England. For more than forty years each Sunday he read the Ten Commandments in the Mohawk tongue from the pulpit of the old Mohawk Church, and Kenyengeh Church, after he removed to that vicinity. The Sunday previous to his death his people for the last time listened to their aged Chief read to them the Ten Great Laws in which he believed, and lived up to.

Each morning for upward of seventy-five years he attached his hunting knife to his belt. In the many years of his peaceful life following the war he never gave up the old Indian custom of carrying his knife at his side.

He was appointed by the white people to lay the corner stone of the Brant Memorial, as he was at that time the only living Indian who knew the great Thayendanegea; but, he being a Mohawk, and the

CHIEF JOHN SMOKE JOHNSON.

Mohawks the leading nation of the great Iroquois Confederacy, they are not, by their laws, allowed to touch the dead. The Six Nations, therefore, would not permit him to accept the intended compliment.

He was working in his garden in the heat of summer when he was overcome by the heat. He returned to the house and asked his daughter for a drink of water, and laid down to rest. But the swift runner, surpassing in swiftness those of his own people, had arrived with his last message. On the 26th August, 1886, Sakayengwaraton died in his ninety-fourth year. His remains were interred in the old Mohawk Churchyard where rest the remains of his wife.

On his coffin was placed a wreath of immortelles in red and black, the war colours of the Mohawks, the former signifying blood, the latter death. Beside it rested his Bible and his tomahawk, both of which had played so important a part in his life. No headstone marks his earthly resting-place, but it is hoped that his descendants will recognize this need before the expiration of the century mark of 1912.

New York, May 24th, 1911.

X.

INFLUENCE OF THE WAR OF 1812 UPON THE SETTLEMENT OF THE CANADIAN WEST.

By Lawrence J. Burpee, Ottawa

At first sight one would be inclined to say that the War of 1812 had no influence, could have had no influence, one way or the other, upon the settlement of what is to-day known as Western Canada—that is to say, that part of Canada lying west of the Great Lakes. The immense territory now constituting the provinces of Manitoba, Sackatchewan, Alberta and British Columbia, lay as completely outside the field of conflict as if it had been in South America. One may safely say that it did not enter into the calculations of the contestants on either side. It contained nothing for the one to attack or the other to defend. Believed at that time, and for many years thereafter, to be a wilderness unfit for civilized habitation, it was not valued by Canada nor coveted by the United States. In any event, it was much too remote from the centres of population on either side of the line to become an element in the conflict. The most westerly military station on the Canadian side was at St. Joseph's Island, near Sault Ste. Marie, and on the American side, the outpost of Michilimackinac, captured by the British soon after the declaration of war.

Nevertheless, although its rays were feeble enough, the dawn of the era of settlement in Western America was already breaking. At the very moment when Madison issued his Proclamation announcing that a state of war existed between the two countries, the pioneers of the Selkirk Settlement were on their way inland from York Factory to the Red River. The origin of that settlement is too well known to need any introduction here. It will be sufficient to note that Lord Selkirk sent out the first party of colonists from Scotland in 1811. They wintered at York Factory, and spent most of the summer of 1812 in making their painful way inland to Red River. A second party followed that year, reaching their destination in 1813. A third party sailed from the Orkneys in 1813, arriving at the Selkirk Settlement in 1814; finally a fourth contingent came out, in charge of Robert Semple, in 1815. Thus throughout the entire period of the war, and for a year after the signing of the treaty of peace, Selkirk continued his laudable but badly-managed efforts to establish a colony in the very heart of the North American continent, more than a thousand miles from the nearest apology for a town, in any direction.

Whatever we may think of Selkirk, in his relations with the North West Company or otherwise, one must at least admire his courage. He seems to have stood at that day almost alone in his belief that the western prairies were capable of supporting a white population. Against him was not only the active hostility of the North West Company (and the Hudson's Bay Company would no doubt have been equally hostile had they not been closely associated with his interests in antagonism to the Canadian fur-traders), but also the passive hostility of public opinion both in England and America. The marvellous western country, which means so much to-day to both Canada and the United States, was believed a century ago—for that matter, half a century ago, as witnessed by much of the evidence embodied in the Hudson Bay Report of 1857, and other public documents of the same period—to be incapable of cultivation. It was said to be a semi-arctic region, throughout which if you dug down a foot or two you came to perpetual frost.

Here, then, we have the beginnings of a settlement on the banks of the Red River, born at the very time Canadians and Americans were fighting, with or without adequate cause, at the other end of the Great Lakes; but we are as far as ever from establishing any influence that the one had upon the other. We know, indeed, that in 1816 Selkirk took out to his settlement a number of officers and soldiers of the disbanded de Meuron regiment, but the influence of these rather turbulent spirits was scarcely noticeable. They did not destroy the colony, and they certainly did not strengthen it. Eventually they moved south, making their homes in what later became the State of Minnesota.

We must, indeed, dig deeper if we are to find the real influence of the War of 1812 upon the settlement of the Canadian West; but first it will be convenient to note here the fact that in the same year that Lord Selkirk sent out his first colonists to Red River, and while they were still at York Factory, an expedition, sent out by John Jacob Astor, arrived at the mouth of the Columbia River, where they built Astoria. As the Selkirk Colony became the nucleus of the prairie provinces of Manitoba, Saskatchewan and Alberta, so out of Astoria, or perhaps rather because of Astoria, grew eventually the far western province of British Columbia.

Now to trace the connection between the War of 1812 and these nuclei of western settlements, or rather between the War of 1812 and the western settlements of which these infant communities were the nuclei. "The war," says Lucas, "was the national war of Canada. It did more than any other event or series of events could have done to reconcile the two rival races within Canada to each other. It was at once the supplement and the corrective of the American War of Independence. It did more than any other event could have done to demonstrate that colonial liberty and colonial patriotism did not leave the British Empire when the United States left it. The same spirit which had inspired and carried to success the American War of Independence was now enlisted on the side of Great Britain, and the successful defence of Canada by regiments from Great Britain and Canadian colonists combined, meant that a new British Empire was coming into being **pari passu** with the growth of a young nation within its limits. The War of 1812 determined that North America should not exclusively belong to the American Republic, that Great Britain should keep her place on the continent, but that she should keep it through this new community already on the high-road to legislative independence." So far as Canada is concerned, probably the most significant result of the War of 1812 was the immense stimulus it gave to the spirit of nationality throughout British North America. Canadians were fighting in defence of their homes; the imminence of the peril swamped all local jealousies; the war emphasized the need of union, if only as a measure of self-defence. Various causes delayed the event, but it is not difficult to trace a more or less direct connection between the War of 1812 and the union of the provinces in 1867. The confederation of the British North American provinces was but the culmination of a movement that had its birth in the War of 1812, and grew to maturity through the Rebellion of 1837; the Union of 1841, and the scheme for a Maritime Union that immediately preceded confederation.

Under the terms of the British North America Act provision was made for the admission of British Columbia, Rupert's Land, and the North-Western Territory. Steps were at once taken for the acquisition of the western country, but it was found necessary to buy out the rights of the Hudson's Bay Company. After prolonged negotiation, the Company finally agreed to accept £300,000, and in 1869 an act was passed for the temporary government of Rupert's Land and the Territories. The following year the new province of Manitoba was created, and in 1871 British Columbia was admitted, the terms of union providing among others things for the construction of a transcontinental railway.

These steps toward the rounding out of the new Dominion were the inevitable consequences of the Confederation movement, and had been contemplated years before Confederation itself became an accomplished fact. The records of the period, however, show clearly enough that the western country was admitted not because it was believed at the time to possess any very great value in itself, but rather because such far-sighted statesmen as Sir John Macdonald realized that it was absolutely necessary to the future welfare of Canada that her territory should extend from ocean to ocean. What the United States had failed to do in 1812, they might still accomplish in the seventies. With the Civil War off their hands, they were entering upon a period of western expansion. The new Western States were rapidly filling up; Alaska had been purchased from Russia; and, if Canada held back, it was quite within the realm of possibility that the United States might step in and absorb the prairie country between the Great Lakes and the mountains. That done, British Columbia would almost inevitably follow, and Canada would be confined to the Atlantic side of the continent. The ultimate destiny of such a Canada one would not care to predict. Certainly the fate of the country would be problematical. It could not hope to reach at any time the stature of a great nation. It must forever be overshadowed by its gigantic neighbour; and American statesmen might then indeed have had some ground for the belief that a few short years would see the peaceful accomplishment of what armed force had failed to do in 1812—the extension of American sovereignty over the whole continent of North America. Nevertheless it must not be forgotten that, while statesmen were directly responsible for bringing in the western provinces, they could not have acted without a widespread sentiment of expansion throughout Eastern Canada—and this sentiment was directly traceable to the influence of the War of 1812.

The project of a transcontinental railway, a vital link in the chain of Confederation, and in the settlement of Western Canada, had been discussed for many years, from every possible point of view. It had been advocated on economic, strategic, and national grounds; it had been pressed for by British Columbia as essential to the safety and welfare of the province, and by the settlers on the Red River as the only effective means of colonizing the western prairies. It was finally accepted by Canadian statesmen as a work absolutely essential to the expansion of the Dominion. One need not attempt to prove what is self-evident, that the building of the Canadian Pacific Railway was a work of supreme importance, to the west and to the east, to Canada and to the British Empire. It made possible the peopling of the western provinces;

it created a trade route between Eastern and Western Canada; it consolidated the Dominion; and it added materially to the strength of the Empire. To-day, when we have a second and a third transcontinental railway approaching completion, with the Hudson Bay route and the Georgian Bay Canal in contemplation, we find it hard to realize what the Canadian Pacific Railway meant to Canada, from the point of view of western settlement, and also from the wider point of view of national development. The following, from an American statesman, William Henry Seward, written when the Canadian Pacific was still a thing of the future, is not without interest at the present day, making allowances for a certain amount of exaggeration:

"British America," he says, "from a colonial dependency, would assume a controlling rank in the world. To her other nations would be tributary, and in vain would the United States attempt to be her rival, for she never could dispute with her the possession of the Asiatic commerce nor the power which that commerce confers."

The Toronto Globe, not usually much given to enthusiasm, had this to say in its issue of Feb. 3, 1871: "Our rulers will be traitors to their country and to British connection if they lose a single session in making it practicable and convenient for settlers to get to Fort Garry through our own territory, and in putting things in a fair way for the Canadian Pacific Railway. It is a question not merely of convenience but of national existence. It must be pushed through at whatever expense. We believe it can be pushed through not only without being a burden pecuniarily upon Canada, but with an absolute profit in every point of view. Without such a line a great British North America would turn out an unsubstantial dream; with it and with ordinary prudence and wisdom on the part of her statesmen, it will be a great, glorious and inevitable reality."

This, however, is getting rather outside my subject. To get back to the initial question, I have attempted to show—although it is nothing more than the mere skeleton of an argument—that the War of 1812 had a distinct influence upon the effective settlement of Western Canada; that out of that war grew a deep-rooted and ever-increasing spirit of Canadian nationality; that from that spirit proceeded the Confederation movement which culminated in the British North America Act of 1867; that as an essential feature of Confederation the western country was brought into the Dominion; and that with the admission of the western provinces came the project of a transcontinental railway—the final link in the chain of western settlement.

I have made no attempt to follow possible lines of influence on the American side, but it might be rather interesting to study the effect of the War of 1812 upon the settlement of the tier of northwestern States along the boundary, and the possible reaction, one way or the other, upon the development of our Northwest. In 1812 Michigan and Illinois only are represented in the population tables of the United States; Wisconsin does not appear until 1840; Minnesota until 1850; and North Dakota and Montana until 1870. Michigan increased from a population of 4,762 in 1810 to 8,896 in 1820; 31,639 in 1830; 212,267 in 1840; 397,654 in 1850; 749,113 in 1860. Illinois grew even more rapidly. She had 12,282 in 1810; 55,211 in 1820; 157,445 in 1830; 476,183 in 1840; 851,470 in 1850, and 1,711,951 in 1860. Wisconsin, starting with 30,945, in 1840, jumped to 305,391 in the next decade; and 775,881 in 1860. These three States could each boast of more than a million white inhabitants in 1870, Michigan having 1,184,059; Illinois, 2,539,891, and Wisconsin, 1,054,670. Minnesota, with 6,077 in 1850, had 172,023 in 1860, and 439,706 in 1870. North Dakota is credited with 2,405 white inhabitants in 1870; and Montana, 20,595.

The real growth of population on the Canadian side was of much later date. According to Dr. Bryce, the Red River settlers numbered in 1815 about 283. Alexander Ross, in his "Red River Settlement," gives the total population of the Colony in 1849 as 5391; and in 1855, about 6,500. A statistical account of the Red River Colony, included in the Hudson Bay Report of 1857, gives the population in 1849 as 5,291, and in 1856 as 6,523. The number of whites and half-breeds in the Hudson Bay Territories in 1856 is stated in the same Report to be about 11,000. J. J. Hargrave, in his "Red River," gives the population of Red River, including the Prairie Portage, in 1870, as about 12,800. This included whites and half-breeds, and also Indians within the boundaries of the Colony. Another authority gives the white population between Lake Superior and the Rocky Mountains, in 1871, as 12,225. In 1881, Manitoba and the Territories had a white population of 118,706; and in 1891—six years after the completion of the Canadian Pacific Railway—the population had increased to 260,573.

One other fascinating, though probably not very substantial, line of influence between the War of 1812 and the settlement of the Canadian West, is through the western fur-trade. There are several possible approaches to the question, and I shall only attempt to very briefly suggest a few of them. On general principles it may be assumed that the fur-trade was inimicable to settlement—or if you are a fur-trader, you may state the case the other way if you please. In any event, the perpetuation of the monopoly of the Hudson Bay Company, through the retention by Great Britain of the western territories north of 49 degrees, in the conclusion of peace, may be taken to have delayed for many decades the effective settlement of Rupert's Land. And yet, on the other hand, the Hudson Bay Company, in one way or another, had a great deal to do with the early settlement of Vancouver Island and British Columbia.

Another point: The Treaty of Ghent, in 1814, finally gave Grand Portage, and with it, the old route of the fur-traders, to the United States. The North West Company thenceforth were confined to the Kaministikwia route. Fort William became for a time the recognized headquarters of the fur-trade. Eventually there grew up at the mouth of the Kaministikwia the twin cities of Fort William and Port Arthur, destined to rival Duluth, and perhaps Chicago, as a mighty inland port, and a connecting link between Eastern Canada and the great west.

One more point: In 1816, when the animosity aroused by the war was still keen, John Jacob Astor secured the passage of an act of Congress restricting trade with the Indians south of 49 degrees to citizens of the United States. This measure was designed, in the language of an American writer, "to put the North West Company out of business on American territory." The North West people sold out to Astor and his associates of the American Fur Company, and confined their operations to the Canadian side of the boundary. The American Fur Company energetically pushed forward into the territory east and west of the Mississippi. Through their influence, military posts were established at Prairie du Chien, Fort Snelling, and elsewhere. Settlement rapidly followed on the American side, coming to a standstill when it reached the boundary line. Meanwhile, the North West Company, confined to British territory, found itself checked in every direction by the Hudson Bay Company. Relations became more and more strained, until finally the only solution was the union of the two companies in 1821. Thenceforward there was peace in the vast territories of the fur-trader. But what of the effect of all this on colonization? Did it tend to accelerate, or to retard, the settlement of Western Canada? I confess I am unable to say.

XI.

HISTORY OF THE HOSPITAL FOR THE INSANE (FORMERLY THE MILITARY AND NAVAL DEPOT), PENETANGUISHENE, ONT.

By G. A. MacCallum, M. D.

The Hospital for the Insane at Penetanguishene is beautifully situated in a locality of considerable historical interest. Perched on a hill, about one hundred and twenty-five feet above the level of the Penetanguishene Bay, which it overlooks, it is so situated as to give a lovely and extensive view of the sloping highlands on the opposite shore, and also of some of the islands out in the Georgian Bay.

Immediately in front of it is Magazine Island, a very pretty little island, on which is still the hewn log magazine, in which during the military occupation were kept the ammunition supplies. The workmanship of this little building is unique. It is built of beautifully hewn squared pine timber, and the joints at the corners have a sort of double dovetailing, the joints fitting perfectly. The roof was shingled with hand-made shingles, nailed on with hand-made nails. It is said that, at one time, this Island was connected with the mainland by a bridge, the one end being where the Hospital now has its dock and boathouse, and the other immediately in front of the magazine building, where indeed even yet, when the water is clear, may be seen the remains of a crib. The middle of the bridge was probably floating. Here, too, is sunken one of the British gunboats, the "Tecumseh," named after the great Indian chief. There are also three other gunboats sunken in this locality, one the "Nawash," named after another Indian chief, sunken near the shore south of the Hospital dock, while across the Bay, in what is known as Colborne's Bay, are sunken the "Tigress" and the "Scorpion."

The name Penetanguishene is, of course, Indian in its origin, and means "The Place of the White Rolling Sands," so named from a high bank of sand on Pinery Point to the right on entering the harbor. It is said to be Abenaki in its origin.

The Bay became first known to white men in 1615, when Champlain and his Frenchmen landed near its entrance and passed around the Bay,

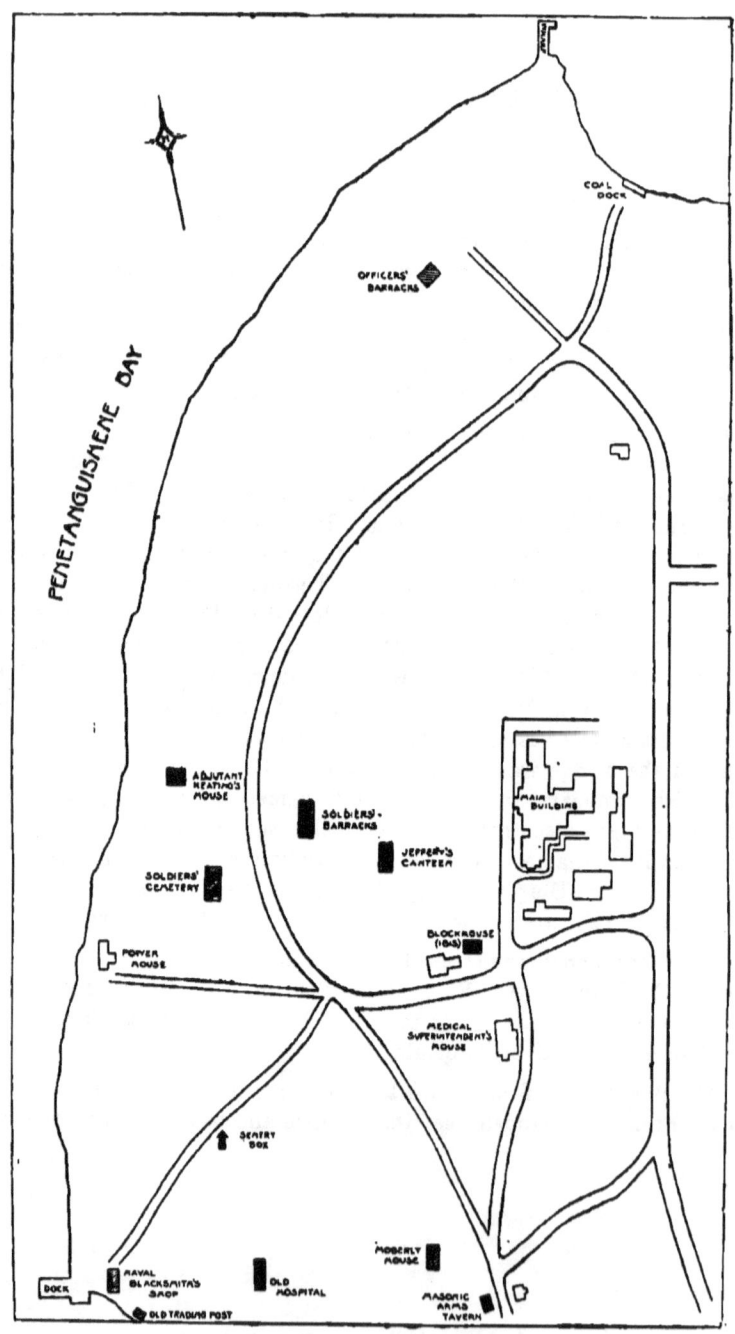

APPROXIMATE POSITIONS OF THE PRINCIPAL BUILDINGS, MILITARY AND NAVAL ESTABLISHMENT, PENETANGUISHENE.
(The buildings marked with hachures were those of the early Establishment.)

HISTORY OF HOSPITAL FOR INSANE, PENETANGUISHENE. 123

visiting many points on his way to the Narrows at Orillia, thence down the Trent Valley waterway to Lake Ontario. The exact spot where Champlain first landed is uncertain, but two places are decided upon, viz., at Ihonatiria, immediately across the Bay from the Hospital, in the small inlet called Colborne's Bay; and at Sawlog Bay, a short distance to the west of the entrance of the harbor.

The Bay was visited by Governor Simcoe in August of 1793, and selected by him as a military and naval base, and a survey of the harbor was completed by his Surveyor, General Aitkin, in November of the same year.

The Military Road from Kempenfeldt Bay to Penetanguishene was opened in November, 1814, and Colonel Poyntz completed another survey of the harbor in December of that year. Sir George or Colonel Head reached the Bay in February, 1815, having traversed the entire country from Halifax, across the Bay of Fundy, up the St. John River to the St. Lawrence, through Quebec, Montreal, Kingston, York and Holland Landing, on snowshoes, toboggans, canoes and horse jumpers, etc.; and built the first block house on the brow of the hill some two hundred yards above the Bay, near the site of the present stable at the back of the residence of the Medical Superintendent. It was 18x21 ft. in size, roofed and clapboarded with shingles cut from cedar trees along the shore in the vicinity of Gordon's Point.

The new Barracks was built near the shore, and later rebuilt in stone, the material in which was in turn transferred to the new building of the Ontario Reformatory, now the Asylum, in 1862-6.

Commander Roberts' establishment was built behind the new Barracks further up the hill; Lieutenant Jackson's, of the Royal Navy, still further up, and Admiral Bayfield's, R. N., a little further east and north along the shore. In the meantime the Naval Store, Hospital, Seaman's Barracks, Guard House, Sergeants' Mess, Shipwrights' Shop and Magazine on the Island, Clerk's Office, etc., were added, and later Adjutant or Captain Keating's dwelling, all of which, except the last, have long ago disappeared. (Since this was written, Adjt. Keating's dwelling was destroyed by fire.)

When the Barracks was rebuilt in stone, the Officers' Quarters (still standing) was built also in stone. The Drummond Island Garrison was transferred to this Post in 1828, and Adjutant Keating's house was built in 1829. The reduction of the Military and Naval Station began in 1832, until in 1849, when Captain Keating died, nearly everything had been disposed of. His house was occupied by Commander Wooten and other naval officers at various times, and during the existence of the Ontario Reformatory served as a Chaplain's residence until the new one was built. Rev. G. A. Anderson,* first Chaplain for the Reformatory, occupied it for many years, followed by Rev. Mr. Lloyd and Rev. Mr. Card.

In 1867, when Confederation took place, over five thousand acres of ordnance lands in the vicinity were transferred to the jurisdiction of the Ontario Government, after which many improvements were made, among these being various additions to the Main Building of the Reformatory, also a brick residence for the Warden, now occupied by the Medical Superintendent.

Much of the above information was obtained by Mr. A. C. Osborne from old residents, and he says there is but one person now living (1912) who remembers the location of the different old buildings mentioned above.

Rev. G. Hallen, recently deceased, was a Military Chaplain for many years, and lived in the Barracks until he built a rectory on his own place, which place was recently purchased by the Government.

The Naval and Military Canteen was known as "Jeffery's Canteen," and there was also a tavern known as "The Masonic Arms," a regular house of entertainment built by the proprietor, and licensed by the military authorities. This was situated immediately in front of the house now occupied by the Storekeeper on the brow of the hill, and among the notables who were at one time or another entertained there were the Duke of Richmond, Earl of Northumberland, Sir John Franklin, Sir John Colborne, Lord Morpeth, Captain Basil Hall, Sir John Galt, and other distinguished travellers.

The year 1815 is the date when Sir George Head, with a small body of soldiers, made his way from Quebec to this point. Their hardships may be imagined when one considers that the journey was made in February, on foot, when the snow must have been very deep, and when there was not a vestige of a road. The soldiers were obliged to clear a pathway ahead of the main body, so that it could make its way with the camping outfit and other necessary stores. Their progress must have been slow, and yet they finally reached Penetanguishene and camped where the buildings now stand. Log huts were first erected, where afterwards a fortress of some pretensions, with the necessary quarters and houses for the officers and men, were built, and to-day some

*See "Papers and Records," Vol. VI., Ontario Historical Society.

of these houses still remain. The Officers' quarters, a very substantial stone structure, with its walls pierced with vertical grooves or apertures for shooting through, and with Masonic emblems and workmen's initials inscribed on each block, is still in a good state of preservation. This, with the fortress, was surrounded by strong cedar palisades, which latter existed until removed three years ago, much to the regret of the lovers of the early history of our country. If the Government, with its local officials, had had a particle of interest in the early history of this portion of Canada, as they should have had, they would never have sanctioned the wanton destruction of such a fine specimen of early fortification as this post evidently was.

Up to 1907 this old fort was visited by many tourists and others interested in historical places, and even yet picnics of schools, etc., are held each season and the children and others instructed in the early history of the place, and the spots of interest pointed out. In 1907, however, those who had charge decided to clear away all traces of the stockaded enclosure for the sake of adding the bit of land it stood on to the surrounding field. It was probably one of the best, if not the best, remains of the stockaded fort in Canada. It consisted of an enclosed space with a path leading to the stone fortification. The stockades were cedar posts from 15 to 18 inches in diameter, sharpened at one end, and about 18 to 20 feet in length. These were sunk side by side in the ground about five or six feet and leaning outward, the sharpened end, of course, pointing upwards and outwards. Whether covered or not, originally, is unknown. The protected path allowed retreat to the safer stone structure.

The whole was in a fair state of preservation and was probably good to last for fifty years yet as far as the cedar stockades were concerned. The stone structure is, of course, permanent, being a single storey building, beautifully built of hewn stone. There was no reason whatever for destroying the fort, for the Institution has nine hundred acres surrounding it.

Across the Bay, and situated a little back from Colborne's Bay, and on each side of a small spring creek, is the site of a large Indian town, said by most of the students of the early history of the place to have been Ihonatiria, the town where Father Brebeuf, early in the seventeenth century, first landed and introduced the Jesuit mission for the conversion of the Hurons, which finally ended so disastrously for themselves. These were the Hurons who were finally almost exterminated by the Iroquois.

The empty houses and other buildings which were left here by the military when they were withdrawn, led to the idea of establishing a penal settlement here, consequently in 1859 a Reformatory Prison was located here by the Cartier-Macdonald Government, in which administration Sir John A. Macdonald was Attorney General West. He took a good deal of interest in the establishment of the Reformatory, and appointed Mr. Kelly of Kingston the first Warden. Mr. Angus Morrison, being the member for the North Riding of Simcoe, was the chief actor in this movement.

The large barracks erected here by the Home Government seemed a suitable building to start with, and the several vacant houses were very suitable for the necessary staff of officers and the heads of the different trades to be introduced.

Mr., or as he was commonly called, Captain William Moore Kelly was appointed the first Warden, and occupied the stone house formerly used as the Officers' Quarters. Rev. Mr. Hallen, late Chaplain to the Military, was appointed Protestant Chaplain, and occupied a log residence where the present Superintendent's residence now stands. Father Kennedy was appointed Roman Catholic Chaplain, and occupied a residence near the barracks. The bursar was Mr. Featherstonhaugh, and he occupied the residence now occupied by the painter. The old log houses which were then occupied by the tradesmen have gradually disappeared, and neat frame houses have taken their place.

The place was first opened in 1859 under the name of a Reformatory for Boys, under Captain William Moore Kelly, and the first inmates were brought here by boat by Mr. Kelly and two guards from the Penitentiary or Prison of Isle au Noix, Quebec. These, of course, were many of them grown up, and from twenty to twenty-five years of age. They were at first housed in the old Barracks, where they must have been kept until about March, 1870, when part of the present building having been built, and the Barracks burned, they were placed in the new building. This was a hewn stone structure, built of limestone obtained from the adjoining islands, and brick made by the prisoners under Mr. James Berry. The first wing built was the part now occupied by the kitchen, the old bakery, and the attendants', nurses', and patients' dining rooms. This building was arranged with three tiers of cells, sufficient to accommodate one hundred and two prisoners. The prisoners were occupied with several industries. First, a cigar factory was started; also a machine shop, and a small laundry was built. After a time the cigar factory was not satisfactory and was abolished, and a match fac-

HISTORY OF HOSPITAL FOR INSANE, PENETANGUISHENE.

tory was started instead, but this too was soon abandoned, and the manufacture of shoes, furniture, broom handles, etc., all tried, to end in the same way.

The cell system was changed and a new wing was added and the dormitory system started. After about twenty-five years of this condition of things under Mr. Thomas McCrosson, who was appointed as successor to Captain Kelly about 1879, the place was changed to a Hospital for Insane on August 14th, 1904, and Dr. P. H. Spohn appointed Superintendent, with Mr. Ronan as Bursar. The insane patients were drafted from other asylumns and came first on August 16th, 1904. They were supposed to be all quiet cottage patients and good workers, capable of taking care of themselves to a great extent, and able to do the necessary work of the Institution, but gradually some acute cases were admitted. Dr. P. H. Spohn resigned, and Dr. G. A. McCallum, formerly of London Asylum, was transferred to this Asylum on January 20th, 1908.

Mr. Ronan, who was Bursar, was transferred to Woodstock Epileptic Asylum, and H. J. Spence appointed here in his stead on March 10th, 1906. James Lonergan resigned as Storekeeper in May, 1908, and he was succeeded by Mr. Charles E. C. Newton. Dr. Cattermole was appointed Assistant Physician early in 1908. Dr. MacCallum resigned in June, 1910, and was succeeded by Dr. W. T. Wilson in October, 1910.

One cannot close this short story of such an interesting historic locality without urging that the Government should devote a small sum for the erection of more or less permanent tablets on some of the more important sites mentioned here, for the use of students in the future, and for the interest of others visiting the locality. The writer has had a roof put on the Magazine on the Island which will preserve it for a number of years yet.

Note.—Through the kindness of Mr. A. C. Osborne I am permitted to make use of his historical notes and researches, which have been obtained during years of study of this subject, and through him I am able to append a map of the approximate sites of the principal buildings of the early settlement when it was a military and naval station.

New York, Oct. 1, 1912.

XII.

THE HISTORY OF THE AMERICAN INDIANS IN RELATION TO HEALTH.

By Peter H. Bryce, M. A., M. D., Ottawa

Like much else that we desire to obtain exact information about in the history of the Indians we find that any statements relating to their health during the period since 1600, when they may be said to have come first into constant relation with Europeans, are almost wholly accidental, and wherever made were by writers, whether as travellers or officials, whose knowledge of diseases and their treatment was naturally imperfect.

But, we must further realize the still more important fact that until at least 1800, the knowledge of medicine in civilized countries was in the matter of causation extremely imperfect, and, viewed from our modern standpoint, the treatment of disease was largely empirical and unscientific.

In Schoolcraft's History of the Indian Tribes may be found an article prefaced by Dr. Zina Pitcher, M. D., late of the United States Army, dated at Detroit, 1853, as a Report for the National Medical Association on Medical Education (Part IV., P. 500), which summarizes more exactly than that of any other writer, so far as I have found, the information then possessed regarding the Indian's knowledge of diseases and their treatment. Introducing his subject he says:

"The aim is to show that he (the Indian) has used faculties as discriminating and arrived at results equally as important and correct as those achieved by his more fortunate neighbours in a far different state of civil advancement .... In the primitive condition of a people who abide in the open air, whose tissue is hardened by exposure over the pursuits which develop therefrom—we find causes for their comparative immunity from disease and reasons for their manifestation of an inherited strong recuperative power."

He further points out how the complexities of the occupations of

HISTORY OF AMERICAN INDIANS IN RELATION TO HEALTH. 129

civilized life develop special diseases and that therefore most of the organic affections are peculiar to the civilized. "The simplest functional diseases are those to which the Indian is liable." To the treatment of these he has a materia medica and sytem of therapeutics, as will be seen in the sequel, very well adapted.

It will be remembered, however, that Dr. Pitcher wrote in the first half of the nineteenth century, after the Indian had been in touch with Europeans in Eastern America for some centuries, and to appreciate the real position of the Indian in relation to diseases and their treatment we must endeavour to obtain information from the earliest periods at which the European writers came into contact with him and referred to such matters.

Various references are found to such in the Jesuit Relations. For instance, in Vol. I., p. 211 (Cleveland Edition), we find the following:

"They believe there are two main sources of disease, one of these in the patient himself, which desires something and will vex the body of the sick man until it possesses the thing required. They think there are in every man inborn desires often unknown to themselves upon which the happiness of the individual depends. For the purpose of ascertaining the desires and innate appetites of this character, they summon soothsayers, who, as they think have a divinely imparted power to look into the inmost recesses of the mind. These men declare whatever first comes to them, or something, from which they suspect some gain is to be derived, is desired by the sick person."

"Therefore parents, friends and relatives, do not hesitate to procure and lavish upon him, whatever it may be, however expensive, a return of which is never thereafter sought. Commonly the sick recover plainly because their illnesses are slight, for in the case of more severe complaints these soothsayers are more cautious, and denying the possibility of ascertaining what the patient desires they bewail him whom they have given up and cause the relatives to put him out of the way."

It is further stated that they were accustomed to kill those suffering from protracted and chronic illness, as well as orphaned infants.

Probably, however, the following instances taken from the somewhat too philosophical hypothesis above given, more exactly illustrate the average attitude of the Indian in his aboriginal state toward disease. It is told how Father Biard visited Membertou, the famous Micmac chief, spoken of in Lescarbot's "History of New France" in connection with M. de Mont's settlement at Port Royal, Nova Scotia, on account of the dangerous illness of his son. Biard was surprised that there was no grief, no lamentation, no tearful dirge, instead of a feast, a dance and two or three dogs fastened together. Asked what all this meant Membertou said the boy would die in a short time. Biard censured them and sent the boy to French headquarters where he recovered.

A similar illustration taken from the narratives of the Pilgrim Fathers may be further quoted as confirming from another source the prevailing practices of the Indians of the East Coast. Mr. Edward Winslow relates the following incident which took place in March, 1622. Word coming to Plymouth that Massassoit, chief of the friendly Massachusetts band, was very ill, Winslow was deputed by the Governor to visit him and shew their sympathy. He says: "When we came to the house it was so full of men that we could scarcely get in, though they used their best endeavours to make room for us. We found them in the midst of their charms for him, making such a noise as greatly affected those of us who were well, and therefore was not likely to benefit him who was sick. About him were six or eight women who chafed his limbs to keep heat in him."

Mr. Winslow then told the chief, who could not see him, that the Governor had heard of his sickness and had sent him and he had brought such things as might do him good. "The chief took his preparation of conserves and seemed satisfied and in half an hour seemed better. The next day they went out to seek herbs, but could find none but strawberry leaves. He took a handful of them with some sassafras root and put them in the porridge. It being boiled, I strained it through my handkerchief and gave him at least a pint, which he liked very well. After this his sight mended more and more and he took some rest." Massassoit recovered and urged Winslow to go from house to house and visit those who were sick within the village and to treat them as he had the chief.

The writer who quoted this incident tells further how in 1622 the people were in great distress for scant rain, and a day of prayer was set apart. "An Indian taking notice that during the former part of the day there was a very clear sunshine and that in the evening the rain fell in a sweet soaking shower was so much affected with the power the English had with their God that he resolved from that day not to rest till he knew this great God." To this end he forsook the Indians and clung to the English. Alongside of these two distinct statements it is of interest to quote from a series of articles just published in a London newspaper of the 13,750 mile journey from Brazil to Peru, through hitherto undiscovered territory, by A. Henry Savage Landor. He tells of how the Barrieros, whom he met, were the first Indians of the Boro tribe.

"The Bororos preceded Darwin in his theory on the evolution of man. Only the Bororos do not say that men or women are the descendants of monkeys. They maintained that monkeys once upon a time were human, were able to speak and lived in huts like human beings."

"These Bororos believe in living spirits; some of them may inhabit the earth; others are invisible. The invisible ones are invoked by them through a special individual called the bireh or medicine man shouting at the top of his voice while gazing skyward and offering gifts of food, meat, fish and fruit to the spirit invoked. The bireh eventually pretends that the spirit has entered his body and he then begins to devour the food himself in order not to offend the spirit of his internal guest."

We have had in these several extracts examples which indicate clearly what the Indian peoples of this continent thought, where uninfluenced by the European, whether three hundred years ago or to-day. That there has been amongst all peoples in every period of the world's history a close relationship between the mysterious influences which affect the body and the mind is common knowledge; and that the thaumaturgist, the wonder worker, has commonly been of the priestly class, whose superior attainments, actual or pretended, have enabled him to exercise, whether as the disciples of the Egyptian god Thoth (Hermes), of Aesculapius in Greece, the priests and prophets of the Old Testament, the priests of the Middle Ages, or the medicine men of the aborigines of America, is equally well understood. That the status of medical practice from earliest to modern times had been, however, one of the most exact measures of social advancement and mental development amongst any people has been curiously illustrated by some notable recent discoveries, both Babylonian and Egyptian.

The Code of Hammurabi, B. C. 2250, discovered at Susa in 1901, gives in a series of 282 clauses a marvellous account of a social state, wherein the King, decreed ruler of the earth by the power of the god Bel, set forth laws regulating almost every conceivable matter, from land laws to medical practice.

Thus he decreed that "if a physician make a successful operation over the eye and saves the eye he shall receive two shekels; but if he make a large incision with the operating knife and kill the patient, he shall have his hands cut off." It will be remembered too that Ebers tells how the papyrus, discovered by and named after him, and written in the 16th century, B. C., in 100 pages, contains the hermetic or sealed book, giving a list of the medical remedies of the old Egyptians. Later in the scroll, diagnoses are drawn up and remedies prescribed for the external and internal diseases affecting the parts of the human body. The numbers referring to the weights and measures are attached to each drug. The prescriptions are accompanied by texts which the physician is to repeat while making the medicine and while administering to his patient. One long chapter is devoted to the optic nerve alone.

But lest we should imagine that the incantations mark an early period we need only recall the fashion in which the sympathetic treatment of wounds by a touch from the weapon which did the cutting was a fad introduced by Sir Kenelm Digby, Knight of Montpelier, in Elizabeth's time; (he stated he had received the prescription from a friar from Persia); or the incantations while mixing the brew in the witches' cauldron in Macbeth, or Soliman's Septasium published in the same period in which he arranges his chapters under the seven heads of Birds, Beasts, Herbs, Man, Fishes, Serpents and Insects, in order to comprehend how even in the period of the literature called "Golden Age," Medicine was empirical, and at its best associated with the mysterious. This was inevitable so long as the idea of sickness, being an evidence of either the anger of God or of the malevolence of demons, dominated human thought. We need not then greatly criticize the poor Indian, a savage in the sense that he inhabited illimitable areas of woodland and prairie, and had usually no settled abode and indeed but little use for medicine, for his superstitions, when so late as 1695 Culpepper's Physick and Astrology commends as a valuable remedy "The skull of a man that has never been buried, beaten to a powder and given inwardly, the quantity a dram at a time in water for palsy and falling sickness," and when Sir James Y. Simpson, the great Scotch surgeon, the discoverer of the use of chloroform, as stated by his daughter in her biography, tells of how his father, David Simpson, was very superstitious, and told them stories of warlocks and bogies. Sir James' favourite story was of how his father's father had buried a cow alive. When he failed to heal his four-legged patients he concluded the witches were interfering with him by counteracting his remedies and so they had to be exorcised. A murrain fell on the cattle about Torphichen, and Alexander Simpson, the old veterinarian, was unable to save them. He decided therefore that to frustrate the malignant designs of the spirits of evil a cow must be interred alive, and interred it was.

But enough has been quoted from different sources to show that in no sense could it be expected that any notable knowledge of medicine as we understand it to-day would be possessed by the Indian peoples beyond what has existed amongst peoples in the pre-scientific age in all periods of the world's history. It is, however, by no means to be supposed, in contact constantly with Nature as they were, that they had not empirically discovered the uses of a very considerable number of plants, which grew about them. As a matter of fact their knowledge is comparable, and its application probably as practical, as that illustrated in Culpepper's Physic.

Dr. Pitcher gives the names of some 53 herbs and the diseases for which they were used by the Indians.

He speaks of the general use by them, as by so many early peoples, of the sweat bath. Curiously the mode of making it, by putting hot stones in a hole in a small tent, or closed-in hut, and then creating steam by throwing water on it, has almost everywhere been the same.

The actual methods adopted in different diseases by the Indians are indicated by Dr. Pitcher. For instance, they began the treatment of fevers with an emetic using commonly the common Euphorbia; while for a cathartic, they used the cambium layer of the bark of the horse-chestnut or butternut. They practised venesection in pleurisy by a sharp piece of flint driven into the vein: but I am inclined to think this was the practice copied from the whites.

In the case of consumption, Dr. Pitcher tells us that they attempted its cure by promoting a free flow of pus by using the bark of the slippery elm and of the mallow.

For asthma they smoked especially tobacco, while for liver complaint they used the leaves of arbutus or the root of the wild gooseberry, and so on through other diseases. As may well be supposed, however, so favorable were nomadic habits to their maintenance of good health and to minimizing the danger of spreading the contagion that the Indian people were helpless, as indeed white people were, in large degree, in the face of such a disease as small-pox or measles if once introduced. How helpless even white people were is illustrated by the record of the Massachusetts colonists when in 1731 a disease, evidently diphtheria, within a few months destroyed in seven towns, one-quarter of the population under 11 years of age.

Old Canada had had her Indian problem and solved it in so far as having had a Superintendent General of Indian Affairs, who was supposed to protect the Indian in his legal rights, encourage missionary effort amongst the bands, in so far as at least establishing schools was concerned, and appointing local physicians at nominal salaries to treat any Indians who were sent to them by the Indian Agent.

Whenever, however, we speak about Preventive medicine in relation to the Indian at or before that date, we have to endeavour to comprehend what the term meant in any ordinary white community amongst us at that period. Many will be surprised to know that the outcome of years of agitation, discussion and legislation, which gave us Confederation in Canada and the B. N. A. Act, resulted in a series of Statutes in which the powers and duties of Federal and Provincial Governments were defined with much breadth and precision, and yet which do not contain a single syllable relating to what we now call Public Health or State Medicine. Hospitals, Refuges, Asylums and Quarantine were dealt with; but the idea of preventive medicine did not really take concrete shape in Canada until 1882, when Ontario passed an Act to appoint a Provincial Board of Health with a permanent Secretary.

It would not be quite correct to conclude, however, that no sanitation was inculcated amongst the Indians. Circulars were from time to time sent to the Indian Agents regarding the necessity for cleaning up premises, limewashing houses and for the regular vaccination of the children. The fatal outbreaks of smallpox had indelibly impressed upon the Indians the necessity for protection, while the value of vaccination was never doubted, in this showing well in accepting scientific medicine as compared with many white people more pretentious of knowledge.

When it is remembered, however, that except smallpox no knowledge either as to the cause or immunization against disease existed, that it was only in 1881 that the dictum **omne vivum ex vivo** or **omne ovum ex ovo** was enunciated by Louis Pasteur as demonstrated in anthrax and chicken cholera and accepted in England when he was the official guest of the Medical Congress Meeting in London, while antiseptic surgery had not yet been introduced into Canada, we need not wonder that the principles of Preventive Medicine were unknown in their practical application amongst our Indians, who as I remember complained that the standard laxative mixture kept in the large bottle of the Indian Medical Office on the Six Nations Reserve was too generously prescribed. As a matter of fact the therapeutics of Medicine in 1881 was still essentially that of the days of empirical Medicine and possessed very few drugs whose action was based upon an experimental basis.

We have through an irregular chronology followed Medicine as it existed amongst the Indians up to 1882, which makes for myself a notable Hegira. This year saw as I have said its official crowning. It is made glorious by Pasteur's triumph and by the further fact that, in April, Robert Koch gave to Germany and the world the first account of his experiments, both laboratory and clinical, which described the discovery of the Bacillus Tuberculosis, which, doubted for years, has now become universally recognized as the cause of that disease, which has been the scourge for thousands of years of the human race, wherever forced to live in closed habitations in temperate and cold climates, and which has done much to decimate the Indian tribes wherever brought into fixed habitations on reserves or around the towns and villages of white settlements. I have examined the oldest official documents and reports in the Department and have noted the statements of early explorers, and, beyond reporting the general health conditions annually, and noting any special contagious outbreak or disease, there is no evidence whatever that any notable effort had been made in either the United States or Canada to investigate the actual health conditions of the Indian people, or any serious idea that it was either worth while or possible to attempt to adopt broad and comprehensive measures for the betterment of their general health conditions.

Every writer, even the most sympathetic, during the past century spoke of them as a dying and vanishing race, unable to withstand the temptations or antidote the degenerating influences of a modern society, whose manners and customs were foreign to their daily habits of life and the traditions of their race. Their's was the story of a proud race, who had recognized the hopelessness of the resistance in the unequal struggle to the force of what is called civilization and progress.

In the introduction by Mr. A. C. Parker to the code of Handsome Lake, the Seneca Prophet, recently published by the New York State Museum, the situation is well set forth. Speaking of the influence of Handsome Lake's teachings, Parker says:

"The encroachments of civilization had demoralized the old order of things. The frauds which the Six Nations had suffered and the loss of land and of ancient seats have reduced them to poverty and disheartened them. Poverty, the sting of defeat, the loss of ancestral lands, the injuries of broken promises and the hostility of the white settlers all conspired to bring despair. There is not much energy in a despairing nation, who see themselves helpless and alone, the greedy eyes of their conquerors fastened on the few acres that remain to them. It was little wonder that the Indian sought forgetfulness of the past in the trader's rum."

It is not without interest to note that in the long message which the prophet Handsome Lake left in his code of life I have found no reference to matters of physical health except in the bringing to life of the sick man Ganiodaio by the touching of Taawonyos.

It is now some thirty years since we in Canada have officially undertaken to deal with the undeveloped work of public sanitation. Individualism, in dealing with health, was inevitable so long as there were no underlying well understood principles of action to guide the energies of Public Bodies, whether provincial or municipal, and least of all was such to be expected in dealing with the Indian peoples who were either settled in their small reserves in the older provinces, or only being brought into areas set apart in the almost unoccupied and boundless prairies of the West. The western bands were still largely nomadic, were far from centres where they could be dealt with in any way other than largely by moral suasion; and the task of keeping these bands peaceable by supplying them with rations fully occupied the energies of the Indian Department, which was well content if by any means they could get in supplies of food adequate to supply the needs of the people, who had seen their natural food supply (the buffalo) diminish year by year. Indeed it is not ten years since, on a large number of reserves, the distribution of rations was a regular practice; nor was it until railways were being constructed and settlement began to surround the various reserves that any serious attempts at cultivation of reserve lands were made.

During all those years the log-hut, too commonly of one room,, was the extent to which the activities of the Department for housing the Indians extended; while the work of education, except so far as carried on in the schools of the various Christian Missions, did not begin until provision was made in 1884 for six Industrial schools. Since then these schools have been supplemented by a goodly number of boarding schools, situated commonly on or near different reserves, which are all under church management, but supplemented by Government grants and supplied with the medical services of physicians paid for by the Department.

The pupils at first were in large degree orphans and sickly children whose care in the Indian camps was deemed a burden, and it was not surprising in view of all the facts that these pupils should have proved only too liable to develop that tuberculosis, which from the placing of the Indians in the houses on the Reservations had spread with remarkable rapidity amongst a hitherto nomadic people, who had as yet no knowledge of the art of living in houses.

The results of a systematic investigation of the schools of the prairie provinces by myself in 1907, showed that they had commonly begun in small buildings, which soon became overcrowded, and few of which had any claims to sanitary construction, were veritable hot-beds of tuberculosis. Indeed, a statistical enquiry into a number of schools from their establishment to that time, a period of some fifteen years, brought out the fact that from 25% to 33% of all the children who had been pupils during the period had died, almost all from tuberculosis, or from measles, or other acute diseases causing the tubercular infection present to develop a fatal termination. As regarded the mortality on the reserves, instances were even found where a mortality rate of 50 or 60, and even more per 1000 in whole bands occurred annually, and the question of how to attack such a discouraging problem became a dominating one.

It will be understood that in almost no case was a medical officer paid for devoting all his time to any band. He was paid only for treating such individuals as applied to him for aid, but almost no facilities such as hospitals for dealing with infection existed. The following two pictures taken from reports by careful observers in two American bands exactly describe what has been too generally the condition of bands whose health has been accurately investigated.

Dr. Jas. R. Walker, resident physician for many years in the U. S. Pine Ridge Agency in Dakota, says:

"The population of the band of full-blooded Sioux was 4,870, regarding whom exact sanitary and vital statistics were kept for ten years. The paper states: 'Tuberculosis among these Indians does not differ in any respect from tuberculosis amongst the white people. The infecting material is the same and is produced and disseminated in the same way; individuals are affected in the same manner and the disease runs the same course, produces the same results and is subject to the same measures, remedial or preventive, as it is among the white people. It does not show any special affinity for the Indian nor affect him under any condition in which it could not affect the white man. There is no inherent peculiarity which renders him more liable to infection from the tuberculosis than is a white man under like circumstances.' After indicating the size of children, their growth and size at maturity, the paper states: 'In person, the Indian is as well adapted to fulfil the requirements of a healthy life as is the white. Yet a much larger proportion of these Indians than of the white people are infected with tuberculosis. This must be the result of external conditions that do not especially pertain to the Indian. . . . . Tuberculosis existed among these Indians before they came into contact with the white people, but at that time the disease was rare among them and remained so until they changed their nomadic to a settled life in houses. When they began to live in houses, tuberculosis began to increase among them, so that the conditions that caused their increase must have been different from those surrounding them when they lived in tepees. They were filthy, both when they lived in tepees and when they lived in houses. It was statistically demonstrated that those who were the most cleanly were the less susceptible to infection by any disease than those who were the most filthy, and conversely, that the most filthy were the most susceptible to infection of every kind. But there is no evidence that this filth ever caused tuberculosis except when it was mingled with the specific germs of the disease.'

When they began to live in houses, the Government supplied them with an abundance of food and in a much greater variety than they had been accustomed to. It also supplied them with cooking stoves and utensils, so that their food was better cooked than when they lived in tepees. Coincident with this increase of food prepared and taken in a more sanitary way was the increase of tuberculosis amongst them."

Again, Dr. Huber, speaking of the Indians in the Cattaraugus reserves in New York State, says: "It is Dr. Lake's opinion that 'young men and women, who perhaps a few months before were apparently in good health, come to the dispensary with some indefinite complaint, which, upon examination, he found to be pulmonary consumption. Whole families die of this disease within a few years.' Dr. Lake states that he finds the chronic affections from which the Indians on this reservation suffer to be very largely of a tuberculous character. He would, he states, 'divide the whole population into two classes, viz., those manifesting tuberculosis on examination, and those who have suffered from tuberculosis as evidenced by the scars and deformities which they exhibit.' The history is common of large families in which but one or two children have survived, the others having died of consumption; and in the survivors' scars remaining from an old gland, tuberculosis is to be observed. 'From babyhood are these Indians tubercular; one among every three children born on this reservation dies of this disease in some form before its fifth year; many children appear at school with glandular enlargements. There is slow progress of the desease until puberty, when a ghastly mortality supervenes, especially among the females.' "

Both in the United States and Canada the deadening effects of a century of official control, following a well-defined routine, have made the attempt to introduce modern scientific methods, in dealing with the health of the Indian, extremely difficult. Every annual report for years has contained the statement, repeated ad nauseam, of Indian Agents, that the health of the band has been good, fair or average for the year; but the report very commonly also made reference to the prevalent diseases, consumption and specific disease, as being the scourges which mean the final extinction of the race. A system of statistics was organized by myself in 1904, and to my surprise it soon became apparent that, excepting tuberculosis, the Indian people were and are remarkably free from other constitutional diseases. Maladies, as dyspepsia, incident to poorly cooked food and irregular habits, were of course common; but it soon became evident that if any adequate measures could be devised for dealing with this house disease, a disease of overcrowding and poor sanitation, there were no reasons why the marvellous results being obtained amongst the poor populations of the crowded cities of Europe and of America, lessening the death rate from tuberculosis, should not similarly follow if adopted on the Indian reserves. There, as elsewhere, where it has become apparent that the prevalence or absence of tuberculosis is the most delicate index possible of the social plane upon which any community lives, it has been shown conclusively that tuberculosis is not hereditary even though there may be a hereditary constitutional debility making the children of tuberculous families less resistant, while examples everywhere illustrate that those who may have the tendency overcome it by developing a resistance under good sanitary surroundings, which include free air and abundant food. .

The same is shown to be true amongst the Indian bands. Succeeding reports for several years have given no deaths due to consumption in some small bands, while others, as the Six Nations at Brantford, show the steady lessening of the annual death rate per 1000, with the falling death rate from tuberculosis, to be but the expression of a steady industrial progress and social advancement.

Six Nations Statistics.

Table.

	Population.	Deaths per 1000.	Births.
1906-7	4,286	18.2	29.2
1907-8	4,236	30.6	20.5
1908-9	4,275	11.9	26.4
1909-10	4,402	19.9	45.2
1910-11	4,466	14.8	25.3
1911-12	4,510	17.0	23.9
1912-13	4,564	12.9	25.4

For four years past there has existed a tent hospital on this reserve to deal especially with tubercular disease. During winter it frequently had twelve patients at one time, and while it was found as elsewhere difficult to get cases into hospital early in the disease and equally difficult to keep them long enough to insure a cure, yet the educational results as well as the directly curative effects have been very satisfactory.

With this there has been a steady improvement in housekeeping and in the management and care of infants. There is still everywhere in the Indian bands an excessive infant mortality; but that its reduction depends upon a steady improvement in general intelligence and knowledge of the social habits of advanced society is proven by the following illustration: The plan for the File Hills Colony was the outcome of the efforts of Inspector W. M. Graham, who resides on the Reservation in Saskatchewan. In 1900 he obtained, after persistent efforts, permission to survey a portion of the Reserve into 160 acre lots and place on neighbouring homesteads young men from two neighbouring Indian Schools. The experiment started with five boys of eighteen years, taken direct from the schools in 1900, and Mr. Graham's letter to me of August 8, 1913, supplies the following statistics to date:

Statistical Return, File Hills Colony, May 31st, 1913.

40 male members joined, 9 died, 2 migrated, leaving 29
24 wives   2 died   leaving 22
82 children   23 died, 1 married,   leaving 58

                            Total members of Colony   109

Religion of	man	woman	children	Total
Presbyterian	8	5	14	27
Anglican	2	2	8	12
Methodist	3	2	5	10
R. Catholic	16	13	31	60
	29	22	58	109

The results are remarkable. In all there have been 24 married families and their average married life is about six years. One married member of the band with three children was admitted; but apart from this I understand all other children were born in the Colony. This would mean, without any deaths in parents, 144 married years yielding 85 children, or one in every 1.7 years for each marriage.

Still more remarkable is the fact that with a population which practically doubled itself within six years, there was, nevertheless, with the remarkable birth rate, an infant mortality of about 80 in 1000 or almost lower than any infant mortality rate in the world.

When it is stated that this Colony was started and maintained on an allowance of only $100.00 per boy for implements and that the Colony has produced for several years nearly 100,000 bushels of wheat annually, with other grain, cattle, etc., the success of the Colony and the natural capacity of the Indian to become an honourable member of the body-politic of Canada, have been proven beyond question. The statistics illustrate a clinical fact which perhaps will not fully appeal to those who are not physicians, viz.: That while every male death was, I believe, caused by tuberculosis contracted as a child at school, the fact of the remarkable immunity of the children, owing, undoubtedly, to the fact of only two mothers having died, and one of these certainly not from tuberculosis, will in the future be cited as a classical proof of what we now know to be true, **that tuberculosis is not hereditary**, and that born of a healthy mother the child has a first-class guarantee with good environment of growing into a strong man or woman.

Another remarkable biological fact is that of males and females in something like equal numbers taken from school at 18 years the child-bearing women have almost all lived, while 9 men, engaged wholly in outdoor occupations, have died.

But I might prolong this essay indefinitely. I trust it may have been of some use in illustrating the problem nearest to me: that of **the future history of the Indians of Canada**. They are not a dead, nor a decaying race in the twentieth century; but the future progress of the aborigines of the American Continent will add another laurel to the achievements of medical science and of a modern humanitarian Christianity, not to be contented with the theological ritual which ensured the Indians a safe entrance to the Christian's Happy Hunting Ground hereafter, but rather to be satisfied only when seeing the once noble Redman a friendly participator in the highest physical, educational, social and spiritual advancements which mark the evolution, and are the glory, of our modern civilization.

XIII.

FEUDALISM IN UPPER CANADA, 1823-1843.

By Miss Marjorie J. F. Fraser, Toronto

The comparatively recent investigations of Dr. C. C. James, A. R. Carman, and A. F. Hunter, M. A., of the origins, and geographical distribution of the various Old World nationalities commingling in the population of Ontario suggest as a subject, suitable in this contest, and fascinating in itself, the story of the Settlement of the Township of McNab, in the County of Renfrew—a story at once unique and important. Although the early settlement of Upper Canada, as a whole, even prior to 1792, when the Province was first separately organized, and subsequent to that date, turned on well-defined regulations*, yet there were exceptions to the general rule, as in the arrangements with Colonel Talbot, and others. The settlement of the Township of McNab, therefore, is singular, and exceptional, not because of the agreement entered into with the promoter of its colonization, but of the manner in which the promoter sought to evade the agreement, and had nearly succeeded in fastening the fangs of an expiring feudalism on an infant community in Canada.

It was in 1823 that a gentleman, from the Highlands of Scotland, presented himself at the town of York, to Sir Peregrine Maitland, the Lieutenant Governor of Upper Canada, and to the members of the Executive Council of the Government, with a request that he be permitted to settle an unoccupied Township with loyal clansmen and fellow-countrymen from Scotland. Archibald McNab, Chief of the ancient Clan McNab, for it was he who preferred this request, was, at that time, in the prime of life. Tall of stature, stately and handsome, of courtly and polite manners, modelled on the French code during a residence of many years in France, social and lavish among his compeers, he made a distinctly favorable impression on the members of the Government, as unpublished but available letters, in this episode, show. The personal factor is rarely unimportant. It is mentioned here, as without the good opinion formed

---

*British Government's Instructions to Governors General; and Instructions to Surveyors General by Governors General-in-Council.

In the History Essay Competition of the Ont. Historical Society of 1913, this paper was awarded first prize.

of McNab, at the outset of his negotiations, his subsequent success in deluding the Government would have been very doubtful. On McNab's arrival in Upper Canada, he visited that shrewd and kindly Scot, Bishop Alexander Macdonell. From him he first received the suggestion of settling a Township, and good advice as to the **modus operandi**. A draft of the plan, so influentially endorsed, was submitted by McNab to the Lieutenant Governor who sent a copy of it to Earl Bathurst, Secretary of State, and to the Executive Council at Toronto, for advice. The subject was not hastily disposed of, and McNab was requested to furnish properly set-forth details of the conditions of settlement in so far as he, as promoter, on the one hand, and the individual settlers, on the other, were concerned. A tolerably clear statement of conditions* (unpublished) were, accordingly, submitted, the gist of which is:

1. That The McNab obtain for settlement an unsurveyed Township on the Ottawa River, free of fees, each lot to consist of 100 acres (Crown and Clergy Reserves excepted).

2. That on arrival of the immigrants and their securing certificates of location from McNab, they be entitled to patents for their lots.

3. That a specific agreement be entered into between McNab and the intending settlers before leaving Scotland containing details of the terms of settlement, so that no misunderstanding could afterwards arise. McNab became bound to pay the expense incurred by the emigrants in coming to Canada, and from the port of entry to destination, and to take all risks and trouble upon himself.

4. That for three years after settlement no repayment of these outlays be payable, but that one bushel of wheat per acre cleared be due to McNab in lieu of interest on monies advanced. If, however, any settler, within that period, was able to repay all or part of the money so loaned, this rent would be proportionately reduced.

5. That, ten or twelve years after completion of the grant, any part of the Township then unsettled would revert to the Crown.

In return for his services McNab stipulated for a large tract of land within the proposed Township.

In due course the Surveyor-General reported on the proposition and McNab was authorized to settle a township newly surveyed by P. L. Sherwood, adjoining the township of Fitzroy, containing 81,000 acres of land, divided into thirteen complete and four broken concessions. McNab named it after himself. The agreement with the Government is, of course, a fundamentally important document and is reproduced in full:

*Department of Crown Lands. Toronto (15th Oct., 1823).

The Committee of the Executive Council to which your Excellency (Maitland) has been pleased to refer the letter of the Laird of McNab, dated York, 15th Oct., 1823, proposing upon certain conditions to settle a township of land with his clansmen and others from the Highlands of Scotland, most respectfully report:

That a township of the usual dimensions be set apart on the Ottawa River, next to the township of Fitzroy, for the purpose of being placed under the direction and superintendence of the Laird of McNab for settlement.

That the said township remain under his sole direction for and during the space of eighteen months, when the progress of the experiment will enable the Government to judge of the propriety of extending the period.

That patents may issue to any of the settlers of said township on certificate from the Laird of McNab stating that the settling duties are well and duly performed and his claims on the settlers arranged and adjusted; or patents may issue to the Petitioner in trust, for any number of settlers, certified by him as aforesaid; the fee on each patent to be one pound, five shillings, and four pence, sterling.

That the conditions entered upon between the Laird of McNab and each settler be fully explained in detail, and that it be distinctly stated that such have no further claim upon the Government for Grants of Land; and that a duplicate of the agreement entered into between the Leader and the settlers shall be lodged in the office of the Government.

That the Laird of McNab be permitted to assign not less than one hundred acres to each family or male of twenty-one years of age, on taking the oath of allegiance, with the power of recommending an extension of such grant to the favorable consideration of His Excellency, the Lieutenant-Governor to such families as have means, and are strong in number, and whom it may be deemed prudent to encourage.

That an immediate grant of twelve hundred acres be assigned to the Laird of McNab, to be increased to the quantity formerly given to a Field Officer, on completing the settlement of the Township.

That the settlers pay the interest on the money laid out for their use by the Laird of McNab, either in money or produce, at the option of the settler; and that the settler shall have the liberty to pay up the principal and interest at any time during the first seven years.

(Signed)   J. BABY, P. C.

Had this agreement been honorably carried out there could be little objection to its terms. It was evident from the beginning that McNab had no such intention. He had come to Canada to escape from his creditors; if possible to amass a fortune large enough to redeem his paternal estates in Perthshire. He unfortunately sought to do so by exploiting the public domain and the way seemed clear to do so when he was entrusted with the settlement of this Township. To this end it was essential that he should conceal from the settlers the real position he occupied and to make it appear that instead of being merely a government locating agent he was the owner of the land. In the first place he did not disclose to them his agreement with the Government, nor did repeated requests to the Government, later on, when troubles arose, enlighten them as to its terms, until towards the close of their struggles in 1841, after Responsible Government had been established. In the second place he did not lodge with the Government as provided in the agreement, the conditions entered into on his behalf in Scotland with the intending settlers; so that, as a matter of fact, the Government was inexcusably ignorant of his power over them.

A near relative of the Laird was Dr. Hamilton (Buchanan) of Arnprior and Leney, to whose friendship he owed his hasty escape to Canada, and to whom he now turned for financial and other help in the work of settlement. Writing jubilantly in August, 1824, he says: "The Township of McNab has today been handed over to me by Sir Peregrine, and it contains 80,000 acres of fine, wooded, arable land—and upward. You will send out to me according to your promise, twenty families, at first. Give them three months' provisions, and make each head of a family, before you give him a passage ticket, sign the enclosed bond, which has been specially prepared by the Attorney General .... I will meet the settlers in Montreal, and see each one on the land located to them, and will provide for their transport to their lands. They should embark early in April, and I should feel obliged if you would personally superintend their embarkation at Greenock. Now I am in a fine way to redeem the estate at home, and in a few years will return after having established a name in Canada, and founded a transatlantic colony of the clan ....."

Dr. Hamilton lost no time in selecting twenty-one heads of families of good character—an emigrant band numbering in all eighty-four souls —McNabs, McFarlanes, McIntyres, McLaurins, McMillans, McLarens, McDermids, Campbells, Drummonds, Carmichaels, etc., names preserved by their descendants in the Township today.

McNab states in his letter to Dr. Hamilton that the bond to be signed by the settlers had been prepared by the Attorney General. That

statement is very questionable. Its truth would imply that the Attorney
General was a party to deceiving his own Government and the settlers
and by so doing become, gratuitously, **particeps criminis** with the un-
scrupulous Chief. The bond provided that every adult bind himself to
pay to McNab "£36 for himself, £30 for his wife, and £16 for every child,
with interest, either in money or produce." Dr. Hamilton was an innocent party to this transaction, for he was given to understand that Mc-
Nab had received a grant of the land from the Government and that the
greater portion of the money thus specified in the bond was for the
purchase of the land from McNab. Assuming that each head of a family
was responsible for himself, wife, and two children, his bond would be
for £98, of which £30 would amply pay for transportation and provisions,
leaving £68, or about $340, for 100 acres of land, a reasonable sum to one
unacquainted with the usual terms of settlement, as was Dr. Hamilton,
and doubtless the settlers thought the amount reasonable at the time.
Consequently they left in good cheer, embarking on the 19th of April,
1825, at Greenock, in the ship "Niagara." The voyage was comfortable
and expeditiously made and on the 27th of May the immigrants landed
at Montreal. McNab, accompanied by his piper, met them with a hearty
welcome there and arrangements were made for the inland journey, up
the Ottawa River.

Proceeding to Lachine they travelled for three days by bateaux to
Point Fortune. Thence to Hawkesbury they went afoot, their baggage
being drawn on ox-carts and sleds. At Hawkesbury they boarded the
steamboat "Union," the journey by which to Hull occupied two days
and one night. Here was the unbroken forest, through which they proceeded with great difficulty and no small danger, to their new Canadian
homes, assisted by a few lumbermen who came from the camps to meet
them. Incredible as it may now seem, it was stated in evidence subsequently, that this pioneer journey, from Montreal to McNab, occupied
twenty-eight days—until the 23rd of June.

The scene, on their arrival, can well be imagined; it need not be
described at length here. Simple, but graphic accounts of it are preserved in letters by some of the settlers to friends in the old land, written
at a time when looming troubles were undreamed of and hope was high;
other accounts, colored by the pigment of dire hardship and unblushing
injustice, were many years later gathered from the recollections of the
surviving pioneers, and found their way to the columns of local newspapers. At first the Chief was pleased to be gracious, and he lodged as
many as he could in Kinnell Lodge, the commodious home he had built
for himself on a commanding position on the banks of the Ottawa River,

near to where the Madawaska joins it. Others were accommodated in tents, and after a few days' rest, they were all assembled before the Laird to be informed of his settlement arrangements. He told them that the Township had been granted to him by the Provincial Government because he was a Highland Chief, and that after they had selected suitable lots he would issue location or occupancy tickets to them. Before the people had left their homes in Scotland, McNab, through his agent, promised them free transportation to their new homes, free provisions for a three months' journey, and for the first year of their settlement; the latter part of the promise being so specific as to designate the storekeeper who would supply the provisions. The need for such having now arisen, the settlers visited the store, kept by a Mr. Ferguson, at the mouth of the Madawaska River. Here their first real disappointment was experienced; for while a few articles of clothing and a large barrel of whiskey were in stock, there were no provisions, nor were any to be had in the Township. The result was that they had to leave for neighboring townships, at considerable distance, hire with the farmers there in order to earn money for bread for themselves and families, and thus were unable to begin clearing their own land for a time. Though the amount of the price of these three months' provisions was included in the bond, McNab neither supplied them nor reduced the bond. Before this migration, however, the lots had been selected and location tickets in the style of the following copy issued:

"I, Archibald McNab, do hereby locate you, ... upon the rear (or front) half of the .... lot of the .... Concession of McNab, upon the following terms and conditions, that is to say: I hereby bind myself, my heirs and successors, to give you the said land free of any quit rent for three years from this date, as also to procure you a patent for the same at your expense, upon your having done the settlement duties and your granting me a mortgage upon said lands that you will yearly thereafter pay to me, my heirs and successors for ever one bushel of wheat or Indian corn, or oats of like value, for every cleared acre upon the said lot of land in name of quit rent for the same, in the month of January in each year.

Your subscribing to these conditions being binding upon you to fulfil the terms thereof.

Signed and sealed by us at Kinnell Lodge, this twelfth day of August, 1825.

        Signed ARCHIBALD McNAB (L. S.)
        Signed SETTLER'S NAME (L. S.)

This was the first attempt, and the written evidence of it, to introduce the feudal system of landlord and tenant into Upper Canada. The location tickets were all signed. The settlers believed McNab when he told them he had received a Crown Grant of the land, and they did not understand the difference between the words patent and quit rent made use of in the ticket. Nor did they realize for many years afterwards that such a document was in itself illegal and non-binding. McNab knowing the people, the inaccessible situation of the Township, and his influence with the Government, felt that this agreement and the bond executed by the settlers for him by Dr. Buchanan Hamilton at Leney House, made him secure in a perpetual tenure of a large estate. For long it looked as if he had rightly judged; the helpless and penniless condition of the people being aggravated by the necessity of hiring out in the spring, harvest and winter, instead of clearing their own lands for crops. The rent, in lieu of interest on the bond, and as quit rent on the locations, steadily accumulated into formidable arrears, and the people were practically serfs, doubly bound hand and foot.

Between McNab and the townships in which they hired—such as Beckwith and Fitzroy, there were no roads, and the hard-earned provisions had to be carried in, most of the way, on the settlers' backs through rough paths and rugged land. For three years this life was bravely endured. The returns were meagre, barely sufficing to keep their wives and families in life. Stories have come down, harrowing and cruel, of the vicissitudes of those years of bitter trial. For weeks women and children were alone in the solitude of the small clearings, subsisting on a few potatoes and nought else, salt being so scarce that it was a Sunday luxury only; the men, the while, absent at a long distance, toiling for a pittance in order to replenish the empty larders at the log shanties in the forest. In their misery no sympathy, or relief, was offered by McNab. In imitation of the barons of yore he held court in his house in which, as a magistrate, he imposed sentences without the semblance of law or justice. He compelled the poor people to apply to him, in his "baron's" court, at Kinnell, to petition for his permission to leave the Township in search of work. He held that they were in a state of villeinage, bound to the soil, a claim, which if doubted, none durst dispute. If, to the least extent, a settler disobeyed him, or seemed to be lacking in the obeisance he demanded, the Chief entered his name in the book known as "The Black List," and the delinquent was marked for punishment unless he made amends—sometimes petty annoyances sufficed, generally serious harrassment was resorted to with the view of creating a "cause" or offence which he could plausibly deal with, as a Justice of the Peace.

Sometimes men were refused leave of absence to search for work; and the result of one such refusal reveals the unlawful power wielded by McNab. Alexander Miller had a very small supply of food on hand and necessity drove him to disobey the chief. He obtained employment readily in the neighboring township. The chief raged with fury. To him such insubordination was intolerable. Miller was arrested at his work and lodged in gaol for a debt of £80, though under the Government agreement McNab had no right to enforce his claim until seven years had lapsed after settlement. But the Governmnt agreement was not forthcoming, only McNab's bond, and, ignorant of it as Miller was, he had no recourse. He was for six weeks in the gaol at Perth, sixty miles distant. before his family or the other settlers knew of his arrest. Then a number of them travelled to Perth and became bail bondsmen for him, thereby incurring the hostility of McNab. The case came to trial. In journeying through the forest Miller was delayed and arrived one day late. McNab, thereupon abandoned judgment and took action against the six bondsmen who were compelled to pay the bond to the extent of £50 each. This case is cited as one of the many ways, by no means the severest, in which McNab persecuted and brow-beat the settlers into dependence on him.

But news of these sufferings reached Scotland. Dr. Hamilton withdrew his help, and the Chief became apprehensive lest the Settlement work should fall through. He proceeded to Montreal, and persuaded Scottish immigrants arriving there to locate in the township of McNab. These were known as the new settlers, the former, as the old. Ignorant of the Chief's designs, the new-comers were innocently entrapped by signing the location ticket and other binding obligations, the nature of which they discovered when too late. For years, thereafter, exasperating tyranny was exercised. Appeals to the courts, petitions to the Government, afforded no relief, while McNab's every request was granted. The original eighteen months allowed him for settlement was extended indefinitely in 1827. His claims and representations were not challenged. He trafficked in locations to his own advantage and the disadvantage of the Township, with impunity. The complaints of the settlers were attributed to a spirit of sedition and revolt. On the suspicion that one, Alexander McNab, had written and forwarded an anonymous account of the Chief's hight-handed actions, to the Governor, McNab issued this ukase:

Degraded Clansman:—You are accused to me by Sir John Colborne, of libel, sedition, and high treason. You will forthwith compear before me, at my house at Kinnell, and there make submission; and if you show a contrite and repentant spirit, and confess your faults against me, your legitimate Chief, and your crime against His Majesty, King George, I will intercede for your pardon.

Your offended Chief,

McNAB.

The "degraded" clansman duly appeared before his offended chief and then for the first time heard of the letter that had been sent to the Governor. On denying the authorship, the Chief exclaimed, "Well, my man, I must send you to gaol, and I assure you that your neck is in danger" (and, indeed, in those days burglary, forgery, etc., were punishable by death). McNab wrote a warrant of commitment, swore in two special constables and sent the innocent settler to Perth gaol where he was detained for six weeks for the Assizes. He was acquitted, but instead of censure for the Chief, he was actually applauded for acting with such promptitude, as witness, prosecutor, and judge.

In 1830 some immigrants from Islay, Scotland, were met by McNab at Montreal, and induced to settle in "his Highland township." The terms were varied from a bushel of wheat per acre to a yearly rent in perpetuity of three barrels of flour per farm. These people had paid their own passage expenses, and had McNab not deceived them, would have obtained Government grants on the usual settlement terms. They too soon fell under the Chief's displeasure and oppression, but the added strength of numbers and the information slowly percolating from neighboring settlements, gradually led to suspicion of the Laird of McNab's honesty. Complaints to Government became persistent; the Chief was openly defied, and threatened, and a bitter, long-drawn-out struggle began.

In 1831, the Government conceded an investigation. But instead of compelling a fulfilment of McNab's original agreement, the Government, now aware of his duplicity, accepted his discredited word that lower rents would be charged. The promise was never kept, nor was it intended to be kept. He added to his exactions by charging a "royalty" on all tumber cut in the township, the amount of which was computed at £30,000. These monies enabled him to play the grand seig017 in the society circles of Toronto and Montreal. He and a neighboring magistrate, as a committee of General Sessions, controlled the location and construction of roads. This power was used to oppress recalcitrant clansmen. No roads were opened in their districts, while their statute labor was forced from them in useless roads far distant from their farms. His sport was to run a road one year in one direction, leave it unfinished, and next year to make a similar pretence in another direction. Life under such conditions was hard to endure; comfort, there was none. The first real relief was when, in the course of a few years, the settlers' sons had grown up, and from their earnings in lumber camps, contributed towards the family expenses. On the expiry of the time limit in his bond, McNab proceeded to serve writs on the old settlers. The people revolted, a defence was organized, the sheriff's officers were baffled time and again; at the end of two years only three writs were served. Feeling grew so bitter that McNab refused the money owing on the bonds when finally offered to him, preferring to wreak the penalties of the law.

Immigrants from Breadalbane, Scotland, reached the Township in 1833, a party from Blair-Athol in 1834, and the Chief's rents began to grow substantial. The location terms were amplified by reserving the pine on the settled lots for the Arnprior Mills. He became increasingly oppressive. The millmen who bought the lumber, cut, slashed, dragged, through the lots, leaving brush and rubbish behind, rendering clearing more difficult, with no indemnification. The law of trespass designed to protect the settler he set at naught. Quasi Municipal law was administered by Quarter Sessions, a body which never questioned McNab's actions. Ejectments were made from the homes in the dead of winter, cattle and furniture seized, houses were burnt to the ground, and hardships cruelly imposed, which caused the worm to turn, and eventually wrought McNab's own ruin. It was found out that he was only a Government Agent, trying by deceit to filch their property.

In the Mackenzie uprising of 1837, the settlers mustered for defence as militia, but refused to serve under McNab as Colonel. They petitioned Government declaring their loyalty, and exposing McNab's grievous impositions. Their expression of loyalty was acknowledged, their grievances ignored: "The arrangements made between The McNab and his followers are of a purely private nature, and beyond the control of the Government," was Bond Head's untrue reply! The Government went further—distributing four hundred copies of the petition and reply among the settlers to terrify them. Sir George Arthur succeeded Bond Head as Lieutenant-Governor. A deep laid scheme to secure by misrepresentation the freehold of the lots on which the settlers were located succeeded in passing the Executive Council, and was only frustrated by the accidental discovery of its true character by a clerk in the Surveyor-General's office. The suspicion of the new Lieutenant-Governor was aroused, and thenceforward the Chief's successes in Council and Court were less frequent. Lord Durham appeared on the scene. Another petition was forwarded resulting in an official investigation. From the Crown Lands' Office condemnatory evidence was produced, and a recommendation was made that the original agreement be enforced. Before this was done, however, Durham resigned, and long-deferred justice was shamelessly postponed. McNab now resumed his lawsuits, in the face of the Commissioner's finding, insisting on his right to rents under his original bond and illegal location leases. He succeeded in the local courts, and the blight of a doubtful issue lay once more on the township. Poulett Thompson (Sydenham) came. The Chief took alarm at last, and hurried to strike terms with the Government, on the basis of a field officer's land grant, offering to compromise for a cash settlement of £9,000. Sir George Arthur thought £2,000 enough, but £4,000 was agreed upon. In the final adjustment £2,500 was paid to him in full.

The settlers petitioned Sydenham, who appointed Francis Allan, Perth, to investigate on the spot the process of settlement from its beginning. Allan's report is in the Public Archives. He found every charge and complaint made by the settlers to be true, and the case against McNab sweepingly proven. The editor of the **Examiner** was the Hon. Francis Hincks. He made Allan's Report the basis of a scathing exposure of McNab's doings in a series of articles remarkable for breadth and public spirit. McNab brought an action for libel. The evidence for the defence, which pleaded justification, exposed shocking details necessitating speedy relief for the settlers and abandonment of McNab to his fate by his friends. Government now stepped in, adjusted the settlers' claims, issued Crown grants, and ended forever the attempt of a Highland Chief to become a feudal baron on the free soil of Canada. The Township of McNab became prosperous, the home of a loyal, contented, and happy people. The ambitious Chief removed to the Orkney Islands, becoming impoverished there he retired to a small village in France, where, after spending many years in seclusion, he died a pensioner on his separated wife's bounty, in 1860, in the 82nd year of his age.

XIV.

BUSH LIFE IN THE OTTAWA VALLEY EIGHTY YEARS AGO.

By John May, M. A., Franktown, Ont.

About the beginning of last century, Ontario was mainly an unbroken forest. I can't go back to the cutting down of the first tree, or the building of the first shanty; but I can cover seventy years or more with what I have myself seen in the Ottawa Valley. There were scattered patches of cleared land—fences, roads of a sort, buildings, cattle, and so forth—before my time; but everything was still in a very primitive condition. Those born here when I was, escaped the very first and worst stage of life in the Bush; but the old folks could tell us of much we never saw: the struggles and the triumphs of men and women who had torn themselves from the homes of their childhood; dared in slow, flimsy crafts the perils of the deep; plunged into the grim solitudes, endless, boundless, and dread; and made for themselves and for all time, free homes in a free land. What hardships they endured! Isolation, rigorous climate, scant clothing and food; church, school, physician, none; or at best few and far between.

As a rule the immigrant had a family, and little money—sometimes barely enough to buy an axe. Were it not for the "Government stores" the people would have perished of want whilst awaiting their first crop. Imagine what it was for men who had never swung an axe to attack that dense jungle of brushwood, that endless array of huge tree-trunks! But by chopping they learned to chop. The novice hacked the tree all round, and it fell where it would. Lives were lost in felling trees. The second generation were fine axemen: to-day good ones are scarce. The brush lay where it fell, the logs tumbled on top. On some hot summer day there were wild roarings and cracklings, terrific blazes and vast volumes of smoke rolling skyward; then—black logs and stumps! Now for the "logging bee." The neighbours assemble. The logs, oxen-hauled, are heaped up, to be burned later on. The white men of the morning are "niggers" in the evening. The heaps burnt, the ashes are scraped up and

In the Society's History Essay Competition, 1913, this article received the third prize.

sold to make potash. Days of the leach and potash-kettle, whence bubbled up some snug little fortunes.

Was life all hardship then? all cloud? no radiance? no social delights? no relaxation? no flashes of fun and frolic? Not so. Why, even the grimy logging bee had its merriments—two men against two, rolling, hoisting the logs, striving to be first! Grave fathers of families were boys again, as the logs swung in, and the heaps arose. And when the sun was set, and the grime washed off, and supper over, did these jaded men drag themselves home to their cabins bewailing their cruel lot? Not a bit of it! In came their wives and daughters, and out came the fiddle and the bottle, and "We'll not go home until morning!" There was a heartiness, a simplicity, a joviality, a mutual helpfulness in those days of common struggle, less in evidence in these days of fine houses, fine feathers, luxuries, rivalries, and vapid conventional socialities.

What a change since eighty years ago! The farmer's work is now child's play. He whistles, not at, but on, the plough. The horse or the engine does nearly all. I have shewn how the land was cleared; but, was it cleared? No; the great stumps, with their wide-spreading roots, remained; also the boulders, rocks, and small stones. These last were picked up and piled pillar-wise; and a field studded with stumps and stone pillars was a sight to see. The hoe put in the potato, and took it out; and a tiresome job it was to plant it in the root-tangle, and "hill up" the growing plant, and keep down the woods. Grain was covered with a "drag," the wooden-toothed crotch of a tree; turnip seed with a bundle of boughs drawn butt-end foremost. Hardwood stumps soon decayed, and were then easily got rid of; not so with pine. On thin or sandy soil its roots spread far and wide, in no haste to moulder. In deep clay lands one could plow right up to the stump.

Two great drawbacks on the prairie are the scarcity of timber and good water. The Ontario pioneer felt no lack of either. Did he want to build a house or a barn? There stood the shapely tree-trunks waiting to be felled. In hardwood regions the rock-elm was the favorite for this purpose. A hard, tough, durable wood, cylindrical and clear of boughs to a great height and usually of moderate girth. Many a primitive shanty or out-house was built of it, just as it grew, in full dress of bark; also many of the first school-houses. In the cabin its own moss stuffed the chinks. Overhead was the roof of basswood "scoops," through which a huge stone chimney thrust its head. Sometimes hungry wolves gained a footing there, to the horror of trembling mother and children, lest they should slip down the chimney's capacious throat!

BUSH LIFE IN THE OTTAWA VALLEY, 80 YEARS AGO. 155

Here, as the winter evening closed in, and the winter wind whistled in the tree-tops, and the children came indoors, and the tallow candle was lit, the father, his cattle housed for the night and his other chores done, might be seen "walking-in" the great elm backlog to its destination at the back of the vast fire-place. No "dogs" or andirons in those days. Small boulders in front of King Log upheld the smaller billets and kindlings. A chill half-hour and much smoke whilst the green stuff hissed and spat before bursting at last into a glorious blaze. All this before the advent of the stove. I remember when the box stove first came into these parts—in the late "thirties" or early "forties," I think—the cooking-stove later on. Soon arose an outcry against it as a generator of headaches! Now, the stove did not cause headaches; it simply failed to remove what did. The open fire-place, on a level with the floor, had never failed to suck up the carbonic acid gas—too low for the small stove-damper. Never since have we had ventilation like that of the forest days; nor shall we have its equal again till the open fire-place, low down, is restored. One of these would be more effectual than all other devices put together, and every school-room should have one.

The open fire, too, has a charm all its own. There's a mystic fascination in vaulting flames and glowing coals. Dim as was the illumination from blaze and candle, it had a cheeriness foreign to the gas jet or the kerosene lamp. Ah! those dear old home evenings in winter, when we squatted on the hearth-stone, reading by the fire-light some pleasing story, or conning over our school lessons, or gazing enraptured on the pictures coming and going on the backlog's fiery face—fancied portraits completed by imagination—men and horses, castles and ships, bears, dragons, and birds! What a training of the youthful imagination, so necessary a faculty in learning anything! But, the backlog is gone, and with it much of the poetry of life. The wise ones would pack after it the fairy tale and the nursery rhyme. What folly may be hid in wisdom!

Many a night, too, before going to bed, did we stand outside the door listening to the dismal howl of the wolves careering along the rim of the clearing, led by one of superior vocal powers, and going like the wind! There was something weird and awesome in these nocturnal lupine concerts, so common in those days. The wolf is reputed a coward, yet a hungry pack was an ugly thing to meet. Many a belated wayfarer was glad to take refuge for the night in some friendly tree-top, the fangs of the famished pack tearing at its trunk to bring him down! No use to climb a tree from a bear, unless it was too small for him to climb. There was a bounty of twenty dollars on each wolf killed, and ten on each bear. One night my father, coming home through the woods, heard a wolf howl, as he imagined, and ran for his life. It was the hooting of an owl!

I learned at school that our winters were growing milder; I have never learned it elsewhere. The immigrant from the British Isles felt the cold less than do his descendants, or than even himself after the first few years. He often went bare-handed in barn or bush on the coldest days. Yet, blood-freezing were the accounts of frost sometimes sent "home." One son of Erin declared that the "tay" froze on its way to his mouth! Sheltered by woods, nobody heeded the cold. Men preferred chopping in the bush to threshing in the barn. The barn is still a cold, wretched place, but you get out of it now in a few hours. Not so in olden times. Threshing was an all-winter job. Did you ever see a flail? two sticks jointed with a thong. Fancy pounding for months at a mow which the machine would shell out in half a day! Thud! thud! thud!—such was your grandsire's winter pastime!

How is it to-day? The engine comes screaming along the king's highway, wheels in at the gate, up the lane, round to the barn-door. Down pour the sheaves, to be chewed, and whisked, and whirled into mounds of empty straw and bins of golden grain; sheaves shooting down the iron throat, straw shooting out in rolls, mows dwindling down, mounds swelling up; bag-heaped wagons wheeling away the precious outcome of a season's toil. A few hours and all is over. What a change from the thud! thud! thud!

And some say the world does not improve! It does improve—at least on its material side. Can the same be said of its moral advance? Do honour, integrity, square-dealing, stand where they stood in the early days? Why, the pioneers seldom or never had writings in their ordinary dealings and contracts with each other. A man's word was his bond; and woe betide him who broke it! He had better pack up and go. How is it now? Not quite the same. A sterling integrity still characterizes the great majority; but "smartness" is more in evidence; and sharp practice seems less severely rebuked and frowned out, than in the early days.

Ninety years ago this Ottawa Valley was an almost unbroken forest —no Pembroke, Ottawa, Smith's Falls, and very little Perth. In 1806 Philemon Wright founded Hull and the great lumber industry; and Col. By founded Bytown in 1826. Richmond was started in 1818 by disbanded soldiers. Roads there were none—hardly so much as a foot-path in the woods! Could a man then have looked down from a balloon on this region, what would have met his eye? One interminable forest, broken only by patches and ribbons of water, and a small opening here and there, indicated by the up-curling smoke from the cabin of the solitary settler. Peering down into the twilight depths of the woods, he might also see a man staggering along from tree to tree, with a bag of wheat on his back. Up hill and down dale he goes; stepping over boulders and roots; climbing over fallen trees; wedging his way through thick undergrowth; painfully skirting dismal, slimy sloughs; now over the shoes in mud; now up to the knees in water; here, struggling through that hideous jungle, the cedar swamp; there, straining across a tamarac muskeag, or the leaf-carpeted hardwood heights; scaling hills and fording streams, his eye ever and anon scanning the tree-trunks for a "blaze," his sole guide through the labyrinth, till at last, weary and worn, scratched and bleeding, and half-famished, he emerges in sight of the mill that is to convert his few pounds of grain into flour for his family and himself. My own grandfather made these trips—fifteen miles to the mill where Perth now stands; and many others had the like delightful experience. I have heard of a woman thus carrying a bushel of seed potatoes forty miles!

To the spot where I write, among the orchard trees bending low with fruit, and fields of waving grain, came, ninety-three years ago, a settler, his wife, and four little ones, from Bytown, through some forty miles of woods. He carried a bed on his back; and, on the top of this, his youngest child. All were on foot. No road, no path. The "blaze," and in wet places, some "string-pieces" to walk on, were all. Around them the wild woods, the wolf, the lynx, and the bear, kept aloof at night by the camp-fire. What a change from the green fields and broad highways of the Emerald Isle! Inside his front gate stands an oak, three feet in diameter, on which, when a sapling, he cut the date of his arrival, 1819. The figures shew there still.

Past that tree, that same year, walked the Duke of Richmond on his melancholy journey from Perth to Richmond village, then but one year old. I had the sad story of his last hours from Mrs. Taylor, a soldier's wife, who kept the "Masonic Arms" hotel, where he lodged with his suite the night before his death. At table, the sight of a glass of water agitated him greatly. All night long he walked the verandah to and fro. Next morning the party started in canoes down the Jock river, making for the Rideau, Bytown, and Quebec. They had gone but a little way when the Duke, in agony, begged hard to be set ashore. No sooner did his foot touch land than he bounded off through the bush with the speed of a deer! About three miles below Richmond he was found prostrate on some hay in a little barn. Before medical aid could be had from Perth, he died. Mrs. Taylor herself laid out the corpse. She said he was a splendid specimen of manhood.

"Blazes" and "string-pieces" in course of time gave way to "corduroy." I wonder how many now living ever jolted over this. It consisted of round logs laid crosswise side by side. To go bumping over these in a springless cart or wagon was an experience not soon forgotten. They said it was good for the liver; but it must have been hard on the teeth, and perilous to the tongue. Oh! the carriages we went so proudly in, to market or to church, in those days! None of your flimsy, frail top-buggies, or luxurious, elastic phaetons; but stout vehicles—solid square boxes on solid square axles, in the solid hubs of solid wheels, bumping over solid logs! You sat on an inch board, laid across the box. Not much spring in that, and still less in the box. Later on, four stout hooks, hung on the box, upheld two poles on which the backless seats rested. This was a great step in advance. Many a pleasant ride was had on these poles and uncushioned seats; and many a jolly wedding party thus went to the church; and more than once have I seen a manly arm steal round a slender waist on the back seat of this same primeval chariot.

In summer time no boots or shoes were worn at school, and not too many even at church. Children actually exulted in freedom from footwear when the snow was gone. Tender at first, the sole of the foot soon thickened and hardened. As the boy grew towards manhood he began to blush for bare feet in church, and took to boots; the girl, somewhat earlier. Yet it was a common practice for girls to carry their shoes and stockings in their hands until they came near the village or the church, when they put them on; removing them at the same place on the homeward tramp. This spared shoe-leather. It was also more congenial to feet that had been six days free, and loathed confinement on the seventh.

To keep a large household shod even in winter was a problem. Skates were not in use as yet—"sliding" was the ice-sport; and it soon wore out the boot-soles. The settler had his calf-skins and cow-hides tanned, and as the winter approached, the peripatetic shoemaker of those days came round and shod the whole family, passing on from house to house. The tailor did likewise, for "homespun" was the prevailing garb. The women of the family, however, usually not only spun the yarn, but "made it up" when converted into cloth or flannel by the local weaver. Both sexes were clad in this, even at church, or social gatherings. No furs on man or woman; no silks or satins; no "fine feathers" of any sort. Dame Fashion had no votaries in the "Bush." Even the dance was done in "homespun."

Still, they enjoyed it to their heart's content—
All cares forgotten in their merriment.
No stiff formality intruded there;
Nor were the ladies' dresses rich and rare.

No pearls or bracelets circled neck or arms,
And yet the forest maiden had her charms;
For, eyes are eyes—an archery that tells
On rustic hearts as those of city "swells."

Hodge sees the blue eyes—not the flannel dress—
And seeks his couch in painful blessedness!
"Fine feathers make fine birds." But love can see
The gem that shines 'neath homespun millin'ry.

Franktown, 35 miles from Ottawa, 15 miles from Perth, and where the stage roads from Bytown to Perth and from Brockville to the upper Ottawa crossed, is now a railroad-killed village. Once it was a stirring place. Its Fair, then a great event, is now a mere name. A big day for the sale of live stock and for fun; the whole population for miles around was there, with buyers from distant towns. When cheap whiskey (a penny a glass) had begun to warm hearts to excessive friendship, and this developed into maudlin embraces, culminating in high voices and angry words—then might you behold a sea of upturned faces, bare heads, and clenched fists, ebbing and flowing, swinging and swaying to and fro, and foaming like a boiling cauldron; nobody struck, as no one had room to strike, and not a soul in the crowd able to tell why he was there, or what the row was about. All whiskey! These wild men were most peaceable citizens in every-day life; in fact, for peace and order, Beckwith was, and is, a model Township.

The live-stock buyer did not then pass from house to house. All animals went to the fair, or were slaughtered and hauled to market. Pork-raising flourished—for the "shanties." The hog reached a venerable age ere his grunting ceased; now all good pigs die young. What monsters they often were! 500 lbs. quite common; fat, six to nine inches on shoulder! These for the "shanty men." And what potato labour they caused! Acres on acres of this tuber to fatten them; thirty to forty wagon loads to the present three or four. Potato-digging meant, for us youngsters, shivering and shaking, and blowing of cold fingers. The Colorado bug had not yet appeared.

The early settler's work was never over; not even in winter and night closed in. All day long was he chopping or threshing, and tend-ing stock; at night there were shingles, spiles, or sleighs to make—perchance also boots and shoes, for some non-professionals made even these. All this before the blazing hearth; the women quilting, sewing, knitting, or plaiting straw for hats, or making these; the juveniles babbling over their lessons for the morrow. A busy, yet cosy, domestic scene, more full of content than are sometimes the palaces of the proud. Pine or cedar blocks gave the shingles and spiles; wheat or rye straw, the hats. No sewing or knitting machines in those days.

Thus passed the winter evenings. At last come the March sun, the hard snow crust, and the sugar-camp. Glorious morning scampers on the crust under crystal skies; reviving suns beginning to shower down new largess of life on a world long dead; Nature rubbing her eyes and coming forth in squirrel and chipmonk, woodpecker and crow; her herald the tapper, with clink of axe and gouge from tree to tree. A sound as music to the boyish ear! It seemed as the first note of a psalm of life, after the long winter death; and it spake of the joys of the sugar season. All this is clean gone now, never to return. A gruesome change is here from the glowing fires beneath the over-arching woods which rang with mirth and song as the young people gathered in for the "sugaring-off," or roamed from camp to camp in friendly invasion, awakening the echoes of the night with clamour and glee, after long months of a quasi-imprisonment. A fine time for the boys—how went it with the women? I see them now with their pails, wading through snow thigh-deep from tree to tree, gathering the sap; trudging over vast areas of bush, heavily laden; struggling to lift and empty the ponderous sap-troughs, and wending their way back to camp, weary and be-drabbled to the knees, boots and stockings soaked! Then to the wearisome boiling again, pelted with rain, sleet, hail or snow; half blinded with smoke, and alternately chilled by the cold blast and fried by the licentious flame. Women did all save tap the trees and lay in the fluel. No roof save the leafless tree tops covered their heads; no friendly wall screend them from the blast. So fared the wives and daughters of the best in the land; the men occupied with matters still more urgent. They sat in no Ladies' Colleges, took no music lessons, had no pianos or organs. Talk of heroes and heroines! The Ontario woods were full of them! For, does it not demand less real courage to flash out in some fiery deed of valour, soon over, and under admiring eyes, than to fight a life-long battle with the wilderness, unnoticed and unapplauded? No costly marble chronicles their deeds, but the maple scars tell a little of their story; a great Dominion is their monument.

As late as the "forties" the housewife still lighted her fire, and the smoker his pipe, by means of "punk," flint, and steel—the blade of a jack-knife "warranted to strike fire," but superseded in time by a steel ring through which the fingers were thrust. The punk in which the spark was caught came from the maple. The clay pipe was universal—sometimes kindled with hot ashes or a coal, and, when black as ebony, whitened in the fire. Lucifer matches were as yet unknown in these parts. They came in with the "fifties" and the decimal currency.

Days of the Axe, the Flail, and the Reaping-hook! There were two kinds of sickles—one toothed, the other plain, and keen as a razor. When a whole family, armed with these, swept across a field, the wheat soon lay bound in sheaves. Many ears dropped, and we youngsters picked them up. The grain crop was often over-ripe ere cut. How particular the farmer was! Every sheaf must be just so. When the cradle came in, there was much shaking of heads over its untidy work. It is now, in its turn, a thing of the past. How many good things are gone!—sickle, flail, frow, ox-yoke, candle-moulds, cradle, potash-kettle, and what not! How many bad things remain!

We boys used to trap the wild pigeon by means of a sap-trough set on edge. What a thrill of delight to see this down! The poor captives were drawn forth, and their necks wrung without a pang! Thoughtless cruelty of boys! I couldn't do it now. I hate even to see anything killed, except a snake.

Where is the wild pigeon gone? Where are the myriads that once blanketed the stooks and obscured the sun?

The "husking bee" was an event. Around a high mound of un-husked Indian corn squatted the invited youth and beauty of the neighborhood, duly paired off. The husks rise higher and higher, under cover of which and a babel of voices, laughter and song, sweet words are said and sweet kisses given. About midnight the floor is cleared for the dance. This was no giddy whirl or stately promenade. The "four-hand reel" was the staple commodity; "steps" the main point—an earnest business. Lacking a fiddle, they danced to a whistle or a "lilt"—danced till dawn. The next night the same—and the next—till the corn season was over. The "quilting bee," as winter set in, afforded a similar means of social enjoyment. These things are all now past, and rural life is dull and prosy. The face of the farmer's son is set town-ward accordingly.

Nearly all the settlers' buildings were log—elm or cedar—neatly dove-tailed at the corners, which only the best axemen could build. A good "corner-man" is now rare. The barn " raisin' " was a big—often a wild—affair. The foundation laid, and a few rounds added, on a set day the neighbours assembled. Corner men are chosen, the rest divide into two rival gangs, one at each end of the log to be hoisted. For the first few rounds there is little excitement; the logs are rolled in and slid up in a quiet, orderly manner. But, with the rising walls rises a rivalry, waxing fiercer and fiercer, till the "wall-plate" is placed, and all is over. It struck terror into the heart of the on-looker to see each gang wildly push to get their end up first. Pushed too fast and too far, it left the skid, then—**sauve qui peut!** Lives were lost in this way.

Were these wild, reckless fellows foolish boys? No. Most of them were grave, middle-aged fathers of families—the self-same sober, serious men who had braved the perils of the sea and the hardships of the wilderness—men earnestly bent on doing their duty to wife and children, King and country. Yes, and not one of them but would have been grieved at heart were any one injured. Bring grave men together—they incline to play. Taking sides, they are boys! These same mad barn-builders built also a nation, and held it at Chateauguay and Queenston Heights!

The polling at elections sometimes lasted two weeks, with royal feasting and merry-making.

> How changed the **School** since that primeval time!
> Young girls had not, as yet, begun to climb,
> In any number, to the Teacher's throne,
> Filled then by men, and almost men alone.
> Rare, curious specimens were most of these;
> Failures in other lines, and glad to seize
> On any lawful means to win their bread;
> The people glad to have their children fed
> On the best mental food that could be got
> Under the circumstances of their lot:
> The grim old soldier, on his wooden leg,
> Thus spared the dire necessity to beg:
> The broken merchant, sunk to penury:
> The sailor, battered on the stormy sea:
> And he who once had sat in college hall,
> But whom the wrestler, Drink, had given a fall.
> Such were the "dominies" of long ago:
> But then, the salaries were also low—
> Twenty or thirty pounds a year, eked out
> Precariously, by "boarding round about,"
> A fortnight with each family, or so.
> But the itinerant soon got to know

The choicest places, and prolonged his stay;
And few had heart to hasten him away.
Studies were few compared with days to come;
The three R's were the whole curriculum.

When we consider the tremendous difficulties and discouragements of pioneer settlement in Canada; the poverty of most of the immigrants; the awful forest to be flung aside; the crushing and incessant toil of both sexes to gain a mere subsistence; the formidable disabilities as to roads, markets, schools, medical aid, the ministrations of religion, and countless other privations—how can we enough admire the pluck, the energy, the perseverance of the long-enduring men and women who surmounted every difficulty, flung aside every obstacle, and handed over to us the foundation, well and truly laid, of this great Dominion, this Canada, this Land of Promise, destined to be a power for good among the nations of the world? The question for us is this:

> Are we the men to guide her course?
> Know we, and feel, and understand
> There is but one Eternal Source
> Of lasting sway on sea and land?
>
> The buried empires of the past
> Tottered and fell when **That** withdrew;
> And England headlong would be cast
> Should she forget the God she knew.
>
> Canada! let thy comely face,
> As flint, for Righteousness be set;
> A Hand shall brush you from your place
> If you forget, if you forget.

XV.

THE PETER PERRY ELECTION AND THE RISE OF THE CLEAR GRIT PARTY.

By Geo. M. Jones, B. A., Toronto

Canada was at a parting of the ways in the year 1849. After over half a century of persistent struggle, she had obtained almost complete self-government, but party feeling still ran high, and commercial depression so aided political hatred that many eminent and many more inconspicuous citizens openly discussed, and advocated separation from the Mother country and annexation to the United States.

The Conservative party was embittered by its loss of power, the passing of the Rebellion Losses Bill, in spite of its vehement protests, the refusal of Lord Elgin either to veto the measure or reserve it for the consideration of the British Government, and, finally, the decision of the British Government to uphold Lord Elgin in his determination to carry out fully, in Canada, the principles of Responsible Government. The Conservatives of the school of Sir Allan McNab did not appreciate a system of government which allowed their opponents to really rule, (1) and some of them were even afraid of full self-government, and shrank from an application to Canada of the system of government established in England.(2)

At the same time Canada was suffering from extreme commercial depression. Owing largely to the abolition of the preference granted to colonial corn and grain, which was a necessary consequence of the repeal of the Corn Laws in 1846, and to the evil effects of the Navigation Laws, which still kept all but British ships out of Canadian ports, the Canadian business community had been nearly ruined. The value of property had fallen 50% in three years, and the Government was forced to pay the public officials, from the Governor-General down, in debentures which were not exchangeable at par.

The judges in the Society's History Essay Competition, 1913, made honorable mention of this article in succession to those awarded prizes.
(1) Toronto Colonist, Oct. 30, 1849
(2) Hamilton Spectator, March 9, 1850.

The result of this political bitterness and the acute, widespread commercial depression was a formidable annexation movement. Many people believed quite conscientiously that the only way out of the political and economic difficulties of the time was through annexation to the United States. Lord Elgin declared in a letter to the Colonial Secretary (1) that "the conviction that they would be better off, if annexed, is almost universal among the commercial classes at present." The movement had its headquarters and greatest strength in Montreal, whence were issued the three famous Montreal Annexation Manifestoes.(2) A determined effort was made by the Montreal Annexation Association to spread the agitation in other parts of the country. They met with little encouragement among the French. The Parti Rouge, led by L. J. Papineau, but small in number and weak in influence, espoused the cause of annexation enthusiastically; but the great bulk of the French Canadians, under the influence of the Church and their political leaders, refused to have anything to do with it. In the Eastern Townships, the Annexationists met with considerable success, and in March, 1850, helped to elect Mr. Sanborn, an avowed Annexationist, in Sherbrooke.

In Upper Canada the annexation movement made only slight headway. A Toronto Manifesto was, indeed, prepared, and a new journal, "The Independent," was issued at Toronto for a few months to advocate independence as a first step towards annexation, but Tories and Reformers united, as a rule, in declaring against any separation from the Mother Country. The Upper Canadian Tories were quite as dissatisfied politically, as were their Lower Canadian associates, but they had already laid the foundations of the modern Conservative party in the platform of "Protection, Retrenchment and a Union of the British American Provinces," which had been adopted by the Convention of the British American League meeting at Kingston in July, 1849. They believed that these policies would rehabilitate the party in public estimation, free the English provinces from the danger of French domination, and check the cry for annexation.(3)

The condition of the Reform party in Upper Canada was peculiar. Between 1843 and 1848, while making the last fight for the establishment of Responsible Government, it had showed a united front under the able leadership of Mr. Robert Baldwin. But, when the victory had been won, and the new system was in operation, a natural cleavage developed in the Reform ranks. Baldwin and Lafontaine felt that, with the establish-

(1) Letters and Journals of Lord Elgin, p 60.
(2) Issued October and December 1849, and February 1850.
(3) For a full account of the Annexation Movement and the various measures taken to combat it see Allin and Jones, Annexation, Preferential Trade and Reciprocity.

ment of Responsible Government, their work was almost done. They were not Radicals, and had no desire to deal with either the Clergy Reserves, or Seigniorial Tenure. The Radical members of the party, therefore, began to feel that Responsible Government, judged by its fruits under Baldwin and Lafontaine, was a failure. George Brown did his best in the Globe to urge the Government, by keen but friendly criticism, to hasten reform, and especially to deal with the Clergy Reserves, the paramount issue in Upper Canada; but the Clear Grit section of the party, which was just being formed in 1849, under leaders like Peter Perry, Wm. McDougall, Jas. Lesslie and David Christie, and which found mouthpieces in the Toronto Examiner and the Hamilton Provincialist, went far beyond the bounds of friendly criticism, and attacked the Government fiercely for its failure to hasten the anticipated reforms. An editorial correspondent of the Examiner declared:(1)

"The ministry came into office after a well fought battle at the polls, with loud professions on their lips; and public expectation swelled high with the hope that a sound, vigorous, intelligent and patriotic course of administration would ensue. The first session was a blank, and one of the principal measures of the second, an unusually long session, was a measure for creating permanent berths for some of the ministers."

The Examiner itself, in a long pessimistic editorial, (2) lamented the extravagance of the civil list and the post office, still under the control of England; the extravagance of the Provincial Government in public works, in the Provincial Penitentiary, in the creation of a new Court, in the appointment of new judges and officials, and in the work of the King's printer; the operation of the English Navigation Laws, still unrepealed; the fact that the Provincial laws had been made more complicated and costly, not cheaper and simpler; and, most important of all, that a "hireling priesthood, feeding on the vitals of the country, is annually abstracting more than £20,000 from our revenues."(3)

William Lyon Mackenzie, still residing in the U. S., although he had now been pardoned, joined in the attack on the Ministry, since he despaired, not only of the existing Ministry, but of responsible government as then established. He objected to their extravagance, to some of their contemplated appointments, especially that of H. J. Boulton to be a justice of the Court of Common Pleas, and to their unprogressiveness. He branded them in one letter(4) as "a mongrel administration," and in

(1) August 22, 1849.
(2) September 5, 1849.
(3) See also Hamilton Provincialist, quoted by Examiner Sept. 5, 1849.
(4) Examiner, Sept. 5, 1849.

another,(1) quoted approvingly the following from the London Spectator of Aug. 11, 1849.

"As it has been administered in Canada, Responsible Government has resulted chiefly in shifting trouble from Downing St. to the colony. It is the letter of 'Responsible Government' rather than its spirit which has been realized under the auspices of Downing St."

But the Radical press went still further. It not only advocated retrenchment, judicial reform and the secularization of the Clergy Reserves, but also the adoption of the elective principle in the filling of all offices from the Governor-General down. Finally, when the annexation controversy became acute, while not supporting the Montreal agitators, it was willing to consider the question dispassionately, and even declared that a failure to deal with the Clergy Reserves would drive the people into a desire for annexation.(2)

While the affairs of the Reform party were in this highly unsatisfactory state, and just prior to the issuing of the first Montreal Manifesto, the constituency of the Third Riding of York was opened on Oct. 9 by the appointment of the Solicitor-General, Mr. W. H. Blake, to the bench. Mr. Baldwin had already heard that one of his parliamentary friends had given in, or was about to give in, to the Annexationists. He thought, too, that he saw through the tactics of his Tory opponents "The tactics of our opponents are transparent. They want to get some of our supporters to commit themselves, and then turn round on them and the whole party, and impute the call for annexation to the Liberal Party."(3) He knew, too, that because of the dissatisfaction in his own party, the rasher among the Radicals might be led to side with the Annexationists; and so, in order to forestall any such action, and to keep the Upper Canadian Reform party clear of the taint of disloyalty, and, most important of all, in order to do something to stop the further spread of annexation sentiment in the country, he addressed a letter on the subject to Mr. Peter Perry, the man most likely to be chosen by the Reformers of the Third Riding(4) to succeed Mr. Blake in the representation of the Constituency.

Mr. Perry had had a very long and honourable record in the Reform party. He had helped to found the party in 1824, and after that time was regarded as one of its stalwart fighting men. From 1824-36, he represented Lennox and Addington in the Upper Canadian Assembly;

(1) Examiner, Sept. 12, 1849.
(2) Hamilton Provincialist Nov. 7, 1849. Toronto Examiner Nov. 14, 1849.
(3) Letter to Lawrence Heyden, of Toronto, quoted by Dent. The Last Forty Years, Vol. II., p. 182.
(4) The Third Riding of York included at that time the townships of Markham, Pickering, Whitby and East Whitby.

but, after the Union, he was overshadowed by Baldwin, and was not included in either of the Reform Ministries.(1) At this time, he was not only highly dissatisfied with the inactivity of the Government, but was reported to be in favor of annexation.(2) It seemed most important, therefore, that the head of the Government and of the Reform party should declare himself. The Globe emphasized the importance of the occasion. "The approaching election for the 3rd Riding of York— the first appeal to the Country since Annexation tendencies developed among us—afforded Mr. Baldwin an excellent opportunity for declaring his views, and the rumoured intention of Mr. Perry to present himself for the suffrages of the electors in the Liberal interest, pointed him out as the proper person to whom the letter should be addressed."(3) Mr. Baldwin wrote to Mr. Perry from Montreal on Oct. 4 as follows:
"My dear Sir:

"The expediency of applying to the Mother country to give these colonies a separate national existence, or to permit them to annex themselves to the neighboring Republic, has bcome a subject, not only openly discussed in some of the leading journals of the province, but appears to be entertained, to some extent at least, in quarters where we would naturally have looked for the existence of very different sentiments. It becomes necessary, therefore, that no misapprehension should exist on the part of any one, friend or opponent, as to my opinion, either on the question itself, or on the effect which a difference respecting it must necessarily produce on the political relations between me and those of my friends (if any there be) who take a different view of the subject. And I take the liberty of addressing this letter to you, as well from the political connection which has so long subsisted between us, as from the circumstance of an election about to take place for the Riding in which you reside. At that election, whether you may become a candidate or not, of which from your letter to me I am yet uncertain, it is due to my friends, that no room should be left to suppose me undetermined upon, or indifferent to, this question. It is but right that they should be made aware that I have not changed my opinions in relation to it, but that I retain unaltered my attachment to the connection with the Motherland— and that I believe now, as I did when I last addressed my constituents from the hustings, that the continuance of that connection may be made productive of mutual good to both the colony and the parent state.

"It is equally due to my friends that they should, in like manner, be made aware that upon this question there remains, in my opinion, no

(1) Dent, The Last Forty Years. Vol. II., p. 185.
(2) Allin and Jones, Annexation, Preferential Trade and Reciprocity, p. 142.
(3) Oct. 18, 1849.

room for compromise. It is one of altogether too vital a character for that. All should know, therefore, that I can look upon those only who are for the continuance of that connection as political friends—those who are against it as political opponents.

"I do not intend to enter here into the question itself, but I will make one single remark respecting it. The mother country has now for years been leaving to us powers of self-government more ample than ever we have asked, and it does appear a most ungracious return to select such a time for asking for a separation from her forever. I can, at all events, be no party to such proceeding, and must not suffer it to be supposed that I have a moment's doubt respecting it; and let the declaration which I have above made, lead to what it may, as respects the relative political position of either myself or others, I feel that I am in the path of duty in making it, and I abide the consequences."

A short time later, on Oct. 22, Hon. Francis Hincks, Inspector-General in the Government, addressed a letter(1) on the same subject to Mr. Chauncey Crosby, of Markham. He pointed out that the annexation agitation was a great hindrance to securing reciprocity with the United States, although he still hoped that it could be secured. He believed that the sentiments of leading Whig statesmen had been misunderstood, and that there was no desire among any numerous party in England to cast Canada off. He said that Mr. Baldwin's views were endorsed by every member of the Government, and that if they were not supported by their party, it would be their duty "to sustain any administration favourable to British connection which could command a larger share of public opinion than themselves."

Mr. Perry deigned no reply to this letter, but, after some delay, it was published in the papers.(2) In the meantime, steps had been taken to bring a Reform candidate into the field. A requisition, signed by over 400 electors of the Third Riding, was presented to Mr. Perry at Whitby, on Oct. 17, asking him to stand as a condidate. The first four signatures were those of officers of two local Reform meetings, which, while disapproving of the method of bringing forward Mr. Perry, did approve of him, and instructed their officers to sign the requisition. Mr. Perry's answer did not mention annexation at all. He declared that he would act independently in Parliament if elected, would approve of truth no matter whence it originated, and would advocate and uphold the true principles of Reform and Responsible Government. He said his former determination not to re-enter public life had been overcome by "the

(1) Globe, Oct. 25, 1849.
(2) Toronto Globe, Oct. 18. Toronto Mirror, Oct. 19. Toronto Examiner, Oct. 21.

numbers, respectability and standing of the parties joining in the request," and declared that he had no desire to hold office in any government.

The full text of Mr. Perry's answer was not published for a week, and when a report reached Toronto that he had declared, in answer to a question, that "he had no sympathy with the Montreal Annexation Movement," the Globe(1) was ready to welcome his candidacy, since he had been such a staunch Reformer for so many years, "and knew so well the wants of the inhabitants, and would be a useful member of the house."

But the suspicions of the Globe were soon aroused by the fact that Perry still did not answer Baldwin's letter, and by a rumor that he had refused to sign a declaration of loyalty. It therefore called on all parties to unite in defeating him.(2) Some of the Reformers of the Third Riding were likewise suspicious of Mr. Perry, and, on Oct. 31, a meeting of delegates from 4 of the 5 townships of the riding was held at Thompson's Tavern, Pickering. It was resolved to present to Mr. Perry for signature the Toronto Anti-Annexation Protest, and in case he did not sign it, to adopt Mr. Wm. Clark of Scarboro as a candidate. In accordance with this decision Mr. W. F. McMaster and Mr. Samuel Hall waited on Mr. Perry, but he refused to sign the Protest.(3)

Before this action was reported, a correspondent of the Globe, and a pronounced British Connectionist, explained in a letter that he had questioned Mr. Perry at the time of the presentation of the requisition, and had received a definite and satisfactory answer. "Mr. Perry is pledged not to advocate annexation during his term of service. . . . . But he has gone further in his explanation to the electors—he has pledged himself that, should his sentiments undergo any change on the leading topic of the day, by which he may not be able to apply himself vigorously to it in conesquence of his pledge, he will at once throw himself again into the hands of the freeholders of East York."(4)

Although this letter left the reader to assume that Mr. Perry believed that annexation to the U. S. was Canada's ultimate destiny, the Globe was willing to withdraw its opposition, since it saw a great "difference between holding an abstract political opinion on any subject, and carrying that opinion into practical life."(5) At the same time it asked

(1) Oct. 20, 1849.
(2) Oct. 23, 1849.
(3) The Globe, Nov. 6, 1849.
(4) Globe, Nov. 1, 1849.
(5) Globe, Nov. 6, 1849.

Mr. Perry "to say plainly and manfully what his sentiments really are." In truth, the Globe was in a tight box. If it came out squarely against Perry, and denounced him as an annexationist, and he were still elected, the opponents of the Government and of British connection would certainly point to Perry's election as a victory for annexation.(1)

The Examiner found fault with the Globe for interfering in the election, and accused it of trying to dictate to the electors of the Third Riding; while a correspondent, not only levelled the same accusation at Baldwin and Hincks, but accused the Government of unnecessarily delaying the issuing of the writ for the election.(2) The Hamilton Journal and Express, the Dundas Warder and the Long Point Advocate all upheld Mr. Perry in his refusal to sign the Anti-Annexation Protest, since it was unnecessary for Reformers to help the Tories out of the hole in which they found themselves.(3)

The Conservative Toronto Colonist seemed to regard the trouble in the Third Riding as a family quarrel, but could not help insinuating that, although the Government and its supporters might indulge in a good deal of newspaper opposition to annexation, or issue election addresses, or, like the Prime Minister, pronounce the movement "impious," yet it would not begin any prosecutions for sedition, since to do so would be to condemn the very state of affairs their course of conduct had brought about.(4)

On Nov. 1, Mr. Perry addressed a meeting of his constituents at Sterling's Hotel, Norwood, and explained his views very candidly. "He looked forward to Annexation as being the ultimate fate of Canada, yet he did not think that time had come." He thought it was a matter of the very greatest importance, and should be thoroughly discussed by the electorate, "and could not, therefore, be properly discussed in Parliament until a general election had taken place, with the question of annexation before the constituency of the country." His reason for refusing to sign the protest was that it would prevent discussion. The other points in his policy were similar to those advocated by the Radical papers.(5)

There was some little delay in bringing on the election, but the writ was finally issued, and the nomination meeting was held on Dec. 4. Mr. T. P. White, who had been spoken of as a Government candidate, had

---
(1) See Hamilton Provincialist, quoted by the Toronto British Colonist, Nov. 20, 1849.
(2) Examiner, Oct. 31, 1849.
(3) Quoted by Examiner, Oct. 31, 1849.
(4) British Colonist, Oct. 26, 1849.
(5) Examiner, Nov. 28, 1849.

been prudently withdrawn; "Col. E. W. Thompson was brought forward in the Conservative interests, but the show of hands being 50 to 1 against him, his friends had the good sense not to demand a poll."(1) Mr. Perry was then declared elected by acclamation.

The Examiner naturally hailed the election of Mr. Perry as a serious rebuff for the Government and a vindication of those men and journals which had been demanding greater progress. But, most interesting of all, it claimed that the election had brought out clearly a new division of parties. "The natural line between parties, which, for some time past, has been dimly shadowed forth, has here been drawn. The Reform and Progress Party has for a long time been confounded with, or swallowed up in the present Government party, but on this occasion stood forth conspicuously, and came out of the contest triumphantly . . . . Mr. Perry's election is the beginning of a movement that will place the real Reform party in its true position. Then we may expect real reforms."(2)

The Annexationists quite erroneously thought the return of Mr. Perry was a victory for annexation. The Toronto Independent, founded only a short time before to advocate independence as a step towards annexation, announced: "Perry's position is that he is ready to make himself the champion of independence and annexation, when the question is submitted at a general election, but that he will oppose it if it is raised in the present chamber. We approve this position."(3)

The results of the election were momentous. The cleavage between the Conservative and Radical wings of the Reform party had up to this time been "dimly shadowed forth," but it was now plain. In January, 1850, the Examiner still objected slightly to the name "Clear Grit," and the Globe was led to reply that it "merely gave the name which they themselves had assumed, to a little miserable clique of office-seeking bunkum-talking cormorants who met in a certain lawyer's office in King St., and announced their intention to form a new party on "clear Grit" principles."(4) But, a short time later, the Examiner had adopted the name, and announced that the Clear Grit party was now a great fact. Its principles had got hold of the public mind. Its platform did not present many new features except that of elective institutions all around; and yet, because the present ministry was divided on that question, all decidedly advanced measures must be left to a Clear Grit ministry, "a

(1) Examiner, Dec. 12, 1849.
(2) Examiner, Dec. 12, 1849.
(3) Quoted by L'avenir, Dec. 28, 1849.
(4) Globe, Jan. 10, 1850.

PETER PERRY ELECTION—RISE OF THE CLEAR GRIT PARTY.

thing which may well be counted among the not very distant certainties of the future.''(1)

At a great political meeting of advanced Reformers, held at Markham on March 12, 1850, at which Mr. Peter Perry, M. P. P., was the chief figure, the following platform was adopted: 1. The abrogation of the Rectories, and the secularization of the Clergy Reserves. 2. Retrenchment in Provincial expenditure. 3. Abolition of the pensioning system. 4. The appointment of all local officials by local municipal councils. 5. Thorough judicial reform, especially the abolition of the Court of Chancery. 6. A very great extension of the elective franchise, and vote by ballot. 7. Repeal of the law of primogeniture. 8. Abolition of Copyright. 9. Election of the three branches of the Legislature by the people. 10. The right of the people to peacefully discuss any question affecting the Government or Constitution of the colony. 11. The amendment of the license law so as to make the liquor dealers responsible for the effects produced.(2)

Many similar meetings were held in other parts of Upper Canada. Between Jan. 16 and Mar. 6, 1850, the Examiner contained reports of meetings at Lawrenceville, Pelham, Jordan, Hamilton and Smithville. The resolutions passed at these meetings varied a good deal, but retrenchment and a settlement of the Clergy Reserves question were always demanded.

The Clear Grits soon had an opportunity to put their platform to the test. The Hon. Malcolm Cameron resigned, early in December, 1850, his office of Assistant Commissioner of Public Works. He said he did so because the office was a useless one; but it is quite certain that he was dissatisfied with the unprogressiveness of the Government, for he at once made common cause with the Clear Grits. Mr. John Wetenhall, the member for Halton, was appointed to the position vacated by Mr. Cameron, and this necessitated a by-election in that constituency. Mr. Caleb Hopkins, who had been elected by the Reformers of Halton to the first Parliament after the Union, now came forward on the Clear Grit platform, and conducted so successful a campaign that (partly owing to the illness of Mr. Wetenhall) he was elected by a majority of 57, whereas Mr. Wetenhall had been elected, in 1847, with a majority of 265 over his Tory opponent.

But the best proof of the growing strength and importance of the new group came in May, when the Assembly met. The Baldwin-Lafon-

1) Examiner, March 20, 1850.
2) Examiner, March 29, 1850.

taine Government had, nominally, an overwhelming majority; but, in reality, the Reform party was now split into two large sections, and, according to the Examiner,(1) the relative standing of the different parties was as follows: Reformers 34, Clear Grits 22, Conservatives 20, Annexationists 7. It would have been possible at any time for the last 3 groups to unite, and oust the Government; but the Clear Grits did not carry their opposition that far. They wished to force the Ministry to be more progressive, but they had no desire to help the Tories back to power. The consequence was that the Ministry held office until 1851, when first Mr. Baldwin and afterwards Mr. Lafontaine retired from political life. Then Mr. Hincks healed the breach between the two sections of Reformers by adopting a progressive platform, and taking Dr. John Rolph and Hon. Malcolm Cameron into the cabinet he was called upon to organize.(2) But the Clear Grit element in the reunited Reform party remained a powerful one; and when, on the retirement of Mr. Hincks, in 1854, a reconstruction of parties took place, it was the radical, Clear Grit section of the party that rallied around Mr. George Brown.

Mr. Baldwin, Mr. Hincks and the Globe could neither prevent Mr. Perry's nomination, nor cause a rival candidate to be brought forward. The authority of the ministers among their supporters in the country had been too much weakened by dissatisfaction and criticism to allow them to influence greatly the Reformers of the Third Riding. At this very time, a meeting of Reformers was held on Oct. 25 at Sharon, in Mr. Baldwin's own constituency. While they expressed their undiminished confidence in the Government, and condemned the Montreal Annexationists, they passed a series of resolutions demanding many of the same reforms that the Clear Grits were calling for, and then invited their representative, Mr. Baldwin, to confer with them, hear their complaints, and advise them.(3)

But Baldwin, Hincks and George Brown did accomplish one very important thing. By their protests, they helped to save the more extreme Radicals from identifying themselves with the movement for annexation. Mr. Perry, it is true, believed that Canada's ultimate destiny was union with the United States, but he expressly deprecated its discussion at the time, or in the immediate future. At most, he was only such a philosophic separatist as Lord John Russel, at that time Premier of Great Britain.(4) In the Halton election, the question of annexation was not brought up at all although the contest was a very bitter one,

(1) May 15, 1850.
(2) Hincks, Reminiscences of His Public Life, pages 251-257.
(3) Globe, Nov. 8, 1849.
(4) Allin and Jones, Annexation, Preferential Trade and Reciprocity, pp. 279-283.

and many personalities were indulged in. When Parliament met in May, 1850, several questions more or less related to that of annexation came up for discussion. But, although there were seven avowed Annexationists in the Assembly, the number voting against the Government on any of these questions was not higher than 14. In the division by which the Assembly, led by Mr. Baldwin, refused to receive a petition from some of the inhabitants of Essex, Kent and Lambton, praying for an address to the Queen in favour of independence, the vote stood 57-7. In the division on the motion of censure on the Government for dismissing from office those officials who had signed the first Montreal Annexation Manifesto, the vote was 46-14. Most of the Clear Grit members, including Perry and Hopkins, did not vote, and only two of the group voted against the Government.(1) While, therefore, Baldwin, Hincks and the Globe had solidified the opposition to the Government, by their interference in the election for the Third Riding of York, they had, nevertheless, helped to save the Radical wing of the Reform party from trifling with annexation, and so had kept the way clear for the reconciliation of 1851. In doing this, they performed a service for the Reform party, but quite as truly did a great service to the people of Canada, at a very critical moment.

(1) Allin and Jones, Annexation, Etc., pp. 338-351.

XVI.

DAVID ZEISBERGER AND HIS DELAWARE INDIANS.

By Rev. John Morrison, Sarnia

To be born in one nation; at five years of age, because of religious persecution toward his people, to be carried like the Christ-child into another nation; to be left there at fifteen to complete his education, when, his parents seeking greater liberty in worship, emigrated to America; to live under a false accusation of thefts, growing out of a gift of gold bestowed by a wealthy man to whom he had rendered a helpful service; to run away with another youthful companion from the school, at seventeen years of age; make his way across Europe, cross the mighty Atlantic; find his parents in the new world; in young manhood to give himself to the church of his fathers; to carry the gospel to no less than thirteen of the great Indian tribes of the American continent, covering seven of the great states, or territories, including Canada; to see all the horrors—including Indians scalping innocent white people, and white soldiers, unworthy of the name, ruthlessly butchering innocent Indians—men, women and children; to spend more than sixty years in such arduous missionary labors; to have established the first Protestant mission, and to have administered the first Protestant baptism, west of the Alleghanies; to have hung the first Protestant church bell and preached the first Protestant sermon in what is now the State of Ohio; to have founded no less than thirteen towns, some at least of which grew into places of importance and hold a prominent place to-day on the map—surely such a list of activities is enough to lift any life from the dead level of mediocrity and also place it on a mountain top of honor before an admiring world. Such was the life of the subject of this sketch.

David Zeisberger was born at Zauchtenthal, Moravia, Good Friday, 11th of April, 1721; at five taken to Herrnhut, Saxony, Luther's land; at seventeen, followed his parents to Georgia. At the age of 87 years ceased at once to work and live, crowned with the glory of God and the praises and honor of men, at Goshen, Tuscarawas County, Ohio, where his body was buried and his grave still is.

DAVID ZEISBERGER AND HIS DELAWARE INDIANS. 177

A marble slab, simple and unostentatious, as was his life, bears the following inscription:

David Zeisberger,
who was born 11th April, 1721,
in Moravia, and departed this life 17 Nov., 1808,
aged 87 years, 7 m. and 6 days.
This faithful servant of the Lord laboured among the
American Indians as a Missionary during the
last 60 years of his life.

This wonderful man, spending most of his life in the forest wilderness of the heart of this American continent, surrounded by savage beasts and yet more savage men, turned the wilderness in many places to smiling farms and gardens, and the untutored Indian in large numbers into Christian, civilized life.

The ancient nation of the Delawares had for him special attraction, and to their Christianization he devoted the greater portion of his long and richly eventful life, proving himself as great in missionary zeal and enterprise in the eighteenth century as David Livingstone, who was born nearly five years after his death, in the nineteenth.

True to the red cross flag of England, under the protecting folds of which he found an asylum when he landed on the American shore, he inculcated the same loyalty very largely into his Delaware Indians, leading his people, his "Brown Brethren," as he affectionately called them, from Ohio, when danger, under the newly flung to the breezes stars and stripes beset their pathway, on the request of the British commandant at Detroit—Major de Peyster—into the state of Michigan. After four years resident there on the banks of the Clinton (then called Huron) River, about three miles from where Mt. Clemens now stands, made to believe all danger past, and hoping to do a yet greater work among the Indian tribes, he led his people back to Ohio, only to discover a danger cloud constantly hanging over their heads. He then, after negotiations with the British authorities, led his band of Delaware Indians into Canada, in 1791, spending one year on the bank of the Detroit River, where Fort Malden was afterwards built. Then a grant of land being made by the authorities, in the County of Kent, in 1792, the year before MacKenzie made his discovery by land of the Pacific, Zeisberger, with his devoted helpers of the Moravian Church—Gottlob Senseman, William Edwards, and Michael Jung—led his "Brown Brethren," part by canoe and part by land, by the route of Detroit River, Lake St. Clair, and the Thames, building a new town—Fairfield—in the unbroken forest.

Here was as true a band of U. E. Loyalists, whether officially given that name or not, as any who crossed at Niagara, Bay of Quinte, or the lower provinces. These men of the ancient race of this continent sacrificed their homes and lands to live under the protection of the British flag, and carve out new homes on the land given them there; and their descendants are with us to this day, at Moraviantown.

In his report of Nov. 8, 1791, Thos. Jefferson, Secretary of State, noted the transfer as follows: "The Indians, however, for whom the reservation was made, have chosen to emigrate beyond the limits of the United States, so that the lands reserved for them still remain in the United States." That is to say, as in the case of the white U. E. Loyalists, their lands were confiscated, without recompense.

For six years did Zeisberger remain at Fairfield, then the mission being well established and his assistants quite capable of full management, his love for souls, greater than his love for the old flag, led him back to Ohio, where he decided he was more largely needed, and there died, as already stated.

Zeisberger was a man small in stature, but big in intellect and soul. He was not missionary only, but a great explorer and pioneer of civilization, and also a voluminous writer, his published works constituting an almost perfect resume of all that entered into the period covered by his missionary life; and what further the thousands of pages of his writings, yet unpublished, may add to our historical knowledge of that period, we cannot tell. This we deeply feel—that what is now Western Ontario was highly favored and honored in having, for full seven years, been the dwelling place of this remarkable, and now almost unknown and forgotten man. We will go so far as to confidently assert that he was one of the greatest men who ever spent that many years in this western part of our Province.

We have carefully read his published diaries; we have read a number of works written by strong men dealing with this wonderful missionary and pioneer explorer; we have searched for, found and photographed the site of New Gnadenhutten (Tents of Grace) on the bank of the Clinton River, Mich.; we have gone over the old ground of Fairfield, photographed important bits of the present life, also the past; we have secured official and authentic maps from original surveys of the town of New Gnadenhutten, showing the exact location of houses, and of old Fairfield on the Thames, afterwards burned to the ground in bitter hatred by the American soldiers after the Battle of the Thames; we have copied from the baptismal register of this, the oldest Protestant cause in western Ontario, seventy years' record of the one hundred and twelve, beginning with January, 1800, and we have found it a most fascinating study.

We have decided that the best way to let you see this remarkable man, his assistants and Indians, following this introduction, is to give you carefully selected items verbatim from his journals,* and in which you will see how truly he entered into every detail of life pertaining to his chosen work. In so doing we will confine ourselves to that portion in time beginning when he and his Indians fled from Ohio to Michigan, still under the British flag, in 1782, and closing with his departure from Fairfield, on the Thames, Aug. 15, 1798.

Extracts from Journals.

Jan. 10, 1782—At Upper Sandusky. Nearly all the brethren went out to dig wild potatoes, on which to live. We have no corn.

Feb. 7—In the Shawanese towns they bought about a bushel of corn for which they paid five dollars. Wild Indians as well as Americans were exceedingly hostile.

March 15—A few of us left today by order from the commandant for Detroit to consult with him.

April 13—Two vessels with a sergeant and fourteen rangers, from the British commandant, to take us to Detroit.

Apl. 20—Arrived safely at Detroit. Major de Peyster told us he called us to save our lives. Detroit is like Sodom, where all sins are committed. There is a R. Catholic church on each side of the Detroit River, but the English and Protestant people have neither church nor preacher, and wish for neither.

July 20—Today David Zeisberger and John George Jungmann, with their wives, Wm. Edwards and Michael Jung, two unmarried missionaries, accompanied by nineteen Delawares, men, women and children, by boat started for the Huron River. Boats lashed together for safety crossing L. St. Clair, in charge of two pilots. Found the Huron River deep, with little current. After several unsatisfactory landings, we, on the 22nd, further up, found on the south side of the river a fine place to lay out a town on a height. On the N. East, between the river and the height, are many springs which flow into the river. Soil is sandy with heavy hardwood timber; splendid cherry, of which in Detroit the most

*The Ohio Archaeological and Historical Society, Columbus, O., has been active in the publication of Leisberger's memoirs. These are of so much interest in the early history of southwestern Ontario that numerous extracts are reprinted here.

beautiful cabinet work is made, and sassafras so large, boards two feet wide can be cut therefrom.

Pitched our tents. The scripture verse for the day—"For ye shall go out with joy and be led forth with peace."

Location data.—He speaks of "the fork a half-mile higher up than we are, to which the water is deep."

July 23—Having brought plants with us, we set them out, sowed turnips and lettuce, planted beans and some garden stuff. We found traces of an old Indian town on the site we had chosen, and holes that had been storehouses, also hills where corn had been grown; now it is a dense wood of trees two to six feet in diameter.

Sat., July 27—We marked out our town, in the first place only where two rows of houses shall be built, and the street four full rods wide, but each lot has three rods in front.

Mon., July 29—We began to fell the trees on our town site, so as to build our houses. No animals to draw them, so we had to carry them.

Friday, Aug. 2—Began to block out our first house (evidently not superstitious).

Friday, Aug. 16—We roofed our first house, and have the timber for a second already on hand.

Aug. 22—At Detroit, the Commandant read us a letter from Gen'l Haldimand rec'd two days before from Quebec, that we might see what he did was done with Haldimand's approbation.

Sat., Sept. 21—We had a love feast and holy communion, the first time in this place.

Six more of our Indians arrived from Sandusky. (Pays tribute to British protection.) Our Indian enemies took all conceivable pains to prevent our Indians coming here, and lied to them on every hand, that they were no longer safer with the English than with the Americans.

Thursday, Oct. 3—Today the first death, Elizabeth, daughter of Ignatius and Christina, two years, ten months and one day old. She was buried on the 4th, the first seed in our "God's Acre," which was thus dedicated, a beautiful, even place on a height, the finest we have anywhere had.

Sun., Oct. 6—A little daughter of the same parents, born in June, was baptized—name Naomi. Our first baptism.

Wed., Oct. 16—Having gone to Detroit by boat, some days before, we received an order from the Major upon the commisary for six months' provisions for ourselves, viz., the missionaries; also full rations of the best provisions for the Indians. The Major told us to keep for further use the boat he had lent us, and promised to visit us during the winter months when the lake was frozen.

Oct. 23—Fine and warm, so that frogs are heard.

Sat., Nov. 2—A pretty and, for the time being, spacious, meeting house was finished.

Tues., Nov. 5—We held the first service in our new chapel. Text—" The Lord will come with strong hand, and his arms shall rule for Him; behold, His reward is with Him, and His work before Him."

Nov. 8—Weather still fine and pleasant. Have had some snow, but it has not remained a day.

Nov. 23—We are very thankful for the exceptionally fine, warm weather which we had not expected.

Where we are located, no open land, all thickly grown with trees, but good land and not hard to clear.

Dec. 7—Lately quite cold, river ran thick with ground ice and froze.

Dec. 12—The brethren went hunting in a body; they form a half-moon or circle, and go through a district where the deer come within shot of one or another.

Tuesday, Dec. 24—We began Christmas with a love feast, the first for two years. He blessed us anew. There were together fifty-three of us, white and brown.

Dec. 25—Bro. Heckewelder (another Moravian Missionary) preached from the gospel about the announcement of the angels to the shepherds and to all mankind, that we should rejoice in the birth of the Saviour. Then was the children's hour. To these was Jesus in the manger depicted, while they reverently sang.

Jan. 3, 1783—Up to date we have had no cold to speak of, for the ground in the bottoms is not yet frozen.

Mon., Jan 27—We heard here to-day loud firing of cannon but knew not what it meant. We hear it was the celebration of the birthday of Her Majesty, the Queen.

Feb. 11—Fine Spring-like weather, the snow went quite away, partly from rain, partly from warm winds.

Feb. 14—This week we made our first sugar. The traders take sugar from the Indians and sell it for three shillings the pound. A whole deer sells for four or five dollars.

March 3—Corn at the fort is enormously dear, and costs more than three pounds a bushel; last summer there was a failure of the crop. Deer meat is exchanged for corn.

April 23—Major de Peyster gave us two cows and three horses. Also Mr. Askin paid us one hundred pounds sterling, received from Montreal; from this we bought two cows; they are very dear, thirty to forty pounds, New York currency.

May 1—Of garden stuff we have already sowed a good deal.

May 16—About forty of our Indians arrived from the Miami and we had to enlarge our chapel.

May 24, Sat.—We began to plant corn.

June 27—Provisions were given us by the Major,— fifty-two barrels of flour, twenty-five barrels of pork, also a quantity of corn and other things, so our people are well provided for.

Early in Sept., corn, cucumbers and beans, were badly cut by frost.

Sat., Oct. 4—Two Frenchmen came here with apples to sell.

The Indians make canoes and the women make baskets, brooms and mats, and also gather acorns. They sell all in Detroit, and with the proceeds buy winter clothing.

Oct. 8—Bro. Edwards went out with a boat-load of potatoes.

Sat., Jan. 10, 1784—Some gentle folk came in sleighs from Detroit, on the ice over the lake, to visit us, simply to see our town, who say according to the thermometer it has not been so cold for twenty-eight years as it is now, being seven degrees lower than in that period of time.

Jan. 29—A hard winter and deep snow, which through the whole country lies full three feet deep.

Feb. 7—Within three days by the use of snow-shoes, more than one hundred deer have been shot, for which, in our hunger, we were very thankful. Our corn did not ripen well last autumn, and we were in distress for food.

Sun. Feb. 22—A merchant from Detroit, who, with his family, came here visiting, asked for the baptism of his two children, as there is no ordained minister of the Protestant Church in Detroit; the Justice baptizes the children, or the commandant, if it be asked of him, but to many this is not satisfactory.

March 3—Again snow has fallen a foot deep upon the old, so that now it lies four feet deep.

March 12—Corn in Detroit is very dear. Twenty to thirty-two shillings a bushel and not to be had.

Wild animals, deer and other, found dead in the woods, owing to deep snow.

April 11—Easter Sunday. We read the litany, partly in our chapel and partly in the grave-yard.

April 15—Now that the corn was gone, our brethren sought to live on wild potatoes, going to the lakes where there are many of them, and bringing back as many as they could carry.

The lake opened on the 19th.

April 25—Commandant well disposed toward us, supplies were few in the King's store-house, and of flour there was none at all, for last autumn three or four ships were wrecked on the lake. Both we and our Indians got some beans and pork.

Mon., May 31—We heard that the commandant, Col. de Peyster, sailed away yesterday from Detroit for Niagara. We wish him every good thing, for he has done well by us; and our Indians would not have been alive here if he had not interested himself in us and helped us.

June 16—The sisters went for wild cherries, of which there are many this year, on which in part they live. Food is scarce, as the deer and other game nearly all perished last winter.

The latter part of summer we lived on whortleberries, of which there was a great abundance about a day's journey away. Sickness usually follows famine, but of sickness we have had no sign.

Oct. 12—We visited Lord Geo. Hay, who succeeded de Peyster. He promised to continue along same line in treatment of our mission; was friendly and promised to visit us sometime.

Tues., Dec. 31—In the midnight watch service, gratitude to God was poured forth for a bountiful harvest.

Holy communion nine times during the year. One woman baptized. Eight births, four boys and four girls. Three marriages, and two adults died.

1785.

Jan. 5—Severe cold weather, snow over a foot deep. Streams frozen over.

Jan. 29—Canoes finished, seventeen in number, to carry us across the lake, where we hope now for safety, and the Chippewa Indians objected to us living in their country.

Mon., Mch. 7—At Detroit. Gov. Hay stated that **the Governor, and Colonels, had strict orders from England to protect our mission in every possible way,** and we were to remain some time longer where we were.

Aug. 3—Heard of Gen'l Hay's death; he was buried on the second of this month.

Mon., Sept. 26—Today many brethren went to the salt springs to boil salt, not far by water and by land only seven miles.

Dec. 9—Smallpox has broken out in Detroit. The English people believe it a punishment from God. They came together in the Council House and are thinking about a church and preacher.

Dec. 17—Have had deep snow; now warm again. The sisters were away this week and made some sugar.

Dec. 31—Baptised this year two adult women and two girls. One death, a child. The inhabitants here on the Huron River number one hundred and seventeen Indian souls.

1786.

Feb. 8—First mention of the new commandant, Maj. Ancrum, who ratified agreements made with his predecessors, and agreed to help them all he could.

Sat., Mch. 4—Major Ancrum, with a couple of officers and Mr. Askin, came in their sleighs; were well pleased with our settlement. In the morning, Mch. 5, they returned.

Mch. 6—Arrangements made at Detroit whereby we are to receive four hundred dollars for our houses and improvements, the missionaries one-half, the Indians the other.

During the past winter our Indians laid out and cut through a straight road to Detroit, twenty-three and one-half miles by measurement.

Mch. 17—Surveyor Frey and Capt. Anderson have surveyed our town and the river to the lake, accurately charting them.

Sat., Apl. 15—Our last love-feast in New Gnadenhutten.

Apl. 16—Easter Sunday. We read the Easter Litany, partly in the chapel, partly in the grave-yard.

Apl. 17—In the ev'g came Capt. Anderson, whose ship lay at the mouth of the river. Mr. Askin had bought our corn and on the 18th our Indians took it down and put it on board.

Thurs., Apl. 20—After we had, early, and for the last time, assembled in our chapel, and upon our knees thanked the Saviour for all the goodness we had enjoyed from Him, and further committing ourselves to His mercy upon the journey, we loaded our canoes, and all went away together in the afternoon. In the evening we camped at the mouth of the River Huron. Just four years today we landed in Detroit.

Apl. 23—Delayed by storms we did not arrive in Detroit until noon today; a fleet of twenty-two canoes.

Apl. 28—On board two sloops, the Beaver and Mackina, we left for Cayahoga, the Major having given us full supplies.

June 8—All arrived safely at Cayahoga, some by canoe, the rest on foot by land, and our vessel safely with all the goods.

Here Zeisberger, his brother missionaries, together with the Indians, built New Salem, on the Cayahoga, continuing there until the spring of 1791. Word being received from time to time of the killing of Indians by the American militia, the missionaries, as well as the mission Indians, grew fearful for their lives, and well they might, with the memory of March 8, 1782, when at Gnadenhutten, in Ohio, ninety Christian Indians, men, women and children, were ruthlessly butchered by the American militia.

1791.

The commandant and Col. McKee were inclined to provide us with a place of abode, ad interim, until the answer from the Governor and Superintendent-General of Canada arrived, and also to help us with ships for transportation.

The latter part of March and first part of April, we moved our belongings to Sandusky Bay.

Sun., Apl. 10—Zeisberger delivered the farewell sermon. Then the bell was taken down and carried away, and on Apl. 14 they bade a last farewell to New Salem.

Tues., Apl. 19—Today went on board the Sagina, and on Thursday, 21st, sailed for Detroit River, part of our men having gone ahead by land, driving our cattle.

Wed., May 4—Owing to opposing high winds, were unable to make the mouth of the Detroit River until today. The Sensemans and others had arrived earlier and greeted us. Our goods were unloaded on McKee and **Elliott's plantation** (Canadian side).

May 6—Officers from Detroit came today and instructed us as to the land we were to occupy, and were very friendly. Only a few white settlers beyond (east of) Elliott's farm.

Tues., May 17—We brought all the cattle over the river by boat, a weary work in windy weather, yet everything went well.

Here, among us, a new trouble has broken out among the dogs, some of which have gone mad and injured the cattle. In Sandusky we were forced to shoot some, for the Chippewa dogs had infected ours.

May 23—Hard rain; our town was overflowed with water. Our brethren had to tear down the huts and build them nearer the water bank.

(Note—This, and another item, when in Aug., 1798, Zeisberger returned to Ohio, viz., "And at the mouth of the River Ft. Malden, building on the site of the Watch Tower," gives us the location of the "Warte," or Watch Tower, their temporary resting-place for one year.)

Sun., May 29—Bro. Senseman preached in the open air. Many blacks and also whites were present. This was the first Sabbath service held by them on Canadian soil.

Sat., June 4—The King's birthday. Heard cannon firing in celebration at Detroit, eighteen miles away.

June 13—Timber had been prepared and today our meeting house was begun, in size twenty-four by thirty-two feet.

June 14—Ten young people went away today without asking us and without orders, with a war party, to fight Americans.

Sun., June 19—Trinity Sunday. Our meeting-house was so far done, we could have our first service in it. Whites and blacks were also present.

Tues., June 21—The meeting-house was today chinked, doors and benches made, and the bell put in place.

Sat., Sept. 10—Bro. Senseman conducted the Lord's Supper.

Mr. Dolson came from the Thames, bringing his two children to put them in our school, of which Bro. Senseman was teacher.

Sept. 13—Day before yesterday twenty vessels sailed by for Ft. Erie. Last night the greatest storm we have seen here; the river rose very high and tonight, with a west wind, it fell five feet.

1792.

Tues., Feb. 28—Under advice from McKee, the Indian Samuel, with five young Indian brethren, set our for Retrenche R. (the Thames) to learn about the country, examine the land, seek out and determine upon a place where we can settle next spring.

Mch. 1—The brethren came back, having met a man at Detroit who told them all was settled by the Government, so no need to go and look.

Mch. 8—Fine spring weather and lake open.

Wed., Apl. 11—Zeisberger's seventy-second birthday.

Thurs., Apl. 12—Assembled early and for the last time in our chapel. The canoes were laden and about noon we went away. Bro. Michael Jung went with the men who took the cattle by land.

Sun., Apl. 15—Owing to contrary winds delaying us at Detroit, did not reach L. St. Clair until the afternoon of today. Our mast broke, delaying us again, so it was after dark before we entered the mouth of the Retrenche. We had added a large hired boat; owing to shallow water we could not land; lay in boat, cold and wet, all night.

Tues., Apl. 17—Came to "Sally Hand," a colony composed of English, German and French settlers. Bros. Senseman and Edwards went with the boat into the settlement. Zeisberger remained in the settlement, waiting the arrival of the men and cattle, which occurrd on Sat., Apl. 21.

Sun., Apl. 22—Zeisberger preached in the settlement; many from the neighborhood came to hear. His text was, "All flesh is grass."

Wed., Apl. 25—All went to Senseman's camp, above the fork (now Chatham), the end of the settlement; further on no white people live. Here unloaded great boat; current too swift to go further; must use our canoes.

Apl. 27—Senseman and party have here built a shelter hut to remain till canoes return for them. Zeisberger and Indians in twenty canoes go up the river; at noon arrive at the rapids. In the evening had a supper of turtles taken on the way.

Wed., May 2—After day spent exploring the river up and down, we today, after examining a height, took possession and staked out our town.

May 3—In the forenoon the town lots were distributed, and each one took possession.

May 5—Senseman and party arrived, and we were all together once more.

Tues., May 8—Moved today to a better town site, three miles down the creek.

May 10—Thomas having died on Tuesday, we buried him this forenoon. We had found and laid out a beautiful grave-yard upon a little height. It is sandy ground.

May 15-16—The brethren cleared, each for himself, and built huts in town. For some days all have been busy clearing land.

Sat., May 19—Got about two acres planted. More than one hundred acres will be cleared and planted this year.

Sat., June 30—Coming here we bought one hundred bushels of corn at "Sally Hand," and now we have bought some more at Monceytown, higher up the river. Corn is one dollar a bushel at Monceytown. We lived in huts under the green trees until after the planting was done.

Sat., June 30—The brethren built a great shed two rods square to hold the meetings in.

July 9—All the brethren went to work on the meeting-house and kept at it all the week, and Thursday, July 12, we had the first service in it from the text—"Which was a prophet, mighty in deed and word before God and all the people."

The Indians are working for the whites to procure food until their crop should be fit for harvest.

June and July very dry; not enough rain to wet the ground. Then came rain and cold, and Sept. 20 and 21, frost, which cut the corn not yet ripe.

Sat., Sept. 22—Received today letters from Bethlehem, Pa., of date May 3 and Jan. 1, last.

Oct. 25—Received kindly messages today by brethren returned from Detroit, from Col. Richard England, 24th Regiment, and now commandant there.

DAVID ZEISBERGER AND HIS DELAWARE INDIANS. 189

Nov. 22—Snowed all day.

Nov. 30—We killed our hogs.

Dec. 15—Our Indians have been making a road to the settlement. They returned today, but the work is not yet completed.

Dec. 26—All the brethren went out to cut, square and then split timber into boards for a school-house. To the young people it was joyful news.

Mon., Dec. 31—Review of year: A perfect wilderness when we came here in May. The building site thickly grown with heavy timber, and now nearly thirty good houses stand here, among them many dressed block houses. More than one hundred acres of land have been cleared and planted. During the year five baptisms, eight marriages, one died. We number here one hundred and fifty-one persons.

1793.

Jan. 10—Our school-house finished.

Sat., Feb. 16—Gov. John Graves Simcoe and party arrived here this morning. He examined everything and was well pleased therewith. We entertained him to breakfast. We told him, "none of us missionaries had either renounced our allegiance to the King, or sworn it to the States." He spent two hours with us.

Mon., Feb. 18—We heard cannon firing in Detroit, welcoming the Governor on arrival.

Sat., Feb. 23—Heard cannon discharged in Detroit, eighty miles away, as the Governor set out on his return journey.

Mon., Feb. 25—Gov. Simcoe and suite arrived and passed the night with us. We presented him with an address. He ordered his commissary to draw for us an order on the King's stores at Detroit, because of our crop having been frozen. Wrote an answer to our address. After asking permission, he, with his suite, attended our early morning service and worship. He expressed his satisfaction with the devout worship of the Indians. He and his party then continued their journey toward Niagara.

Mch. 12—The ice in the river broke up.

Sat., Apl. 20—This week we sowed our garden vegetables.

Sat., May 4—Surveyor McNeff and party arrived to survey townships below us.

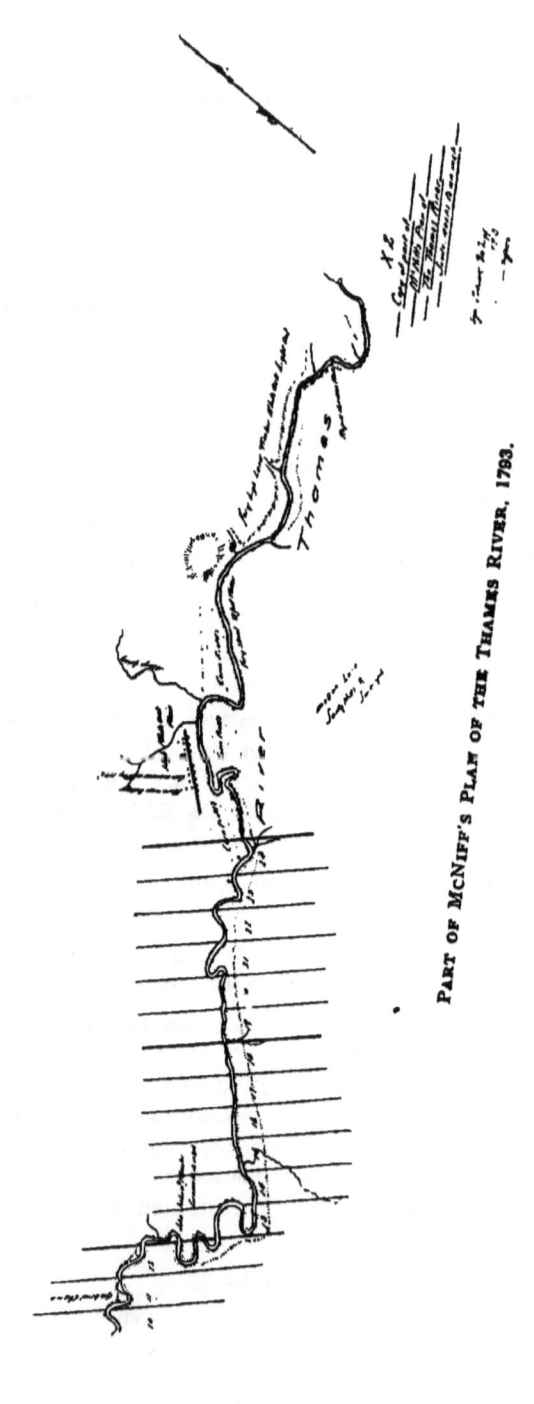

PART OF McNIFF'S PLAN OF THE THAMES RIVER, 1793.

Wed., May 8—The Surveyor surveyed our town in order to make a draft of it. (See map.)

Thurs., June 27—The Indian Peter's hive of bees, which he brought here from Pettquotting, swarmed today for the second time. **There are none here in the bush in the whole neighborhood.**

(**Note**—At Pettquotting, bee trees were abundant in the forest, and they could easily secure honey in plenty.)

(Bees are not native to N. America, but were brought by the Puritans, and the Delaware-Moravian Indian, Peter, was evidently the pioneer apiarist of Western Ontario.)

Aug. 12—Indians at work on houses in the middle of the town for Zeisberger and Sensemann, their former houses being temporary only, afterwards to be stables.

Sat., Sept. 14—This week the brethren began to harvest their corn, which this year has all thriven as well as could be wished.

Sept. 2—Our corn good and perfect; nothing injured by frost.

Oct. 3—Our people found, hardly half a mile from the town, on the bank of the creek, a salt spring of which no one knew, at a place where the bank is so steep cattle could not get to it, else it had been found before. Earlier, an oil spring had been found lower down the river.

Oct. 14—Our school-house covered with clapboards.

Oct. 18—The Zeisbergers moved into their new house facing the **street.**

Nov. 6—The wolves began killing our young cattle.

Nov. 19—The weather mild with a south wind. The sisters boiled sugar. (See map for location of sugar bush.)

Nov. 22—Sisters made a good amount of sugar this week.

Mon., Tues., Dec. 9-10—It has been like a yearly market. Mr. Dolson came with goods for sale, displayed them, and the whole town traded, buying from him for cattle, corn and skins.

Tues., Dec. 31—There live here now one hundred and fifty-nine Indian souls—eight more than at the close of last year.

1794.

Wed., Jan. 1—Many strangers from the upper town (Monceytown, we presume) were here during the holidays and attended the services.

Tues., Jan. 7—The surveyor, Mr. McNeff, came from Detroit to survey our township. In the river he lost ten of his people, soldiers, who broke through the ice and were drowned.

Jan. 14—The surveyor finished surveying, thirty-six lots in all. Senseman and Indians blazed the line on both sides of the river.

Sat., Mch. 22—This year there is a poor sugar harvest, such as we have never had. First it was furiously cold and then all at once it came such warm weather it was soon over.

Mon., Mch. 31—Towards evening Gov. Simcoe arrived with a suite of officers and soldiers and eight Mohawks, by water from Niagara. He at once asked for our school-house as a lodging. It was cold, having snowed during the day. He was much pleased when Bro. Sensemann offered his house, where he, together with his officers, then lodged. Two of his officers had been here with him last year. Our sisters entertained them. The soldiers lay close by in the school-house, but the Mohawks were divided between two Indian houses, whom also our Indian brethren abundantly supplied with food. The Gov. was glad to see so many houses built since he was here before; also that our Indians had cleared so much land, and he praised their industry and labor. Still more, he wondered at seeing in the place such a great pile of timber, and when he learned that it was destined for a meeting house, and also that the Indian brothers and sisters had brought it in on sleighs, without horses, he said, "Would that I could have seen this."

Tues., Apl. 1—After friendly leave-taking, the Gov. and his party set out for Detroit in four canoes.

Toward the end of March Mr. Parke came here with a boat and took away to Detroit about one thousand bushels of corn, and Mr. Dolson has taken away quite as much.

Wed., June 11—White people came through here from Niagara with cattle for Detroit.

Frid., Aug 6—Weather has been very hot and dry, so that many fruits and vegetables have wilted and the corn begins to wither. The thermometer for several days has been at 96 degrees, which it never was before.

White people went through here Wed., the 4th, from Detroit, with cattle. They have begun a settlement forty or fifty miles up this river. They are thirty families strong, having lately come from Europe.

Wed., Oct. 1—The temporary meeting-house having been removed, a new and substantial one was being built. Our people were industrious about the meeting-house. Today they finished the roof and also the little tower, and the bell was hung up.

Sun., Oct. 19—Our new meeting-house having been completed yesterday, we dedicated it today to the Lord, in the first service held by Bro. Zeisberger; the sermon was by Bro. Sensemann, from the text, "In all places where I record my name I will come unto thee and I will bless thee." In the afternoon a love-feast was conducted by Bro. Zeisberger, and at the concluding service of the day Michael Jung preached from, "Turn us again, O Lord God of Hosts, cause thy face to shine and we shall be saved." Several strangers attended the church opening.

Oct. 24—A runaway negro from Detroit came here, and was taken back by Mr. Parke.

Sun., Nov. 16—We chose a name for our place and township—namely, Fairfield—(that is, Schönfeld).

Nov. 19—Mohawks went through with two American prisoners.

Wed., Dec. 31—In Fairfield, one hundred and sixty-five Indians.

1795.

Wed., Apl. 8—From MacKenzie, the trader, we heard that his uncle had made a journey by land to the northwest as far as the sea, being two years about it, and is now come to Detroit.

Apl. 20—The Indians got a dozen canoes into the water, made near here, most of them of walnut wood. MacKenzie took up by consent his abode here.

June 26—We got in our hay.

Wed., July 1—White people went through with horses for Niagara.

Thurs., July 16—The Indian brothers went to make a deer fence from here to the lake, from which they expect much advantage and good hunting.

White people brought children to be baptised and also some came to be married. Sensemann goes at times to the settlement to baptise and also to marry folks.

Aug. 19—An Indian in Monceytown has had a vision and revelation that the world will last four years more, and then be destroyed.

Mon., Sept. 14—We mowed our after-grass.

Frid., Oct. 2—White people arrive almost daily. The road to Niagaga is much used.

Thurs., Oct. 15—There was a severe wind, which began with a thunder storm and lasted the whole day. It unroofed houses, and in the fields much damaged the corn, and in the bush around made great devastation, yet no one was injured.

Tues., Oct. 20—There being many chestnuts, which the wind has lately shaken down, the sisters brought home great quantities of them, which are very helpful in their housekeeping.

Oct. 27—Our neighbor, Kessler, ploughed for some Indians, and sowed wheat for them (the first mention of wheat at Fairfield). We have again a good harvest and a burden of corn.

Nov. 5—Chestnuts and walnuts very plentiful this year, and freely gathered.

Dec. 7—Bill Henry and others came with wheat and corn they have had ground, from the mill, seven miles from here.

Dec. 31—In Fairfield there now live one hundred and fifty-eight Indian souls, great and small, seven less than last year.

1796.

Wed., Jan. 15—It is now known that in the spring the States will take possession of Detroit, for which preparation has been made by laying out a fort on the east side of the river.

Sat., Feb. 20—Michael Jung went to the settlement, seven miles away, to deliver a sermon, having been invited so to do. On his return, reported a fine audience and requested to come again.

Feb. 22—Our young people, who go to school, are so set upon it, they make it their chief business and prefer it to everything. Went and cut wood for Bro. Sensemann at his sugar hut, so he might not be hindered by work from keeping school. Many of them can write a good English hand, better than many clerks with merchants at Detroit.

Sun., Apl. 10—Bro. Michael Jung went early to the next township and preached to the people assembled there, and in the afternoon came home.

Apl. 11—Bro. Sensemann came back from the lower settlement, where he preached yesterday and baptised eleven children. The people live like Indians; hear no word of God and have little longing therefor.

Apl. 19—The Chippewas went away to their home on the next river northward, the Sneycarty (Chenal Ecarte). Our people sowed much wheat.

Fri., Apl 22—Bro. Sensemann came back from the Fort, where the soldiers are evacuating Detroit and going to the east side of the river.

Tues., May 3—A hat-maker from the settlement came here with hats to sell, almost all of which he disposed of.

Wed., May 25—The hat-maker, Choates, came here to sell hats.

(Note—As the diary proceeds, it becomes evident that reasonably regular preaching service was established in a number of places around the settlement near by.)

Wed., June 29—A taylor whom we had sent for to make us needful clothing, came yesterday, took our measure, and went home again.

Thurs., Aug. 23—Indians busy cutting summer wheat and bringing it into their barns, the like of which has never been seen in any of the places where we have been, and all are wishing to raise wheat but not to give up corn.

Wed., Sept. 14—Work was begun upon the new school-house, which will stand near the chapel.

Sept. 17—Window glass and nails were brought from Detroit for the new schoolhouse.

Sept. 29—We sowed our winter wheat. This was a month earlier than last year.

Oct. 3—We harvested our potatoes and pumpkins.

Wed., Oct. 5—This is a year quite apart by itself; it was a late spring, a cool summer and early autumn. There were early frosts, which kept on, but since we made good use of planting-time, the corn ripened in good season. Racoons, squirrels, bears, wolves and wild turkeys came in great numbers, and did great harm to the fields. Besides, all sorts of vermin came from the south, tried to get over the river and were drowned, whole heaps of which could be seen.

Oct. 8—Brethren came back from the settlement with canoes full of apples, which they paid for with baskets.

Oct. 18—Michael went to mill with wheat. (The first intimation of wheat supplanting corn.)

Oct. 22—Bro. Sensemann came back from Detroit, where he had dinner with Gen'l Wayne, who inquired kindly about our mission. When Gen'l Wayne marched in with his troops, the English commandant went away with the garrison by water, discharging in salute his cannon from the ship and was saluted in return, whereupon the new owners moved in with music, undisturbed. It was in July the change was made.

In the settlement Bro. Sensemann was offered a place in the Legislative Assembly, but he declined.

Oct. 29—Our Heavenly Father has again blessed us by giving us a good harvest. The squirrels have not done so much damage here as in the settlement, where they have laid waste whole fields.

Dec. 31—In Fairfield live one hundred and sixty-nine Indian souls.

1797.

Jan. 22—After a funeral conducted in the settlement by Michael Jung, some of them brought a law-suit to him to settle; he declined.

Mon., Apl. 3—The river having broken up Mch. 16, and fine weather continuing after, many today sowed summer wheat.

Apl. 15—During these days many rafts of pine lumber went by which came down from "The Pinery," far above.

Mon., May 20—Inasmuch as the frosts lasted so long, the corn rotting in the ground did not come up, we had to plant again. A very late spring. The white settlers came to us for seed corn for second planting, as their first had all rotted.

Frid., June 16—So strong a wind from the N. west, with thunder, lightning and rain, few houses remained uninjured, and much damage was done in the fields. For three miles west the road was blocked with fallen trees. The corn crops appear to be ruined.

Oct. 23—Harvesting our corn; it was planted late, has not ripened, and is frost bitten. Blackbirds in flocks have damaged it much.

Frid., Nov. 3—The sisters went for chestnuts and brought home many bushels.

Winter set in with much snow, early in Nov. Much corn in the settlement not ripe. Whites in trouble because of it.

Sun., Dec. 31—At present there are living at Fairfield, one hundred and seventy-two Indian souls.

1798.

Tues., Jan. 2—The townships below have been laid out and the road cleared to our township. Our Indians set to work on the road through our township and finished.

Sat., Feb. 3—Fine thawing weather for several days; the brethren made sugar, the earliest in the year since coming here.

Mon., Feb. 19—All last month and this fine weather and without snow. Today winter set in in earnest.

Feb. 28—Several went to mill and to the smith. (First mention of the latter.) There is a godless people and much drinking along the river.

Frid., Apl. 13—A doctor arrived whom we had asked to see our sick. He came from the States and gave them medicine.

Apl. 14—The Indians brought a boy of Dolson's here to go to school to Bro. Sensemann.

Mon., Apl. 16—Very cold weather and snow, as at Xmas Day.

Early in April the river broke up and rose twenty feet.

Wed., May 9—Our fields were planted somewhat earlier this year than last, and generally the weather has been finer.

Tues., May 22—John Heckewelder and Benjamin Mortimer came to us from Bethlehem by way of Niagara, Mortimer to remain, Heckewelder going on to the Muskingum. The Zeisbergers, with some Indians, to follow in July or August.

In Aug. preparations were made for the Zeisbergers' departure. A religious service was held and Mortimer preached the sermon. The day following Sensemann again called them together and spoke of Zeisberger's departure, of his fearless courage, his self-sacrificing spirit, his readiness to lose his life for the Indian's sake, and all that had rendered illustrious the many years of his missionary service.

Zeisberger left the mission in a prosperous state, spiritually, and of growing importance as a settlement. Three hundred acres were under cultivation; two thousand bushels of corn were annually furnished to the Northwest Trading Company; and extensive trade in cattle, canoes, mats and baskets was carried on, and five thousand pounds of maple sugar were made and sold every winter.

August 15, 1798—The entire population of Fairfield gathered by the river to bid farewell to their leader, counsellor and friend. He came among them, grasped each one by the hand with emotion too deep for utterance. Precisely at noon, he entered a canoe, paddled by three young Indians who had begged for this honor, and put off from the bank amid the sobs of the converts. Thirty-three of them, forming the colony for the Tuscarawas valley, followed in other canoes.

The settlement below on the river consisted of more than one hundred families; they flocked to the river to hail the missionary canoe and give Zeisberger gifts from garden and orchard as he passed on his way. He found opposite Detroit the English were building a town, and at the mouth of the river, on the site of the "Watch-Tower"—Fort Malden.

After a journey by canoe and land of fifty-one days, the missionary and his party again halted, and in Tuscarawas County, Ohio, established his last mission station, and called it Goshen.

On Nov. 17, 1808, it was seen that his end was near. The chapel bell was tolled and his people gathered together; thus surrounded by those with whom and for whom he had laboured long, this illustrious missionary passed peacefully away in his eighty-eighth year.

Never would he consent to have his name put down on a salary-list, or become a "hireling," as he called it. He received no financial reward, from his sixty-two years of missionary labours, other than his living, only the actual necessities being accepted. He was an affectionate husband, a faithful friend.

Sun., Nov. 20, was a clear, warm, radiant day, when his mortal body was laid to rest in the Goshen burying ground. Benjamin Mortimer, one of his companion missionaries, preached the funeral sermon from the text—"And they overcame him by the blood of the Lamb, and by the word of the testimony; and they loved not their lives unto the death." This sermon was in English, translated into Delaware. Then George G. Mueller preached in German from the text—"The memory of the just is blessed."

Zeisberger's widow died (and was buried) at Bethlehem, Pa., Sept. 8, 1824, aged eighty years. They were childless, and so the name of Zeisberger died with them.

Sarnia, Ont., 1913.

XVII.

TRIBAL DIVISIONS OF THE INDIANS OF ONTARIO.

By the late Alexander Francis Chamberlain, M. A., Ph. D.

The question of tribal affinities of the Indians still to be found in the Province of Ontario, and of others formerly resident within its borders, does not require lengthy exposition, since the problems involved are comparatively simple ones and the ethnological complications present in some other regions of the New World appreciably absent.

Ontario has not been the scene of origin of man in North America, nor do archaeological, ethnological, or linguistic arguments induce us to believe the residence of man here has been remarkably ancient; in other words, man is here a much more recent comer than in many other parts of the continent.

So far, not the slightest evidence has been produced to show that, previous to the coming of the whites, Ontario (as at present, or as formerly constituted geographically or geologically) was ever inhabited by human beings of other affiliations than tribes of American Indians past and present. To these can safely be attributed all the pre-Columbian works of man, hitherto discovered or likely to be discovered in the future within the boundaries of the Province. The pre-Indian "Mound-Builder," still believed in by some writers as "a race distinct from that of the modern Indian," is as much a myth for Ontario as it is elsewhere. The makers of the mounds of Ontario were Indians, just as were the mound-builders of the Ohio-Mississippi valley, etc.

Of the fifty or more independent linguistic stocks of American Indians north of Mexico the following have at times had representatives in the Indian population of the Province of Ontario, past and present: **Eskimoan, Siouan, Algonkian, Iroquoian**, but the great mass of aborigines has always belonged to the two last, of which the **Iroquoian** is intrusive from the south, and the **Algonkian** from the north and west. The **Eskimoan** and **Siouan** stocks have been represented but incidentally, and not in very large numbers at any period of the history of the Province.

Ontario has not been the scene of origin of any of these linguistic stocks, all of which, late or early, are immigrants within its borders.

1. **Eskimoan.** The old theory that the Eskimo represented pre-glacial man, retreating northward with the melting ice-sheet, is no longer held by the best authorities, there being abundant evidence to show that this Arctic people is simply an aboriginal stock that has reached its present habitat from somewhere in the region between Hudson's Bay and Alaska—they are, in other words, an interior people who have become largely coast and island dwellers. It is, therefore, very improbable that the Province of Ontario was at any epoch largely inhabited by Eskimo, a view set forth by certain archaeologists chiefly by reason of Eskimo-like implements (e. g., the so-called "woman's knife") discovered in various parts of the country. It is only in the newly-acquired portion of the Province, bordering on James' Bay, that in times past Eskimo may have been temporarily resident, perhaps before its occupation by the Algonkian Indians of the Cree-Montagnais division. As an ethnic and a culture factor in the history of the Province, they can, perhaps, be omitted altogether.

2. **Siouan.** Like the Eskimoan, the Siouan stock has been represented in Ontario only temporarily and intrusively by accident of war, immigration, etc. In the far western portion of Ontario, bordering upon Manitoba, during the period of Sioux-Ojibwa warfare, Indians of this stock made many forays, and roamed about the country in the neighborhood of the Lake of the Woods, etc. In the 17th century (they drifted northwestward to the region about Lake Winnipeg by 1670) the **Assiniboins**, a Siouan people, migrating from the head-waters of the Mississippi, settled about the Lake of the Woods, and some of their movement to the north and east of that location would bring them within the boundaries of the Province of Ontario, as at present constituted. They have not, however, been, during the period of their temporary residence there, an important factor in the history of the Province itself, in so far as its aboriginal culture is concerned. A curious fact in the history of the American Indians of Ontario is the presence (the last surviving full-blood died in 1871) among the Cayugas of the Six Nations Reserve (Grand River) of some **Tutelos**, representing a people of the Siouan stock, belonging originally in North Carolina. The Canadian Tutelos were descended from some of this tribe who fled with the Cayugas to Canada, after the destruction of their settlement at Coreorgonel (on L. Cayuga, New York) by Gen. Sullivan in 1779. The Tutelo language is now extinct (but a brief vocabulary was obtained in 1911 by Dr. E. Sapir from a Cayuga Indian, who heard it spoken in his childhood). A few

individuals having more or less Tutelo blood in their veins still survive.

3. **Algonkian.** The great majority of the Indians at present residing within the borders of the Province of Ontario belong to the widespread Algonkian stock, representatives of which at one time or another were found over a vast area from the Rocky Mountains to the shores of Newfoundland, and from Churchill River in the north to Pamlico Sound (N. C.) in the south—the Blackfeet, Cree, Ojibwa, Montagnais, Mississagas, Micmacs, etc., are well-known members of the stock. Of the Indians of Ontario the following belong to the Algonkian stock:

i.—Certain so-called "**Algonkins,**" of which a few hundred survive at Golden Lake, North Renfrew, Gibson, etc.

ii.—The **Abittibi, Nipissing** (on the Lake of this name) and a few other closely related Indians, by many classed with the "Algonkins" just mentioned.

iii.—The Indians of the region between Lake Abittibi and James' Bay—**Saulteaux-Ojibwa** and closely related Indians of the **Cree-Montagnais** division of the Algonkian stock. All the Indian population of this section of the Province is Algonkian.

iv.—The **Ottawa,** now on Manitoulin and Cockburn Islands and the adjacent shore of Lake Huron, with a few settled with the Ojibwa, etc., on Walpole Island, Lake St. Clair.

v.—The **Potawatomis,** who number altogether about 200, of whom most are settled with the Ojibwa and Ottawa on Walpole Island. There are also a few with the Ojibwa and Munsees of the Thames, in Caradoc township, Middlesex Co. There may be likewise a few among the tribes of the north shore of L. Huron.

vi.—The **Ojibwa** (or **Chippewa**) and the **Mississagas**, the latter existing in small numbers at Mud Lake, Rice Lake, Alnwick, Scugog, New Credit (some 800 in all), but once of much greater distribution and importance in the earlier aboriginal history of the country. The Mississagas and Chippewa or Ojibwa are very closely related and are often classed together. Besides the Chippewa of northern and western Ontario (the tribe once occupied both shores of Lakes Superior and Huron) the Ojibwa are represented by settlements in various parts of the Province (Walpole I.; River Thames with Munsees, etc.; Georgian Bay, etc.).

vii.—Certain immigrant Algonkian peoples who found refuge with the Six Nations or with other Indians of the Thames-Grand River Reserves, etc., in the latter part of the 18th century. Included among such are the **Munsees** of the Thames, in Caradoc township, Middlesex Co., settled with the Chippewa; some of the "**Moravians**" (chiefly Munsee) of Oxford township, Kent Co.; the **Delawares**, settled on the Six Nations Reserve (Grand River), etc.

4. **Iroquoian.** This stock, of great importance in the aboriginal history of the Province by reason of the long wars with the Algonkian tribes, and the remarkable extermination of the Hurons by other Iroquois in the first half of the 17th century, is represented in Ontario to-day by some 6,000 Indians, of whom about two-thirds reside on the Six Nations Reserve, Grand River. The Iroquoian population of the Province includes the following: "Iroquois" of Gibson (Watha), some 60 in number; **Mohawk** of Bay of Quinte; **Oneida** of Thames; Indians of Six Nations Reserve on Grand River—**Cayugas, Mohawks, Onondagas, Senecas, Tuscaroras;** a few **Wyandots (Hurons)** in Anderdon, Essex Co. In the early part of the 17th century practically all of the region between Lakes Erie and Huron, and Lake Ontario and Georgian Bay was occupied by, or roamed over by Indians of Iroquoian stock, of whom many tribes became extinct. It was formerly believed (e. g., by Dr. Brinton and Horatio Hale) that the primitive home of the Iroquoian stock was "somewhere between the Great Lakes and Labrador," but the best ethnological opinion now places it far to the south, even beyond Ohio. According to this view, the whole Iroquoian population of Canada is exotic. This is a point of great importance in connection with the aboriginal history of the country. The advent of the Iroquoian stock into Canada is, therefore, more recent than has generally been supposed.

In conclusion, it may be repeated that the Indians of Ontario show no evidences whatever of pre-Columbian white influences, all stories and speculations to the contrary notwithstanding. All that has yet appeared is Indian and Indian alone.

XVIII.

BEAR CUSTOMS OF THE CREE AND OTHER ALGONKIN INDIANS OF NORTHERN ONTARIO.

By Alanson Skinner

Among all the animals with which they are familiar, there is none more impressive to the minds of the Eastern Cree than the black bear. Its courage, sagacity, and above all, its habit of walking man-like, upon its hind legs, have convinced the Indians of its supernatural propensities.

The Eastern Cree are convinced that all living animals have souls or spirits whose good will must be secured or else they will prevent their species from being captured by the hunters. Because of this belief they take pains to return the bones of the beaver to running water, and prevent them from being devoured by dogs. The heads of ducks and geese, the teeth of the caribou and moose, the claws, chins, and skulls of bears, are carefully preserved as talismans and trophies, and mystical paintings are placed on the skins of fur-bearing animals to appease their manes. But the customs concerning the capture and treatment of the bear have become much more elaborated.

If a hunter, while in the forest, comes upon a bear and wishes to slay it, he first approaches and apologizes, explaining that nothing but lack of food drives him to kill it, and begging that the bear will not be offended at him, nor permit the spirits of other bears to be angry. On killing the bear, he cuts off the middle toe and claw of the right fore foot and returns with it to his camp. When he arrives he first smokes for some time, saying nothing of what he has done, but meanwhile mentally deciding whom he shall ask to take care of, bring in, and butcher the carcass. Usually, if he is a married man, the person chosen is the wife of the hunter. When the proper time, perhaps an hour, has elapsed, he gives the announcing claw to the person whom he has picked out, and states where the bear may be found. The recipient of the claw understands what is required, and, asking no further questions, takes a companion, goes out, and brings in the carcass. The announcing claw is wrapped in cloth, beaded, or painted, or both, and kept as a memento of the occasion.

In case two or more men kill a bear, it is laid out on its back in their canoe, and carefully covered. When the hunters approach their camp or post, the burden is seen from afar, and all the Indians crowd the river bank with cries of congratulation. When the canoe grates on the beach, it is at once surrounded by the small boys, who run down and draw back the blanket or covering enough to expose the bear's head, or at least, its teeth. It is then carried up and laid out, like a man, in front of its slayer's wigwam. After the bear had been laid out, and tobacco placed in its mouth, the hunter and the chief men present smoke over it.

Nowadays, when the bear is brought in, it is laid out upon a new blanket purchased from the Hudson's Bay Company for the occasion. While the ceremony is going on, the bear must be called **Kawipätc mitcem** (black food). Pointing with the finger at the carcass during this ceremony is strictly tabooed.

After the hunter and chief men have smoked, the bear is butchered, and the flesh distributed to all the camp. Certain parts of the bear's flesh are at once burnt ("given to its spirit to eat"), including a small piece of its heart. The rest of the heart is at once eaten by the slayer, in order that he may acquire the cunning and courage of his victim.

Women are not allowed to eat of the bear's head or paws, nor men of its rump. The bones are never given away, unless the bear's flesh is served as a feast in the lodge of the slayer. In any event, they are carefully cleansed, saved, and hung up, or placed on a scaffold where the dogs cannot reach them. If wild animals, other than dogs, reach and devour them, no harm is done. The skull of the bear is cleaned, and the brains removed. It is dried and painted with vermillion and is placed in a safe place and kept from three to six months, when it is secretly taken by its owner and hung up on a tree in the forest.

Formerly, the Cree of Moose Fort, instead of smoking over the carcass of a dead bear, like those of the Eastmain, went through the following ceremony:

The head of the bear was first cut off and cooked, after which the men and boys of the camp sat down in a circle about it. A large stone pipe was laid beside the head and a plug of tobacco placed upon it. Then the man who had killed the bear arose from his place in the circle and filled the pipe with the tobacco, after which it was lighted and passed about the circle from left to right, the slayer smoking first. Each person had the alternative of smoking the pipe for several moments or merely taking a single puff before passing it on. After this the bear's head was passed about and everyone strove to bite out a piece of its flesh without touching it with his hands.(1) The same ceremony was sometimes also gone through after the slaying of a caribou.

Another bear ceremony observed by the Moose Cree was as follows: The bear's intestines were removed, slightly cooked and smoked, after the passing of the head. They were then coiled up on a plate and passed about the circle by the slayer and offered to all the men present, each of whom bit off a piece. Women were allowed to be present at this part of the function but were not allowed to partake of the meat. This ceremony was quite recently observed.

The Cree of Rupert's House and Eastmain River Fort taboo pointing at a bear with the finger even if it is a live bear in the woods, for if this was done, the bear would turn and run away, even if he did not see the offender, for his medicine would warn him of the approach of danger. At the feast, after the slaying of the bear, a certain amount of food is always set before each guest, who is obliged to finish it at one sitting. If, however, he cannot eat it all at once, he is privileged to leave it at the house of the giver of the feast until the next night, when he must finish it. The Moose and Albany Crees do not now observe the majority of the bear customs, nor have they for many years. Those at Albany have forgotten their significance.

It is permissible to speak of a bear as **Muskwá** (the "angry one" or "wrangler") in his absence only, unless one wishes to anger it, or as an expression of reproof. It must never be used before his carcass. If a hunter comes upon a bear in the woods, and is obliged to speak of it, he may call it **Kawipätc mitcem** (black meat, or food) because this is the bear's proper name, and it will not be offended or frightened. This name may also be used before the dead body. Under the same circumstances as above, or when it is not desirable to let it know that it is being spoken of, it may be called **Tciceäk** ("old porcupine") because it will not know who is being talked about. When making fun of a bear, or joking about it, it may be called **Wakiuc** (crooked tail). This name must never be used before the carcass, but **Tukwaiâken** (short tail) may be used. **Pisesu** or **Pisistciu** ("resembling a cat," or lynx) is another term applied to the bear to avoid calling him by his real name. **Wakiu** may be another form of **Wakiuc**, and **Matsue** may be a variant of **Muskwá**.

The skin of the bear is dried, but never tanned and painted. The skin of the under-lip or chin is sacred, and with a piece of bone from the tongue is saved. The bone is placed in a little pouch or bag, and

---

(1) The writer saw an almost identical ceremony of passing the bear's head during a midnight ceremony of the Little Waters, or Secret Medicine Society, of the Seneca Iroquois on the Cattaraugus Reserve, New York. This time a bear's head was not obtainable, and a chunk of salt pork was used.

fastened to the point of the chin on the inside. The skin is folded (sometimes being first painted with vermillion) and sewed together.* The edges of the skin and of the pouch containing the tongue bone are beaded. At Eastmain River Fort, the skin is folded, but not fastened, so that the little bag cannot be seen, as at Rupert's House. These chins serve as charms, and as tallies or hunting trophies. A string of these which was perhaps used as a necklace was collected at Eastmain River Fort. Single claws are also kept as trophies, the bony part being rejected and the horny nail saved; often a number are fitted together, one inside of the other, to form a ring. A skinning tool of the thigh bone of a young bear, and a worked scapula, from the same animal, perhaps intended for a spoon, were obtained at Rupert's House, and the writer was informed that these were kept as charms, and never used. A bear's foetus skin, obtained at the same post, was kept for the same reason.

Anciently, the Eastern Cree never used the bow and arrow in taking the bear, as they did not consider these weapons strong enough. Bears were invariably hunted with the war club and knife, especially in winter, when their hibernating dens might be found. The hunter always endeavored to strike the bear a fatal blow on the head with his club, or approach at still closer quarters to stab him.† Dogs were used to worry the bear, and the Indians affirm that when standing on his hind legs neither the polar nor black bear can turn well on the right side, making it comparatively easy for an agile man to run in closely and stab it to the heart.

Bears are supposed, as will be seen, to understand everything said to them. One man whom we saw at Eastmain River Fort in 1908 was horribly scarred and mangled by a black bear which he had attacked and wounded, but which finally set him free when he pleaded with it for mercy. A "bear dance" was formerly held, but no information could be obtained concerning it, other than a meager description.

Among the northernmost bands of the Ojibway in Ontario, kindred customs are found. The animal to whom the Saulteaux show the most consideration, if not veneration, is the black bear. When an Indian catches a bear in his trap, a few words of apology and explanation are addressed to the animal, which is then killed and dressed up in all the finery obtainable, and is laid out to look like a human being. A Saulteaux at Sandy Lake, not far from Dinorwic, gave the following reasons for this custom: "The bears have a king, or chief, and the orders of this

*This custom was observed among the Montagnais by the Jesuits.
†The Seneca seem to have had a similar custom according to information gathered by the writer in New York.

chief must be obeyed. Sometimes he orders a bear to go to an Indian trap. When a dead bear is dressed up it is done as an offering or prayer to the chief of the bears to send more of his children to the Indians. If this were not done, the spirit of the bear would be offended and would report the circumstances to the chief of the bears who would prevent the careless Indians from catching more." When an Indian eats a bear he puts up a pole upon which are hung the skin of the animal's muzzle, his ears, skull, and offerings of tobacco and ribbons. On the lower part of the pole the bark was allowed to remain intact, but at intervals of about three feet, peeled spots about a foot in length were rubbed with red ocher. The skull, ears, and skin of the muzzle were fastened on with offerings to the spirit of the dead bear.

At Sandy Lake the writer saw an old Saulteaux woman take the shoulder blade of a bear and make transverse marks across it with charcoal, each bar meaning a prayer for a successful year of life for the slayer. This should have been hung on the bear pole but was obtained by the writer before the pole was erected.

Some of the Saulteaux claim that in erecting the bear pole the skull should be painted with charcoal, but with no other pigment. Tobacco should be hung at the center of the pole and the skin of the bear's chin should also be suspended from it. The bear's skull is not painted, as is the custom among the Eastern Cree, nor is it kept in the house of the slayer before hanging it up; nor do the Saulteaux ever paint the bearskin inside. A bear which for any reason is not eaten after it has been killed is not honored in this way. Bears' bones are never given to the dogs, but are hung out of their reach. Bear poles are very frequently seen on the journey from Lac Seul to Lake St. Joseph on deserted camp sites, but were not found north of this.

Long says that near Lake Abittibi, "On one of the islands we discovered two Indian huts, but from their appearance no person had visited them for a length of time. About half a mile from the place we saw a high pole, daubed all over with vermilion paint; on the top were placed three human skulls, and the bones hung around: The Indians suppose that it had been erected many years."

The tongue and heart of the bear may not be eaten by women. In the event of a bear being killed by a member of a camp, the slayer always receives the brisket, head, and heart, as his portion. This is true of other large game. A young man who has killed his first bear or other big game has a feast made in his honor, and sits up the entire night drumming and singing prayers for his future success.

Should a man find a bear's winter den during the summer and desire to slay the animal the following winter, he takes a bullet from his pouch and after warning it not to tell anyone and to prevent others from finding the spot, he lays it by the hole, expecting it to guard his prize until he returns. Bears slain in their lairs in winter should never be shot, but rather knocked on the head with a club. According to the Saulteaux, when the bear makes his hole, he takes all kinds of animals with him to live on in the winter. They, however, believe that if he takes them from the territory covered by the route of a single trapper, the man will have bad luck; but if he draws them from the trails of several trappers, no harm will be done. If the bear sees a trapper he may throw out game to him, counting on the man's mercy in return for his charity. If a man kills lean animals at the beginning of his winter's hunt it is a sign that he will kill a bear, but if the animals are fat he will not kill one.

The Saulteaux admit that like the Eastern Cree they have various names for the bear, but they refuse to tell these to white people for fear that ill success will attend them. While the proper name of the bear is **mukweh**, he is also known as **oputowan**, but the meaning of the latter term could not be found.

Some light is thrown on Cree and Ojibway beliefs by information more recently obtained from the Menomini, a small Algonkin tribe dwelling in Northern Wisconsin. Among this people the belief is that the gods are divided into two groups, the Powers above, and the Powers below, the world lying between. Each division of the universe is further subdivided into four tiers, each ruled over by a particular god. The chief of the Underworld is **Waiäbskinit Awäse**, the Great White Bear. He is represented on earth by the ordinary black bear, to whom the Menomini formerly apologised before slaying as the Saulteaux and Cree do today. In certain medicine formulae tobacco is sacrificed to the Underground Bear by burying it with prayers for success on the chase. The Menomini formerly preserved the skulls of slain bears and the Woodland Potawatomi still do so. Le Jeune, in his relation (Jesuit Relations, vol. 6, p. 217) says of the Montagnais, 1633-4:

"When some one of them has taken a bear, there are extensive ceremonies before it is eaten. One of our people took one, and this is what they did:

"First, the bear having been killed, the man who killed it did not bring it back, but he returned to the cabin to impart the news, so that some one might go and see the prize, as something very precious; for the savages prefer the meat of the bear to all other kinds of food; it seems to me that the young beaver is in no way inferior to it, but the bear has more fat, and therefore the savages like it better.

"Second, the bear being brought, all the marriageable girls and young married women who have not had children, as well as those of the cabin where the bear is to be eaten, and of the neighboring cabins, go outside, and do not return as long as there remains a piece of this animal, which they do not taste. It snowed, and the weather was very severe. It was almost night when this bear was brought to our cabin; immediately the women and girls went out and sought shelter elsewhere, the best they could find. They do this not without much suffering; for they do not always have bark on hand with which to make their house, which in such cases they cover with branches of the fir tree.

"In the third place, the dogs must be sent away, lest they lick the blood, or eat the bones, or even the offal of this beast, so greatly is it prized. The latter are buried under the fireplace, and the former are thrown into the fire. The preceding are observations which I made during the performance of this superstition. Two banquets are made of this bear as it is cooked in two kettles, although all at the same time. The men and older women are invited to the first feast, and, when it is finished, the women go out; then the other kettle is taken down, and of this an eat-all feast is made for the men only. This is done on the evening of the capture; the next day toward nightfall, or the second day, I do not exactly remember, the bear having been all eaten, the young women and girls return.

"If the bird which they call **Ouichcatchan**, which is nearly the size of a magpie, and which resembles it (for it is gray in the places where the magpie is black, and white where it is white), tries to get into their cabins, they drive it away very carefully, because, they say, they would have a headache; they do not give any reason for this, but have, if they are to be believed, learned it by experience. I have seen them take the throat of this animal, split it open, and look into it very attentively. My host tells me, 'If I find inside a little bone of the Moose (for this bird eats everything) I shall kill a moose; if I find a bone of the bear, I shall kill a bear;' and so on with other animals."

These or similar customs are widely distributed in Ontario, the adjoining provinces, and in the eastern United States; indeed, there is probably no part of the world where the bear is found where he does not make a strong appeal to the emotions of mankind.

American Museum of Natural History, New York City.

XIX.

AN INTRODUCTIVE ENQUIRY IN THE STUDY OF OJIBWA RELIGION.

By Paul Radin

Although the present paper is concerned almost exclusively with the Ojibwa of South-Eastern Ontario, there is little doubt that the data presented hold likewise for all the other divisions of the Ojibwa group, except perhaps for the extreme western branches in western Manitoba and Saskatchewan, and the so-called Northern Saulteaux, where they have come in contact with the Cree. Even there, however, we do not anticipate any great changes, for the investigations of Wm. Jones on the Manito belief of the Sauk and Fox, and those of Alanson Skinner among the Cree and Menominee, seem to indicate that the Ojibwa beliefs differed only in detail from those of these other tribes.

In dealing with the subject of the religion of primitive peoples, it will be well to bear in mind that it must be treated in the same manner in which that subject is treated among civilized people. The unjustified and unsubstantiated assumption that there is any real difference has been the cause of considerable confusion hitherto and has resulted in the development of some erroneous conceptions on cardinal points in the religious life of the North American Indians. But, perhaps, more harmful than any erroneous point of view, has been the utter absence of critical analysis with which the sources for religious life have been treated. Rarely have investigators made an attempt to go behind the data, to realize its individual significance, the character of the individual or individuals from whom it has been obtained, his relation to the tribe, and numerous other pertinent points, and as a result we see primitive religious beliefs discussed as though they pertained to some vague social unit. No suggestive or correct view-point can possibly grow out of such a treatment.

Just as among us, there are religious and unreligious people among the Indians, and it is a matter of the very gravest consequence—of far more consequence than among us—from whom our information is obtained. By "unreligious" is meant not "unbelief," but a passive attitude toward religious beliefs; their acceptance, but accompanied only by a modicum of religious thrill or emotional response. The Indian system of education—from now on, we will refer exclusively to the Ojibwa and Winnebago (a culturally kindred Siouan tribe)—is possessed of great elasticity and permits an individual within certain limits to stress that particular bent of mind which fits him most naturally. If he is religiously inclined, he will prepare for the life of a shaman, and preparation means essentially, endless and ceaseless repetition on the one hand, and persistent fixation of the attention upon religious life, on the other. Those individuals who do not prepare for such a life are deficient in just these points. However, in addition to the shamans, almost all the gifted individuals, those who excel in any walk of life, be it as hunter, fisherman, warrior, craftsman, etc., attain to a great degree of knowledge, much of which is associated with a high development of religious feeling and consciousness, for in their education a large amount of attention is fixed upon religious practices. And when it is remembered that success and efficacy of individual powers depends not so much upon the performance of a rite and the attitude of prayer, but upon the individual's emotional attitude—the power of complete absorption while at prayer, in his religious emotion to the exclusion of all others, then it will be easily realized how intense the religious life of these individuals must be, and how far removed from that of the other members of the tribe. Such an intense participation, while it does, on the one hand, act as a bulwark for the conservation of past beliefs, must, on the other, lead, in a number of cases, to an assertion of individual points of view, that become in time centres for the development of innovations both in belief and ritualistic practice. This two-fold function of the "gifted" man, it is of great importance to bear in mind.

The conclusion to be drawn from the above remarks is certainly a common-place one, namely, that there exists among the Ojibwa a group of men possessed of "esoteric," and another group of "exoteric" knowledge. These terms have generally been used in connection with secret societies, but there can be no objection to extending their meaning to include the grouping given above.

The majority of the Indians are what we have called unreligious, their attitude being one of passive acceptance. However, it may be well to define this passivity more clearly. It is to a large, preponderating extent, not the passivity of choice, but what may be called the "passivity of fact." These individuals, representing the normal run of men, simply did not have the necessary temperamental make up; manitos did not appear to them, or having appeared to them were of an inferior order, or bestowed upon them "blessings" of a minor kind. Certainly they regarded the religious beliefs, the religious manifestations, with all the awe and veneration they were capable of, and showed themselves punctilious in the observance of such religious injunctions as they were taught. In order to obtain a moderate degree of success in the pursuits of life, in obtaining food, success on the war-path, etc., they purchased from their more successful brethren efficacious herbs and medicines, to which offerings had to be made in a prescribed way, deviations being regarded as nullifying their efficacy. The most punctilious observation of ritualistic details was for them what a complete and consciously directed absorption in their religious-emotional selves, was for the shaman.

Now, it follows from the fact that so much attention was paid to the formal expression of beliefs by the "exoteric" element of an Ojibwa community, that nothing pertaining to the beliefs handed down from generation to generation, was ever touched, and that some had already become formulae and others were on the road of becoming such. For the average individual religious education consequently consisted in the learning of a certain number of formulaic beliefs, which might or might not call forth a religious thrill.

We have used the phrase "religious education" as though there were other kinds of education for the Ojibwa child. But with the exception of etiquette, every activity of life to him was so intimately associated with a religious sanction, that to speak of "religious education" is to speak of the entire system of education. It goes without saying that for the average Indian of whom we have been speaking, as for the average individual among us, a fact is a fact, standing out strongly from among other things. The killing of a deer or the catching of a fish are real facts to him, even though he may be thought inclined to attribute some of his skill to the efficacy of certain ritualistic practices. There can be no question that when they are asked, they will answer that lack of success is due to failure to properly perform certain ritualistic injunctions. But it does not follow that the converse is true, that he consciously realizes the connection of cause and effect, between the performance of ritualistic observances and his success in killing a deer, **when he is actually hunting.** These observances are formulaic in nature; are associated with hunting; are accepted by him as always occurring together; but it is to him certainly not a cause and effect relation, and calls forth little or no religious response.

Thus far we have been speaking of **normal success**. The moment the question shifts to that of exceptional success, which is of course due to exceptional ability, and deals with events out of the ordinary run of life, then the point of view is entirely changed. Exceptional success places a man immediately in the "esoteric" group. But how about this other element, the crises of life, or as the culturally kindred Winnebago say, "the narrow places of life?" And the idea of life's crises is not an assumption. It is insisted on from earliest childhood. The old grandfather says, "Life is full of crises. What will you have, when they come upon you, to successfully surmount them? Fast and obtain power to use on these occasions." In other words, for the average man the religious aspect stands out prominently in relation to all the material and immaterial possessions of life, during the crises of life. At such a time, we do not doubt that ritualistic observances are regarded by the individual as directly responsible for increased skill, for normal skill even.

This discussion has taken us somewhat afield. But it was essential, and before leaving it we wish once again to insist not only upon the materialistic side of the "exoteric" but also upon that of the "esoteric" religion. There are no religious observances given merely for the glorification of a manito or manitos. They are always associated with undertakings of practical consequence for the tribe and the individual, and for the specific furtherance of these undertakings. To say, then, that religion is an attempt at the explanation of life is erroneous, in this case. It has assumed this aspect among certain shaman, but to the majority of Ojibwa, religion is essentially a means of strengthening life, of enriching the contents of life specifically.

If we now look at religion in its various manifestations we will find that it assumes among the Ojibwa those forms found among other peoples. There is a general animism taking the rather concrete form of the manito; the religious fasting at puberty; the religious exaltation; the auto-suggestion, prayer, etc.

There is an indefinite number of manitos. They are found associated with practically all material objects and with many immaterial objects, from our point of view. Their form is indefinite, the large majority having an animal form, although some have human form when they appear to individuals. Any attempt to divide them into spiritual and corporeal beings would be futile, owing to the general belief in a possibility of transformation possessed not merely by them, but also by powerful shaman. Many of them are associated with specific powers; some "bless" individuals with success on the war-path; others with success in hunting, or fishing, or love. Almost all "bless" individuals with long life. A man fasts on many occasions in life, but his important fast is that which takes place at the age of puberty. He is then given some charcoal to blacken his face and told to go out to some deserted place and fast. It will be best to give a first-hand description of such a fasting experience.

"I was about ten years old when I fasted, that generally being the age at which grandparents want you to fast. I don't suppose I should ever have fasted if I hadn't had a grandparent living at the time.

"About the middle of Little-Bear month (February) she came and took me to her house. I did not know what she wanted of me, at the time. About two days afterwards she told me that she wanted me to fast. The next morning I received very little to eat or drink. At noon nothing at all was given to me. In the evening I again received a little food and water. There were seven of us fasting together, and all day we would play and carefully watch each other so that no one would break his fast. We were to fast for ten days.

"About the end of the fifth day, I became so hungry that after my grand-parents retired, I got up and had a good meal. They must have found out what I had done, for I had to start all over again. This time I resolved not to break my fast, for I did not wish to start from the beginning again.

"At the end of the tenth day, they built me a wigwam under a tree not far from their house so that they could watch me conveniently during the day. My grandmother had told me before not to accept the first manito that appeared to me in my dreams, for some would try to deceive me and the acceptance of their "blessing" would lead me to destruction.

"The first four nights I slept very soundly and dreamt of nothing, but on the fifth night, I dreamt that a large and very beautiful bird appeared and promised me many things, but as I had made up my mind to refuse the 'blessing' of the first manito who appeared, I did not accept his offers. As the bird disappeared in the distance, I saw that it was only a chickadee. In the morning when my grandmother came, I told her that a chickadee had appeared and that I had refused its offers. She told me that I had done well, for chickadees had deceived many people already.

"After that I did not dream of anything until the eighth night. Then a large bird appeared to me, and I determined to accept his blessing, for I was getting tired of waiting and staying in the wigwam.. The bird took me far away north where everything was covered with ice. There I saw many other birds of the same kind. **Some were very old and they offered me long life and immunity from disease.** This was quite different from what the chickadee had offered. I accepted, and the bird brought me back to my wigwam. As he was starting he told me to watch him as he disappeared from view, and I saw that he was a white loon.

"In the morning my grandmother came and I told her all that had happened. She was delighted, for she said people were rarely blessed by loons. From that time on, I have been called White Loon."

Now this is emphatically the experience of an "unreligious" man. Although it does not seem entirely correct to assume a highly developed degree of religious susceptibility for children between the ages of ten and twelve, still it was greater among Indians than among us. However, there is an entirely different consideration to be borne in mind here. These fasting experiences are only told long after the age of manhood has been reached (i. e., if they are ever told), and an individual sees them of course through the vista of what life has given him, in emotional development and in practical experiences. The shaman reads his puberty experience in terms of his success in life and the "unreligious" man in terms of his; and while it would perhaps be erroneous to deny a different religious temperament for the two from the start, yet the other factors must be recognized and given their full value.

Let us now give in outline the fasting experience of a Winnebago shaman,(1) identical we believe with that of Ojibwa shaman.

"When I had reached the age of puberty, my father wished me to fast, that I might become holy; invincible and invulnerable in war; become like one of those about whom tales are told in the future. Thus I would become **if I made special efforts in my fasting.** I would be "blessed' with long life, he told me; I would be able to cure the sick; life would not be able to harm me in any way. No one would dare to be uncivil to me for fear of incurring my enmity. He pleaded with me to fast long and intently, for only then would the various spirits 'bless' me.

"There was a hill near my father's wigwam called the Place-where-they-keep-weapons. **It was a very high hill, steep and rocky. They said it was a very holy place.** Within that hill lived spirits called Those-who-are-like-children (i. e., liliputians). There were twenty of them and they possessed arrows. My father was in charge of these (i. e., some powerful manito had in his 'blessing' placed these under his control). When he

1) The father of this man was himself a very famous shaman.

wished to 'bless' a man, he would do as follows: He would take his bow and arrows in both hands and take the spirits around the hill into his wigwam (into the middle of the hill), where stood a stone pillar. On this pillar he drew the pictures of various animals. Then he danced around the stone and sang, and when he was finished, commenced to breathe upon it. Then he walked around it again, shot at it, and it turned into a deer with great antlers......... So I could do if I wished, and if I poured tobacco and fasted........ My father was a great hunter, and I would have been delighted to be like him........

"Through fasting one obtains the power of curing disease. While I was fasting the spirits came to me from a doctor's village up above. The shaman gathered around me and told me it would be difficult. Then he who was in front began to breathe audibly and all those in the wigwam helped him. When they finished this, they began to sing. This they showed me and they said, 'When a person is sick and in a critical condition and all others have failed to cure him, they will call upon you and offer you tobacco, which you are to direct toward us'...... Certainly I should have been holy, for very earnestly I labored."

These two examples illustrate all the important points in the fasting experiences of the Ojibwa. The two most essential elements are the control exercised by the older generation and the formulaic character of what is taught.

It will be seen by a glance at the first fasting experience that a great control is exercised by the parent or grandparent on the blessings to be accepted. How minute this control is has not been determined, but it is extremely probable that practically everything is given with the possible exception of the specific individuality of the manito itself. In other words, the youth does not go out to fast vaguely, for some indefinite, hazy object, but as we have seen, for something definite; something sharply circumscribed and which he is subsequently to clothe in religious-literary formulae that have been handed down from generation to generation. That there are variations of detail must not be overlooked, but they are not essential.

In the second example, the control of the parent is exercised in another way. Being himself a powerful shaman he has the natural desire to have one of his children inherit all his supernatural powers and the material wealth it has brought him, and to do so he surrounds his son with conditions that practically make it certain that he will be blessed by the same spirits in the same way. Practically the son inherits these powers and gifts, but only that son who duplicates those religious conditions his father submitted to when he "was blessed," and consequently only that son who shows especial aptitude and conscientious endeavor will obtain them. If no son should show such an aptitude, the powers will pass to some more distant relative.

The religious intensity of the shaman, of the gifted man, thus turns out to be not a question of chance variation, but one due to conscious selection of specially endowed individuals, from generation to generation, within a small number of families.

A number of other points relating to the manito belief will now have to be discussed, namely, the localization of the manitos; the existence of two great manitos, and the nature of manito as a general "force."

It is extremely significant that in many instances where individuals are "blessed" by animal manitos, these are always found to be definitely located. An individual is "blessed" not by some general manito-snake, for instance, but by a definite manito-snake, located in some definite place. For instance, a person is crossing a certain lake, and a terrible storm comes up; but he has been "blessed" by the particular manito in control of this lake and by the appropriate prayers and offerings, the storm is allayed. A man is "blessed" by a number of manitos, but he does not call upon them indiscriminately. Had the foregoing Ojibwa not been "blessed" with the particular manito in question, he would have been drowned.

The question of the belief in two all-powerful manitos, one in control of all the good, the other in control of all the bad spirits, is extremely difficult to discuss in the present state of our knowledge. Christian influences may have penetrated here. Still the belief is found among the linguistically kindred Pottawattomie, Ottawa, Menominee and the culturally kindred Winnebago. There is no question in our mind that the belief will turn out to be a development of the shaman, for it is always found in the great ritualistic legends that have undoubtedly been developed by them. It seems likely that the "exoteric" group did not possess this belief in the beginning and that the influence of the whites and its similarity to that of the Christian God and devil made it spread more generally among these Indians than it would have done had there been no contact with the whites.

Of the "manito-force" discussed by Wm. Jones for the Sauk and Fox, and which has been taken by all investigators to apply to the Woodland Indians generally, we find no evidence, and we are strongly inclined to believe that Jones' formulation is over-systematised. The difficulties encountered in obtaining adequate and precise information on this subject are, it is known, almost insurmountable. Yet the overwhelming balance of the data, and it seems to us even that quoted by Jones himself, indicates that the Indian regards an object as manito, sacred, because it contains a manito, and if the conditions were propitious, he could be "blessed" by it. If a belief in a manito "essence" or "force" exists it is as a characteristic of a manito. That the "essence" exists apart and separate from the manito is, we believe, an unjustified assumption, an abstraction created by investigators.

But there is a vagueness about the nature of the manito which has perhaps led investigators, and even Indians, astray when they attempted to translate the concept into words, for purposes of explanation, and which is paralleled by that which exists in their belief in the transformation of individuals at will, under certain conditions, into animals, trees, immaterial forces (from our point of view), ghosts, etc. The nature of the manito is properly that of a tertium quid, from our point of view. The whole question is, is it that from the Indian's point of view? We do not think so; for he does not make the opposition of corporeal and noncorporeal; data obtained through direct sense impressions and that through mediated sense impressions, in anything like our way. To investigate exactly, what, if any, opposition they make in regard to these matters is, perhaps, the most fascinating, as it is certainly the most difficult of ethnological problems.

We have dealt only with the most characteristic and fundamental points of Ojibwa religion, for the space at our disposal will not permit us to discuss more.

XX.

A NOTED ANTHROPOLOGIST (DR. A. F. CHAMBERLAIN).

The death occurred on April 8, 1914, of Alexander Francis Chamberlain, professor of anthropology in Clark University, Worcester, Mass. Prof. Chamberlain was a son of the late George and Maria Chamberlain, of Toronto, and was born at Kenninghall, Norfolk, England, January 12, 1865. He came with his parents to Canada in early youth, and received in Peterborough, Ont., his primary school education, as well as a training in the Collegiate Institute of that city. He took an Arts course in the University of Toronto, where he received the degree of Bachelor of Arts, 1886, and Master of Arts, 1889. During his college course he showed a rare capacity for the rapid mastery of languages. Immediately after taking his bachelor degree in 1886, he was appointed to the fellowship in modern languages, in his alma mater, and in 1890-92 held the fellowship in anthropology in Clark University, Worcester, Mass., where he received his Ph.D. degree in the last named year. He was then appointed to a lectureship in the same university, and afterwards to an assistant professorship, which position he held up to the time of his death. In 1898 he married Miss Mary Isabel Cushman of Worcester.

The Toronto Globe, after reciting the main facts of his life, referred to his distinguished career in the following terms: His rapid mastery of foreign languages was a form of ability that stood him in good stead when later in life he had to pick up as best he could under serious difficulties the languages of the Indian tribes whose characteristics he had under observation.

Early in his academic career Prof. Chamberlain began in his own neighborhood his observations on the languages, manners, customs, and folklore of the Indians on the reserves in Ontario. The publication of the results of his researches brought him and his work to the attention of anthropologists, generally, in Canada, the United States, Great Britain and other countries. In 1891, for a Committee of the British Association for the Advancement of Science, he conducted protracted investigations of the tribal peculiarities of the Kootenay Indians in British Columbia.

He edited, from 1901 onward, the Journal of American Folklore, and, in addition to many papers contributed to scientific periodicals, he prepared articles for several encyclopædias, including the new Encyclopædia Britannica.

He leaves behind him (the Globe added editorially) at his untimely passing a high reputation as an original investigator of anthropological phenomena. By sheer force of ability and untiring work he made his way into the front rank of research toilers in the field of anthropology, where he was ultimately recognized as an authority. His observations of the customs and languages of Indian tribes involved long journeys and much physical hardship, but for this he was amply repaid by his interest in the natives and their regard for him. He was the recipient of many honors that came to him absolutely unsought, and left him as shy and unaffected as if he had never earned such distinctions. His death has created a blank in the republic of science which it will not be easy to fill, and in his dual academic environment which cannot be filled at all. He was pre-eminently an altruistic and lovable man.

In recent years, Prof. Chamberlain has devoted much attention to the Indian languages of South America, and had just completed, a short time prior to his death, a survey of the languages of that continent, in which he reckoned eighty-three distinct families or language-stocks, each of which was subdivided into different branches which were related to each other like English and German, and yet were quite as unintelligible to those using them.

The brief article by him, on the Indians of Ontario, which appears on earlier pages of this volume, and which was contributed to the Society at its Annual Meeting in Chatham, September, 1913, accordingly has a pathetic interest, inasmuch as his death occurred while the book was passing through the press.

Publications of the Society

Papers and Records, Volume 1, pp. 140, 1899. 18 historical articles and copies of original documents.

Papers and Records, Volume 2, pp. 128, 1900. "The United Empire Loyalist Settlement at Long Point, Lake Erie," by L. H. Tasker, M.A.

Papers and Records, Volume 3, pp. 199, 1901. 22 historical articles and copies of original documents.

Papers and Records, Volume 4, pp. 115, 1903. "Galinee's Narrative and Map," Part 1, Translated and edited by Dr. James H. Coyne.

Papers and Records, Volume 5, pp. 236, 1904. 10 historical articles and copies of original documents.

Papers and Records, Volume 6, pp. 170, 1905. 16 historical articles and copies of original documents.

Papers and Records, Volume 7, pp. 237, 1906. 12 historical articles and copies of original documents.

Papers and Records, Volume 8, pp. 228, 1907. 12 historical articles and copies of original documents.

Papers and Records, Volume 9, pp. 200, 1910. 8 historical articles and copies of original documents.

Papers and Records, Volume 10, pp. 85, 1913. 7 historical articles.

Papers and Records, Volume 11, pp. 81, 1913. "Place-Names in Georgian Bay," by James White, F.R.G.S.

Papers and Records, Volume 12, pp. 220, 1914. 20 historical articles.

Annual Reports are also printed each year, which contain a record of the work of the Society during the year, reports of the annual meetings, reports of affiliated Societies, lists of members and other historical information.

www.ingramcontent.com/pod-product-compliance
Lightning Source LLC
Chambersburg PA
CBHW032042230426
43672CB00009B/1431